Anthony Powell
A LIFE

'A lovely book, and a real delight to live with' Paul Fussell

'[Barber] has done a remarkably good job ... This study of Powell is very readable ... I have read it twice with immense enjoyment'
Hugh Massingberd, *Spectator*

'Barber is well-read and perceptive. His textual analysis of the Powell novels, for the origins of people and scenes, is especially pleasing'
Max Hastings, *Sunday Telegraph*

'Barber takes the trouble to build up the secondary characters; essential in this case ... because Powell liked to see himself as observer, noting from the wings the absurdities and aberrations of his friends in bohemia and high society, and transmogrifying them into the characters in his books'
Jeremy Lewis, *Literary Review*

'Barber's intuitive perceptions are often very sharp'
Financial Times Magazine

'Barber is very good on Powell's Bohemian connections in the polyglot world of late 1920s London ... and adroitly emphasises a side of his life not conspicuously apparent in the late period journals - his liking for people who existed on or beyond the margins of his own social catchment area'
D.J. Taylor, *Independent on Sunday*

'Barber is at his best describing bohemia and the literary world that Powell by choice inhabited – once again very far from the aristocratic one of the gossip-writer's imagination'
Antonia Fraser, *Evening Standard*

'One of the appealing things about Barber as biographer is that he never proposes to know things about his subject that the poor subject never knew about himself ... What strikes one first and last about Barber is how much he truly likes the man and writer he's engaged with, and how his aim is no more nor less than to put events in orderly compass so as to share with readers the story of an original life and sensibility'
The Hudson Review

'One can recommend this book ... as an unpretentious romp through the story of Evelyn Waugh, Malcolm Muggeridge, George Orwell and Weidenfeld, Peter Quennell, Cyril Connolly and all'
Times Literary Supplement

Anthony Powell sketched by Ronald Searle in July 1956,
when they were colleagues at *Punch*.

ANTHONY POWELL
A LIFE

Michael Barber

Duckworth Overlook
London • Woodstock • New York

First paperback edition 2005
First published in 2004 by
Duckworth Overlook

LONDON
90-93 Cowcross Street
London EC1M 6BF
inquiries@duckworth-publishers.co.uk
www.ducknet.co.uk

WOODSTOCK
The Overlook Press
One Overlook Drive
Woodstock, NY 12498
www.overlookpress.com
[for individual orders and bulk sales in the United States,
please contact our Woodstock office]

NEW YORK
The Overlook Press
141 Wooster Street
New York, NY 10012

A CIP catalogue record for this book is available from the
British Library and the Library of Congress

ISBN 0 7156 3420 8 (UK)
ISBN 1-58567-710-8 (US)

Typeset by e-type, Liverpool
Printed in Great Britain by
Bookmarque Ltd, Croydon, Surrey

Contents

For My Family

Illustrations

1. Maud Mary Wells-Dymoke.
2. Lieutenant-Colonel Philip Powell.
3. Powell as a fag at Eton.
4. Detail from a group photo at an Old Boys' match.
5. Drawing by Powell for *Cherwell*.
6. Hubert Duggan as a subaltern in the Life Guards.
7. Constant Lambert.
8. Nina Hamnett.
9. John Heygate.
10. Henry Lamb's portrait of Powell.
11. Powell with Tequila bottle.
12. Violet in her nurse's uniform.
13. Landscape with Figures – I, by Osbert Lancaster.
14. Landscape with Figures – IV, by Osbert Lancaster.
15. Field-Marshal Montgomery putting the attachés in the picture.
16. Powell and Malcolm Muggeridge outside the National Gallery.
17. The Chantry seen from the rear.
18. Barbara Skelton and Cyril Connolly.
19. Widmerpool as seen by Mark Boxer.
20. X. Trapnel as seen by Mark Boxer.
21. The Powells at a Cairo nightclub.
22. Powell in 1973.
23. Powell at his writing desk.

Preface and Acknowledgements

The strains of *Cwm Rhondda* are rarely heard in Mayfair, but at about 12.30 p.m. on Thursday 4 May 2000 they echoed across South Audley Street from the Grosvenor Chapel, where the memorial service for Anthony Dymoke Powell was drawing to an unmistakeably Cambrian close. For despite the quintessentially English character of his writing, Powell thought of himself as Welsh. This was brought home to me in 1975 when I was preparing to interview him for the *Paris Review*. Nigel Hollis, the genial publicity manager of Powell's publishers, Heinemann, took me on one side.

> For God's sake [said Nigel], don't raise so much as an eyebrow if he talks about his Welsh ancestry. I once told a journalist he wasn't in the least bit Welsh and the silly bugger went and printed it. Next thing I know Tony's on the phone giving me a terrific ballocking. What on earth was I playing at, telling that person he wasn't Welsh? Of course he bloody well was.

It was because he was Welsh that Powell pronounced his name to rhyme with Noel and not, as you might expect, with towel. Unfortunately nobody thought to inform the Grosvenor Chapel's vicar of this, so that the service began with the sort of gaffe that was made for a Bateman cartoon. Though Powell would undoubtedly have deplored such an egregious solecism, I think he might also have acknowledged, albeit wryly, that it conformed to an established pattern and was therefore 'appropriate', like 'most things in life – perhaps all things', according to his *alter ego*, Nick Jenkins.

Equally appropriate was the quantity of incense burned at his pyre by obituarists, most of whom pointed out that because he was, in his own words, 'frightfully buttoned-up', he never became a household name like Evelyn Waugh, Graham Greene and John Betjeman, to name but three of his more uninhibited peers. His reputation rests solely on his writing, the craft he pursued for more than sixty years. This is not to say that he was a recluse. His first novel, *Afternoon Men*, was described as 'the party novel to end all party novels'. And when, late in life, an interviewer asked him what he had sacrificed for his art, he replied, 'Rather a lot of time actually ... I have fairly often *not* gone to parties because I was writing.' He was also, like his seventeenth-century exemplar, John Aubrey, a virtuoso gossip. 'On *no* account tell Tony,' wrote Edith Sitwell to her brother Sacheverell, having just informed him about her other brother, Osbert's, sufferings at the hands of his boyfriend.

I discovered Powell in my early twenties, attracted, in the first instance, by Osbert Lancaster's cover for the Penguin edition of *A Question of Upbringing.* This showed an Eton boy's study, with a top-hat in the foreground, a hunting print over the mantelpiece, from which dangled an umbrella, and a distant prospect of the school chapel through the window. Forty years on I can still recall my disappointment with the story. Compared with Simon Raven, another recent discovery, Powell seemed long-winded and staid. Only Peter Templer showed a bit of dash, losing his virginity in a manner identical to Raven himself (though I didn't know this at the time). Still, I bought volume two and was immediately taken with Mr Deacon, who satisfied my youthful hunger for the *louche.* However, it was not until Jenkins arrived at Mrs Andriadis's party that I realised what all the fuss was about. And by the time he encountered Widmerpool in the Stourwater dungeons – for my money, the funniest episode in the whole sequence – I had signed on for the duration.

Soon afterwards I went to live in Sydney, where, I was glad to find, Powell had a following. On my return to London I gravitated to Grub Street, where the opportunity arose of interviewing Powell. He was, to borrow an expression of his, 'perfectly civil', but would only talk about his writing, not himself. Three things in particular struck me about him. His nasal drawl, particularly apparent whenever he emphasised a word, which he did repeatedly;* antiquated vowels – 'orf' for 'off', 'gorn' for 'gone' and so on; and the extraordinary mixture of overstatement and understatement that characterised his speech. A corollary of this was his attachment to conciliatory adverbs like 'frightfully', 'awfully' and 'decidedly'. He was also fond of expressions like 'sort of' and 'I mean'.

Powell said he didn't want to talk about himself because it would prejudice his Memoirs, which he had just begun to write. But he is no more the hero of his Memoirs than Jenkins is of *Dance* (as I shall call his long novel). As James Lees-Milne noted: 'He discloses nothing about himself, but is revealing, albeit cautiously, of his contemporaries' follies.' Whatever the reason for his reticence – nature, nurture, or a combination of the two – it left a lot of readers, myself included, wanting to know more. Hence, in part, this

---

*e.g. 'They *abound,* eccentric soldiers.' And: 'It was *sheer, extraordinary* coincidence … I mean there was no *earthly* reason why she should have married a Spaniard.'

book, whose primary purpose is to try and relate the man to his work. I think this is a legitimate exercise. *Dance*, like *A la recherche du temps perdu*, is a creative autobiography. Very little of it is invented, though most of it may have been changed. Disentangling fact from fiction does not, I believe, diminish Powell's achievement, or overlook the amount of 'appallingly hard work' he said went into it.

Another reason for writing about Powell was suggested by Perry Anderson, who emphasised the historical sweep of *Dance*, unmatched 'in the annals of European fiction'. Powell lived through interesting times, which began in earnest the day that Billson, the Jenkins's parlour maid, gave notice. His life, and the lives of his characters, were shaped by large impersonal forces over which they had no control. Luckily they were left alone for long enough to experience 'the post-war spirit', that euphoric cocktail which intoxicated so many of those who were young in the Twenties. Powell's early novels were written under the influence of this, though by the time *Afternoon Men* appeared in 1931 it had already gone out of fashion, replaced by 'Vin Audenaire', a sulphurous red that Powell couldn't stomach. The conflict between enthusiasts of these converse cultural stimulants is a major theme of the first half of *Dance*.

Powell said that one of the reasons he embarked on *Dance* was to try and recapture the epoch that ended with the Second World War: 'Nothing was ever the same again.' Unlike Evelyn Waugh, who in 1940 abandoned *Work Suspended* because 'the world in which and for which it was designed had ceased to exist', he thought, correctly, that there would still be people who would pay to read about that world regardless of whether or not it still existed. In fact you occasionally come across vestiges of it today. A year or two ago, in a television programme about Anthony Eden, I saw the inimitable Bill Deedes loose a parting shot that Powell himself might have primed. He was talking about Eden's fondness for double-breasted waistcoats – 'Always had doubts about that. So did my tailor.' Then: 'Here you had this very strong character, a very brave man, and a very able man, dressed, ever so slightly, like a shopwalker.' It could have been Stringham putting down Templer: 'I am devoted to Peter … but really I'm not sure one could have him in the house.'

Powell said of his father that mentally he remained an Edwardian subaltern all his life. He was not without Edwardian characteristics himself, one consequence of which was his objection to the promiscuous use of Christian names. 'My friends call me Tony,' he would say, emphasizing 'friends'. Since I was not a friend of his I could not bring myself to refer to him here as 'Tony'. Nor would 'Anthony' have done. 'Mr Powell' was out of the question, but to call him 'Powell' would be to promote myself to his social equal. I trust readers will overlook this presumption.

*

Anthony Powell was still alive when I had the idea of writing about him. My then agent, Giles Gordon, approached Powell's agent, Bruce Hunter, who reported that his client was opposed to any biography appearing in his life-time. Later it became apparent that he had someone else in mind for the job. As a result certain doors were closed to me and certain resources withheld,* so I am grateful to all those who were prepared to help. Top of my list are Malcolm Muggeridge's biographer, Richard Ingrams, and Muggeridge's son, Leonard. Richard lent me Muggeridge's unedited Diaries for 1948, 1949 and 1950, a period when Muggeridge and Powell met almost every day. Leonard Muggeridge gave me permission to quote from these, and also from his father's two published volumes of autobiography and the notes that exist for volume three. I am also indebted to Michael Meredith, the Eton College Librarian, and his assistant, Nick Baker. Michael put his library and archives at my disposal and then read, and amended, the chapter on Eton. Any howlers that remain are mine.

Powell was an assiduous correspondent and his letters are scattered far and wide. I am particularly grateful to Mrs Chloe Teacher, who showed me the correspondence between Powell and her father, Sir Henry d'Avigdor-Goldsmid, and also to the late Frederick Bradnum, who gave me all Powell's letters to him in connection with the radio adaptation of *Dance*. I was able to read Powell's letters to Evelyn Waugh at the British Library, which also supplied me with various books and periodicals which had slipped through the London Library's net. Powell's first letter to George Orwell is in the Orwell archive at the University College London Library.

In America I received every assistance from Nicholas Scheetz, curator of manuscripts at Georgetown University Library (correspondence with John Monagan and Christopher Sykes) and from Kathy Henderson and Tara Wenger at the Harry H. Ransom Humanities Research Center at the University of Texas at Austin (correspondence with David Higham, Jocelyn Brooke, Kay Dick, Alan Ross and Julian Maclaren-Ross). I must also thank Judy Truesdale at the Buswell Memorial Library, Wheaton College, Illinois, for sifting through Malcolm Muggeridge's extensive papers; Gayle Richardson at the Huntington Library, San Marino, California, for extracting

* e.g. Heinemann's archives at Rushden.

material from the Kingsley Amis collection; Vincent Giroud, curator of the Beinecke Rare Book and Manuscript Library, Yale (correspondence with Alan Pryce-Jones and James Lees-Milne); and Paula Deitz, editor of *The Hudson Review*, for briefing me on the Bennett Award and sending me a programme of the ceremony honouring Powell in 1984. Gary Conklin, of Gary Conklin Films, Pasadena, not only sent me a videotape of *A Question of Class*, his documentary about British writers between the wars, but also an audio tape of Paul Fussell's interview with Powell, most of which was cut from the film.

In Luxembourg Paul Caemer of the *Luxembourger Wort* was kind enough to mail me copies of Powell's articles for his paper. And in London, Mike Patterson at the Imperial War Museum Library was very helpful about details of Powell's military career and that of his father, Lieutenant-Colonel Philip Powell. I am also grateful to Sue Knowles of the BBC Sound Archives at Caversham and Nick Roberts and Helen Wanaseck of the *Punch* archives in Basil Street, London SW3.

The kernel for this book was a piece about Powell commissioned for the *London Magazine* by Alan Ross, whose memory I salute. The following were also helpful in one way or another: the late Sir Kingsley Amis, Perry Anderson, Phil Baker, John Bayley, Lieutenant-Colonel Sir John Baynes, Michael Bloch, Miranda Carter, Lieutenant-Colonel Robert Cartwright (for information about the Companion of Honour), John Coldstream, Jilly Cooper, Arthur Crook, Susan Crosland, Timothy d'Arch Smith, Basil Davidson, Michael Davie, Peter Dickinson, Willie Donaldson, M.R.D. Foot, Alistair Forbes, Paul Fussell, Roger Graef, the late Celia Goodman, Laurence Harbottle, Lady Harrod, Dominick Harrod, Richard Heygate, Bevis Hillier, Anthony Hobson (for permission to quote his account of Powell's funeral), Miles Huddleston, Chester Kemp (whose horoscope of Powell I could not, alas, find a place for), Jonathan Kooperstein (for details of Powell's correspondance with Dennis Wheatley), Paul Kronacker (for a copy of his father's memoirs), Peter Lawrence, Deirdre Levi, Jeremy Lewis, Michael Luke, Keith Marshall and Hugh Massingberd (respectively Secretary and President of the Anthony Powell Society), James Michie, Brigitte Mitchell, John Monagan, Neil Morgan (of The New Beacon school), Andrew Motion, Richard Ollard, Lucy Phipps, the late Sir John Plumb, David Pryce-Jones, the late Simon Raven, John Richardson, James Sandilands, Raymond Seitz, John Sloan, Jeremy Treglown, Kenneth Trodd, Alan Watkins, Donald Cameron Watt and Paul Willetts.

Powell was employed by Duckworth for ten years so it is appropriate that a book about him should appear in their list. I must thank Sarah Such, who commissioned it, and, in particular, her successor, Eleanor Birne, who has had the daunting task of trying to hold me to some sort of deadline. I am also very grateful to two friends, David Elliott and Mel Minnett, who have rescued me on several occasions when my computer has proved recalcitrant.

But my greatest debt is to my family, who have had to put up with someone present in body but, all too often, absent in mind. I hope they will feel it has been worthwhile.

M.B.
January 2004

1

In the Beginning

'An ounce of heredity is worth a pound of merit.'
Olive Lloyd-Baker, quoted by James Lees-Milne:
Through Wood and Dale

Anthony Powell thought it was rare to find exceptional people without exceptional antecedents, though he added that the unusual nature of those antecedents might not be immediately apparent. He spoke from experience, having dug down to the fifth century AD in order to trace the roots of his family tree. What he found was a pedigree that had seen better days, notably in the early middle ages when one of his ancestors, Rhys ap Gruffydd (1132-97) ruled much of South Wales. By Elizabethan times, when the family had begun to call themselves Powell, their estate had shrunk to a few hundred sparse acres on the border of Radnor and Hereford.

Unscathed by the Civil War and its aftermath, the Powells were undone in the late eighteenth century by the author's great-great-great-grandfather Philip (1746-1819). Reputedly irascible, demonstrably improvident, Philip Powell seems to have been in and out of hot water all his life, long before the conclusion of which he had lost all the family's land. Luckily for Philip his wife, Alice, whom he married before the rot set in, was an heiress; and although much of her dowry went to pay his debts, there remained a house at Marloes in Pembroke, overlooking St Bride's Bay, where Philip ended his days.

Philip Powell had three legitimate sons, the eldest of whom, Philip Lewis (1775-1832), was procured a commission in the Marines, then a dowdy corps by any standards. But Lieutenant Powell evidently had something to recommend him, because while serving in Great Yarmouth he met and married Elizabeth Turner, daughter of a wealthy local banker and sister of Dawson Turner FRS, botanist, antiquary and friend and patron of the watercolourist Cotman. On his marriage to Elizabeth, Philip Lewis Powell retired from the Marines. Presumably his in-laws obtained a job for him in Norfolk, because his seven children were baptised at Old Buckenham, a village near Attleborough. Eventually he moved back to Wales, to a house beside

Milford Haven called Landshipping. At his death he was described as being agent to Sir John Owen, a local magnate.

So Philip Lewis Powell had made some amends for his father's follies. But what sort of person was he? To the chagrin of his great-great-grandson, whose purpose as a novelist was to show how people behave, this was a question that could not be answered. 'I know next to nothing about my great-great-grandfathers as *men*,'[1] he told Evelyn Waugh.

Of Philip Lewis Powell's five sons, three entered the service of the East India Company. Two died young, while the third, another Philip Lewis Powell (1805-56), rose to the rank of Commander in the Company's Naval Service, retiring on the grounds of ill-health at about the time of his marriage. This occurred in 1840, his bride being Eliza Sophia Galliers, one of a large family whose home near Presteigne in Radnor was on the site of a medieval castle levelled during the Civil War. The couple went to live in Jersey, where in due course they had a son, Lionel Lewis, grandfather of Anthony Powell.

With Lionel Lewis Powell (1847-1912) we at last meet a recognisable character, albeit one whose formative years are a bit of a mystery. For instance his obituary in the *Melton Mowbray Mercury*[2] states that following the death of his father he spent several years in Italy with his mother. Yet the same year his father died, 1856, he was enrolled as a day boy at Berkhamsted Grammar School. Why Berkhamsted? Possibly because of John Dupré, a Jersey man who was Headmaster of the school from 1790 to 1805, during which time it became customary for the Jersey gentry to send their sons there.

In 1861 Mrs Powell seems to have moved to Edinburgh, where Lionel would later train to be a doctor. He spent a few terms at Edinburgh Academy, leaving in 1862; then the trail goes cold for several years. Perhaps this was when he and his mother went to Italy, which had recently become a united nation. Mrs Powell's sister Charlotte had married an English officer serving with the Bourbon army in the Kingdom of the Two Sicilies. Eliza Powell may well have been anxious to see how her sister and brother-in-law were faring under the new regime.

At his death Lionel Powell was described as a good linguist. Foreign travel in his teens would account for this. It might also explain his unrealised ambition to become a soldier, since Europe in the 1860s was a far more militaristic society than Great Britain, its big cities teeming with uniforms. Possibly his mother put her foot down, or maybe there simply wasn't the money to purchase a commission in a decent regiment; either way Lionel Powell had to settle for thirty years of part-time soldiering with the local Volunteers, whose honorary Colonel he eventually became.

1. In the Beginning

There are no clues as to why Lionel Powell decided on medicine as a profession, but in 1872, having qualified as a physician in Edinburgh and having obtained his MRCS in London, he put up his plate in Melton Mowbray, a town famous for foxhunting and pies. It was a happy choice. When not hunting himself, which he did three days a week in the season, he was profiting by its consequences. The rest of his spare time was devoted to the Leicestershire Volunteers. Although not without charm, Lionel Powell was evidently someone who had to be taken on his own terms, which included a taste for practical joking. His party piece when out for a stroll with a companion was to trip them up with his walking stick and catch them before they hit the ground, a feat that must have required split-second timing and a degree of forbearance on the part of his victim.

In 1878 Lionel Powell married Jessie Adcock, daughter and heir of William Adcock, a self-made brewer and vintner with whom he served in the Volunteers. Financially this made sense: on the death of her father in 1890 Jessie inherited £16,000, worth over a million in today's money, some of which may have been used to buy The Elms, the large and gloomy house Anthony Powell remembered as a small boy. But in other respects there was a price to pay. Because of her father's humble origins Jessie was not received everywhere in the county. Furthermore her character was markedly different from her husband's. He was a hearty extrovert, happiest in the saddle or, latterly, at the wheel of Melton Mowbray's first car. She, by contrast, was lazy and imperious, reclining on the sofa all day with a risqué novel, but quick to impose her will on anyone within range. She was also a bit of a sorceress, skilled, like Mrs Erdleigh, at reading the cards, and reputed to discomfort her enemies by means of spells.

Lionel and Jessie Powell had two children, Philip and Katherine, both of whom were largely raised by servants. In those days that was normal enough, but Philip took it hard, convinced he had been neglected. He blamed Jessie for this, but she cannot be held responsible for the mess that was apparently made of his education. I say 'apparently' because Powell, normally precise about such matters, gives no details of his father's schooling. All he says is that having failed his naval entrance exam at the age of twelve (like Evelyn Waugh's Apthorpe), Philip continued to be educated in a 'hand-to-mouth fashion' (again like Apthorpe) until it was time for him to cram for Sandhurst, a longish period being spent with a French family in Brittany. Whether this was negligence on Lionel's part, or a deliberate attempt to spend as little on his son's education as possible, is anybody's guess. But there were plenty of good schools nearby, notably Uppingham, where Philip could have gone.

Like the narrator's father in *Dance*, Philip Powell (1882-1959) grew up to be a difficult man, highly strung, caustic, often morose. No doubt the fault lay in his stars, not his irregular education; but in an Army where nine out of ten officers were public school men, he may have felt that through no fault of his own, he had got off on the wrong foot. It made no difference in the long run: he enjoyed a distinguished career that was cut short by ill-health. But just as some people are very obviously the product of their school or university, Philip Powell was defined by the terms he spent at Sandhurst and his earliest years in the army. Despite having a good enough brain to take a Second in Law at the age of 48, he was never able to refocus the perspective on life he had first acquired as a gentleman cadet. (But could not something similar be said of Winston Churchill? It is, to echo Powell himself, an interesting question.)

Philip passed out of Sandhurst at a time when the Army's shortcomings were being mercilessly exposed on the South African veldt. But while the Boer War kick-started long overdue reforms in tactics, policy and administration, it did nothing to broaden the intake of officers, all of whom were expected to possess a minimum private income of £100 a year, though in most regiments you needed at least £150. Consequently Philip, with not much money behind him, would have known that there were only a limited number of regiments he could afford to join. On the recommendation of his kinsman, Major-General (Sir) Alfred Turner, he chose the Welch Regiment, a socially undistinguished unit, but said to be good and cheap. In March 1901 he was gazetted into the 1st Battalion, then on garrison duty at Pretoria.

Commenting on his father's choice of profession – and we must assume Philip had some say in the matter – Powell notes that although it was difficult to imagine him doing anything else, he was by no means a typical soldier. He was certainly not a typical subaltern in one very important respect, for in December 1904, a few months after his return from South Africa, he became a married man. While not in breach of King's Regulations, this was simply not done, which in those days was reason enough. But this is what he did. At the age of twenty-two he married a woman fifteen years his senior – and one, moreover, who he must have known was not cut out to follow the drum. Clearly he loved her very much. And, as we shall see, time and chance offered other, more congenial avenues for advancement than regimental soldiering.

Philip's bride was Maud Mary Wells-Dymoke (1867-1954), second daughter of Lionel Wells-Dymoke (1814-92) by his second marriage, his first marriage, to another of the Galliers sisters of Presteigne, having been childless. A qualified barrister who neither needed nor bothered to practise, Lionel Wells-Dymoke was the son of an obsessive Lincolnshire squire who almost beggared himself trying to prove that he was the legitimate King's Champion and also heir to two mediaeval baronies. Lionel, who did not share his father's dynastic aspirations, got to know the Powells through his first wife, becoming godfather to Lionel Powell, who was named after him. In time his daughters would visit The Elms, and although they didn't much care for the atmosphere of the house, they were there often enough for Maud and Philip to become acquainted. To say that Maud was in danger of being left on the shelf before she and Philip reached an understanding may be an exaggeration, since she had kept her looks and was, moreover, wealthy enough in her own right to remain a good catch. Nevertheless she must have been flattered by the young man's attentions, which began while he was still at Sandhurst.

Philip would have known that a young officer's first duty – some said his only duty – was to his regiment, and that this precluded early marriage. In some regiments a newly-joined subaltern was required to sign a document promising to pay a hefty fine should he marry before becoming a captain,[3] which would probably not be for at least ten years. That this practice was illegal shows the lengths to which officers would go to prevent one of their brethren defaulting. But assuming a young officer did defy convention and marry, he could expect no preferential treatment; indeed there was a risk that he and his bride would find life so irksome that he would either send in his papers or apply for a less demanding job outside the regiment. This latter course was the one chosen by Philip Powell. In January 1908, two years after the birth of his only son, he took up the post of adjutant to The Kensingtons, a battalion of London Territorials whose Honorary Colonel, by a happy chance, was Major-General Turner.

Given his interest in military matters it is odd that Powell seems unaware of the risks his father ran in marrying when he did. Reading *Infants*, you are left with the impression that such objections as there were to the marriage came from Philip's parents, and that these were based solely on the couple's disparity in age (incidentally a further embarrassment in regimental circles, since Maud, thirty-seven when she married, could have passed for a Major's wife). Happily the marriage proved a great success, Maud dedicating herself to the welfare of her far from tranquil husband. But having had to move nine times in their first two years together she must have been relieved when Philip got his new job and they were able to settle down in a large flat in Albert Hall Mansions overlooking Kensington Gardens. It was here that Powell's memories began.

*

Anthony Dymoke Powell, an only child, was born in Westminster on Thursday 21 December 1905. In view of the great age he attained it should be recorded that he was a very sickly infant whose life hung by a thread for several days. But perhaps, even in the cradle, he knew better than to draw attention to himself, something his mother deplored.[4] At any rate, not only did he pull through, he also proved resilient enough to survive the dislocations that preceded the family's removal to Albert Hall Mansions. There, for the next five years, he was looked after by a kindly nursemaid called Clara, a martyr to 'the curse' whose sufferings, he reckoned, 'should have prepared one in the future for feminine disorders of health and temper at these regular intervals'. I think this is stretching a point. But it does suggest how ill-informed about such matters young men of Powell's sort could grow up to be. For instance Peter Quennell, later sent down from Oxford for heterosexual misdemeanours, arrived there thinking that a baby was born through the navel, while Cyril Connolly, aged eighteen, feared he'd caught syphilis after shaking the gloved hand of a French prostitute.

Reviewing a life of Compton Mackenzie, Powell noted that at Mackenzie's christening the Bad Fairy's gift had been 'just the right element of moderate unhappiness in childhood'[5] to help him to become a writer. From this it is natural to conclude that when he describes his own childhood as 'lonely ... but not unhappy', he may have left something out. Brought up to do 'ordinary things',[6] it did not escape his notice even then that his parents' marriage was out of the ordinary. No doubt there was always a certain amount of tension in the air, some of it seeping under the nursery door. A man who could literally foam with rage, as Philip Powell was once seen to do, cannot have been easy to have around the house. Still, there is no reason to disbelieve Powell's assertion that he never wished for brothers or sisters. As long as he could draw, his favourite pastime as a small boy, or play with his large collection of lead soldiers, he was content. In due course he learnt to read, but it is indicative of the part that pictures would play in his life that for many years he valued books as much for their illustrations as their words, a taste he shared with his father, whose large collection of art books included volumes devoted to Beardsley and Bakst and also a certain amount of classy erotica.

Beardsley – 'our greatest satirical artist'[7]– became a particular favourite of Powell's, and was one of those he would have invited to his 'ideal luncheon' party (the other diners being Shakespeare, John Aubrey, Byron, Wilde and Kipling).[8] Long before posters of Beardsley's work became commonplace Powell had covered a filing cabinet with copies of his drawings. Interestingly enough the novelist Jocelyn Brooke compared his writing to Beardsley's drawings: in both cases 'the blank spaces are as essential to the total effect as the lines and masses which surround them'.[9] Of course young Master Powell did not spend all his time in the nursery. He also went out every day with Clara – to Kensington Gardens, where they might meet other children and their nannies; to the Natural History Museum, another haunt of nannies and their charges; to Kensington High Street, site of new-fangled department stores like Barkers and Derry and Toms; and even to the cinema, though visits there had to be carefully vetted. His old friend Osbert Lancaster, growing up in Bayswater, used to say that what he associated with Edwardian London was the smell of hot tar and horseshit. For Powell that time and place meant the grotesque yet oddly endearing Albert Memorial, a short walk away from the flat, on the steps of which Nick Jenkins's unavailing passion for Barbara Goring is kindled.

Philip Powell was promoted to Captain in 1910. In early 1913 he left the Kensingtons and rejoined his regiment, as second-in-command of D Company in the 2nd Battalion, who were stationed at Bordon Camp near Aldershot. A few years before the Powells arrived there Christopher Isherwood's mother Kathleen, married to a Major in the York and Lancaster regiment, gave this unflattering assessment of the area:

> … half-built villas, market gardens, cemeteries and later heather, camps, pines and soldiers. Horrid atmosphere of soldiers nearly everywhere and nothing intimate or restful about the country. *How can anyone* like living in this restless sort of atmosphere![10]

Maud Powell must have found it especially trying. Intensely shy with all but her family and a few intimate friends, she relished the anonymity of London. As consort of a Territorial Adjutant her social duties were minimal. Now she had to be an 'Army wife', offering tea and sympathy to tongue tied subalterns half her age. Albert Hall Mansions was exchanged for 'Stonedene', a large, isolated bungalow in extensive grounds on a hill beside Ludshott Common. Like its fictional counterpart 'Stonehurst', Stonedene was surrounded by a sandy wilderness of heath and pine, terrain good for nothing but military exercises and golf. And like Stonehurst it was haunted, by a white spectre similar to the one seen by Billson, the Jenkinses' maid, and also by an unidentified 'thing' which would crawl up Mrs Powell's bed, later supposed to be the spirit of a much-loved dog belonging to a previous tenant. Built in about 1890, Stonedene survived until the late 1980s, being redeveloped as 'Stonedene Close', an upmarket estate.

Just as Stonehurst stands for Stonedene, I think it is fair to conclude that although about a year younger, Master Nicholas Jenkins in *The Kindly Ones* is in every other respect a dead ringer for Master Anthony Powell. An only child in a house full of adults, alert, inquisitive, articulate, self-possessed; probably too old for his years to be popular with other children, but likely to make a good impression on grown-ups, as Nicholas does when cross-examined about Army lore by General Conyers. Already he has begun to think of soldiering as 'the *natural* profession',[11] hence his disappointment at the absence of troops in the area, Stonedene being so remote.

Another feature of the Stonedene landscape to find its way into the novel is the mystical 'New Life' sect presided over by Dr Philip Oyler, who would lead his curiously garbed flock on jogs across the Common. Powell gave Dr Oyler's long hair, silky beard and white robe to Dr Trelawney, the sinister mage whose name alone is enough to give the young Jenkins an uneasy thrill. In other respects Trelawney is a projection of Aleister Crowley, later described as 'the wickedest man in the world'. There is also a sort of precedent for the interest taken in Trelawney's teachings by General Conyers: Crowley had a disciple called Captain (later Major-General) J.F.C. Fuller, a friend of Captain Powell. Fuller was an odd mixture of crank and visionary. His advanced theories on tank warfare were eagerly embraced by the Red Army and the Reichswehr in the 1920s, but his endorsement of Crowley and later of Sir Oswald Mosley, and his contempt for the 'clubbish' regimental system, meant he never got a proper hearing in Britain.

Powell's education at Stonedene was in the hands of Miss Judkins, a 'droll' spinster who bicycled round the area giving lessons to officers' children. But in the summer of 1914, when he was eight and a half, he was warned that he would soon be shipped off to prep school. Then, as told in *The Kindly Ones*, the Austrian Archduke Franz-Ferdinand was assassinated at Sarajevo, whereupon Mrs Powell rapidly went off the idea. On 4 August Great Britain declared war on Germany. Eight days later Captain Powell came into his son's bedroom and made a 'very emotional speech about going away to fight'.[12] Then he was gone, and with him went Powell's childhood and a whole way of life. Within a couple of months almost all the fathers of Miss Judkins's pupils had been either killed or wounded and Kitchener's New Army, clad in odds and ends of uniforms, were drilling on Ludshott Common. By Christmas Maud Powell and her son had left Stonedene and begun to follow the drum in earnest.

Always prone to digestive disorders, Captain Powell probably owed his life to his delicate insides. Some time towards the end of October, having taken part in the gruelling retreat from Mons and seen the Germans advance shoulder to shoulder in their suicidal attack at Langemarck, he suffered such a severe attack of dysentery that the following month he was invalided home. In his absence the 2nd Welch were all but annihilated at Gheluvelt, a strategic village on the Menin Road that barred the way to Ypres. Of the twenty-seven officers who had sailed for France with Captain Powell only one remained unwounded three months later; among those killed were the Commanding Officer, the Adjutant and his company commander.[13]

On his recovery Captain Powell was admitted to that promised land of all soldiers, the Staff. There he remained for the rest of the war, serving in France throughout 1916, otherwise at home. That he was very good at his job there can be no doubt. Three times mentioned in dispatches in the space of a few months, he was awarded the DSO in July 1916. In 1918 he was made CBE and promoted to Brevet Lieutenant-Colonel.

Wherever possible Mrs Powell tried to find quarters near her husband, a resolution that took mother and son from London to Wensleydale, from Wensleydale to Salisbury Plain and thence to Cambridge, finally fetching up again in London. Logistically it must have been a nightmare: they lived in hotels, boarding houses and furnished rooms; the houses or flats of friends, an estate cottage and undergraduate digs. But for Powell, whose life so far had been very sheltered, the experience was salutary. He began to appreciate 'the vast extent of human oddness', which phrase he would later use to explain what genealogy had taught him. Another discovery made at this time was not so welcome: how unpleasant other small boys could be. This became apparent at Gibbs's, the London day-school he entered shortly after his ninth birthday, remaining there for four terms. Then, rather late in the day, he was sent to The New Beacon, a prep school near Sevenoaks, most of whose pupils were the sons of professional soldiers or sailors.*

In his essay on Eton, 'The Wat'ry Glade', published in 1934, Powell wrote that his prep school 'reflected in some degree the atmosphere, if not the conditions, of Dotheboys Hall'. Forty years on he saw no reason to dissent from this judgement: 'I should be unwilling to live five minutes of it again.' Part of the trouble was the war, which by 1916 had begun to squeeze the pips on the Home Front. This meant that school food was not only worse than before – an achievement in itself – but in short supply. Then again, as Powell himself conceded, he had had it pretty cushy up to now. Most boys went away to school at eight. He was ten and a half, old enough to know when he was well off, particularly in wartime. Still, it is a measure of how miserable he became that he was 'almost inclined to doubt [the Headmaster's] often-repeated assertion that life was worse in the trenches'.

* The New Beacon thrives to this day. A history of the school – Hugh Barty-King, *The New Beacon* (The Bath Press, 2000) – contains a brief and inaccurate entry for Powell.

The Headmaster was a short-sighted and irascible little man in his late sixties called John Stewart Norman, whose life's work had been his school. When the war robbed him of all his able-bodied male staff he simply took on more duties himself, teaching every subject, coaching every game and devising means by which the boys might 'do their bit', such as chopping wood or helping at a local farm. With several generals among parents and Old Boys, he was able in 1916 to visit the British army's GHQ in France and quiz the top brass about the conduct of the war. When he returned he divided the school into six companies and made them drill with wooden rifles twice a week.

Norman's approach to life was spartan. In the words of Powell's friend Henry Yorke (in future known by his pseudonym of Henry Green), he 'praised the boy who, seeing he could not make a catch, put his face in the way and broke his nose'. Green, while not disputing that Norman was bad-tempered and tyrannical, says that in the end he came to 'reverence him'.[14] In *Infants* Powell laughs up his sleeve at such Old Boy sentimentality and then notes that although Green, unlike Powell himself, found Kipling unreadable, he is the one to praise 'a famous man of little showing'. The explanation for this otherwise rather ponderous allusion must lie in the fact that a few pages previously Powell had likened Norman, with his thick spectacles and shredded-wheat moustache, to the photo of Kipling that hangs beside the main stairs in the London Library.

Every schoolboy has the right to rubbish his teachers if he chooses, so Powell's verdict on Norman – a sadistic old philistine with an uncontrollable temper – must stand. But in one respect at least the regime at The New Beacon was enlightened: boys were allowed to talk for half-an-hour after lights out, and it was then that Powell and Green began their careers as storytellers. I mention this concession because at my own prep school in the 1950s talking after lights out was a beatable offence, as I discovered to my cost within a few weeks of going there. I suspect that this was always the case at most prep schools – and at a good many public schools as well.

At Gibbs's Powell had spent just enough time on the playing fields to conclude that he would never be any good at games. At The New Beacon, when he became, briefly, quite a sturdy little boy, he played for the First XV and won his weight at boxing. But this was an aberration. Sport would play no part in his life or his books. Without being particularly averse to hearties as such, he would often point out that to be good at games was not, as so many schoolmasters then believed, a prerequisite for success in life. For instance, he knew of several distinguished soldiers and sailors who were not in the least physically tough as schoolboys.

Powell still hoped to become a soldier himself, as indeed did many of his schoolmates. Despite the shortages, the chores and the casualty lists, which included fathers and brothers of boys at the school, they were not downhearted. Then one November morning when they were doing Livy with the Headmaster, his wife burst in with news of the Armistice. A holiday was declared, so that the rest of the day was spent in playing football and chopping wood, neither activity very congenial to Powell. Then Mr Norman had second thoughts: there would be prep after all, he said, otherwise the timetable would be disrupted. The following term Powell took the Common Entrance exam for Eton, experiencing a feeling of 'indescribable wellbeing' on learning that he had passed.

Why Eton, rather than an 'Army' school like Wellington, which would certainly have been cheaper? Because Philip Powell was leaving nothing to chance. The product of a botched upbringing himself, he was determined that this would not be the case with his son. No doubt snobbery came into it too, but that is beside the point. What matters is that without Eton and the habit of mind he acquired there, Anthony Powell could not have written *A Dance to the Music of Time*. The £300 a year it then cost was money well spent.

2

The Best of Schools

'Being a gentleman is the priceless heritage we receive from Mother Eton.'
General Sir Henry Rawlinson, in a speech to his old school

'If a single idea can be caught running through such diversity it is the idea of style.'
Richard Ollard: *An English Education*

Eton boys wear black, it is said, because they are still in mourning for their great benefactor, George III. But in May 1919, when A.D. Powell first appears in the School List, the sombre uniform had an immeasurably grimmer significance. In the war that had just ended, 1160 Old Etonians had been killed, approximately one in five of those who had marched away, the equivalent of a whole generation. What impact did such a tragedy have on Powell and his contemporaries? This is hard to assess, not least because, as Richard Ollard says in his book on Eton in the first half of the last century, 'Before a horror so universal, so immediate and so huge, imagination and analysis retire scorched.'[1] Another point to remember is that in 1919 there was a concerted effort on the part of institutions like Eton to turn back the clock to 1914. As the *Eton College Chronicle* reminded its readers, the Eton and Harrow match would resume at Lord's, while that 'remarkable festival', the Fourth of June, would once again be celebrated with all its tribal pageantry.

Powell saw a link between Eton's pomp and the magnitude of its sacrifice: 'If the prizes offered [at Eton] were splendid, the oblation was no less unstinted.' In other words, *noblesse oblige*. But that is a retrospective comment. During his first couple of years there he would have been far too busy keeping his head above water to brood over the roll of honour, which was not officially unveiled until 1922. By then, as he told the American writer, Paul Fussell, he had made two very significant discoveries. First, he became aware that this was 'an incredibly exciting period for the arts. There was this curious sort of flowering, coupled with an urge to beautify things. I think the war had a lot to do with this. Modern art had gone about as far as it could go before 1914. The war closed everything down. Then it burst out afterwards, just as the song said it would: "*Après la guerre/* There'll be a good time everywhere".'

Powell's second discovery was that there were other boys in the school, some very talented, who shared his passion for the arts. 'It seemed a very exciting thing in one's life and is what I am most grateful to Eton for.'[2]

*

When people want to know what Eton was like immediately after the Great War they generally turn first to Cyril Connolly's full-blooded account in *Enemies of Promise*. Shorn of all its intellectual and romantic baggage this describes how, after a hellish couple of years as a junior, an ugly boy who has nothing to offer but wit and charm somehow achieves the most glittering prize of all, membership of Pop, the self-elected oligarchy dominated by athletes. But 'early laurels weigh like lead': his life since then, he confesses, has been an anti-climax. He now regrets that 'moral cowardice and academic outlook' prevented him from befriending a set of literary and artistic boys, among them Powell, 'who in fact gained most from Eton because of the little they gave'.[3] Powell objected to this. He and the others, he told me, 'gave just as much as Connolly did', the difference being that Connolly was 'enormously ambitious' as a schoolboy and they, for the most part, were not.[4] But I think that where Powell is concerned, Connolly had a point. Powell's essay on Eton, 'The Watr'y Glade', published a few years before *Enemies of Promise*, is a droll account of four years spent in 'well-deserved obscurity' at the 'worst' house in the school. Neither then, nor forty years later in *Infants*, does Powell express anything but quiet satisfaction at belonging to such a disreputable house, which had not got through the first round of the football ties for more than ten years. He also has a dig at Pop, noting that while membership was 'considered life's highest ambition', there were limits to its authority, as witness its humiliating failure to control an unruly mob of junior boys during the official Peace celebrations in the summer of 1919.

This is not the place to discuss Powell's ambivalent attitude to Connolly, whom he knew only by sight at Eton. But it's interesting to observe that however different their school careers, both grasped the point of Eton immediately. Here is Connolly enjoying a break from the rigours of the Foundation Scholarship:

> I looked over the bridge as a boy in an outrigger came gliding past like a waterboatman. Two Etonians were standing on the bridge and I heard one remark,

'Really that man Wilkinson's not at all a bad oar.' The foppish drawl, the two boys with hats on the back of their heads, the graceful sculler underneath, seemed the incarnation of elegance and maturity ... There was no doubt that this was the place for me.[5]

Two years later, on his second day at the school, Powell looked out of his study window 'in the hope of seeing something of interest'. Here is what he saw:

A boy of about fifteen was walking slowly along the far side of the road with one hand in his pocket and the other supporting a pile of books, which rested like a field-marshal's baton against his thigh. His top hat was at the back of his head and he wore exceptionally short trousers and light-coloured socks. One of his shoulders was higher than the other and a slight sag at the knees made him an almost perfect specimen of the world-famous Eton slouch. While he walked he whistled ... This was the most sophisticated thing I had ever seen. I realised at once that the boy was a figure from a new world.[6]

Of course the fundamental difference between Powell's experience of Eton and Connolly's is that Connolly was a scholar and Powell was not. In a school of about eleven hundred boys, the seventy scholars, derisively known as 'tugs',* were herded together in College, an intellectual fastness to which Oppidans (the other boys) were rarely admitted. It was Connolly's bad luck – and his readers' good luck – to be a junior there when authority was vested in a succession of bullies, but even had this not been the case, his perspective would still have been very different from Powell's.

That said, Oppidans were just as likely to be knocked about as Collegers (to give tugs their official title). In a school where robust adolescent boys ruled the roost a fair amount of brutality was inevitable. For instance this was the welcome Powell's contemporary Oliver Messel got as a new boy: 'What the f*** you think you are doing, you ruddy little c**t?' Messel learnt to dread the shout of 'Boy!' Every task he attempted as a fag 'was met with disapproval and resulted in a flying leap with a switchy cane'.[7] Yet his house, Robeson's, was considered pretty lax. Powell was exceptionally lucky to be in a house that set so little store by the traditional shibboleths of games, fagging and corporal punishment; indeed someone who was at the school a few years later was astonished to learn that he had not once been beaten – 'Are you *sure* you've got that right?'[8]

Powell was at Goodhart's, so called because at Eton the houses are known by the surname of the housemaster rather than the title of the building, in

* From *toga*, Latin for a gown, which scholars wore.

this case Walpole House. A classical scholar, educated at Eton and King's College, Cambridge, A.M. Goodhart (1866-1941) was acknowledged as something of an enigma. His mastery of the black arts of the Wall Game, which he still played in his fifties, was legendary, yet he was also the most accomplished musician on the staff, earning this valedictory tribute from the Headmaster, Dr Cyril Alington: 'As skilled to guide sweet music's dying fall / As organise mere murder at the Wall.'

Like many Eton masters Goodhart was considered a little odd, sharing with Isherwood's Mr Norris an obsession with women's footwear, though there is no evidence to suggest that he did more than pore over catalogues devoted to these items. A bachelor, who reminded Powell of Swinburne's friend, Watts-Dunton, to look at, he was rumoured to have proposed to the distinguished pianist, Irene Scharrer, who married another musical house-master, S.G. Lubbock. Perhaps this was a lucky escape for Goodhart, since it has been said that there is no unhappier creature on earth than a fetishist who yearns for a woman's shoe and has to embrace the whole woman.

Powell thought that in addition to being 'kinky', Goodhart was probably a repressed bisexual. But bisexual or not, Goodhart was determined that there would be no hanky-panky in his house, annoying everyone by his habit of prowling round after lights-out with his ears cocked for sounds of depravity. One evening an unidentified boy eased open the door of his study and threw a tray at the patrolling housemaster's back. The same thing happened on the two floors above, prompting Goodhart to ring the fire alarm at 6.30 the next morning and order the house to report to him immediately – 'just as you are'. Some of the more quick-witted pretended to take him at his word, arriving either stark naked or wearing just a shoe or a sock, which made a nonsense of his attempt to find the culprits.[9] This happened about a year before Powell arrived, a particularly disorderly period at Goodhart's which culminated in a mass sacking. One of those ejected subsequently became a bootlegger, which suggests that Scott Fitzgerald was on the right lines when he had Gatsby boast of being 'an Oxford man'.

Powell used to say that Goodhart represented 'a far more exotic form of life' than Jenkins's housemaster, Le Bas. All they had in common was a funny way of standing with both feet pointing in the same direction, and the habit of bringing out unexpected quotations. But according to Malcolm Muggeridge, who heard it from Powell, Goodhart was the victim of a famous joke like the one Stringham plays on Le Bas, kidding the police that his housemaster is 'Braddock alias Thorne', a local fraudster. The perpetrator was a character called Bill Allen, at Goodhart's before Powell and later a sidekick of Sir Oswald Mosley's. Allen saw a notice in a local shop saying that someone had lost his umbrella in St George's Chapel:

> He answered this advertisement saying that Goodhart had the umbrella. The chap in due course applied to Goodhart for it and of course there was a row. Goodhart ordered Allen to go to the man and apologise for what he'd done. Allen went along, but instead of apologising, told the man that he'd a message from Goodhart that, after all, he'd got the umbrella.[10]

What punishment Allen received is not recorded, but it comes as no surprise to learn that despite his Mosleyite past he was recruited by MI6, later becoming their bureau chief in Ankara. He is also one of many Old Etonians mentioned in *White Mischief*, James Fox's lurid account of Happy Valley and the murder of Lord Erroll.

Powell's affectionate memories of Goodhart are in sharp contrast to those of Lord David Cecil, three years senior to him, who considered his housemaster 'a deplorable figure – perfectly futile'.[11] To judge from my researches Lord David was in a majority, but what matters here is Powell's opinion. He could live with Goodhart, a far less oppressive figure than Mr Norman and one, moreover, whose snooping posed no threat to the fastidious young heterosexual he was growing up to be. Too fastidious? Goodhart hints at this in the reports Powell quotes from in *Infants*. He regrets that such a sensible, conscientious and dignified boy appears to have difficulty in making friends, and fears it may be because he comes across as 'superior and coldly critical'. ('Why are you so stuck up?' Gypsy Jones asks Jenkins. 'I'm just made that way.' 'You ought to fight it.' 'I can't see why.') It says something for Goodhart that he recognises that his pupil's demeanour 'may simply be due to shyness'.

Another interesting comment on Powell at Goodhart's was told me by John Bayley, who heard it from Lord David Cecil, briefly Powell's fagmaster. Tony, said Lord David, was 'always extremely neat and tidy – like a little pixie. He was quaint.'[12] You have only to see the photograph of Powell as a fag in *Infants* ('sitting there cross-legged and very fetching'[13] according to Simon Raven) to appreciate what Lord David was getting at. Perhaps this was why Lord David hadn't the heart to punish him when he let his fire go out, the nearest he seems to have come to a beating.

What were the other boys at Goodhart's like? This is a difficult question to answer because, with one or two exceptions like Hubert Duggan and Denys Buckley, Powell virtually ignores them. But to judge from the School List, which gives every boy's home address and the name of his parent or guardian, all Goodhart's pupils, as you would expect, were out of the top drawer or the one below it. In 1919 about a third of the house either had titles or would inherit them, quite a high proportion even for Eton. But if A.D. Powell seemed a little aloof, it would not have been because he deliberately put on airs to compensate for his relatively modest background. Snobbery at Eton in the Twenties began and ended on the playing fields and the river. A more likely explanation is that he already had the makings of a highbrow and could not always conceal his impatience with boys less gifted than he. The habit of grading people according to their intelligence would remain with him to the end of his days.

We shall never know for sure whether Powell would have had a harder time of it at another house, let alone another school. Still, Eton afforded one priceless amenity no other boarding school could offer: a room of one's own from first term to last. This undoubtedly encouraged a measure of individualism, even eccentricity, without which the pressure to conform might well have been overwhelming. Revisiting the school after twenty years, in the company of Malcolm Muggeridge, Powell insisted that far from the boys looking odd in their tailcoats and top hats, he felt everyone else was out of place, and 'almost felt the flaps of his own coat as he walked along'.

While watching a game of cricket on that same visit, Powell said something to Muggeridge that contradicts the impression he liked to give of being a committed 'scug', as boys who had no colours were known:

> Tony said it was extraordinary, looking back, with what passionate intensity he had longed to have the right to wear some of the coloured caps the boys we watched were wearing. I said it wasn't really extraordinary since, in the context of the school, they represented power and authority, therefore infinitely desirable to the will.[14]

This is probably the place to summarise Powell's athletic record at Eton. Loathing cricket, he opted for the river, coxing the Junior House four in 1921 and rowing at two in the same boat the following year. In the winter he either went beagling with the school pack or played the Field Game, a code of football so arcane that it was never in any danger of catching on elsewhere. Powell eventually captained Goodhart's second Field, earning this ironic accolade from Hubert Duggan: 'always a good type of boy does that'.

Hubert Duggan, the younger brother of Alfred Duggan, the historical novelist, was one of several well-connected boys Powell knew at school whom Evelyn Waugh would subsequently annex. The model for Stringham as a schoolboy, he also, on his deathbed, inspired the scene in *Brideshead*

Revisited where the dying Lord Marchmain appears to return to the Church. In photographs Duggan always looks immaculate, yet I associate him – and Stringham – with the dishevelled young dandy Powell glimpsed through the window of his study, all three defined by the debonair insouciance that Eton was then thought to bestow. The fact that Duggan had not a drop of English blood in his veins is a reminder that the English upper classes have always rated manners above extraction.

Eighteen months older than Powell and a year senior to him, Duggan was the stepson of the Foreign Secretary, Lord Curzon, who married his beautiful American mother following the death from drink of his father, a wealthy Argentinian of Irish extraction. Neither Hubert Duggan nor Alfred, being Catholics, was down for Eton, but at the last moment their mother personally persuaded Dr Alington to find places for them. Alfred, in the same house as Harold Acton, gave early notice of the dissipation that became his hallmark. He broke out once too often to meet a local girl and was sacked. Hubert, less of a rebel than his brother, survived to become house captain.

Given the disparity in their ages, the friendship between Powell and Hubert Duggan could probably only have flourished at Eton, where Oppidan houses averaged a mere forty boys. It must have been thanks to Duggan that Powell was elected to the house Library, five or six senior boys whose status was roughly that of prefects in other schools. Powell, Duggan and Denys Buckley, later a Lord Justice of Appeal, used to mess together, Eton slang for the high tea boys laid on for themselves in their studies, the 'predominant' meal of the day according to Powell's contemporary, Harold Acton.[15] They also went about together outside the house, and one day overheard themselves described as 'Goodhart's bloody trio' by a small boy Powell identifies as Evelyn Waugh's future commanding officer, (Major-General Sir) Robert Laycock.

At school the gulf between Powell's background and Duggan's could be ignored. Both professed the tolerant scepticism that Powell saw as characteristic of Goodhart's; both had a taste for ironic understatement. Duggan, although far from being a highbrow, could sometimes surprise Powell by the breadth of his reading, while Powell, a soldier's son, could tell his friend a thing or two about the profession for which Duggan was theoretically destined. But just as Stringham leaves Jenkins behind once they become adults, so the friendship between Duggan and Powell effectively ended with their schooldays. Money, in each case, was what divided them.

Interestingly enough, Powell's friend John Heygate (about whom more anon) explored the same theme in his Eton novel *Decent Fellows*, which generated volumes of hot air when it appeared in 1930. The hero, a solicitor's son called Denis, gets in with some swells and neglects his work. His housemaster reminds him that the rich are different: they can afford to loaf.

> 'Many boys in the house will never have to do anything for a living, though I don't say they won't. Peter Ockley, for instance. But your father told me it was essential for you to get a scholarship if you were to go up to the Varsity…[a]nd at the moment I can't see you getting one … By all means mess with Peter and Oliver Harbord. First rate fellows, but you must remember the difference. You've got to work for your living and they haven't.'[16]

Decent Fellows probably contributed to one of the myths about Eton that Powell refutes in *Infants*, namely, that only Collegers ever did any work there. On the contrary, says Powell: until a boy passed the School Certificate – roughly speaking GCSE – he worked longer hours than a German boy of the same age. And what did he study? Latin, Latin and yet more Latin (as General Conyers might have said), plus Greek and yet more Greek if, like Powell, he had done it at his prep school. Classics masters, better paid than their colleagues and in a majority, ran the show, teaching English, History, Geography and Divinity in addition to their own subjects. Only Maths, French, Science and Drawing were out of their hands. Junior boys also had to learn something by heart every week, an activity known as a Saying Lesson, and everyone, without exception, was subject to Sunday Questions, a religious test which had to be handed in on Mondays.

Such an intensely literary education was bound to leave its mark on even the least receptive boys, which must explain that occasion at the Ritz when Peter Templer, to Jenkins's surprise, quotes Rowland Egerton-Warburton, a minor Victorian poet. But very little time was spent in teaching boys to write good English, which it was assumed they would pick up from their classical studies and their familiarity with, for example, the Prayer Book and the Bible. Powell did not regret this, despite the stick he received from reviewers for bad grammar. The great thing about English, he maintained, was its flexibility, which pedants were always seeking to confine. He thought Latin was 'an enormous help' in writing English and presumed that people like Clive James who objected to his 'copious employment of dangling participles'[17] had probably never done Latin, which was not true of James, or of another persistent critic of his grammar, Simon Raven.

After taking the School Certificate Powell became a History specialist, being taught by (Sir) Henry Marten, who later tutored the future Queen Elizabeth the Second. Powell awards Marten full marks for presentation, but implies that he was too inhibited to see the full picture; for instance he could only conceive of homosexuality as 'beastliness'. One wonders if Marten ever discussed the matter with Mrs Warre-Cornish. This formidable dowager, whose husband had been the school's Vice-Provost for twenty years, was once asked whether there was much homosexuality at Eton. 'Oh indeed,' she replied, 'it's an ancient, aristocratic, traditional vice here, but quite unknown in the sanitary, linoleum schools.' Powell himself thought there was a book to be written about 'the extraordinary lack of experience of schoolmasters' He marvelled at the determination of another Eton master, George Lyttelton, to remain 'intensely prim and buttoned-up' throughout his correspondence with Rupert Hart-Davis, whose revelations about his private life – he lived with his mistress during the week, with his wife at weekends – must have shaken Lyttelton 'to the core'.[18]

But Powell was impressed by one aspect of the teaching at Eton which he doubted was to be found elsewhere:

> [I]t was assumed, or so it seemed to me, that every boy would at one time or another be in some such position as viceroy of India and must be brought up with this end in view ... The government of the country was somehow made almost a personal matter. It was as if, instead of saying, 'If you don't learn to speak French properly, you will never be able to enjoy yourself in Paris,' our mentors said: 'If you don't learn some sort of civilised behaviour, England will become uninhabitable for everybody.'[19]

Powell's contemporary, Lord Home, put it rather more pompously at an Eton Ramblers' dinner: 'Life is service and the foundation of service is integrity and it is because Eton teaches integrity to her sons that we hold the proud conceit that as Eton flourishes so too does the country.'[20]

*

Life at Eton could be claustrophobic for someone who was no good at games. The playing fields, the fives courts and the river, not the classroom, were where you acquired friends from other houses. But luckily for Powell there existed a meeting place for boys of all ages 'whose adventures', as he put it, 'took place in the world of the imagination'. This was the old Studio, situated about fifty yards up the road from Goodhart's, a long, low dusty room, lit by two skylights, smelling of paint and turpentine and full of artistic clutter. It was in this 'nook of the Latin Quarter', a cross between a workshop and a salon, that Powell found 'a retreat from surrounding school life so pleasant that even the holidays were scarcely in competition'. Here he first learnt about avant-garde painters like Matisse and Picasso. Here he attended lectures by Sir William Rothenstein and Roger Fry, whose aesthetic puritanism he soon came to reject. Here, in the debates that took place on Saturday evenings, his critical faculties were unleashed. Years later Malcolm Muggeridge would write that 'everyone has a "*real*" something in their lives. Tony's is "*real kultur*"'.[21] The Studio was where this preoccupation began.

Presiding over the Studio until Powell's final year was the Drawing Master, Sidney Evans, whose father and grandfather had held the same post. A genial bohemian from the pages of *Trilby*, Evans had the good sense to realise that however pretentious some of the talk that went on round him, it was motivated by a genuine passion for the arts. 'We felt we had a mission', wrote Harold Acton, 'and chafed at the restrictions of a life regulated by games and the winning of colours.'[22] Powell was not so militant. Unlike Acton, whose housemaster was a pothunting philistine, he had no pricks to kick against. Nor was he consumed by ambition, like Acton's friend and ally, Brian Howard. Nevertheless when, in February 1922, the Eton Society of the Arts was formed, his was one of eleven names on the teamsheet pinned to the Studio's wall (the twelfth man was their President, Mr Evans).

Of 'the Characters of the Eleven' assessed by Powell, three need not concern us here because they played no significant part in his life after school. A fourth, R.L. Spence, is only worth mentioning because of the way Powell sums him up, in a sentence that reveals as much about himself as it does about his subject: 'Doing his duty, behaving well, being quietly agreeable, seem entirely to have engaged his life.' Hugh Lygon, at Goodhart's with Powell, is another of the Etonians referred to earlier whom Evelyn Waugh latched on to. The younger son of Earl Beauchamp, chubby and blond, he had no artistic pretensions and probably owed his inclusion to his *beaux yeux*. Like several of the others he died comparatively young, achieving posthumous fame as the suggested model for Sebastian in *Brideshead Revisited*. Harold Acton's younger brother, William, beefy enough to play lock for the Eton rugby XV, showed promise as a painter, the profession he followed in the Thirties, but his health was permanently impaired at Oxford by a drunken fall from a third-storey window, and after an exacting five years as a ranker in the Pioneer Corps, he died mysteriously in his bath at the end of the war.

The secretary of the Society was Powell's friend from The New Beacon, Henry Green, whose treatment of their proceedings in his enigmatic memoir, *Pack My Bag*, endorses Powell's description of him as 'very, *very* complicated and tricky'.[23] One minute he says their debates were 'like a conversation between women, whoever got up to speak only did so to show off'. Then he says their conversations were like those you were supposed to have at university, but which he himself never did, 'in which the course of life is plotted so they say like bringing a smack into Southampton'. He is equally undecided about the members' motives. Were they really cocking a snook at the strutting athletes who thought them all 'awful'? Or did some of them secretly hope to use the Society of Arts as a way of getting into Pop by the back door? Powell says, with some justice, that he is condescending. But buried in the elliptical prose is the admission that joining the Society was a watershed: 'I determined to be a writer.'[24] A year or so later, while he was still at Eton, he had begun to write his first novel, *Blindness*, a *roman à clef* which is set at a public school called Noat.

Green, incidentally, may well provide the answer to the mystery of Widmerpool's overcoat, which was 'wrong' in a way that is never disclosed. In *Pack My Bag* he reveals that as an act of rebellion he deliberately bought an overcoat that came down well below the knee.* While this was not a beatable offence it was certainly 'not done', and for some time he was not allowed to forget this.[25] Even though Green was in another house Powell must have known about his friend's aberration. In the absence of any other clues it seems reasonable to suppose that Widmerpool's overcoat was cut from the same cloth as Green's.

Robert Byron, no relation to the poet, was the most belligerent member of the Society, noted for what Harold Acton called his 'provocative tirades'.[26] He specialised in butchering sacred cows, tearing into classical sculpture one minute, Post-Impressionist painting the next. Shakespeare was a particular *bête noire* of his, but even terms like 'intellectual' and 'good taste' could set him off. He was equally vehement in defence of the things he liked: at Eton and Oxford, Victoriana – a deeply unfashionable cause in the Twenties; later, Byzantine art and architecture (reviewing his second book *The Station*, D.H. Lawrence wrote: 'Byzantine is to Mr Byron what Baroque is to the Sitwells'). A genuine eccentric, the 'Englishman abroad' *par excellence*, Byron was killed in the war when the destroyer taking him to Egypt was torpedoed. Powell saw the point of him and thought that had he survived the war he might have become that essentially continental type, the intellectual man of action (the role Widmerpool pretends to after the war). But he and Byron were never close: he didn't care for people who liked nothing better than a good row.**

---

* I have been told that (Sir) James Goldsmith committed the same offence.

** According to his biographer, James Knox, Byron thought Powell 'very boring' at Eton and Oxford. He thought better of him on hearing Powell's bloodcurdling account of the 'golf and bridge' world he encountered as a probationer in the Territorial Army.

Powell cared even less for the Society's *louche* founder, Brian Howard, who was probably the person Green had in mind when he talked of getting into Pop by the back door. This Howard failed to achieve, but, such was his panache, he could scarcely have been more conspicuous in Pop than out of it. Tall, lean and pallid, with unusually long eyelashes, sensual lips and a voice that Osbert Lancaster likened to heavy scent, Howard could amuse and abuse with equal facility. An exemplar of Cocteau's dictum that the secret of life is knowing how far to go too far, he eventually overstepped the mark, but in the Twenties he made the bright young people dance to his tune.

At Eton, after a wobbly start, Howard used his calculated impertinence for aesthetic ends. While 'most of us' as Cyril Connolly admitted, 'had not yet caught up with Brooke or Flecker', Howard was reading and quoting Eliot and Pound. Aged fifteen he brought off a precocious double-whammy, contributing a satirical piece about modernist poetry to the influential weekly, *The New Age*, and exhibiting a sketch at the 1920 International Exhibition. The following year, on reading some of his poems, Edith Sitwell called him 'a born writer'. It was his idea to mark the founding of the Society with a one-off avant-garde magazine, *The Eton Candle*, dedicated to the memory of Swinburne and incorporating an Old Etonian supplement as well as contributions by boys. The result was a triumph, the only one of its kind that Howard would enjoy. At Oxford, pressurised by his snobbish American mother, he gave up the arts for 'Lordolatry', the first false step down a primrose path so brilliantly mapped by Connolly in *Where Engels Fears to Tread*.

If Brian Howard was the most sophisticated Etonian of his generation, the most cultivated was undoubtedly Harold Acton, a stylish and extravagantly mannered Anglo-American whose cosmopolitan background was straight out of Henry James. He had been brought up near Florence at La Pietra, a serene Renaissance villa with Baroque embellishments which was already on the discerning visitor's map. The house had been bought by his mother, an heiress from Chicago (like Hubert Duggan's mother), and furnished and restored by his father, an English artist and collector whose family had lived in Italy since the eighteenth century. Surrounded by works of art, indulged by the steady stream of cognoscenti who visited La Pietra, young Acton had acquired a sensibility that several years of team games and house spirit could not shake. An unrepentant muff, he positively gloried in the name of aesthete. Powell enjoyed his company at Eton but felt he did the arts a disservice at Oxford with his camping about.[27]

Powell himself was not a mover and shaker, preferring, as Harold Acton put it, to participate 'discreetly'. He organised an exhibition of portraits by members of the Society, spoke briefly in defence of the Post-Impressionists and did a pen and ink drawing for the *Candle* of a fierce-looking Colonel of Hussars. His interests at this period were still primarily visual: military regalia, Regency costume, and illustrators, particularly Aubrey Beardsley and Claud Lovat Fraser. But more important was his belief in the integrity of art, which he thought the Society ought to reflect. He did not want it to become a kind of Bohemian alternative to Pop, which had begun life as a debating society and then been overrun by athletes.

The athletes did not arrive at the drawing school and the *Eton College Chronicle* continued to devote far more space to Junior House cricket matches than the Society's goings on, which were lucky to get a couple of lines. But in July 1922 Sidney Evans retired and his replacement, a master who had formerly taught French, was in Powell's opinion a disaster. He stuck it until the following January, by which time Harold Acton and Robert Byron had left for Oxford and a majority of the Society seemed in favour of working with marionettes. 'Puppets', as he calls them, did not appeal to Powell, and he resigned.

*

The night before he left Eton, Powell had one drink too many in the course of saying his goodbyes and woke up with what sounds like his first serious hangover. This would not have mattered so much had he been going straight home, but unfortunately he had ten days of Corps camp ahead of him, which meant parading in full fig at about 7 a.m. and marching through Eton and up Windsor Hill to the main-line station where they would entrain for Salisbury Plain. The effort of presenting himself more or less correctly proved too much and, rather than fall over, he fell out. Some boys would have laughed it off but Powell, a sergeant, took the Corps more seriously than most. Even worse, his default was witnessed by his company commander, referred to by Powell as 'someone who had been almost entirely responsible for winning the war', a vainglorious master who had never forgiven him for once pointing out that his left puttee was unravelling. But this 'bitter moment' was redeemed when someone suggested he bring up the rear in a local cab, which in those days were still horse-drawn. For once he had no qualms about drawing attention to himself, rattling along in state like 'one of the tableaux in the Lord Mayor's Show'.[28]

Powell was barely seventeen and a half when he left Eton. Had he been a games player he might well have fancied staying another year and adding to his collection of colours. As it was, he was ready to go. Although he couldn't have foreseen this at the time, none of the boys he had known there would become close friends of his. Nor was Eton much of a help in 'getting on', at least before the war. But without being in the least sentimental about his schooldays, the true *vice Anglais,* he retained a great affection for Eton and her ways, sent both his sons there and was truly sorry his grandson chose to go to Dulwich College, a London day school, instead.[29]

What did Powell gain from Eton? Primarily, I think, familiarity with the 'new world' he had glimpsed through his study window, a world in which there was always something of interest to see. It can be no coincidence that thirty years later, in the blurb to *A Question of Upbringing,* he should invoke that epiphany and explain that his object in this, and subsequent volumes, was to convey what he had seen through the window 'during the course of these last three strange decades.' Of course this new world stretched far beyond Eton; indeed its charm lay in the number of different bases it touched, from Chancelleries to Charlotte Street, peeresses to *poules de luxe.* But whether Powell would have got to know it so well had he not been to Eton is debatable. Talent, for a man without the right social credentials, was not enough in those days: you had to sing for your supper and, if necessary, put up with snubs. Neither of these came easily to Powell, as I think one can infer from what Jenkins says here:

> Later in life, I learnt that many things one may require have to be weighed against one's dignity, which can be an insuperable barrier against advancement in almost any direction.

Another benefit of his being at Eton in the early Twenties is obvious. He was there with some remarkable characters, most of whom he captured, Aubrey-fashion, in his Memoirs and Journals, and a few of whom he cannibalised for *Dance.* Interestingly, the ones he actually knew at school, like Acton, Byron, Howard and Green, had rather less impact on his life than some of those with whom he simply overlapped, like Cyril Connolly and George Orwell, Alan Pryce-Jones, John Heygate and Rupert Hart-Davis.

Then there is style, which was always going to make a greater impression on Powell than on his grander schoolmates, to whom it was second nature. Aristocratic in origin, it made for elegance, amiability, easy manners and absence of fuss, qualities that had been largely absent from Powell's life so far. Within a few weeks of his arrival Powell had succumbed to its charm:

> I felt that at last I was among men. Later on in the half I coxed a boat for two of the more senior members of my house. Their manner and the terms with

which they greeted disobliging circumstances confirmed me in this opinion. Many of the phrases used by them were still unfamiliar, but the words had a vigour which demanded immediate respect. There was a certainty about the standards of the people I found myself among which was to make the assurance even of undergraduates seem vapid and self-conscious.[30]

Powell never mentions Eton by name in *Dance*. Nor, with the exception of the verb 'to mess', does he use any Etonian slang. Yet the school Jenkins attends – a congeries of ancient and modern buildings set in a damp river valley not far from London – is readily identifiable as Eton, its status underlined by the pedigrees of its pupils, among them Lady Isobel Tolland's four brothers. One critic, irritated by how many of Powell's characters were old Etonians, said the book ought to be retitled *A Dance to the Eton Boating Song*.[31] But if anything, *Dance* is a wry inversion of that song's message. Sadly for Jenkins, the chain that binds him to Stringham is all but severed by the end of volume one. Instead, like a galley slave, he finds himself rowing a full course with Widmerpool, the last person with whom he would choose to share an oar, let alone a life.

But what is Widmerpool, the antithesis of style and swagger, doing at Eton in the first place? Jenkins never answers this question, though he gives us plenty of reasons for asking it, beginning with the symbolic overcoat. Widmerpool, he says, is 'comfortless', 'inelegant' and 'indigestible'. He looks a fright: his lips are thick, his nostrils distended and he walks like a robot whose motor has gone wrong. Then there are his hands, 'small and gnarled, with nails worn short and cracked, as if he spent his spare time digging with them deep into the soil'. Add to these stigmas poor delivery, 'as if his tongue were too big for his mouth', and a susceptibility to boils and it's hardly surprising he looks permanently aggrieved. Even his comparatively unusual name, with its territorial association, turns out to be bogus. He ought really to be called Geddes, the name his hypergamous grandfather bore until he changed it to that of his bride, a Miss Widmerpool.

In a school the size of Eton there must always be a few misfits. But Widmerpool, whose deceased father, we later learn, sold liquid manure, is so grotesque by comparison with the other Etonians Jenkins knows that he comes dangerously close to engaging our sympathy on account of this. Such was the complaint of James Tucker, reviewing the sequence in the *New Review*: 'Fail to fit in at school and end up the dead-beat of dead-beats. That's some endorsement for the percipience of an in-clique at the top school.'[32] I think Tucker exaggerates: Widmerpool was not blackballed for Pop (like Powell's future brother-in-law, Lord Longford). On the other hand his presence at Eton, essential though it is for the plot, is never satisfactorily explained. Perhaps the war had something to do with it. Or maybe the formidable Mrs Widmerpool camped on the Provost's doorstep, as Robert Byron's mother did until a place was found for him.[33]

But whatever his social shortcomings, Widmerpool is no dunce. His decision to 'cut out' Oxford or Cambridge and become an articled clerk is based on financial considerations. 'There was not much money when my father died,' he tells Jenkins when they unexpectedly meet at La Grenadière, not one of Balzac's old haunts but a recommended *pension de famille* for language students. It is here that Jenkins first sees Widmerpool in action, settling the dispute between Orn and Lundquist. He is impressed, but not for long, because almost immediately the joke is on Widmerpool again, in the shape of a 'crude, though not unaccomplished' caricature of him scratched on the lavatory wall. This pattern is repeated over the next five volumes. Whenever Jenkins begins to take Widmerpool seriously, something happens to make him recant. It's only when he becomes Widmerpool's dogsbody in the army that Jenkins realises how unwise he has been to underestimate him. There is no more chilling sentence in the whole sequence than this: 'I saw I was now in Widmerpool's power.'

And talking of power, I am puzzled that Powell ignores the one lever by which a mediocrity like Widmerpool could have obtained this at school, the Corps. Most boys regarded the weekly OTC parade as a chore, particularly now that the war was over; all the more reason for Widmerpool to take it seriously.* Unlike on the playing fields or the river, where no amount of training could compensate for absence of natural ability, keenness was the number-one requirement in the Corps. Powell's failure to pick up on this is all the odder given what he says here in one of the last interviews he gave. Why, asked the interviewer, did Widmerpool join a hippy commune if what he wanted was power? Powell replied that John Bayley had made the same point in his *Times Literary Supplement* (*TLS*) review of *Hearing Secret Harmonies*:

> My answer to that was that I remembered, when I was at school, somebody saying of the then captain of the house that he would much rather boss Watkin-Williams around in the rifle range for an hour than have the most beautiful woman in the world. Now that seems to me to be a terrific sort of true saying about certain people ... The point was that this captain of the house would prefer to have the power to boss around in this frightfully minor way than have some great romantic thing happen to him. It seems to me to be a

* Powell told Serrell Hillman of *Time* magazine that Widmerpool was 'ambitious about things that other people aren't, so he gets away with a lot.'

frightfully good image of what some people are like. This is what I meant with Widmerpool. It is really in the hope of getting more worldly power that he joins this commune ... because in the long run he felt that there was more power there than, so to speak, in being Prime Minister.[34]

By the same token Widmerpool would, I feel sure, have grasped that the only way he could hope to throw his weight around at school was by earning promotion in the Corps, something he would have made it his business to achieve.

*

The end of the war had allowed Powell and his mother to catch their breath after four years on the move. Although Lieutenant-Colonel Powell was still, militarily speaking, nomadic, his wife no longer felt obliged to follow him everywhere. She took the lease on a house in Melina Road, St John's Wood, the address given for Powell on the School List during his first three years at Eton.

London suited the sort of young man that Powell was becoming: reserved and bookish, yet with graphic ideas about what metropolitan life had to offer if you could only get your foot in the door. He got a glimpse of what lay beyond the threshold at Nigel Playfair's production of *The Beggar's Opera*, a show as seminal in its way as *Oklahoma!* or *Hair*. Partly this was a tribute to Lovat Fraser's stunning costumes and sets, which were immediately ripped off by all and sundry so that their originality is now hard to grasp. But the opera itself, as Paul Fussell noted, 'overflows with images of irresponsibility and freedom',[35] two concepts in short supply since the passing of the Defence of the Realm Act (DORA) in 1914. It was also about sex, something else that contravened the spirit, if not the letter, of DORA, most of whose puritanical restrictions would remain in force for years to come. Listening to haunting melodies like 'Were I Laid on Greenland's Coast' the fifteen-year-old Powell was simultaneously torn by romantic yearnings and adolescent lust, his first inkling of how closely the two were linked.

Although a little too remote from central London for Powell's liking, St John's Wood harboured at least one fully-fledged bohemian with whom he not only struck up an acquaintance, but also infected with his enthusiasm for Lovat Fraser. This was Christopher Sclater Millard (1872-1927), a self-confessed bibliomaniac and practising pederast who had compiled a monumental bibliography of Oscar Wilde and written an account of his three trials. The son of an Anglican clergyman, educated at Bradfield and Oxford, Millard had been destined for the Church himself until, aged twenty-three, he became a Roman Catholic. His interest in Wilde arose from his own homosexuality, for which he was twice imprisoned. Chronically hard-up, he was only able to work on Wilde's bibliography thanks to the generosity of Wilde's friend and literary executor, Robert Ross. When Ross died he bequeathed Millard a small annuity, on the strength of which he set up as a dealer in rare books and manuscripts. He worked from home, a tiny two-roomed bungalow in the garden of a house about ten minutes' walk from Melina Place. Here, probably in the spring of 1921, he received Mrs Powell, who had seen something in his catalogue she thought her husband might like for his birthday. Knowing nothing of Millard's past she took him as she found him: he was 'odd', she told her son, but not in the least off-putting. She particularly liked his deep, 'musical' voice.

Intrigued by his mother's description of Millard and his surroundings Powell went round there in the holidays. He found someone who could not have looked less like the popular conception of a disciple of Wilde. Tall and gaunt, with grey curly hair and craggy masculine features, Millard dressed like a progressive schoolmaster: old tweed jacket, faded blue shirt and red bandanna, grey flannels rolled up to expose his ankles and, in the summer, sandals. To complete the picture he invariably carried a haversack slung over one shoulder when out and about.[36] Rather conventional in his own approach to dress, Powell may well have had misgivings about Millard's turn-out. If so, they were soon dispersed by Millard's easy manner: he was the first adult to treat him as an equal. You can see this, I think, from Millard's letters to Powell about Lovat Fraser, which are reproduced in Montgomery Hyde's short book on Millard. They begin 'Dear Powell' and are identical in tone to his other business correspondence; only the occasional reference to Eton indicates that the recipient is a schoolboy.

By choice a loner, who cooked and chored for himself at a time when this was almost unheard of among men of his class, Millard made occasional forays to Bloomsbury and Soho where he would drink draught Bass and consort with other free spirits, among them the artist and model, Nina Hamnett. It would be interesting to know if he ever told her about his young Etonian acquaintance because some years later she and Powell had an affair. Millard fancied Powell himself: he told him so to his face, an admission Powell managed to laugh off without any subsequent awkwardness. Intriguingly, Millard also seems to have met Brian Howard, presumably through Powell. He calls him 'an exceptionally talented young man', and says he reminds him of Proust's translator, C.K. Scott-Moncrieff, at the same age. Howard, for his part, thought Millard was '*very* sinister'.

About a year after Mrs Powell met Millard her husband learnt of his proclivities. Powell was warned off in no uncertain terms, though to their credit his parents refrained from any further action. By chance, this injunction coincided with the family's removal from St John's Wood to Salisbury, Philip Powell's new posting, so Powell had a plausible excuse to give Millard for not visiting him any more, though they continued to correspond for a short while. Millard died in 1927, before Powell had a chance to meet him again, which he might well have done given the sort of bohemian circles he had begun to frequent. As it was he had seen enough of Millard to resurrect him as Mr Deacon, something he says he could not have done had Millard still been alive. He also says in his Journals that Millard was 'more of a gent'.[37] Perhaps this was prompted by his discovery, rather late in the day, that unlike Deacon, who spends the war shirking in Paris, Millard enlisted in the Army at the age of forty-three and may even have served at the front before being invalided out with a bad heart. This is revealed by Montgomery Hyde, whose book Powell obtained in 1991. Another curious fact to emerge is that during the General Strike Millard sold copies of the strikers' paper, the *Workers' Gazette*, something Powell was unaware of when he had Mr Deacon and Gypsy Jones sell *War Never Pays*. Odder still, when out selling this rag Millard took a tumble like the one that does for Mr Deacon; he and two others were bundled down the stairs of a dive by some drunken volunteer strike-breakers.[38]

Salisbury, where Powell was based for the next few years, had far less to offer than London, though it does seem to have given him the idea for Zouch's demise in *From a View to a Death*. Riding his father's charger down a wet road used by buses, he was run away with, but unlike Zouch, kept his seat. The fact that he had gone for a hack in the first place shows how bored he must have been, since he had no more taste for country pursuits than for ball games ('You're not the sort of chap who likes to take a gun and get a bit of rough shooting,' said his father). He read of course, and drew, and accompanied his parents on the foreign holidays they liked to take. But what he really wanted was to meet some girls. Their absence was to cast a pall over his days as an undergraduate.

3

Oxford Blues

'Silly young man, he's been gilding our dreaming spires.'

'Colonel' George Kolkhorst on Brian Howard

'The cloakroom where I left my youth.'

Cyril Connolly

In September 1964 Evelyn Waugh sent Powell a copy of his autobiography, *A Little Learning*, some forty pages of which are about Oxford in the early Twenties. In his letter of thanks Powell commented: 'Oxford, I felt, presented a rather different picture to myself.'[1] You can say that again. For Waugh, Oxford was a 'Kingdom of Cokayne'. For Powell, it was more often like the Slough of Despond, hence the arresting opening sentence of *Books Do Furnish a Room*: 'Reverting to the university at forty, one immediately recaptured all the crushing melancholy of the undergraduate condition.'

Why was Powell's experience of Oxford so different from Waugh's – or indeed from that of Harold Acton, John Betjeman, Osbert Lancaster and all the other wits and aesthetes for whom it was 'very heaven'? The short answer – and one that Powell himself hinted at – is that he was neither rich nor queer. But of course there was a bit more to it than that, as I hope to show.

First, though, I think it is important to remember that when we talk about the 'Brideshead Generation' – to use a lazy but convenient term – we're talking about a tiny minority whose impact on most undergraduates was practically nil. Powell himself doubted whether one in twenty undergraduates had heard of Brian Howard.[2] But I bet two out of three could name the captain of the Oxford rugby XV – and with good reason. The Twenties was a golden age for Oxford rugby. In 1924, Powell's second year up, they scored three tries against the All Blacks, which was more than England managed. And they beat Cambridge. Things like that mattered then.

In the long run, of course, the force was with the aesthetes. They wrote the books. They gave the interviews. But from time to time there was a protest from someone who said, 'Hang on a minute. It wasn't like that at all.' For instance in December 1967 *Oxford* magazine ran a piece which sought to correct 'the rather odd impression' of Oxford life in the early Twenties conveyed by the memoirs of 'bright literary and other figures'. Purportedly written by 'Sir Derek Slocombe KBE', a Whitehall mandarin, at the request of his old chum Vernon Fork, a don, it describes the life of an average undergraduate *c.*1924. He plays rugger for his college, belongs to the Student Christian Movement, has an occasional binge, but never loses sight of the fact that on his degree depends his future livelihood. 'True but dull,' he concludes. 'No publisher would look at it for a moment.'[3]

In his efforts to distance himself from anything remotely decadent, the author, the then Master of Pembroke, Ronald McCallum, lays it on rather thick. There is a bit about 'gathering after a game in one of our rooms, before a glowing fire and eating incredible quantities of buns and toast' that is straight out of Orwell's essay, *Boy's Weeklies*. Still, it is probably nearer the mark than the picture later given by television: that of simpering young nobs swigging Château d'Yquem to the sound of trumpets.

As it happens I interviewed Powell just as *Brideshead Revisited* was being repeated on television. When I asked him what he'd thought of the whole series, he said he'd enjoyed it 'as entertainment', but that in the early episodes Jeremy Irons and Anthony Andrews were 'all wrong' as Charles Ryder and Sebastian.

> Waugh was writing about retarded adolescents, young men who by today's standards were sexually and emotionally very immature. So it simply doesn't ring true when you see these two beefy matinée idols gazing into each other's eyes. In the long run I think the chap who played Hooper would have made a better Ryder because the whole point about him is that he isn't supposed to be especially good-looking. But some of the supporting parts were very well done. Whoever played Anthony Blanche, the character based on Brian Howard, was absolutely spot-on. Sebastian's German friend, the ex-Legionnaire, was also very good.

Powell's wife, Lady Violet, put in a word for Jeremy Sinden as the oafish Boy Mulcaster – 'I remember only too well trying to impress people like him at parties.'

With his customary eye for dress Powell observed that they'd made the mistake of showing the undergraduates in caps and gowns as if these were *de rigueur*. In fact they were only worn when 'absolutely necessary', i.e. when there were likely to be proctors about. And Ryder was courting 'social death' by appearing in a tweed jacket with a band at the back* – 'They went

* It cropped up again in the awful *Cambridge Spies*.

out with the ark. We were just as keen to be up to date as young people now. That's why you never saw anyone my age at Oxford with a moustache. We associated them with the war, which we were very anxious to forget.'[4]

Powell was well aware how difficult it was to present a coherent yet unstylised picture of his life as an undergraduate. 'Oxford isn't one long round of Evelyn Waugh and Maurice Bowra,' he told an *Isis* interviewer in 1973.[5] But when, shortly afterwards, he came to write the Oxford chapters of *Infants*, Bowra topped the bill and Waugh was one of the supporting acts. This, he used to insist, was why memoirs were so unreliable: you had to amuse people, which would not be the case if you went on about how miserable you'd been most of the time. Powell also did his best to refute the idea that the Brideshead Generation had all been up at the same time and been to the same parties. 'You're the person who always knows who's two-and-a-half years older or two-and-a-half years younger than somebody else,' George Orwell once said to him, and it showed in his irritation with people who wrote as if Waugh had overlapped with Betjeman, or Connolly with Alan Pryce-Jones. 'It's all there in *Who's Who*, but nobody can be bothered to check these things now.'[6]

(Powell enjoyed research of this kind, particularly if the end result was deflationary. In *Strangers* he says that at *Punch*, whose literary editor he was in the Fifties, there were shelves full of sports annuals from the past, which 'were useful for checking up on the sometimes dubious claims to athletic distinction, "blues" and the like, claimed by acquaintances'. And Alan Pryce-Jones records how, by consulting the Army List, he exposed an Etonian contemporary who claimed in *Who's Who* to be the son of a full General 'without so much as an OBE'. The father, it transpired, had not been a General but a Lieutenant-Colonel in the Indian Army.[7])

*

Graham Greene, we learn from his biographer, was dispatched to Balliol in 1922 because it was 'anti-athletic'.[8] No doubt this also appealed to Powell, a year behind Greene, though he rather liked its reputation for 'effortless superiority' as well. 'So you are one of the clever men!'[9] people said when they learnt where he was; and while the college no longer stood as high as it did in Jowett's day, its academic standards excluded the rich nincompoops and dim-witted hearties found elsewhere. Cyril Connolly, who went up the same year as Greene, pronounced it 'blokey',[10] for which read middle-class. But to judge from the Register it was no more middle-class than College at Eton. There were several Rhodes Scholars, several Rugbeians – including a future headmaster of Eton, (Sir) Robert Birley – several Baronets and the next King of Norway, Prince Olaf* – though he, admittedly, did strike the writer Philip Mason, who went up in 1924, as being 'rather middle-class' by comparison with some of his snooty contemporaries, whose 'polite, defensive, glacial veneer' the talkative young Mason resented.[11]

What Mason saw as snootiness, Powell characterised as the Balliol tradition of undergraduates minding their own business, which he wholeheartedly endorsed. There was no question, as there was in some of the smaller colleges, of being pressurised to 'join in', though of course you could join in if you wanted. As a consequence some Balliol contemporaries never exchanged a word during their entire residence. Powell and Greene had the same tutor, Kenneth Bell, yet they met just once in the two years they overlapped. Again, it was not until almost the end of his first year up that Powell met Connolly, who like Greene lived in a world of his own.

Balliol had its disadvantages too. Many of its buildings, nineteenth-century in origin, were ugly and inhospitable, while the standard of cooking in Hall was dire. It was also, despite the presence of several Etonians, a progressive college, soon to acquire a Master who would align it squarely on the Left. This was A.D. Lindsay, who took over in Powell's second year. A Christian Socialist, passionately committed to the underdog, Lindsay was one of the first dons to take an active part in politics, standing against Quentin Hogg on an anti-appeasement ticket in the Oxford City by-election of 1938. Later, like Sillery, he became a Labour peer. Powell had no cause for complaint against Lindsay while he was up, but grew increasingly angry on Balliol's behalf at the consequences of his long and partisan tenure.

If Lindsay represented the way forward for Balliol, the Dean, F.F. Urquhart, commonly known as 'Sligger', was a link with its illustrious past. The first Roman Catholic since the Reformation to be elected a Fellow of an Oxford college, Sligger exemplified the don as *éminence grise*. Nothing gave him greater pleasure than to see one of his protégés succeed in the great world; many of them did. Monkish, self-effacing and benign, he had a warm heart, a deep purse and the ability to put young men at their ease. For years he kept open house from 10.30 to midnight in his fusty rooms above the college West Gate, where despite offering them nothing stronger than lemonade or barley water he could usually induce even the shyest undergraduates to talk. Some people have since described Sligger as a snobbish old neuter, fawning over handsome Etonians and Wykehamists, but in those

---

* Described in Powell's *Journals* as 'not very bright', he is one of the minor royalties with whom Jenkins's CO, Finn, liked to hobnob.

days universities and public schools were full of snobbish old neuters, so I don't think that can be held against him. Kenneth Clark compared him to the perfect hostess, adding that 'like all hostesses, he preferred those who had contributed, or were likely to contribute, something to society'.[12]

Powell was on good terms with Urquhart, who put him up for the Travellers' Club, but did not regard himself as a 'Sliggerite'. He turned down an offer to join one of the Dean's annual reading parties at his chalet in Switzerland, having no stomach for the allegedly spartan régime of long walks, cold showers and prison diet. There remains the connection a reader might legitimately make between Sligger and Powell's manipulative don Sillery, usually addressed as 'Sillers'. This so upset the economist, Sir Roy Harrod, that he raised the matter with Powell in the course of a fan letter:

24 October 1960

There was only one thing that grieved me ... It was the name Sillery (Sillers) that offended me. This name, together with some of the description of the way people lounged about in his room, or suddenly burst in addressing him in familiar terms, were strongly reminiscent of Sligger ... I could not dismiss the idea that owing to some fleeting impression, some unfortunate personal misin-terpretation, or some malicious gossip, you might really have supposed that Sligger was somewhat like the character you described ... Never in my own time did he show any inclination to anything that could reasonably be described as intriguing or seeking power.

In his reply Powell chose to ignore Sir Roy's point about the names. Instead, he rehearsed the argument he would use in his Memoirs. Sillery, like Sligger, had an undergraduate salon, but 'in other respects – as you say – he bears no sort of resemblance to Sligger'. He then considered the wider implications of Sir Roy's complaint:

29 October 1960

Suppose one was to write a novel about contemporary London, and introduce a hostess who gave little luncheon parties for distinguished people, everyone would say: 'Of course it is a composite figure of Pam and Annie* (or 'obviously Annie' or 'obviously Pam'), and unfair on Pam because, etc. etc., and libellous to Annie because etc. etc.' Yet what is more reasonable than to give meals to lions, and what more reasonable than to write about ladies who do? But do you suppose it would be humanly possible to produce a figure not identified with one or other by people we know?

* Lady Pamela Berry (1914–81) and Ann Fleming (1913–81).

I produce this one from a million examples of the hopelessness of trying to convince people the novels are – or should be – works of the imagination which has fed on experience.[13]

This debate will run and run, and we have not heard the last of it by any means. I should, however, like to suggest a possible source for 'Sillery' as a name. In a contemporary issue of the undergraduate magazine *Isis* I came across a rather solemn account of an International Students' Conference at Budapest. The author, an undergraduate from St John's, was called Sillery. I like to think that Powell read this piece, gave a mocking laugh, and filed the name away under the heading of 'half-baked progressive causes'.

No greater contrast to the costive Sligger could be imagined than Powell's tutor Kenneth Bell, a rollicking war veteran, winner of the MC, who swore like a trooper and sometimes got tight at bump suppers (he coached the college Second Eight). Whereas Sligger had barely written a word since taking his Finals, Bell was a distinguished scholar, a fellow of All Souls as well as of Balliol, who told his students, 'Give me the facts and I will give you the ideas.'[14] Beery, heterosexual and extrovert, he was every bit as dedicated to undergraduates as Sligger, but went about it in a different way. On Sunday afternoons, arguably the most dispiriting period of an undergraduate's week, he would take parties of them on a long walk through villages round Oxford, enlivening the proceedings with his talk.[15] It was, in Powell's opinion, a tragedy for the college as well as for Bell himself when he was obliged to resign his fellowship at the beginning of the war after leaving his wife for another woman.

The year before Powell came up Bell had told the Balliol freshmen, among them Graham Greene, that the one thing they would all be taught at the college was to take their drink like gentlemen.[16] Greene, never one for half measures, immediately embarked on a long and punishing novitiate. Powell, not yet eighteen when his turn came, was more circumspect. Invited to lunch at The Hypocrites Club during his first week in residence, it was as much as he could do to finish a pint of the club's potent dark beer, let alone sink a tankard of burgundy, the lunch-time tipple of his host, Alfred Duggan, Hubert's elder brother, who was in his second year at Balliol.

Duggan had been drunk when he issued the invitation. The son of an alcoholic, he was well on the way to becoming one himself and already needed a keeper in attendance whenever he went abroad. It might therefore seem appropriate that he belong to a club whose name is explained by its motto, 'Water is best'. In fact he was not really typical at all, being equally keen on hunting, whoring and gambling, none of which appealed to the prancing aesthetes like Harold Acton who had infiltrated the Hypocrites and were busy making it a byword for lewd behaviour as well as drunkenness. Powell, despite his distaste for homosexuality, found the atmosphere congenial. He became a member, got to grips with its beer, and steered well clear of the fumblings that sometimes took place when Robert Byron commandeered the piano and there was a knees-up. Eventually, after a riotous fancy-dress party towards the end of Powell's first year, the club was shut down by the authorities – probably because it was too far off the beaten track for the proctors to keep an eye on, though there had also been complaints about noise. By then, according to Powell, it was in danger of becoming chic, having attracted the attention of Brian Howard and the rich lordlings whose mentor he had become.

Powell once wrote of Proust's detractors that their objections might well have sprung from the belief that he had attended more amusing parties than they had themselves.[17] I think this may account for some of his own antipathy towards Brian Howard, who certainly seems to have had a whale of a time in the Twenties. Powell told Howard's biographer, Marie-Jacqueline Lancaster, that 'at Oxford, Brian was snobbish in the least attractive use of that often abused term'.[18] Elsewhere he has implied that Howard was almost single-handedly responsible for promoting the cult of the rich, so that people 'who would have cut no ice at school' were run after simply because they had pots of money.[19] But according to Henry Green, this 'money snobbery' was inevitable, and reflected the change in values between school and university, with wealth replacing athletic success as the desideratum:

There was also a realignment between those who had been at the same school at the same time ... For London and the great country houses were calling and a man one had been happy and safe to kick on his knee-cap ... every day at school ... was taken up as they say. It did not follow that because his father was an enormously rich man he need yet be in receipt of a huge allowance, it was the potentiality of the vast wealth that one day should be his which made him an irresistible attraction.[20]

Significantly, Nick Jenkins endorses Green's point about the lure of a vast inheritance when he notes how popular Stringham has become in a very short time at Oxford:

Stringham was, in fact, not substantially richer than most undergraduates of his sort, and, being decidedly free with his money, was usually hard-up, but from the foothills of his background was, now and then, wafted the disturbing, aromatic perfume of gold, the scent of which, even at this early stage of our lives, could sometimes be observed to act intoxicatingly on chance acquaintances; whose unexpected perseverance, and determination not to take offence, were a reminder that Stringham's mother was what Widmerpool had described as 'immensely wealthy'.

Stringham can't see the point of Oxford and leaves after a term to become Sir Magnus Donners's secretary. His prototype, Hubert Duggan, lasted no longer. Originally destined for Sandhurst, Duggan had concluded that his poor health – Powell says he was tubercular – disqualified him from the rigours of life as a gentleman cadet. After a long convalescence in Argentina, whose girls he spoke favourably of to Powell, he arrived two terms late at Oxford and immediately took against it. In *A Little Learning* Evelyn Waugh wrote that Duggan 'languished at the House (Christ Church) without feminine company' and left complaining of 'damp sheets and immature society'.[21] His brother Alfred, in a letter to Waugh, put it rather more bluntly. 'Hubert,' he wrote, 'had a real horror of homosexuality, which was very much in the air of Oxford at that time'[22] (which can hardly have been news to Waugh, who was actively homosexual as an undergraduate).

Duggan was twenty by then and the presumption must be that like Stringham, who sleeps with a divorcée in Kenya, he had had his first woman. Most undergraduates hadn't, for the sort of reasons advanced here by the cultivated Canadian, Charles Ritchie, who entered Pembroke a year or two later:

[T]hese English undergraduates do seem remarkably young. It's the way they've been brought up. For one thing they have never had anything to do with girls except sisters and the odd girl they have met at a tennis party or dance. They are mostly virgins, though they would rather die than admit it, and they don't know anything about petting as we practise it at home. They talk about sex a lot but it is mostly smut and endless limericks.

The trouble was, as Ritchie acknowledged, that 'there don't seem to be any available girls at Oxford except undergraduettes and whores ...The undergraduettes are hardly to be regarded as girls. They are to be seen bicycling to lectures with unpowdered noses, wearing hideous regulation Tudor-style black velvet caps.'[23] Unchivalrous? Yes. But not untypical. Early in 1924 *Isis* ran a competition whose first prize was a choice between tea with an undergraduette every Sunday for the remainder of term, or two guineas. The winner took the money, saying he 'really couldn't stand a dowdy [*sic*], beside her chaperone'.[24] Chaperones were compulsory for women visiting men's colleges; they even sat in at tutorials. Small wonder that the girls lacked sex-appeal (a daring new term) and so many young men thought it sapiens to be homo.

Charles Ritchie's problem was solved by a local floozy who lived on an allowance from her estranged husband. But he was far more mature than his peers, having graduated in Canada and spent a year at the Sorbonne. For someone like Powell the cupboard was bare and there was nothing for it, he told Kingsley Amis, but to 'torse oneself orf',[25] a practice recommended by Maurice Bowra, who was also, at this early stage in his career, an ardent advocate of homosexuality, 'the natural condition of an intelligent man'.

Few dons have left their mark on a generation so indelibly as Bowra, the *fons et origo* of the Oxford wits. 'You made us what we are,' wrote John Sparrow,[26] while for Osbert Lancaster Bowra possessed, 'to a degree which I have never encountered in anyone else, the power to stimulate the brilliant response even among those whose reactions were not normally lightning-quick'.[27] Yet because he set his face against radio, television and film Bowra is as mythical to those who never heard him talk as Hector and Achilles. When Powell met him he had only been teaching for two years, yet such was his charisma that every gifted undergraduate was eager to attract his notice. To a conventional young man like Powell he was a revelation, deriding good form and making the joke in bad taste acceptable. Self-denial was abhorrent to him: he insisted that a lot of what you fancy does you good. He was also a trenchant critic of the *ancien régime*, whose values, he argued, had been powerless to prevent the slaughter in Flanders, if indeed they were not responsible for it.

Bowra, born 1898, had served in the war – like Kenneth Bell he was a Gunner officer – and this gave him an authority that character alone could not have achieved. His hedonism was not simply the product of his Hellenism, it was the affirmation of someone who had stared into the abyss. 'Whatever you hear about the war,' he told Cyril Connolly, 'remember it was far worse: inconceivably bloody – nobody who wasn't there can imagine what it was like.'[28] Convinced as they might be of the merits of their own generation, Powell and his fellows always knew that this was one rite of passage they would never have to experience. Recalling the noisy dinner parties Bowra gave for undergraduates, Powell doubted whether their host, even at his most exuberant, ever quite banished the war from his thoughts.

Bowra used to quip that he was 'more dined against than dining', presumably a reference to the stories that were told behind his back at High Table. His undergraduate dinner parties, though they had their malicious moments, were primarily designed to loosen his guests' tongues and get them, if possible, to say things they did not know they had it in them to say. To this end he provided plenty of champagne and a torrent of provocative talk. No quarter was given in argument. You had to keep your end up and return his fire or risk being pulverised by what Kenneth Clark called his 'outrageous cannon'. Clark caught the blast of this and thought it did him good: 'My priggish fears and inhibitions were blown to smithereens.' Bowra, he wrote, became 'the strongest influence in my life'.[29]

Clark and Powell had much in common. Both had solitary childhoods; both were instinctive aesthetes; both were staunch heterosexuals and both were thought rather aloof. But although, like Clark, Powell profited by his association with Bowra, he was, in the end, rather relieved when an incident occurred which loosened Bowra's grip on him. Whereas Clark, as Bowra himself noted, 'knew from an early age what he wished to do and where his talents lay',[30] Powell was still finding his way. He wanted to keep an open mind, particularly about the arts, on the subject of which Bowra struck him as being too dogmatic. But the breach, when it came, had nothing to do with the arts. It arose from the sort of misunderstanding that is always on the cards when juniors are encouraged by their seniors to speak their minds.

One afternoon during the Long Vacation of 1925 Powell was twiddling his thumbs in a dreary private hotel in Andover, his parents' latest billet, when a car drew up outside. To Powell's surprise, since he supposed no one knew where he was, the car contained Bowra and another Balliol undergraduate, Pierce Synnott, an extremely handsome Anglo-Irish dandy who had introduced Powell to Bowra the year before. Bowra turns out to have been besotted with Synnott, as indeed was Cyril Connolly, something Powell doesn't mention, though he may not have been aware of it at the time. Over tea Bowra invited Powell to come and spend a few days with him in Oxford, an offer he accepted with alacrity – anything would be better than Andover – without giving much thought to what might be expected of him 'at the receiving end', an intriguing phrase in the circumstances.

Synnott, it transpired, was on his way home and Bowra was busy all day so that Powell had to amuse himself until dinner-time, a process almost as tedious in out-of-term Oxford as in Andover. This reminded him how disenchanted he was with the university, not least because you had no chance to meet any girls (in three years he met just one undergraduette). One evening, flown with wine, he said as much to Bowra, whose immediate response is not recorded. But the following term Powell understood that he had given offence, resulting in a coolness that apparently lasted thirty-five years.

While acknowledging that it was probably for the best, Powell gives himself a severe wigging for this gaffe. How could he have been so tactless as to run down the very institution whose ladder of preferment his host was busy climbing? It was inexcusable, a breach of good manners and so on. Well, yes. But he was only nineteen, an age when tact does not come easy, particularly after a few drinks. And in any case, tact was not something Bowra himself recommended. True, Bowra was notoriously sensitive to criticism, a grave handicap in one so prone to making enemies, as he himself admitted: 'A skin too few. Yet one continues to go out of one's way to court hatred.' But Powell could be forgiven for thinking – if he gave the matter any thought at all – that Bowra would not take it personally.

We only have Powell's word for what went on. Bowra's papers contain no mention of the incident, and apart from one brief anecdote in his memoirs there is nothing to link him with Powell at all. Why then did he take the trouble to establish where Powell was staying, seek him out and invite him to stay? If Powell had been a star attraction like Acton or Howard or Connolly (another of Bowra's crushes) it would have been easier to understand; but though welcome at Bowra's table he did not, in the words of Synnott, 'seize the front stage or talk loud'.[31] Fifty years later Powell was at a loss to explain how Bowra tracked him down, though presumably some explanation was given at the time. Another odd thing is that this visit is supposed to have taken place after Powell had already 'walked a social tight-rope' with Bowra. But that incident, a dinner party to which Kenneth Bell, mistakenly in Powell's view, was also invited, could only have occurred in the autumn of 1925 at the earliest, since the meal was given in the digs Powell shared with Henry Green during his last year up.

Why dwell on this story? Because, as I have suggested, it raises more questions than it answers. Did Bowra make an unsuccessful pass at Powell (as he certainly did at Synnott)? Or was Powell's complaint about the absence of girls spiced with some savage asides about the authorities' indifference to homosexuality (something he mentions in Infants)? Either would seem a more plausible explanation for their long estrangement than Powell's admission that he longed to go down, which Bowra ought to have been resilient enough to take in his stride. Then again, Powell may deliberately have decided to keep the reader guessing, as he sometimes does in Dance. We never know for sure what passed between Widmerpool and Gypsy Jones (except of course money), or between Miss Weedon and Stringham once she began 'helping him'. (If, as John Bayley says, there is an element of Steerforth in Stringham, then there is also an element of Rosa Dartle in Miss Weedon.)

The writer Alan Watkins doubted whether Bowra did take Powell's outburst so hard. In his portrait of Powell in Brief Lives he suggested that what the story really illustrated was Powell's 'hyper-sensitivity in social matters'.[32] There is plenty of evidence for this, so Watkins may be right. In any case, as Powell conceded, he and Bowra would probably have fallen out sooner or later, 'seeds of disagreement existing at the stage each of us was approaching, a break inevitable'. Exactly. Bowra was an anti-Establishment agitator. Powell, most definitely, was not. Within a few years such a fundamental difference would have been hard to overlook.

Powell often said that the more realised a person is in life, the harder it becomes to turn them into fiction: 'It's more likely to be one's bank manager or dentist.'[33] Bowra was one of several people he knew – Evelyn Waugh was another – who came into this category. Nevertheless, two distinguished dons who had known Bowra, Hugh Lloyd-Jones and John Bayley, both found echoes of him in Sillery; and when Powell himself reread *Dance* in the late Eighties he found himself agreeing with them, while insisting that it must have been involuntary. This underlined another of his theories, 'the degree to which a writer lacks absolute control over a novel'.[34]

One character whose provenance Powell could hardly have disputed is Mark Members, the posturing young poet first encountered in Sillery's rooms. Tall, skinny and boyish (he sports a floppy fringe at a time when most young men brushed their heavily oiled hair straight back), Members is clearly based upon the young Peter Quennell, of whom Harold Acton wrote: 'I had thought Brian Howard precocious, until I met Peter Quennell.'[35] Because he played to perfection the role of aesthete – Acton invokes some lines of Wilde's to describe his 'dancing gait' – people assumed on first acquaintance that Quennell was homosexual. They were wrong. Quennell was one of those feline charmers whose success with women can drive their macho rivals to distraction. At Oxford he began by laying siege to undergraduettes, a forlorn hope in the days of chaperones, and then, after losing his virginity in Paris, was taken up by a notorious Thames Valley vamp. Detected in this depravity he was rusticated at the beginning of his third year and elected to stay down.

Quennell never fulfilled his early promise as a poet (like Members, he was singled out for praise by Sir Edmund Gosse) becoming, instead, the last of the men of letters. Five times married, he also found time to bed a succession of Bohemian nymphs, two of whom subsequently took Cyril Connolly's name. Years later, noting that Randolph Churchill's bride 'had passed through Peter Quennell's hands', Malcolm Muggeridge wrote, 'Tony [Powell] and I agreed Quennell really ought to set up as a sort of finishing school, which would ensure social advancement to those who passed through it.'[36]

3. Oxford Blues

Quennell and Connolly had more than lovers in common. As Connolly noted, they held the same intellectual rank, which formed the basis for their long, but by no means unbroken, friendship. At various times they lived under the same roof, laboured in the same vineyard, belonged to the same club and graced the same salons. On leaving Oxford both turned down the job of secretary to the Reverend Montague Summers (q.v.), and both also suffered at the hands of Evelyn Waugh and his son Auberon. So if Quennell contributed to Members it is surely worth considering whether traces of Connolly can be discerned in J.G. Quiggin, with whom, in Jenkins's eyes, Members is indissolubly linked. At first sight this seems unlikely. Quiggin, as an undergraduate, is what Maurice Bowra would have called 'unpresentable'. He is dour, chippy, charmless, seemingly a product of the Thirties, not the Twenties. You could never say of Quiggin, as E.M. Forster said of Connolly, that he gave Pleasure a bad name.

But there are similarities. Powell calls Connolly 'a master of flattery; flattery of the best sort that can seem on the surface almost a form of detraction'. He elaborated on this to his American friend, John Monagan,* recalling Connolly's 'fantastic power' of 'flattering you ... while apparently attacking you. He was brilliant in gauging how much one could take'.[37] Quiggin employs the same technique. When out to ingratiate himself, says Jenkins, '[he] was far too shrewd to confine himself to mere flattery. A modicum of bullying was a pleasure both to himself and his patrons.' Again, Connolly, though far from handsome, enjoyed considerable success with women; so also does Quiggin, whose conquests include Templer's beautiful first wife Mona, and the recalcitrant art tart, Lady Anne Stepney. You could also describe them both as spongers and, arguably, as shirkers, though perhaps this is harsh on Connolly, who did his bit with Horizon. Finally Quiggin, like Connolly, is an arch procrastinator whose 'survey', Unburnt Boats, takes ten years to appear, following which he abandons all hope of producing a masterpiece. It's almost as if he and Connolly were 'excused books', like those old sweats in the pre-war regular army who were 'excused boots'.

At Eton Powell had been intrigued by Connolly from the moment he 'burst through the Pop-barrier', but owing to Connolly's exalted status their paths never crossed. Arriving at Balliol a year after Connolly he found to his surprise that far from coveting fresh social laurels Connolly had become a recluse, his circle virtually restricted to a few old Collegers like himself and

---

* John S. Monagan, 'The Congressman', is that rare literary phenomenon, a fan who became a friend. His correspondence with Powell, which began in 1969, is at Georgetown University Library, Washington DC.

two dons, Urquhart and Bowra (from both of whom he extracted a dole). Powell thought he might well have been formally introduced to Connolly in Sligger's rooms, but the first time they ever did anything together was towards the end of his first year. Bizarrely, since he used to say that the only exercise he ever took at Oxford was running up bills, Connolly persuaded Powell to share a canoe with him, piloting them up a sidestream and over some rapids. Later, in one of his celebrated letters to Noel Blakiston, Connolly called Powell 'harmless',[38] an understandable estimate at the time. Powell, for his part, was still rather in awe of Connolly whose true colours had yet to emerge.

The same term he went canoeing with Connolly, Powell contributed some reviews and drawings to the *Cherwell*, which had just been relaunched under Robert Byron's editorship as a lively alternative to the official undergraduate magazine, *Isis*. One of the drawings is entitled *The Four Seasons*, but it is not Poussin, but the American writer and illustrator, Edmund Gorey, whose style it brings to mind. The other drawing, *A Son of the Caesars*, is of an exquisite Italian cavalry officer who looks too tightly corseted to mount a horse. He wears what Powell insisted on calling an eyeglass, as opposed to the 'alien and odious' word monocle.[39] Of the reviews, one is worth quoting from because it reveals the deep roots of Powell's Toryism. Assessing a life of Marat by Sydney L. Phipson he notes how 'almost without exception' the leaders of revolutions

> [m]ay be classified as unqualified scoundrels or tiresome and ill-informed pedants. A hereditary monarchy by the law of averages produces a certain number of good rulers, but a democratic upheaval ensures only that the reins of government are given over into the hands of the morally and intellectually deficient.

Marat, he concludes, is 'one of the most contemptible characters in history'.[40]

Powell could get away with this unchallenged in 1924. Politics had yet to become an issue with the educated young, most of whom, as Connolly later noted, 'wanted to keep the security and opulence of 1913 with the avant garde ideas and sexual emancipation of 1923'.[41] What really mattered were love and art. And since neither of these was on offer at Oxford you had to travel to find them, a defining experience for a whole generation who, profiting from the strong pound, would henceforth associate pleasure with abroad. Powell, though more reconciled to England than many of his contemporaries, clocked up a respectable mileage in his vacations. In 1924 he went as far east as Belgrade – 'in those days not without all Comic Opera allure'. A year later he visited Vienna where, like Pennistone, he was bowled over by the sight of 'those four staggering Breugels' in the Kunsthistorisches Museum. He also spent two vacations in Helsinki, where his father was attached to the British Military Mission, aspects of which are reproduced in *Venusberg*, his only novel to be set entirely abroad.

In December 1925, shortly before his twentieth birthday, Powell had a short break in Paris with his parents. Maurice Cheke, an Oxford acquaintance of his, was also there, cramming for the Foreign Office. Powell went with him to a tea dance, which were all the rage then, where a pretty girl caught his eye. Greatly daring he managed to make a date with her the following day, a rendezvous rhapsodised in his dreams that night. Much to his surprise his dreams came true. 'Lulu', it transpired, was on the game. After some hesitation on Powell's part – he and his unconscious were at odds – they took a cab to an *hôtel de passe* where after the usual hygienic formalities Powell contrived to bring it off. (Strange to relate, both he and Peter Quennell, who lost his virginity in equally unpropitious circumstances, use the same word, 'fiasco', to describe what they narrowly managed to avoid.[42])

*

In his final year Powell moved out of Balliol and into digs in King Edward Street, which he shared with Henry Green. Green was almost the only old friend of his still at Oxford; most of the others had either gone down, been sent down or, like Hubert Duggan, left of their own accord. They spent a lot of their time discussing Proust, whose long novel, then in the process of translation, had already joined the Ballets Russes and *The Waste Land* as one of the most formative influences of the period.

Despite an addiction to billiards – he represented Oxford against Cambridge – and the cinema, which he visited every afternoon, Green had not only managed to complete *Blindness*, the novel he had begun at Eton, but also place it with a publisher. Even at a time when according to Powell, 'every articulate young man was writing a novel', an undergraduate novelist was an event. Green was invited to Garsington, the country house near Oxford where Lady Ottoline Morrell held court. On subsequent visits he took Powell, who was shaken but not stirred by his first excursion into High Bohemia. The problem was that Lady Ottoline made no concessions to age or inexperience. She was a curious mixture of groupie and grande dame who assumed her guests were as well informed about high life as the arts (which were treated, Powell reckoned, in a somewhat 'middlebrow' manner). You might also find yourself confronted by a token bohemian 'wild man' who would throw down a gauntlet it was uncommonly difficult for a novice to pick up. There is an echo here of the distinction Jenkins draws between the Huntercombes' dance and Mrs Andriadis's party, the latter 'far more intimidating' because the rules of engagement were not immediately apparent. But whereas Jenkins involves the reader in his unease, Powell omits to say exactly how he put his foot in it at Garsington – if indeed he did put his foot in it, and this is not another example of his 'hyper-sensitivity in social matters'.

That Powell was by no means as sure of himself as you might suppose from his education and background is suggested by Pierce Synnott. Reviewing *Infants of the Spring* he says the most dramatic utterance he heard Powell make at Balliol was when a group of them were having a 'Socratic dialogue' about their parents, particularly the difficulties they experienced with their fathers. 'I consider my father to be a gentleman,' declared Powell, apparently taking pride in 'this piece of one-upmanship'.[43] Well, we don't know what else he said about him, but unless his listeners had very exacting standards I can't think this announcement came as much of a surprise. Who at Balliol then did not consider his father a gentleman? Still, the fact that Synnott describes it as 'one-upmanship' underlines the importance Powell attached to his claim. It would be interesting to know if Philip Mason was present, since fifty years later he wrote a book about the English Gentleman himself.* Mason's view of Powell as an undergraduate is essentially the same as Synnott's, quoted earlier: '[He] was already playing to perfection the part for which he casts the narrator in his novels, the almost invisible man, the universal unobtrusive confidant and observer.'[44]

Powell does not mention Mason in *Infants*. With one or two notable exceptions like Connolly, Quennell and the historian, Wyndham Ketton-Cremer, he seems not to have kept up with any of the people he mixed with at Balliol. Years later Malcolm Muggeridge reports him saying of the journalist Bernard Cawston: 'Now you can see why, arriving a moderately sensible youth from school at Balliol, I was set back for at least a decade by having to consort with crackpots like Cawston.'[45] As it happens Cawston was at Christ Church, not Balliol, but this doesn't really affect the point Powell was making. Although he never regretted going to Oxford he felt he suffered an 'intellectual recession' there, hence, in part, his poor performance in his Finals.

Expecting a Second, hoping for a First, Powell took a Third. So, as it happens, did Evelyn Waugh, Cyril Connolly and Robert Byron. But they at least could console themselves that a Third was no more than they deserved.

---

* *The English Gentleman* (Andre Deutsch, 1982).

3. Oxford Blues

Powell's case was different: he had worked hard and gone unrewarded. What went wrong? Powell offers a variety of explanations. Bell, he says, 'taught history for itself, not as medium for acquiring a good degree'. Rather than rattle through the whole syllabus, which was huge, he chose certain subjects and taught them thoroughly, a gamble that didn't come off in Powell's case. At his *viva*, instead of getting a chance to show what he knew, as Bell had predicted, he was grilled about a period he had scarcely glanced at. He also made a nonsense of his special subject, inexplicably choosing to study the Congress of Vienna, for which proficiency in German, which he didn't have, was required.

Powell must have been one of Bell's rare failures. At his death Bell was remembered as someone who 'wrote like an angel', but whose 'real work' as an historian went into his pupils, many of whom got a better class than they deserved.[46] In the event Powell's Third was of no material consequence: he already had a job lined up. But fifty years later, writing about it in *Infants*, his disappointment was still apparent.

Powell was by no means the only Etonian to be unimpressed by Oxford. Apart from Hubert Duggan, who had not wanted to go there in the first place, and the dashing Lord Knebworth, who said he would 'rather be at a girls' school for knitting',[47] the most notable critic was Cyril Connolly, who thought 'the dismal emptiness and ugliness of Oxford' was bound to depress anyone who had been happy at Eton.[48] Unlike Connolly, for whom school was paradise lost, Powell had not the slightest desire to return there. But his experience of Eton may well have been a handicap to making the most of Oxford. In many important respects – its location, its buildings, its tutorial system – Eton was a microcosm of the university, so to exchange one for the other was no big deal. But to someone like John Betjeman, arriving from a Darwinian rookery like Marlborough, it was as if he had gone from the barrack room to officer's quarters:

> Privacy after years of public school;
> Dignity after years of none at all –
> First college rooms, a kingdom of my own ...[49]

In a piece he wrote about Robert Burton, author of *The Anatomy of Melancholy*, Powell noted that education, in Burton's opinion, was one of the main causes of melancholy,[50] so perhaps this explains everything. My own feeling is that he went up a year early. At seventeen years, nine months when he arrived, he was at least eighteen months younger than almost all the other Balliol freshmen, and could well have been one of the youngest undergraduates at the university. If, as he says, he was ready to leave Eton when he did, it doesn't necessarily follow that he was ready to enter Oxford. A year out could have made all the difference, though I suppose it's equally possible that in the course of it he might have grown up too quickly, discovered girls (and so felt their absence more keenly, like Hubert Duggan) and acquired some expensive habits. As it was he came down with no debts, an achievement as extraordinary in its way as not being beaten at Eton.

Powell summed up his Oxford career like this: 'I'm glad I went. It was tremendously useful to me in all sorts of ways. But I don't look back on it as a golden period in my life.'[51] As to the broader question of his upbringing, what better answer than this, from a review he wrote of Arthur Calder Marshall's *The Magic of My Youth*: 'The book brings out the point that – to the egotism of adolescence – understanding is not enough. There is nothing to be offered short of growing up and a life of one's own.'[52]

4

A Good Time Everywhere

'What happy days – compared with our own – when the world was interested in art.'

Anthony Powell

'It was a joy then to be alive.'

Cyril Connolly

Reviewing a life of Saki (echoes of whom can be heard in asides by Dicky Umfraville and Peter Templer), Powell rebuked the author for trying to absolve Saki of Edwardianism on the grounds that most of his work had been published during the reign of George V: '[I]t is where an author's feelings lie which colours the books, not the date when they are published.'[1] The same principle applies to him. His pre-war novels may all have been published in the Thirties, but the Twenties is where they belong. For Powell, the Twenties was a golden age, the one and only time in his life when it was possible to feel reasonably optimistic about the future. Politics had not yet begun to matter. The arts were enjoying a boom. And a little bit of privilege went a long way.

In *Messengers* Powell insists that apart from the 'vague intention' to write a novel – something 'every reasonably literate young man' professed in those days – he arrived in London with no particular ambition other than to enjoy what was on offer. It took him about a year to achieve his goal, his progress delayed by the absence of a cicerone and also by his (unspecified) 'ineptitude at dealing with people'. But once he established a foothold in the 'Art-Smart' world things began to look up. The 'great charm' of the Twenties, he later recalled, was that 'the bohemian world of that period faded imperceptibly, on all its sides, into other worlds of an entirely different kind. It was then possible for the most unlikely people to meet each other in a manner which today [1951] would be, to say the least, unexpected.'[2]

Perhaps this was a symptom of the experimentalism, in behaviour as well as in art, which contributed to the Twenties' zeitgeist – or as Powell would have it, the 'post-war spirit'. Noel Annan, also writing in 1951, refers to 'the demi-mondaine quality of the Twenties' which expressed itself in a 'restless

51

quest for new dresses, dances, faces, in the hope that ultimate security could be found in some new method of living. In a peculiar way art got mixed up with life.'[3] It can be no coincidence that at parties, fancy-dress was the rule rather than the exception. Not only was this a reaction against the war years, when the streets were full of khaki and black, it also encouraged social mobility, as anyone who lived through the Sixties will attest.

*

The job awaiting Powell when he left Oxford was with a publisher, Gerald Duckworth & Co. Ltd. Given the sort of young man he was this seems a natural enough choice. In fact, once it became apparent at Eton that he was not cut out for the Army Powell had only the vaguest idea of what he might do for a living. That he became a publisher was thanks to Thomas Balston (1883-1967), a director of Duckworth, who had served under Philip Powell during the war and kept up with him afterwards. Balston, the model for Dan Tokenhouse in *Dance* and Hugh Judkins in *What's Become of Waring*, had already imposed himself on Powell's life. It was he who tipped off Philip about Christopher Millard's liking for boys, and it was largely on his recommendation that Powell had gone to Balliol. Now he proposed that Powell serve a three-year apprenticeship with Duckworth, his salary of £300 a year being heavily subsidised by his father, as was customary in those days. If all went well Philip would then invest directly in the firm and Powell would become a junior partner.

Powell reported for duty at 3 Henrietta Street, Covent Garden, in the autumn of 1926. He would remain there in one capacity or another for almost ten years. It was a fruitful association: his first four novels were published by Duckworth while his fifth, *What's Become of Waring*, was inspired by his experiences there. Equally satisfying for someone who passionately desired a vibrating social life, his duties were not too onerous, so that parties could safely be savoured to the dregs. Like Jenkins at the same age, he was never in any doubt that 'Pleasure before Business' was a truism and not, as Bill Truscott supposed, an epigram or paradox.

Balston had recruited Powell in an effort to revitalise Duckworth, which for some years had been living off fat. Their back list was impressive and eclectic: Ibsen and Galsworthy, Chekhov and Virginia Woolf, D.H. Lawrence and Hilaire Belloc, Ford Madox Ford and Elinor Glyn; but there was nobody young except the Sitwells. One reason for this was short-sightedness – some alleged snobbery – on the part of the founder, Gerald Duckworth, who in 1920 had refused to offer a directorship to Jonathan Cape, his very hard-working but humbly-born manager. Cape, who had flair and initiative, went on to found his own imprint and then poached Duckworth's reader, Edward Garnett, the greatest talent-spotter of his day. Balston, conscious that Duckworth probably appeared rather stuffy to anyone under thirty, hoped that Powell's presence would reassure them. So, up to a point, it did. But Balston had underestimated the founder's bloody-mindedness, which not only cost them the services of Evelyn Waugh as a novelist, but eventually resulted in a showdown at which Balston himself was voted off the board.

Whereas Balston had always wanted to be a publisher, only lacking the capital to achieve his goal earlier, Gerald Duckworth (1870-1937) seems to have entered the trade for want of anything better to do during daylight hours (after dark he found plenty to occupy him). The stepson of Sir Leslie Stephen and half-brother of Virginia Woolf, whom he traumatised as a child by inspecting her private parts, Duckworth was a typical Edwardian clubman, portly, pompous and self-indulgent. An avid theatre-goer – hence the presence of Ibsen, Chekhov and Galsworthy, a close friend, on the firm's list – he had, by the time Powell joined Duckworth, relinquished what little pleasure he ever took in books and reading. Nor did the third partner, George Milsted, contribute much except capital and proficiency in proof-reading. A figure from the pages of the *Pink 'Un*, nattily attired in loud check tweeds and a brown bowler, he turned up about once a week, otherwise devoting himself to country pursuits.

Powell's earliest days at Duckworth were spent perched on a high Dickensian stool writing invoices, something for which, unsurprisingly, he showed little talent. But before long he found himself assisting Balston in the Augean labour of scanning the five or six hundred unsolicited manuscripts that plopped through the letter-box every year. It was, he always maintained, an invaluable lesson for an aspiring young writer like himself. 'It's part of the mystery of writing that the great hands always conceal how they do it. But when a book is bad its faults are pretty obvious, so you say to yourself, well, here's how not to do it.'[4]

If Gerald Duckworth and George Milsted were period pieces, so too was A.G. Lewis, Duckworth's manager, with whom Powell shared an office. Powell's evocation of 'Mr' Lewis allows him to engage in some social hair-splitting, a process he enjoyed. His colleague, he says, knew precisely his place, which was bang in the middle of the social scale, and adjusted his stance accordingly. What he doesn't tell us is how Lewis reacted to him, his social (and intellectual) superior but professional inferior. There is a hint, no more, that Lewis could be very bit as obstructive as Gerald Duckworth, particularly where the production costs of highbrow books were concerned.

The situation was complicated by the esteem in which Balston held Lewis, giving him a free hand in all but editorial matters. It's possible that Balston, having served in the Army, took the same trouble with Lewis as a prudent officer did with commissioned Quartermasters, who could be a terrible nuisance if antagonised.

Perhaps, after all, Lewis had a soft spot for Powell. At any rate he apparently clung on to his inscribed first editions of Powell's early novels for as long as he could afford to, eventually selling them to Sotherans in the 1960s, by which time, as an elderly pensioner, he had begun to feel the pinch. His copy of *Afternoon Men* must later have been bought by Powell's friend, Sir Henry d'Avigdor-Goldsmid, because I was shown it by his daughter, Mrs Chloe Teacher. Powell's inscription is worth quoting:

> For A.G.L.
> Who works next to me on the chain gang.

*

Needing a base in London, Powell, like Jenkins, opted for the 'seedy chic' of Shepherd Market, long a haunt of tarts and scene of the seduction that occurs in the opening chapter of Michael Arlen's racy bestseller, *The Green Hat* (which Quiggin manoeuvres a reluctant Jenkins into lending him at Oxford). Powell admitted that the seduction had 'chiefly influenced' his decision to live there, though he was also attracted by its convenient location, in the heart of Mayfair and halfway between 'those two vital centres, Chelsea and Bloomsbury'. He was lucky enough to find what he wanted immediately: two small rooms on the ground floor of a shabby-looking building on the corner of Shepherd Street and Carrington Street, with breakfast and a cleaner thrown in, for £2 a week. There was barely room to swing a cat, but at least he could come and go as he pleased, no small consideration for any young person in those days. The key to a thrilling social life was another matter. It took him a while to obtain that.

In an interview he did with Lynn Barber in 1992 Powell admitted that it had pained him to discover that he was not considered 'grand enough' as a young man to get all the invitations he would have liked.[5] Without being at the bottom of the barrel, like Widmerpool, he never made the 'White Four Hundred', identified by his future sister-in-law Lady Mary Clive as a list of 'every single man in London who was truly marriageable, morally, financially and physically'.[6] Someone who came into this category was Hubert Duggan, whose friendship with Powell was now at an end. Just as Stringham cuts his date with Jenkins when something better turns up, so Duggan put Powell off for the same reason, the difference being that Duggan's action proved to be irrevocable: he and Powell hardly spoke again.

Powell says that after quitting Oxford Duggan was, naturally enough, swallowed up by the beau monde. In 1924 he entered the Life Guards as a probationer, thus avoiding the rigours of Sandhurst. 'One is said – for some reason – "to have a good time in The Tins"' reports Stringham, and so, for four years, did Duggan, whom one of his contemporaries described as 'the rage of London and the *adoré* of the girls'.[7] Eventually, however, he fell out with his Colonel, who told him he could no longer go skiing at St Moritz every winter, but must hunt instead. He was briefly married to Joan Dunn, the daughter of Beaverbrook's millionaire crony, Sir James Dunn, and then in 1931 became the Tory MP for Acton. In the early Thirties, probably through his lover Lady Mary Lygon, whose brothers had been at Goodhart's, he met Evelyn Waugh, who became a close friend. In 1940 he rejoined the Life Guards, but the exigencies of wartime soldiering told on his health and in 1943 he died, with Waugh, and a priest, at his bedside. The previous year he and Powell, both captains, met for the last time. 'Of course you don't get into the big money until you're a major,' he said, which is also what Chips Lovell says to Jenkins at their last meeting.

Powell said that any parallel between Hubert Duggan and Stringham ended once Duggan went into the Life Guards. Stringham's drinking, never satisfactorily explained, owed nothing to Hubert, though it may have been partially suggested by the example of his brother Alfred, who was finally cured after the war. His appeal to women was emphasised by Daphne Fielding (née Vivian), one of the reigning beauties of the Twenties, who said she had 'more fun with him than anyone else. In his company everyday events took unexpected turns, but in spite of his high spirits he had a melancholy side which made him gentle and engaging.'[8] It is also pertinent to remember that Duggan was one of the thirty-three rebel Tories who in May 1940 helped to bring down Chamberlain, thus earning the undying enmity of 'Chips' Channon, formerly a protégé of Duggan's mother, Lady Curzon, and an arch-appeaser. This may be the reason why, when Powell met him after the war, Channon was so rude about Hubert, something Powell was at a loss to explain. Another odd thing is how Powell and Duggan managed to avoid bumping into each other for so long. You might suppose from reading *Dance* that the rhythm of life would have brought them together from time to time, but for some reason it didn't.

Powell did not take his exclusion from the smart set lying down. He tried to 'ingratiate' himself with the sort of people who might otherwise have ignored him.[9] So did all sorts of other young men on the make. As Cyril Connolly put it:

> To be accepted by the upper class, then in possession of money and authority and even glamour, was a natural ambition. Just as the following generation was to try and join the working classes and become communists to try and get away from their parents, we tried to escape from middle class homes by rising above them. This explains such meteorites as John Betjeman and Evelyn Waugh.[10]

Betjeman and Waugh had higher to climb than Powell. They also had more stamina, thicker skins and, crucially, a gift for role-playing, something Powell lacked. But whether any of these attributes would have tipped the scales in his favour when first he fell in love is doubtful. Quite simply, he was out of his league.

Her name was Adele Biddulph, though everyone called her Dig, and like Barbara Goring in *Dance* she was the daughter of a Peer. When Powell met her she was in her mid-twenties, a charming, intelligent and attractive young woman who before the Great War, when there was no shortage of eligible young men, would probably have married within a year or two of 'coming out'. Neither she nor her equally enticing younger sister Mary had jobs, dividing their time between Belgravia and Herefordshire, where the Biddulphs had lived in the same house for 300 years. Dig's younger brother Rupert, an unstable character who was later committed, had been at The New Beacon and Goodhart's, something Powell doesn't mention, so presumably it didn't signify. Powell must have met Dig through her cousin, Henry Green, who was paying court to Mary.

Green, well-born and wealthy, was Powell's oldest friend, someone who meant a great deal to him and whom he trusted. So what happened next rocked him back on his heels. While assuring Powell that he was still keen on Mary, Green secretly began to pursue Dig. By the time Mary's engagement to a Guardee was announced in 1928 Green and Dig were going steady. They were finally married in July 1929.

More than sixty years later Powell admitted to Green's biographer Jeremy Treglown that while he'd 'had rather a passion' for Dig, the idea of marriage 'wasn't *on* at all' because he had no money[11] (precisely the explanation Widmerpool gives Jenkins for not proposing to Barbara Goring). There was no falling-out; Powell went to Green's wedding and kept up with him until the war, after which they gradually drifted apart. But he never got over his old friend's duplicity, writing in his *Journals* that he was 'really rather a shit'.[12] It can't have helped that after marrying Dig, Green started carrying on again with Mary, or that he should later have put it about that he was the model for Stringham, a claim that incensed Powell. In fairness one should add that at the time when Powell was supposed to be so keen on Dig, he was also regaling Green with stories of bohemian routs 'where there was every kind of incredible creature ... and some of the most lovely women I have ever seen'.[13] Stuck in Birmingham, where he was working on the shop floor of his family's engineering business, Green may well have concluded that Powell had other fish to fry.

Much has been written about the famous parties of the Twenties, not least by Powell himself. What seems generally agreed upon is that you might meet 'anyone' at them, meaning that some, at least, of the barriers erected by the *ancien régime* had come down. Money and birth still counted for much (as Powell knew to his cost) but they were no longer the only criteria. In all but the stuffiest circles beauty, brains, talent and wit commanded equal respect, so that people were not necessarily shown the door if they looked a bit odd. This last is one of the lessons Jenkins takes home from Mrs Andriadis's party. Anxious, for snobbish reasons, to distance himself from his *outré* companions Mr Deacon and Gypsy Jones, he finds to his surprise that they 'fade unobtrusively into the general background'.

Powell had especially fond memories of the 'huge, eccentric parties' that took place on the *Friendship*, a riverboat moored beside Charing Cross Pier:

> They consisted of a curiously incoherent group of people. I mean, at one end of the scale there'd be quite smart people, Diana Cooper-ish sort of figures and so on. And then there'd always be a lot of these girls who were sort of living on the margin – you know, they'd do a little modelling, and at the same time they were not quite tarts, but they were being half kept. And then it would tail off into the queer, almost criminal world – lesbians dressed as admirals, that sort of thing.[14]

Formidably discreet as a rule about his private life Powell does indicate in his Memoirs and Journals how bitter-sweet his relations with one or two of these bohemian nymphs proved to be. Compared to the average deb they were liberated. They would undoubtedly have endorsed what Hemingway had to say about morals: 'So far, about morals, I know only that what is moral is what you feel good after and what is immoral is what you feel bad after.'[15] But this didn't mean that they were going to hop into bed with any young man who caught their fancy. In the background there was invariably someone with a prior claim because he paid the bills. Powell learnt this the hard way. It became the theme of his first novel, *Afternoon Men*.

*

Powell, as I have said, had no talent for role-playing. This was brought home to him when, in an attempt to put Oxford well and truly behind him, he took the drastic step of enrolling as a probationary officer in the Territorial Army. The unit he chose was a Gunner regiment, reckoning that what was good enough for Tolstoy was good enough for him. Two evenings a week he slogged out to their headquarters in Brixton, where he rode round and round a dusty shed and learnt the rudiments of gun-aiming. Aware that he had practically nothing in common with the other officers, many of whom were City types who referred, in a Woosterish way, to their 'mater' and their 'guv'nor', he said little and swore a lot. To no avail. One evening he was introduced to an officer he hadn't met before. 'This is Powell,' said the Adjutant. 'He's a Senior Wrangler or something.' After that he packed it in.

Ten years later, when the idea of joining the TA no longer seemed so bizarre, Powell wrote a piece about his experiences for *Night & Day*, London's short-lived answer to the *New Yorker*.[16] He also had some mild fun at the TA's expense in *What's Become of Waring*. Curiously enough, support for the Adjutant's appreciation of Powell was provided during the war by the Inspector of Military Intelligence, Brigadier Barker-Benfield, whose courses at Cambridge and Matlock Powell attended. In a letter to Malcolm Muggeridge Powell reported that 'someone met Barker-B[enfield] recently who said, "Powell – he isn't much to look at; but as soon as he opens his mouth you can see what an astonishingly intelligent person he is."'[17]

Not long after Powell had made his excuses and left the Gunners his father was the victim of ill-health and Army regulations. Although he had spent very little time with The Welch since being invalided home in 1914, Major Powell (the rank to which he had reverted) was now in line to command the 'home' battalion, the other being stationed in India. Unluckily for him the government suddenly decided, early in 1927, to send a Defence Force to Shanghai, whose International Settlement was threatened by Chinese Nationalist insurgents. The Welch formed part of this force and Major Powell sailed with them to China. On arrival his insides soon got in such a state that he was sent back to England to convalesce. Army regulations were that an officer must be fit to serve anywhere, so he had no option but to send in his papers, retiring with the rank of Lieutenant-Colonel.

Philip Powell read for the Bar, took a Second and went into Chambers but his temperament got the better of him and he soon ceased to practise. Aged forty-seven he had thirty years of increasingly cantankerous retirement ahead of him, growing ever more dependent upon his long-suffering wife. Until the Blitz they lived in Clarence Terrace, Regent's Park, next door to the novelist Elizabeth Bowen and her husband, Alan Cameron. Then, like Uncle

Giles, they took to living in residential hotels, the last of which was near the Star and Garter Home on Richmond Hill.

Incurious about other people, Philip Powell was positively affronted by family history, the study of which would be bound, he thought, to end in tears. I think it is reasonable to assume that Powell's abiding interest in genealogy, which began while he was still at Oxford, was in part a gesture of defiance against his father, whom he found a great trial. Aside from Philip's chronic embitterment, exacerbated by his failure to find employment during the Second World War, there was also his stinginess, the full extent of which was not revealed until his death. Not only did he fail to keep his side of the bargain with Balston, so that Powell remained a hired hand, he also became increasingly reluctant to put his hand in his pocket at all. So hard-up did his son assume he had become after the war that whenever they lunched together at Philip's club he would refuse the offer of a sherry beforehand.

*

In later life Powell was apt to be dismissive about his duties at Duckworth, saying he wasn't really a publisher, 'just a young man employed to empty the inkpots and compose the ads and that sort of thing'.[18] In fact, less than a year after his arrival, he had begun to trawl on Duckworth's behalf among his contemporaries. One of the first he netted was Evelyn Waugh.

Although two years behind him at Oxford, Powell had seen just enough of Waugh to recognise that he was bound to make his mark in the world somehow. They met again in the spring of 1927. Waugh, a schoolmaster, had just been sacked for making a drunken pass at the new matron, who as he noted in his *Diaries* had formerly been the Dame at Goodhart's, a coincidence everyone seems either to have overlooked or misinterpreted.* Still at a loose end socially, Powell warmed to Waugh, whose self-confidence had not been dented by the many setbacks he had experienced since leaving Oxford. At one of their meetings Waugh presented Powell with an inscribed copy of his privately printed essay on the Pre-Raphaelites, written at the suggestion of Waugh's close friend Alastair Graham, then working for a small press. Powell showed the essay to Balston, who promptly commissioned Waugh to write an up-to-date life of Dante Gabriel Rossetti. This was successfully published in 1928, by which time Waugh had not only completed his first novel, *Decline and Fall*, on which Duckworth had an

* e.g. Christopher Sykes, who thought Goodhart's was a house at Waugh's old school, Lancing.

option, but also married the Honourable Evelyn Gardner, a distant relative by marriage of Gerald Duckworth. The juxtaposition was unfortunate.

Waugh had married Evelyn Gardner ('She-Evelyn') in the teeth of opposition from her mother, Lady Burghclere, whose sister was married to Gerald Duckworth's brother, George. Being the sort of pompous body he was, Gerald Duckworth sided with Lady Burghclere, so imagine his indignation when he learnt that *Decline and Fall* contained ribald passages that might well land its publisher in court. Conscious of Gerald looking over his shoulder Balston applied too much blue pencil, causing Waugh to reclaim the manuscript and submit it instead to Chapman and Hall, his father's firm. They also insisted on changes, but not as many as Duckworth. These Waugh consented to, leaving Balston to wring his hands for ever more over the one that got away. It was small consolation that Duckworth retained the option on Waugh's non-fiction.

Powell played no active part in this cause célèbre, but shortly afterwards he became embroiled in what was, for Waugh, a far more traumatic event, the break-up of his marriage. Why She-Evelyn left her husband need not detain us; what matters is who she left him for, a raffish friend of Powell's called John Heygate, the author of *Decent Fellows*. Although an innocent bystander, Powell had often been present on those occasions when Heygate and She-Evelyn met, and as luck would have it he and Heygate were on holiday together in Germany when the balloon went up. Incorrectly, but understandably, Waugh saw this as proof of Powell's complicity in She-Evelyn's defection, and while their friendship was never formally dissolved, their intimacy was at an end. But even before the collapse of his marriage Waugh had set his sights on social peaks that Powell had no inclination to climb, so a parting of the ways was probably inevitable.

A few years after Waugh's death Powell was asked by Little, Brown, his American publisher, whether he would consider writing Waugh's biography. 'Other things being equal,' replied Powell, 'I can imagine nothing I should like less.'[19] And yet it's clear that Waugh was one of those people – Cyril Connolly was another – who fascinated Powell to the end of his days. In the last volume of his Journals he devotes more space to Waugh than to anyone except his family and closest friends. While Waugh was alive he took a keen interest in his writing (a compliment Waugh returned) and as a young man is on record as asking Connolly for his opinion on them both. Nor were their worldly ambitions so dissimilar: it was Powell, not Waugh, who told Malcolm Muggeridge that the two things he most wanted in life were a wife with a title and a house with a drive.[20]

*

At about the same time that Powell began seeing Evelyn Waugh he met Constant Lambert (1905-51), who became probably his closest friend as a young man. A few months older than Powell, Lambert was a musical prodigy. Already famous for having become, aged twenty, the first English composer to write a ballet for Diaghilev, he would soon be hailed as a genius for his jazzy composition *The Rio Grande*, which put the Queen's Hall 'in a frenzy' on its opening night. Powell himself was not musical, but this didn't matter because Lambert was one of those very rare beings who could claim to be an authority on three different arts, two of which, writing and painting, meant so much to Powell. Their tastes, particularly in art, were different, as indeed were some of their appetites, but they talked the same language. For the first time in his life Powell had found someone with whom, intellectually speaking, he was wholly at ease.

Lambert grew up in Chelsea, but there was nothing fancy about his upbringing, which was often hand-to-mouth and marred by a succession of agonising illnesses that left him lame and partially deaf in one ear. George Lambert, his father, born in England but raised in Australia, was a moderately successful portrait painter whose career in London was curtailed by the Great War. Always a remote figure to his younger son, he played no part at all in his life after 1920, abandoning his family in order to execute a series of commissions in Australia, where he died suddenly in 1930. Sadly, Lambert himself was to prove an equally negligent father. A true bohemian, his promiscuous, pub-crawling, after-hours way of life did not sort with domesticity.

At the age of ten Lambert went to Christ's Hospital. More than once it looked as if the school would be his final resting place – 'Boys who die during the term-time,' noted the prospectus, 'are usually buried in the churchyard' – and his mother took a cottage nearby so that she could nurse him herself. Confined to the infirmary for months on end with nothing to do but read, write and think, he made up for his physical shortcomings by his intellectual maturity. According to the politician Michael Stewart, a contemporary of his, Lambert had, at the age of sixteen, 'the mind and interests of a well-informed adult: there was no affectation about this – it simply was the fact'.[21]

In later life Lambert would sometimes complain that compared with contemporaries of his like Powell, who had received a gentleman's education, he had been made to feel like a 'Charity boy'.[22] But there can have been few people in his circle who had read so widely and indiscriminately, or who had retained so much of what they had read. The range of his interests is suggested here by the painter Michael Ayrton, whose house Lambert lodged in after the war: 'early aeronautics, nineteenth-century French verse, numerology, Jacobean tragedy, the topography of French seaports and London rivers, cats for whom he had a passion and bats for whom he had a more cursory enthusiasm.'[23] To this list should be added lewd limericks, many of his own devising and literally hundreds of which he knew by heart.

Powell shared Lambert's passion for cats, but what chiefly impressed him in the early days was how Lambert combined devotion to the arts with a loathing for artiness, the besetting sin, so Powell thought, of his Oxford contemporaries. Another bond between them was Lambert's disdain for Bloomsbury, which Powell fully endorsed, and, later on, his disregard for the Auden Group, whose didactic verse he compared to back-numbers of the *New Statesman*. Many of Lambert's prejudices were aired in *Music Ho!*, a book for which Powell had tremendous admiration. Although essentially a study of contemporary music, it is also concerned with such topics as chemical beer, loudspeakers, the redevelopment of Regent Street ('an appalling example of modern degeneracy') and the impact of Modernism. More than once Powell quoted Lambert's theory that by 1913, writing, painting, sculpture and music had all of them, in advanced circles, reached their furthest limits of obscurity for the man in the street. They both agreed that the Twenties really began, both in the arts and general social loosening up, before 1914.

The music critic Cecil Gray, a hard-drinking, much-married and misogynistic Scot who probably contributed to Maclintick in *Dance*, described Lambert as 'a disconcerting blend of the *fin de siècle* Frenchman and the bluff and hearty Englishman'.[24] Lambert's *fin de siècle* side is hinted at here in a letter he wrote from Marseilles:

My dear Tony,
   As I write I am surrounded by so many negros and dwarfs that I can hardly believe I am not in the heart of Old Bloomsbury. In fact the only real difference between Marseille night life and a Gt. Ormond St. party is one of expense. One feels that at any moment the homely figure of Dick Wyndham may emerge from a bordel or that Wadsworth will be seen trying to retrieve his hat from some old hag or other. All the female whores look like Greta and all the male ones like Brian Howard ... You will excuse the shaky handwriting I'm sure – it's all I can do to hold a pen these days. My obsessions are becoming more pronounced I'm afraid but not quite so narrow. I feel rather like Walt Whitman --all races, all colours, all creeds, all sexes etc.[25]

Two points arise from this. First, while Powell would certainly have wanted to hear in more detail about Lambert's 'obsessions' (he was insatiably curious about other people's sex lives), it's doubtful whether, given the chance, he would have joined him on his escapades, except perhaps as an observer. Though no stranger to lust, on which he once delivered a radio talk, he was far from being a libertine. But neither, on the available evidence, is Jenkins's friend Moreland, the composer. Which brings me to my second point, the connection between Moreland and Lambert.

Powell, as we saw with Sillery and Urquhart, was very guarded about the extent to which his characters were based on real people. But he could hardly deny the link between Moreland and Lambert. Not only do they look alike, they talk alike. For instance in *Infants* Powell recalls Lambert saying of his elder brother Maurice, a sculptor, 'The amount of work my brother does is limited only by the hour he gets up in the morning.' Moreland says practically the same thing about Ralph Barnby, the painter. Again, it's clear that as a young man Jenkins enjoys the same sort of conversational intimacy with Moreland that Powell enjoyed with Lambert, an intimacy unattainable with anyone else, however sympathetic, after the age of about twenty-five. Although they see increasingly less of each other as they grow older, Jenkins and Moreland remain on the same wavelength. When Moreland dies, that frequency shuts down. Their last talk together, when Moreland is dying, is also the last talk of its kind that Jenkins has with anyone.

Powell was sometimes criticised for making his characters too well read and witty, but if we accept that Moreland is in some sense a memorial to Lambert, then in this instance he did not exaggerate. Lambert was, said another friend, 'somebody whose conversation could cover anything that might seem relevant to the subject under discussion – Shakespeare, Ibsen, Oscar Wilde, the Sitwells, Russian Ballet, Impressionist painters, as it might be – in a single flight'.[26] Moreland measures up to this, but not to the compulsive womanising indulged in by Lambert. Though we're told that he beds the occasional fan, Moreland is too diffident to be a womaniser; whereas Lambert, in the words of Frederick Ashton, was 'highly sexed, if he saw someone he wanted, he had to have them.'[27] Given that he started sleeping with Margot Fonteyn when she was eighteen it is hard to imagine Lambert showing the same restraint towards the young Priscilla Tolland as does Moreland.

Some readers must wonder why Powell took so long to introduce Moreland, who despite being a Twenties figure does not appear until volume five, *Casanova's Chinese Restaurant*. The answer, I believe, is that he was an afterthought. Where possible, Powell preferred not to use living models for his leading characters, particularly if they were old friends, and at the time when he was doing the spade work for *Dance*, in the late Forties, he cannot have known that Lambert had only a few years to live. When Lambert died, unexpectedly, in August 1951, Powell was finishing *A Buyer's Market*, which is when, chronologically, you might expect Moreland to appear. It was partly I suspect out of delicacy, but also for technical reasons, that Powell delayed his entrance for several years.

*

If Constant Lambert was a milestone in Powell's life, so too was Nina Hamnett (1890-1956), the rackety artist and model whose life was like one of Hogarth's satires. According to Peter Quennell, 'Nina was Anthony Powell's first grown-up love affair. He was rather pleased with it at the time. She satisfactorily deprived him of his innocence, which is a thing people were anxious to get rid of in those days. He built her up as a romantic *femme de trente ans*, a bohemian mistress.'[28] Typically, Powell does not confirm this in *Messengers*; the most he will admit to is visiting her studio so that she can draw him, a sketch reproduced in the book. Nina, in her memoirs, omits any mention of Powell at all, which given the profusion of other names she drops is a curious omission.

Powell met Nina in 1927 when she delivered to Duckworth the drawings she had done for Osbert Sitwell's waggish guide-book, *The People's Album of London Statues*. She was then thirty-seven, a veteran of Montparnasse in its heyday and the Edwardian Café Royal, loud, promiscuous and alcoholic, but still capable of the draughtsmanship that had so impressed two of her mentors, Walter Sickert and Roger Fry, ten years before. Though far from beautiful – she was tall and angular with a long nose and receding chin– she had abundant zest and what Powell called 'an unshakeable, if not always very judicious, belief in her own myth'. Her father, a colonel in Uncle Giles's old unit, the Army Service Corps, had been cashiered for taking a bribe, bequeathing nothing to his daughter except a 'county' accent and manner which even in the most indelicate of situations she never lost. Probably Powell was reassured by this. At any rate for a short while he took the place of the boxers and sailors who were her usual consorts, being referred to by Nina as her 'little Etonian'.[29] The writer Maurice Richardson, in what turned out to be his last published piece, recalled seeing them, 'one blue October Saturday afternoon', at a table in Nina's local, the Fitzroy Tavern:

> And as Nina, getting as she often did, a little noisy, raps on the table with her pink gin glass, and trolls out her 'waxworks' song, half hoping her fiancé might join in (which of course he was far too diffident to do) a barrel organ opens up its myxolidan jangle ...[30]

Powell was enraged by Richardson's description of him as Nina's fiancé. It was, he told John Monagan, 'a complete invention ... I can't imagine why he dragged the subject in, but he was struck dead for it, the review itself being posthumous'.[31] However that might be, I think Richardson does convey what a sight for sore eyes they must have been, as incongruous in their way as Widmerpool and his merry widow, Mrs Haycock. He also hints at one of those 'uncomfortable truths' that Powell himself was fond of emphasising, the bitter joys of bohemian life.

Still, there can be no doubt that Powell profited by his association with Nina. For a start she had no sexual hang-ups, confiding in a friend that she couldn't see what all the fuss was about, 'but they seem to like it so I let them get on with it'.[32] Powell, one suspects, would have been far too busy 'getting on with it' to bother about the underlying frigidity that permitted such liberties. The fact that she was, by now, barren removed another potential source of anxiety, and also helped preserve her figure, her greatest asset, which had been sculptured in marble by Gaudier-Brzeska and drawn by Modigliani – 'He said I had the best tits in Europe, m'deah!'[33]

Nina was not exactly a 'free poke' (as Jenkins's old comrade Borrit would have put it): chronically hard-up, she expected to be bought several drinks and would not say no to the occasional 'fiveah'. But she offered more than sex in return, notably the mana that came from knowing many of the artists and writers who made the weather in London and Paris before and after the Great War. Even if Powell sometimes wilted under 'the inimitable machine-gun fire of her conversation',[34] he would undoubtedly have relished hearing at first hand about people like Picasso, Modigliani and Joyce (who thought Nina was one of the few 'vital' women he had ever met).[35] It must also have been thanks to Nina, whose studio was nearby, that he infiltrated the colony of painters who had settled round Charlotte Street, the main artery of what would soon be known as Fitzrovia. Observing them live and move and have their being, 'the professional necessities of painting were all at once revealed'.

Powell had other cause to be grateful to Nina. For instance in *Afternoon Men* the hero, hoping to 'amuse' the cool adventuress he has fallen for, takes her to a rather crummy boxing tournament, not the sort of milieu one associates with Powell, but one he almost certainly experienced with Nina, who was an aficionado. She also introduced him to the original of the Marquis de la Tour d'Espagne, the excitable opium-smoking French Count who appears in *Agents and Patients*, a meeting which took place at the Cavendish Hotel in Jermyn Street. Nina was *persona grata* with Rosa Lewis, who owned the Cavendish. Powell went there often enough to take the measure of this tough Cockney dowager and her legendary establishment. Despite the hotel's reputation for upper-class depravity he found its atmosphere as chilly as the champagne, 'the fact never forgotten that dissipation must be paid for'.

The price exacted from Nina Hamnett was a heavy one. Within a few years of meeting Powell the pub, rather than the studio, was where she was most often to be found. This led, inevitably, to penury, degradation and decrepitude, an end of which was made when she fell forty feet from her squalid room in Paddington and was impaled on the railings below.

Powell deplored sentimentality. One of the reasons he so admired *The Beggar's Opera* was that Gay 'is absolutely true to life. He is witty, satirical, tender, moving – but he is never *sentimental*.'[36] It follows that any attempt to exaggerate the strength of his feelings for Nina Hamnett would be a mistake. At bottom, it was 'just one of those things' (to invoke, as he sometimes did, a popular song). And yet ... recalling Nina's connection with Modigliani, I'm also reminded that if, as has been said, the central theme of *Dance* is Art versus Power, it is surely significant that the outcome should be determined by the fate of a drawing by Modigliani.

*

One of the painters Powell met through Nina Hamnett was Adrian Daintrey (1901-88), whose studio was next door to hers. This proximity was by accident rather than design, because although Daintrey could see the point of Nina she was definitely not his style. As he explained in his memoirs he had first encountered her in Montparnasse, where her reputation as a famous English bohemian had led him to expect 'a sultry, if blowsy beauty',[37] not a raw-boned daughter of the regiment from Tunbridge Wells or Cheltenham. Nor was the rough trade she picked up to his liking, so Powell must have come as a pleasant surprise. They got on immediately, a friendship which endured for sixty years. Though Daintrey had not yet had an exhibition he was already a drinking companion of Augustus John, having introduced himself to the great man while still a student at the Slade. It was thanks to Daintrey that Powell met John, no longer 'the young painter who had dominated the serious studios of the century's opening years', but 'almost ...the figurehead of the demi-god round which the post-war carnival was danced'.[38]

Like John, Daintrey was a dedicated philanderer, and what he says here about John was equally true of himself: 'His attempts at seduction were unending and often successful, but I do not think he felt any grudge if rebuffed.'[39] Moreland says something very similar of Barnby: '[I]f he sees a girl he likes, all he has to do is to ask her to sleep with him. Some do, some don't; it is one to him.' Daintrey's nerve is illustrated by a story I was told about his involvement with the wife of a wealthy friend. Returning home one evening this friend saw the silhouette of a couple embracing in his drawing room. When he went in he found Daintrey alone with his wife. At the time he said nothing, but meeting Daintrey a few days later he challenged him with what he had seen. 'Yes,' said Daintrey, 'I did kiss her. But only on the mouth.'[40]

In his memoirs Daintrey was frank about the impact of love affairs on his art. They were, he said, competitors rather than stimuli – 'and very formidable ones at that'.[41] Himself a believer in the need for complete dedication to art, Powell would certainly have endorsed this. But he did concede that because of their privileged position as regards seduction – 'Time, place and a respectable motive for a visit', to quote Moreland – painters were more exposed to temptation than other artists.

Although they are both womanisers, the resemblance between Daintrey and Barnby is pretty superficial. Barnby not only paints like a Frenchman, he looks like one too, wearing overalls in the studio and sporting a bristly haircut. Daintrey, on the other hand, was described in the Thirties as 'the most English of all young painters'. He smoked a pipe, dressed conservatively and used to say that drawing required 'the same application as sinking a putt'.[42] He specialised in gracious interiors, evocative cityscapes – particularly of London – and beautiful women, and like his coeval, Rex Whistler, was popular with the more go-ahead members of Society. But if, as he once implied to Powell, there was a period in his life when he was 'always at the Ritz',[43] it must have been at somebody else's expense, because although 'semi well-known', he never commanded high prices for his work and ended his days at Sutton's Hospital in Charterhouse Square, an alms house for indigent gentlemen.

Daintrey was also thought by some to have inspired Zouch, the predatory, social-climbing artist who comes a cropper in Powell's third novel, *From a View to a Death*. But Zouch is undoubtedly a shit, whereas Daintrey, by all accounts, was not. He had the knack of remaining on good terms with old lovers, some of whom would have been no help at all in his getting on. Much as he valued his social connections he was always prepared, so he told Powell, to pass up a smart party if he got the scent of a fresh conquest on his way there.

Powell thought that 'in certain respects' his old friend was 'a simple soul'.[44] He may well have had in mind Daintrey's friendship with the spy Donald Maclean, a Chelsea neighbour of his during the late Thirties.

Daintrey, unpolitical but conscious of how indebted artists like himself were to the liberal intelligentsia, was very taken with this tall, outspoken and unkempt young diplomat who was so different from the usual run of starchy Foreign Office types. They often played golf together at unfashionable courses in the suburbs, Maclean having a horror of anywhere smart like Sunningdale or Wentworth.

Daintrey got Powell along to meet Maclean, whom he described as 'more or less a Communist'. The fact that Powell did not demur at this shows how used he must have become by then to mixing with people so described. But Maclean was no more his style than Nina Hamnett had been Daintrey's. He found him 'vain, pompous, snobbish and shifty'. They did not meet again until after the war, by which time Maclean's star was in the ascendant, largely, it was said, because he dared to be different (though in his biography of Maclean, Robert Cecil suggests that by the beginning of the war he had smartened up his act and was known in the typing pool as 'Fancy-Pants' Maclean).[45] In Powell's eyes he was just as objectionable as before; even so whenever they met, at parties, or in pubs and clubs, they got on 'perfectly well'. At this period Powell was laying down the foundations for *Dance*, in the second volume of which there appears a young man cramming for the Foreign Office called Tompsitt, who is not only large, fair and scruffy, like the young Maclean, but also lacking in the social graces traditionally associated with a diplomatic career. Much to Nick Jenkins's annoyance Barbara Goring, the deb he's in love with, seems to find Tompsitt 'not unattractive', this despite his being as offhand with her as with everyone else. When they meet again during the war, at a Cabinet Office meeting presided over by Widmerpool, he has a more sinister cause for complaint. News of the Katyn massacre has just come through and Tompsitt, like Widmerpool, thinks the Poles are behaving unreasonably by demanding an explanation from 'our second most powerful Ally'. He is last heard of as ambassador to the Eastern Bloc country with which Widmerpool is suspected of having had treasonable dealings.

5

The Party's Over

'Art is memory: memory is reenacted desire.'

Cyril Connolly

'Mr Powell is by far the most amusing and incisive observer of what has been known vulgarly as the "bright young people".'

Edith Sitwell

The air of Mayfair in the Twenties was thick with noise and dust as mansions were demolished to make way for mansion flats. Shepherd Market did not escape the carnage, one consequence of which was that in 1928 a wooden stanchion was plonked in the middle of Powell's sitting room to support his ceiling, supposedly at risk from the wreckers next door. Already cramped, his quarters became too tight a fit, so in the spring of 1929 he began to look for a new address, finding somewhere suitable almost immediately in Tavistock Square, Bloomsbury, where Dickens had lived in the 1860s and since 1920 the site of Leonard and Virginia Woolf's Hogarth Press. For £110 a year, roughly a third of his annual income, he took a three-year lease on an unfurnished basement flat at No 33, consisting of three rooms plus kitchen and bathroom, with a small patch of garden at the back. In those days young bachelors like Powell didn't cook,* so his kitchen was redundant; nor did he ever use more than two of the three rooms at one time. But once settled in, the 'vague intention' he had of writing a novel became a deliberate attempt to set out his stall. He had a subject: life and love in the London he knew. And thanks to Robert Burton, a title: *Afternoon Men***– a good description, he thought, of characters whose mornings were clouded by hangovers. The problem was presentation. He needed to find a style that would express, in contemporary terms, what he wanted to say. It was no use trying to write like Galsworthy, Bennett or Wells: that would have been as *de trop* as a Norfolk jacket in a night-club. Nor could he learn much from Bloomsbury, since they now seemed 'scarcely less stick in the mud than the philistines they had formerly attacked'.[1]

---

* In later life he prided himself on his 'farmhouse' curries.

** 'They are a company of giddy-heads, afternoon men.' (*The Anatomy of Melancholy*)

Literary influences are sometimes hard to detect. Who, reading *The Naked and the Dead*, would automatically connect it with E.M. Forster, the writer from whom the young Norman Mailer said he learnt so much?[2] In Powell's case the difficulty arises because many of the writers he doffs his cap to – E.E. Cummings, William Gerhardie, Ronald Firbank, Mikhail Lermontov and Wyndham Lewis (whose painter's vision he shared) – are nowadays unlikely to be found on the common reader's shelves. There is, however, one name that should be familiar to everyone: Hemingway. 'It is largely due to [Hemingway],' he wrote in 1955, 'that people are not still writing like Hugh Walpole.'[3]

Powell was introduced to Hemingway's work in 1927, when *The Sun Also Rises* (called *Fiesta* in Britain) was published. He is honest enough to admit that he did not, at first, grasp what a break with the past it represented. Only after a second reading did the penny drop. 'You really need to have lived then to realise what a revelation he was. Everybody writes like that now, which wasn't at all the case then. We thought it was absolutely extraordinary. I mean people literally used to talk to each other in Hemingwayese. It became a craze, like the latest dance.'[4]

At that stage Hemingway the hearty was still subordinate to Hemingway the aesthete, striving to pare his sentences to the bone. Young highbrows like Powell were prepared to put up with hairy-chested characters who boxed and shot and went to bullfights because they had yet to become a cliché; and in any case, 'after D.H. Lawrence and Virginia Woolf, they offered a certain exhilaration'.[5] No doubt the cosmopolitan setting was a factor too. Powell's was the first generation to visit the Mediterranean in summer, for reasons which Hemingway makes abundantly clear in *The Sun Also Rises*. As Cyril Connolly, an early advocate of Hemingway, noted: '[He] alone of living writers has saturated his books with the memory of physical pleasure, with sunshine and salt water, with food, wine and making love, and with the remorse that is the shadow of that sun.'[6]

Unlike Hemingway, Powell is not a sensuous writer. He never attempts, as Hemingway does so successfully, to convey the taste of a cold beer on a hot day. He is more interested in showing what drink does to people, though Hemingway did that as well. 'I admired the way [Hemingway] made drunk people talk,' said Evelyn Waugh.[7] So did Powell, and it shows:

> Atwater said: 'But what has made you so depressed?'
> 'Depressed?'
> 'Yes, depressed.'
> Fotheringham finished his drink at a gulp. He said:
> 'I suppose I must have sounded rather depressed. You see, I had a rather heavy lunch.'

'I see.'

'You know how a heavy lunch always lets you down.'

'About this time in the evening.'

'Yes,' said Fotheringham. 'About this time in the evening. You know I'm afraid I must have been boring you.'

'Not a bit.'

'I feel I have. You must forgive me. Do you forgive me? Say you forgive me, Atwater.'

'I do.'

'It's not the weather to eat and drink a lot in the middle of the day.'

Powell was also impressed by Hemingway's mastery of British idiom, much of it derived from his friendship with the controversial and enigmatic 'Chink' Dorman-Smith, who stood godfather to his son. Strangely, since he reviewed several books about Hemingway, Powell never mentions Dorman-Smith, a soldier as unconventional in his way as his father's friend, 'Boney' Fuller, and a beau ideal to the young Hemingway. He does however mention meeting Duff Twysden, the model for *The Sun Also Rises*'s heroine, Brett Ashley, who struck him as surprisingly suburban – 'a type from the bar of a Surrey golf club, rather than what I supposed appropriate to Montparnasse'.

There was also a model for Powell's heroine (as I suppose one must call her). In *Messengers* he describes how, shortly after moving to Tavistock Square, he suffered a *coup de foudre* at a party in Chelsea, receiving just enough encouragement to raise his hopes. This was unfortunate, because as Constant Lambert later told him, the girl in question, a chic little brunette 'of ravishing prettiness', already had a lover, who was not only older than Powell but considerably richer. By then, however, it was too late: he was hooked, and would remain wriggling for about a year.

Who was this Dark Lady? Writing in 1977 Powell drops a hint or two but nothing more. He says that she and her half-sister had a flat in the King's Road and that Peter Quennell had compared them, unjustly, to '*Les Demoiselles de Bienfilatre*', two mercenary little tarts in a story by the nine-teenth-century French Symbolist, Villiers de l'Isle-Adam. But a few years later, in his first volume of Journals, he refers to a Chelsea beauty, Enid Firminger, with whom he was 'fruitlessly' in love. And then, in the entry for 6 March 1991, he says he's received a letter from Firminger's stepdaughter asking if it was indeed 'Enid Firminger I mentioned in my memoirs'. We aren't vouchsafed his answer, but why bother to write about it if the step-daughter is mistaken?

In *Afternoon Men* the Chelsea beauty is called Susan Nunnery. She is, we're told immediately, 'a bit of a menace', but naturally this doesn't stop the hero, Atwater, from pursuing her. He gets off on the wrong foot by taking her to a restaurant where 'one meets everyone':

> 'Do you know everybody?' said Atwater. He hoped that lots more people would come and talk and drink and sit at the table and make assignations with Susan and give him good advice and argue with each other, because then it would become funny and he would feel less angry.

On their next date she stands him up. And by the time he has tried, and failed, to amuse her with a night out watching boxing – '"All this blood is rather much, isn't it?"' – it's clear he ought to throw in the towel. The *coup de grâce* is delivered by her father, a broken-down City gent, who announces that Susan has gone to America with a rich admirer called Verelst – '"Not a companion I should have chosen myself. But there it is."' For once dizzy with grief rather than alcohol, Atwater can't really take this in. He stumbles back to Soho where, as usual, someone knows of a party, which is precisely where we came in.

As a love story *Afternoon Men* lacks conviction. Even though one or two women seem to find him attractive, Atwater never really lives down his unpromising introduction:

> [A] weedy-looking young man with straw-coloured hair and rather long legs, who had failed twice for the Foreign Office. He sometimes wore tortoise-shell spectacles to correct a slight squint, and through influence had recently got a job in a museum.

Impossible to imagine him getting off with a stunning gold-digger like Susan Nunnery, who is the first of Powell's many 'difficult' women.

But as a corrective, *Afternoon Men* takes some beating. How appropriate, for instance, that there should be no hot water in the country cottage taken by Atwater's risible painter friend, Pringle, since Powell pours cold water on the whole idea of a bohemian house party. He's equally unimpressed by the quality of their London lives: the foetid dives they meet in, the nasty cocktails they drink, the boring parties they gatecrash, the loveless affairs they pursue. The message was not lost on reviewers. 'This is a book,' said the *Cherwell*, 'which anyone who has the intention of becoming a Bright Young Person should most certainly read; for those who have escaped this temptation it will remain a salutary warning.'[8] In *The Bookman*, R.S. Forman (who can only have lived in Tunbridge Wells) went even further: 'I can remember few books which contain such a gallery of futile and disagreeable people. It is the story of the semi-smart and pseudo-artistic minority which from time to time forces itself upon our notice, and is inclined to be a good deal more noisy than its numbers and importance warrant. I can think of nothing more salutary for its members than to take 'Afternoon Men' and let the rivet-hammer stroke of its sentences impinge on their souls. For a time at all events, and probably for ever, they would surely blush to hear themselves uttering their usual inanities.'[9] Even Harold Nicolson, who gave Powell himself a pat on the back in the *Evening Standard* ('A style as deft as Mr Powell's imposes admiration') described the book as 'a study in the utter absence of purpose in intellectual and social promiscuity'.[10]

It was left to L.P. Hartley in the *Week-End Review* to give *Afternoon Men* its most thoughtful review. He began by invoking Hemingway:

> It was inevitable, I suppose, that Mr Ernest Hemingway should have imitators, and he has been lucky to find such an able disciple as Mr Anthony Powell. Mr Powell has not only adopted the letter; he has entered into the spirit; if his little group of English Bohemians encountered Mr Hemingway's cosmopolitan Americans they would find themselves speaking the same language and thinking the same thoughts.

But not, reckoned Hartley, drinking at the same pace: '[B]y the standards of Mr Hemingway's men without women, or even of his men with women, they hardly drink anything at all.'

Hartley then took issue with the 'explosive, staccato method' of writing dialogue employed by Hemingway and Powell. 'Most people are not laconic at all: quite the reverse in fact ... It is difficult to tell what [they] are like if they only say a few words at a time.' (Powell's answer to this, given in *Messengers*, is that 'Hemingway's dialogue at its best is a brilliant representation of "naturalism", not necessarily "how people really talk".') However, concluded Hartley, 'If one can keep one's ear in, so to speak, one finds much that is subtle, witty, humorous, brilliant.' He thought the characters were 'certainly worth writing about once'; but hoped that 'Mr Powell, who has clearly a good deal of talent, will find a different subject for his second book'.[11]

What you won't find in any of these reviews are protests on behalf of Verelst, Atwater's suave rival, who despite having 'bags under his eyes and rather a thick nose ...hardly looked like a Jew at all'. The same point is made more subtly later, when he's described as 'telling the story well, using his hands, but not at all as if he wanted to sell something'. Such slights would be unacceptable in a modern novel, but they were commonplace then. If anything Powell lets Verelst off lightly. In *The Sun Also Rises* Hemingway is far nastier about Robert Cohn.

Nearly sixty years later, when there was a row about T.S. Eliot's alleged anti-Semitism, Powell devoted an entry in his Journals to defending himself against the same charge. He began by saying that there was an awful lot of 'humbug' nowadays about how Jews were spoken of before the war, mostly on the part of young people who were being wise after the event. To insist, as some of them did, that they would never have dreamt of cracking a Jewish joke was absurd; in a free country Jewish jokes were as legitimate as any other kind of joke, and indeed there were plenty of Jews he knew then who had made a point of telling them. Then Powell dealt with Verelst, whom he described as 'a rather attractive middle-aged man'. I would agree with this, though it's not necessarily apparent at first reading. Powell sought to clinch the matter with an afterthought. He recalled that the ridiculous Pringle, whom no one would have taken for a Jew on account of his name, was actually modelled on Gerald Reitlinger, a Jew he later got to know very well. 'In other words I went out of my way not to appear anti-Semitic in days long before the Nazis.'[12]

Well, yes. Powell certainly had several Jewish friends besides Reitlinger, notably Sir Henry d'Avigdor-Goldsmid MP, who gave him much valuable advice on Widmerpool's career in Parliament and the City. It is also the case that Rosie Manasch is one of the few really sympathetic women in *Dance*. But in his eagerness to refute the charge of bigotry Powell seems to have overlooked this passage in 'The Wat'ry Glade', which was written after Hitler had come to power:

> Worse still, there had been a period in the immediate past, happily drawing to a close at the time of my arrival [at Goodhart's], when the non-Aryan proportion in its membership had seemed to many unnecessarily high.

Whether or not this was the case, Powell chose an unfortunate way of putting it.

*

Where the arts were concerned, Powell's was a very competitive generation. So he must have been gratified by *Afternoon Men*'s reception, which was markedly better than that accorded to Peter Quennell's first novel which appeared in the same week. But Powell thought most reviewers had got it wrong in one important respect.

> I set out to show what a love affair was like in that sort of world at that period. I wasn't attacking that world – far from it. But reviewers thought I was. They confused me with Evelyn Waugh, which was understandable, but mistaken.

Waugh was a satirist, and satirists have an aim. I didn't have an aim. I simply wanted to show how the sort of people I was writing about behaved.[13]

I myself think that in this instance there is a fine line between attacking something and sending it up, which is what Powell does. Characters like Pringle and Fotheringham and Lola, the tiresome girl who is inspired by Bertrand Russell 'when he talks about mental adventure', may take themselves very seriously, but I don't see how we can. Significantly the original blurb, which Powell would certainly have approved if he didn't actually write it himself, makes no mention of a specific love affair. The author, it says, 'deals from inside, critically but not unmercifully, with the lives and loves of a cross-section of society which is chiefly known to the public through its artists and parties'. Twenty years later, when the novel was reissued, it was the 'dullness' of the parties that Jocelyn Brooke* recalled in a retrospective piece for *Time and Tide*: 'Mr Powell had, once and for all, exploded the long-cherished myth that parties were fun. Most of us, after that, realised just how bored we had really been.'[14]

But what neither Brooke nor Powell realised at the time was that, dull or not, the party was over. *Afternoon Men* was published in early June 1931, when it still seemed that Great Britain could rise above the Depression. But that summer there was a steady run on the pound, culminating in a financial crisis. On 21 September Britain went off the Gold Standard, 'the biggest shock', according to Evelyn Waugh's brother Alec, that 'my generation and their predecessors had ever known'.[15]

Overnight the Roaring Twenties were silenced, a point made abundantly clear that autumn by of all publications, the *Bystander*. Instead of gushing over the sumptuous Red and White party given by Arthur Jeffries, an American millionaire, it complained that 'ill-bred extravagance' at a time when Hunger Marchers were descending on London was exactly the sort of thing 'that breeds Communists'.[16] By the following spring, when *Afternoon Men* was published in the United States, the *New York Times Book Review* thought it was already dated: 'Novels about cocktail parties of the younger sophisticated set seem somewhat stale today.'[17]

Powell was already at work on *Venusberg*, his second novel, when *Afternoon Men* appeared. Unlike its predecessor it was written on a typewriter, purchased out of his advance. He had no problem with what Jenkins calls the 'awful bareness' of typescript, which reflected the somewhat austere approach to the arts that he had as a young man. Sometimes he

---

* In 1931 Brooke himself had completed a 'party novel' called *Spare Men*. It was never published, possibly because of its homosexual theme.

would spend hours looking at a blank sheet of paper, but as a rule he wrote with a fluency that in later life he could only marvel at.

> When you're young you do have this sort of inner energy that bubbles up all the time. I remember bits of dialogue would come into my head when I was sitting on a bus perhaps, and I would write them down on whatever came to hand – the back of an envelope or even the evening paper. It didn't necessarily have anything to do with what you were writing at the time. You just thought it might come in handy one day.[18]

Powell had also begun keeping a Notebook, which was published after his death. Quite early on you come across this entry, which could well apply to Pamela Flitton: 'She's the sort of woman who if she'd been taken in adultery would have caught the first stone and thrown it back.' In fact it is said of Frau Ortrud Mavrin, the doomed heroine of *Venusberg*. Although undeniably tough, she is a far more sympathetic character than Pamela: a bartered bride, married to someone her father's age, who falls for Powell's pink-cheeked young hero, Lushington.

The setting is a small capital city on the Baltic where Lushington, a journalist, has been sent to cover the political violence that is threatening the regime. It's the sort of place where foreigners, in particular, see the same old faces all the time, a situation Powell experienced when he spent a couple of university vacations in Helsinki, where his father was attached to the British military mission. The characters include two émigré Counts, one very louche, the other melancholic, various diplomats including an old school friend of Lushington's called Da Costa, Da Costa's valet, Pope, an unctuous clown, and Ortrud's husband, Professor Mavrin.

Because he seems such a proper young Englishman no one suspects that Lushington is Ortrud's lover, though given her circumstances, it's assumed that someone must be performing that role. At one point her husband actually discusses the matter with him, an exchange that anticipates the scene in *Dance* when Duport regales an increasingly uncomfortable Jenkins with Jean Templer's infidelities. By now Lushington has begun to acknowledge to himself that he loves Ortrud more than Lucy, his estranged mistress in London.

> She smiled at him, making him think that perhaps he would give up his job on the paper and try to find a post on the spot, a waiter's or something of the sort where it would not be necessary to learn much of the language. Anything so long as he could stay with her.

But it's not to be. Sharing a cab home from a ball, Ortrud and Da Costa are caught in the crossfire when some local Communists try to shoot General Kuno, the Chief of Police. Both are killed. Lushington is recalled to London, where his affair with Ortrud seems so unreal that he barely hesitates before taking up with Lucy again.

Despite having what the blurb calls a 'Ruritanian' setting, *Venusberg* is the nearest to a 'Thirties' novel that Powell wrote. I'm sure Powell didn't intend this – indeed the idea of a Thirties novel had yet to be promoted in October 1932, when *Venusberg* appeared. But as he later admitted, 'novels have a life of their own in which one only partially partakes'.[19] The equivocal Count Bobel, with his face cream and his amber cigarettes, would not be out of place in Isherwood's Berlin or on Graham Greene's Orient Express, and a modern reader, aware of what was in store for the Baltic states, is bound to be struck by passages like this:

> 'Why do they try to kill General Kuno?' Lushington said.
> Baroness Puckler said: 'During the troubles he shot many Bolsheviks. Many, many Bolsheviks. Once he made a mistake and shot a great lot of men who were not Bolsheviks. In those days it was hard to tell. Therefore he has enemies. He is head of the police too. That may cause him to be disliked by some persons.'

Intended or not there is also a grim parallel between the shooting of Ordrun and Da Costa and the assassination of Franz-Ferdinand and his wife at Sarajevo, the prelude to Armageddon and 'the birth', as Jenkins says, 'of a new, uneasy age'.

Venusberg proved that *Afternoon Men* was no flash in the pan. L.P. Hartley thought it was 'as good as [its predecessor], perhaps better. It is full of fire and wit'. The *TLS* said it was 'often very amusing' and praised Powell's talent for dialogue. Other reviewers were again struck by the irony and understated humour, as when we glimpse the American Minister at a night-club, 'who with the help of the German leading lady was energetically lowering his country's prestige at the far end of the room'. Nobody linked the shootings, which happen off-stage, with the ideological conflicts that had begun to divide Europe.

*

Powell had now been working at Duckworth for six years. Although under no illusions about his prospects following the refusal of his father to invest in the firm, he apparently made little or no effort to look elsewhere. Why?

asked more than one reviewer of his Memoirs, forgetting that the Depression encouraged people to sit tight. Another reason may be deduced from a confession he made in one of his *Cherwell* reviews: 'The sin of Innate Inertia is not without its appeal for me.'[20] Add to these what he later called, in a letter to Evelyn Waugh, 'the luxury of seeing all my early books through the press personally'[21] and his reluctance to move on is understandable.

But like everyone else Duckworth had to tighten its belt, uncomfortable though this must have been for the fat founder. In the summer of 1932, a few months before *Venusberg* appeared, Powell received an ultimatum from Balston: either he could go back to square one, working full time for £300 a year, probably less if trading did not improve; or he could work mornings only for £200 a year. He chose the latter, partly out of prudence, but also because he thought this would give him more time for writing. In the event he found that when it came to writing fiction, he was not an afternoon man. Nor, at that period, was there much in the way of reviewing or other free-lance work, so he ended up reading or going to galleries or seeing friends, among them the couple to whom his third novel is dedicated, John and Evelyn Heygate.

A few years ahead of Powell at Eton and Balliol, (Sir) John Heygate – he inherited the title from his uncle in 1940 – was the son of a one-time Eton housemaster who was so stuffy as a young man that Edwardians coined the verb 'to heygate', meaning behave in an ultra-conventional manner. Whether Heygate deliberately set out to live down this inheritance is unclear (Powell says that 'in principle' father and son rubbed along pretty well); but certain it is that after leaving Oxford, where despite hobnobbing with Alfred Duggan and other swells he managed to take a Second, he never showed much respect for 'good form'. For instance, in *More Memoirs of an Aesthete* Harold Acton describes how, while serving with the RAF in Colombo during the war, he was approached by an unidentified Old Etonian corporal with a 'singular request': could he help find a room for the corporal's 'juvenile concubine' – a young girl he had purchased for 'hard cash' while serving up-country?[22] The Old Etonian was Heygate, whose lowly rank is explained by an article he wrote in September 1941 for *Horizon*, attacking the snobbish ethos of the OCTU he had bailed-out of and concluding with these words: 'I had no wish to be taught over again, what I trusted I had forgotten, how to be a gentleman.'[23]

Powell first got to know Heygate through the Evelyn Waughs, whose friend he then was. Naturally Waugh soon changed his tune when She-Evelyn defected, calling Heygate 'a ramshackle oaf'.[24] But Powell found him an attractive figure, the ideal 'spare man', tall, good-looking, well turned-out, often witty, a generous host, and 'prepared for any sort of adventure, with any sort of people'. Later it would become apparent that Heygate was neither as debonair nor as insouciant as he seemed. If Powell suspected this he chose to overlook it, presumably on the grounds that it is advisable to take people as they come. As Jenkins says in *The Kindly Ones*, 'One passes through the world knowing few, if any, of the important things about even the people with whom one has been from time to time in the closest intimacy.' Heygate, with his 'easy rather lounging carriage', had every appearance of someone for whom life would not prove too much of a struggle.

Heygate was then working as an assistant editor in the BBC newsroom, a job he had to give up when Waugh sued for divorce because Sir John Reith, the BBC Director-General, would not employ anyone involved in a divorce. But just before the scandal broke he and Powell went on holiday together in Germany, a country Heygate had fallen in love with five years before when learning the language in Heidelberg. Heygate's account of this trip, written just before the war, is a good deal more detailed than the two pages it warrants in *Messengers*. He describes how he and his friend 'AP', a writer, were determined to investigate Weimar Germany's two most obvious attractions: '*Nachtleben* and *Naktkultur* – Night Life and the Culture of Nakedness.'[25] As there was a heat wave they had plenty of incentive to take their clothes off and mingle with the hordes of Germans for whom nudity had become almost a religion. Some of Heygate's descriptions of the bronzed torsos they saw at lake-side camps are reminiscent of Spender and Isherwood, though it is fair to say that it is the women – 'the most naturally and physically *female* women in the world' – to whom he awards the palm.

In Berlin, a baking hot city of the plain, they exchanged the world of the *Sonnenkinder* for that of George Grosz. In the mornings they went to art galleries and museums; in the afternoons they lay perspiring on their beds until the sun went down and a breeze sprang up; and in the evenings, so Heygate says, they went in search of 'some satisfaction of the senses which had eluded us up until now, something more, something *further*'. Lest anyone protest that this is at odds with the portrait of Powell so far presented, I should make it clear that their search was apparently in vain. They had to settle for 'looking on'. There was plenty to see. Live shows, at which bored girls performed 'heroic orgies'; a hermaphroditic freak called Voodoo who offered 'monstrous spectacles in a salon in Berlin-East'; and in the Potsdamer-Platz, 'scarlet-heeled or spurred grenadiers, whose handling of the willing recruit was said to be as disciplinary as the treatment meted out to the men of the old Imperial Army'. Returning to their hotel they had to run the gauntlet of a crowd of famished part-time whores who blocked the way to their room, bidding each other down in a desperate attempt to get a client.

A week early Heygate was summoned home by Waugh to explain himself. He was soon in more hot water over *Decent Fellows*, his icono-clastic Eton novel, which dared to suggest that even at the best of schools, boys would be boys. This did however lead to a job in films, then an expanding industry, where Heygate's fair grasp of German was also an advantage at a time when UFA, the big German studio, was making trilin-gual movies. Powell visited him in Berlin, an interlude that found its way into his fourth novel, *Agents and Patients*, in which Heygate appears as Maltravers. But before that Heygate had produced his own Berlin novel, *Talking Picture*, which deserves a mention because the narrator has a friend called Rightlaw, a Welsh writer living in Bloomsbury, who closely resembles Powell.

We meet Rightlaw briefly on page one, seeing the narrator off at Liverpool Street Station:

> 'But wait a moment,' said Rightlaw, 'I must tell you how the dream ended – The girl was just coming down the stairs and the funny thing about her ...'
> And then the whistle blew, and my friends began to slip away from me, Rightlaw his mouth open with his unfinished dream, the others waving hands and already turning away to resume their chatter.[26]

Two hundred pages later Rightlaw turns up at the studio.

> At this moment the commissionaire made his way on to the set and behind him I saw the unconcerned face of Rightlaw ... Impressed as he was by this novel world, I knew that Rightlaw was going to continue the conversation exactly where it had been suspended by the train's departure from Liverpool Street.
> 'And the funny part about the dream,' said Rightlaw, tripping over a sound cable, 'was that the girl was wearing my own evening trousers. I know, because the braid has got frayed all down one side. By the way, I'm not inter-rupting, am I?'[27]

Rightlaw's visit is a short one, but the glimpses we get of him are in char-acter. When he is not appraising everyone else on the set, particularly the girls, he is dishing up all the latest London scandal or discussing modern art. The business about the dream is in character too. Like many of his contem-poraries Powell did for a time try and record his dreams, there being a fashionable theory that they sometimes forecast what would happen to you in real life. The problem was that dreams are not easy to describe on paper, particularly first thing in the morning, which is when you were supposed to do it. He gave up after three months, not long enough to test the theory, but having taught himself to set down his dreams intelligibly. Years later he said writing a novel was 'like having dreams which you then somehow rationalise and get into some sense'.

Powell gave the game away about Rightlaw in his review of *Talking Picture* for *Now and Then*, the house magazine of Heygate's publisher, Jonathan Cape. He observed that although the Berlin Heygate described – 'a Teutonic Babylon' – was gone, its legend would live on through his characters, among them Rightlaw.

> There will be few readers who do not succumb to Rightlaw's charm, even though he appears for a few pages only. His considered, brusque remarks about himself, followed up by equally brusque questions about other people, make us feel at once that we have been privileged to meet a really delightful person, intelligent, sensitive and reserved. If there were more Rightlaws about, the world would be a pleasant place to live in; if there were more characters like Rightlaw in literature, novels would be a joy to read.[28]

It was at Heygate's urging that Powell saved up for his first car, a £100 Morris Minor, possession of which widened the horizons of his social life. The car also helped determine where he moved to next when the lease on Tavistock Square expired. A wealthy and cultivated acquaintance of his, Michel Salaman,* whose house-parties were of a higher order than those depicted in *Afternoon Men*, had offered him the ultimate room with a view, a flat on the corner of Haymarket overlooking Piccadilly Circus. At present the view was obscured by an advertisement hoarding which brought in £100 a year. Salaman said he would remove the hoarding and let Powell have the flat at the same rate. For a fan of the passing parade like Powell the chance to look down on the hub of the Empire was hard to resist. That he did so was largely because, even seventy years ago, parking space in the West End was at a premium (and besides, there were a great many stairs to be climbed).

In the event he moved a few hundred yards east to Brunswick Square, swapping his basement for a top-floor flat in a terrace that has long since been demolished (unlike 33 Tavistock Square). By chance, the flat immediately below his at No 26 was occupied by E.M. Forster, yet in the two years or so that they shared the same address they never once met. Even allowing for the fact that Forster divided his time between London and Abinger, where his mother lived, this will strike some people as odd; it was as if, like Balliol undergraduates in Powell's day, they were determined to mind their own business. In fact, had Powell knocked on Forster's door he might well

---

* Salaman's daughter, Merula, married Alec Guinness, who quotes Humbert Wolfe saying of his father-in-law: 'You can't be an artist, a country gentleman and Jew.'

have met two of his coevals, William Plomer and Christopher Isherwood, both of whom Forster had recently got to know. Plomer, as shrewd a literary tipster as Edward Garnett, whom he succeeded at Cape, was a fellow contributor to *The Old School*, published in 1934, which Forster himself reviewed in the *Spectator*. Isherwood, whose background was almost identical to Powell's, had just written *Mr Norris Changes Trains*, with which Powell was so 'immensely taken' that he personally recommended it to all his friends.[29]

Forster, like the other two, was homosexual, which was probably reason enough to deter Powell from knocking on his door. But the animosity he later showed towards his distinguished neighbour was consistent with the low opinion he held of almost all the Bloomsbury Group. This was not simply on aesthetic grounds – though even as a young man he thought their work was very overrated – but also as a matter of principle. He blamed the 'tiresome Edwardian Liberalism' they espoused for the sorry state, as he saw it, of the modern world. Furthermore, he had nothing but contempt for their conduct during the Great War, arguing that 'In their much admired France the men would have been conscripted if fit.'[30] He thought pacifist agitators like Lady Ottoline Morrell were no better than 'those patriotic girls [Siegfried] Sassoon was always complaining about who, just because they enjoyed the glamour, persuaded men to become soldiers'.[31]

As it happens Forster might well have enjoyed Powell's next novel, *From a View to a Death*, though there is no evidence that he read it. Set somewhere in the shires, it contains some of the funniest passages Powell ever wrote and also, in a matter-of-fact way, one of the most poignant:

> Joanna went upstairs to her bedroom. She could do the shopping in the afternoon. She wondered whether this was called having your heart broken. Anyway it was very unpleasant. She wished that she could cry. She lay on the bed and found that later in the morning she was able to. A short time after that it occurred to her that it was early closing day so that she had to go out and do the shopping after all.

Joanna's heart has been broken by Arthur Zouch, a facile young artist on the make who treats life 'as a sort of quick-lunch counter where you helped yourself and all the snacks were free'. Having helped himself to Joanna, he is now after something more substantial, the local squire's daughter, Mary Passenger. The only problem is her father, Mr Passenger:

> He too, as Zouch had recognised at once, was an *Übermensch*. A pretty grim figure in fact. Indeed part of Zouch's uneasiness at that moment was due to an instantaneous fear that in Mr Passenger he might have met his match.

He has. But only because in order to try and win Mary, he is forced to play Mr Passenger on his own ground and according to his own rules. Persuaded by Mary that her father will be won over if he takes up hunting he deludes himself into thinking that 'the will to power should teach him how to ride'. But Mr Passenger mounts him on a lethal horse called Creditor which 'pulled a little' and that is the end of Zouch.

The sub-plot involves a running battle between Mr Passenger and his neighbour Major Fosdick over shooting rights. The latter looks 'more of a country gentleman than perhaps any country gentleman could hope to look'. But appearances can be deceptive. Major Fosdick is a closet cross-dresser:*

> Major Fosdick undid the knots of the first parcel and took from out of it a large picture-hat that had no doubt been seen at Ascot some twenty years before. The second parcel contained a black sequin evening dress of about the same date. Removing his coat and waistcoat, Major Fosdick slipped the evening dress over his head and, shaking it so that it fell into position, he went to the looking-glass and put on the hat. When he had it arranged at an angle that was to his satisfaction, he lit his pipe and, taking a copy of *Through the Western Highlands with Rod and Gun* from the dressing-table, he sat down. In this costume he read until it was time to change for dinner.

As the story progresses we see the Major becoming more and more careless about concealing his fetish. Finally he comes face to face with his old enemy Mr Passenger, who in the dim light of the Fosdicks' hall mistakes him for Mrs Fosdick – until he recognises the Major's 'heavy grey moustache':

> All at once, in spite of the winter weather, Mr Passenger became bathed in sweat. With brutal suddenness he was made aware of the fact that he was in one of those situations when it was necessary to keep his head.

What follows is an example of pure sang-froid. Neither man alludes to the Major's get-up; instead they settle their quarrel about shooting rights in Mr Passenger's favour. But his is a hollow victory:

> He was overcome with a sense of failure. He had not risen to the situation. As a superman he had let himself down. In this moment of emergency he had been thrown back on the old props of tradition and education and when he might have enjoyed a substantial revenge he had behaved with all the restraint in the world.

* In a letter to his agent about a new paperback edition, dated 13 May 1992, Powell said how extraordinary it was that it had taken 'fifty years for anyone to depict Major Fosdick in drag, rather than a man falling off a horse'. (Copyright 2004, Estate of Violet Powell.)

From a View to a Death was written at a time when it was still, just, possible to make fun of people who thought of themselves as Nietzschean Supermen. But when, twenty years later, Powell reviewed a study of Nietzsche, he was quick to point out that while 'Nietzsche's philosophy undoubtedly provided Hitler with some sort of flimsy intellectual background', there was nothing the philosopher would have disliked more than Nazi Germany.[32] His own interest in Nietzsche stemmed from the philosopher's theories about coincidence and its part in everyone's life, which he would sometimes invoke when critics complained about the incidence of this in *Dance*. He also endorsed two of Nietzsche's theories about human beings: that the individual when closely examined is always comic; and that there is no such thing as human equality. What about Nietzsche's contempt for women, his belief that they need the whip? Zouch subscribes to this. Powell, I am sure, did not – even though, in his Notebook, he compares training a wife or mistress to 'the training of the Spanish Riding School'.[33] But I doubt if he understood women any better than most men of his class and background. In an interview published in the American magazine, *College English*, which he checked and approved, Powell was asked which were easier for him, male or female characters. Here is his reply:

> Females are very hard to do. I don't think any male writer has ever done one right. Pope says somewhere that, 'Nothing so true as what you once let fall, "Most women have no characters at all."' I agree. Women are terribly, terribly difficult.[34]

But not as difficult as children. Powell found most children in novels 'embarrassing to a degree',[35] which is why, in his books, they are rarely seen and, with one exception, never heard. The exception is Bianca, Mary Passenger's niece, a pert six-year-old with 'a snub nose and a malicious expression' whose goading of Zouch suggests that she could audition for a role in *Dance* when she grows up.

Considering the status it now enjoys *From a View to a Death* had a slightly disappointing reception. Eric Crickman, in the *Sunday Referee*, thought Powell's '[acid] wit left a bitter taste in the mouth.' He did, however, allow that Zouch was Powell's 'best character to date, and something more than mere cleverness has produced Mr Passenger and Major Fosdick'. Harold Nicolson in the *Daily Telegraph* had a more fundamental complaint. 'Mr Powell essentially is metropolitan. I regret to find him in rough brogues tripping across the fields. I always rejoice in the bland cruelty of Mr Powell's style. But I do not think this is his best book. I think it is his worst.' But there was an unexpected bouquet from Evelyn Waugh, who chose to overlook that the novel was dedicated to 'John and Evelyn', his ex-wife and her husband. In a retrospective of 1933 for *Harper's Bazaar* he proposed that the only novelist 'who seems really worth watching [is] Mr Anthony Powell, whose *From a View to a Death* delighted me'.[36]

*

From a View to a Death marked the end of Powell's 'lyrical' phase. It also coincided with the arrival of 'Stormy Weather', a hit song of the moment that summed up the political situation in Europe as well. Clouds had been gathering since March when the newly empowered Nazi party had burnt hundreds of thousands of copies of books by those writers and savants deemed by Goebbels to 'threaten the very roots of Germandom'. In October, the same month that Powell's novel appeared, Hitler withdrew Germany from the League of Nations and began rearming. To a young writer like Stephen Spender, four years junior to Powell, the message was clear:

> As artists, what is most important to writers today is their freedom. The warning of Germany is clear enough to show them that the enemy of that freedom is fascism.[37]

For the remainder of the decade young writers like Powell whose commitment was to literature would be overshadowed by those like Spender who were, increasingly, committed to a cause. In the long run this did Powell nothing but good; indeed he had the satisfaction of seeing almost all the literary fellow-travellers admit that they were dupes – or as Quiggin puts it, guilty of 'over-enthusiasm'. When, in 1977, Powell reviewed *Christopher and His Kind*, Isherwood's memoir of the Thirties, he could not resist quoting, without comment, what Isherwood said to W.H. Auden as they sailed away to America in 1939:

> 'You know,' [said Christopher], 'it just doesn't mean anything to me any more – the Popular Front, the party line, the anti-fascist struggle. I suppose they're okay, but something's wrong with me. I simply cannot swallow another mouthful.' To which Wystan answered, 'Neither can I.'[38]

But at the time Powell's detachment was undoubtedly a handicap. He was writing for intelligent readers in their twenties and thirties. Some might share his belief that writers should concern themselves with art, not polemics, but there must have been many others who wrote him off as at best frivolous, at worst a lackey of the Old Gang. Roy Fuller, later a friend and admirer of Powell, admitted that this was probably the case with him.

> Though I was of an age to do so, I never at the time read his novels that came out in the Thirties. I was well aware of them, knew their titles, but through their reviewers imagined them to be mere imitations of Evelyn Waugh. Moreover, involved on the left-wing side of Thirties literature I expect I thought also that their attitude would be uncongenial.[39]

Noting how many writers began to call themselves Marxists in the Thirties, Powell declared that 'it took much more courage' to steer clear of politics and get on with trying to write your books.[40] This was particularly so once the Spanish Civil War started. As Cyril Connolly recalled, 'The fellow travellers could mount a very solid cold-shoulder, and controlling, as they did, so many columns and corners in the Press, they put up a barrage of innuendo.'[41] Connolly, despite his addiction to Pleasure, was briefly a fellow-traveller himself, before 'reason and scepticism' persuaded him to jump ship. But Powell was never tempted by any of the 'isms', Right or Left, transcendental or materialist. He had convictions, prejudices and opinions, but they were dictated by feeling rather than thought. Theorists were particularly distasteful to him, as he admitted to the *College English* interviewer, Douglas Davis: 'People get me down who claim, you know, to have the answer to life.'

Much to the annoyance of some critics the views of Nick Jenkins on the 'European Situation' are never stated explicitly. The most he will admit to, when the first rumble of thunder is heard, is his failure to grasp the 'broader aspects' of Quiggin's ousting of Mark Members as secretary to the elderly St John Clarke. It seems just another exchange in the ongoing duel between them. Only later is it apparent that this 'could almost be regarded as a land-mark in the general disintegration of society in its traditional form'. Presumably Mona Templer's decision to ditch her dashing husband Peter for Quiggin is another example of this. But neither can compare with the 'positively cosmic change in life's system' suggested by Widmerpool's manhandling of Stringham after the Old Boy dinner. Conscious that he, as well as Stringham, had submitted to Widmerpool's authority, Jenkins has to reassess Widmerpool's status. He is no longer merely ludicrous, but ludicrous and alarming – the very adjectives people had begun to apply to Hitler.

6

The Coming Struggle for Power

'The voice of the Tempter: "Unless you take part in the class struggle you cannot become a major writer."'

W.H. Auden

'The real test of a man is the sort of woman he wants to marry.'

Anthony Powell

If literary influences are sometimes hard to detect, literary reputations can be equally difficult to assess, particularly at a distance of seventy years. Powell's first three novels had gone down well with the Art-Smart set, but selling at the very most between two and three thousand copies each, they had a limited readership. One reason for this was advanced, long after the war, by Powell's friend Alan Pryce-Jones, writing as 'George Cloyne':

> As a young novelist, Anthony Powell had a stroke of bad luck: he happened to be just two years younger than Evelyn Waugh, so that his own *Afternoon Men* came into a world already conditioned by *Decline and Fall* and *Vile Bodies*. This did not mean that he was dismissed as an imitator – Mr Waugh himself has always been among his warmest supporters – but it concealed from the public that a very unusual talent, slow to ripen, but capable of astonishing extension and modulation, had made its first appearance.[1]

In fact, as Roy Fuller said, Powell did come across to some people in the Thirties as an ersatz Waugh. He was certainly bracketed with Waugh by reviewers – to Powell's irritation, as we have heard. But I think that what Pryce-Jones says about Powell being a few years behind Waugh is one reason why, unlike Waugh, he never became a household name. Another reason is that he lacked Waugh's appetite for self-promotion. Waugh grasped almost immediately that getting your novel reviewed was not enough; you had to get people talking about it – and, better still, about you. 'A fashionable wedding is worth a four-column review in the *TLS* to a novelist,'[2] he told Henry Green. To this end he cultivated gossip columnists, some of whom, like Tom Driberg and Patrick Balfour, were already personal friends. He also had the knack of turning out immensely readable articles for the popular press, something Powell was not prepared to stoop to. (Reviewing *I Want to be a Success* by Peter Opie, he wrote: '[I]t is possible to assure the author that he *will* be a success – because no one could produce such a flood of slush at the age of eighteen and fail, sooner or later, to make a success of popular journalism.'[3])

But although they enjoyed, at best, a *succès d'estime*, Powell's first three novels put him on the map. When, in 1935, Cyril Connolly revealed which modern first editions he was determined to acquire, he mentioned the complete works of Powell in the same breath as those of Hemingway, Waugh and Scott Fitzgerald. Powell's novels, he said, contain 'much of the purest comedy that is now being written'.[4] A little later, in *Enemies of Promise*, he named *Afternoon Men* as a prime example of the 'New Vernacular' style that was carrying all before it.

Connolly thought the best work exploded with a delayed impact, so that ten or even twenty years later it would seem as vivid to another generation of intelligent readers as when it was newly minted. Happily, this would prove to be the case with Powell's early novels. When, after the war, they were reissued, it was clear from the reviews that they had stood the test of time. Jocelyn Brooke thought that '[l]ike *Ulysses*, *Afternoon Men* is a cul de sac – nobody could ever write another novel quite in the same manner',[5] while V.S. Pritchett compared Powell to Jane Austen:

[She] would stiffen at the antics of a society now gin-scented, leadened by businessmen and penetrated by successful Bohemia; cocktails have loosened the eyes, voices and shoulder straps; but she would recognise the comedy of character, self-interest and the un-square deals of behaviour as her own.[6]

Another quality of Powell's that impressed reviewers the second time round was the maturity with which, as a young writer, he had handled love and sex, avoiding any trace of sentimentality or self-pity (which Powell regarded as an essential ingredient of the popular bestseller). Did this indicate a rather cold-blooded technique in real life? Or was it simply a literary device? Almost certainly the latter. A rake would hardly have written something like this: 'The really extraordinary thing about professional seducers is the drivel they talk, there is not a single cliché they leave unsaid. That is why they have such a success with women.'[7]

Powell liked women, but in his Notebook he writes about them with Stendhalian astringency:

After a hundred lovers women have still drawn no conclusions about life – Nothing is so humiliating as to be liked for the qualities one hasn't got, and women always do it – Some women seem to imagine that one has nothing better to do than to sit up all night listening to anecdotes about their first husband – It is an illusion of every woman that she is less tiresome than other women.[8]

Powell greatly admired Stendhal, as he did several other nineteenth-century French writers. Their influence can be seen in Jenkins's meditations about women and love in *Dance*, and the exchanges he has with Barnby and Moreland on the subject. These exchanges remind me a little of the *Goncourt Journal*, in praise of which Powell used much the same dinner-table analogy that he would cite when asked about the narrative of *Dance*:

The entries should be thought of as the most amusing sort of dinner-table conversation – alas, all too rarely encountered – in which the speaker is highly intelligent, passionately interested in life and literature, not at all discreet, able to express himself briefly and well. It is not the evidence of a witness speaking on oath.[9]

Where his own relations with women were concerned Powell was inclined either to plead the Fifth Amendment or be immensely coy, as in this admission from *Messengers*: 'Painful as love can be, I cannot pretend to have abandoned all attempt at finding consolation.' A clue as to who did console him is contained in his Journals, where there are one or two references to a lady called Juliet O'Rorke, *née* Wigan, whom he meets again after an interval of more than forty years. Now a great-grandmother, she was once, we learn, a very talented, if wayward, illustrator who was on the party circuit in the *Afternoon Men* period. Her death, a few years later, causes a pang, as does the discovery on his shelves of a book she inscribed to him. Then he recalls that two of his early novels inscribed to her 'with Love' turned up in a sale at Sothebys during the Sixties, which is enough to banish any 'sentimental twinges'.[10]

Photographs of Powell in his twenties show someone who is neat, well-groomed and, as yet, without the sardonic cast to his mouth that was so noticeable later on. He does not look the sort of young man for whom *la boue* would hold any attraction, so it is with some surprise that one reads what he said to James Lees-Milne in the Seventies. Lees-Milne wondered how young men could possibly fancy 'today's grubby girls'.

Tony said he did [understand]. He had always been attracted by girls who looked as if they'd slept under a bush for a week.[11]

All at once the fancy Jenkins takes for Gypsy Jones is explained. Small, sooty and dishevelled, she looks like 'an ill-conditioned errand boy'. When, in 1976, Mark Boxer submitted his preliminary sketches for the covers of the paperback edition of *Dance*, Powell said he had made Gypsy 'rather too much like a tart ... I think her boy-like appearance can hardly be exaggerated'.[12] A lot of girls looked like boys at that period, when breasts were out and Eton crops were in, so I don't think this has a bearing on Jenkins's proclivities, though it may have been an incentive for Widmerpool, whose sex life, like the camel's in the rugby song, 'is stranger than anyone thinks'. Another reason why Jenkins fancies Gypsy is that she reminds him of Barbara Goring, the noisy and impetuous deb he has been fruitlessly pursuing. Though physically unalike, they are, so Powell told Frederick Bradnum, 'sisters under the skin as regards narcissism',[13] a failing he was quick to detect in real people as well, including Juliet Wigan.

Powell always said that he needed 'some sort of inner calm'[14] to write fiction, which was why he could not have written a novel during the war – even if, like Evelyn Waugh, he'd had the time to do so. He also thought that in love, as well as in war, anxiety was the 'predominant feeling',[15] something that Nick Jenkins has cause to ponder when he gets mixed up with Jean Templer. Does this mean that once launched as a young novelist Powell did his best to avoid stressful entanglements? A remark in his Journals lends weight to this theory. Writing about the photographer and artist Barbara Ker-Seymer, who drew the chic flapper on the cover of his novella, *O How the Wheel Becomes It*, he says he found her attractive and thinks she liked him too, 'but some sense of self-preservation prevented running into trouble with her'.[16] No doubt an incident he witnessed while on holiday in the south of France, involving a very pretty friend of Ker-Seymer's called Irene Hodgkins ('Hodge'), made him doubly wary.

Hodge, accompanied by her friends Edward Burra, the painter, and William Chappell, the dancer, was staying at the same hotel as Powell in Toulon. Her fiancé, a charming and cultivated Jewish publisher called Dennis Cohen, founder of the Cresset Press, was joining her there a week or so later. Finding it hard to concentrate on the novel he was writing Powell saw quite a bit of Hodge and Co and was there one evening when they were joined by a boatload from the artists' colony at Cassis. The party included Powell's Dark Lady, Enid Firminger, who moved in similar circles to Hodge, and the painter Tristram Hillier, described by William Chappell as 'a suntanned blond god, quite clearly the offspring of Apollo and Venus'.[17] It soon became apparent that Hodge was gone on Hillier, who promptly whisked her off in his fiery chariot to a ruined castle in Provence, where a year later she gave birth to twins. Meanwhile Dennis Cohen, who had installed Hodge in a '*cocotterie*'[18] off the King's Road, arrived to find her gone. In his account Chappell suggests that Powell, who knew Cohen slightly, broke the bad news, whereas Powell says he heard it from Cohen himself over breakfast. What matters is that according to Powell Hodge's conduct was typical of that milieu at that time.

There is a curious footnote to this story, which bears out the inbred nature of English society, something Powell's critics thought he exaggerated. The Hillier-Hodge ménage broke up a few years later and Hodge, after further adventures, married Colonel Alfred Varley, of the advertising triumvirate Colman, Prentis and Varley. She died of cancer during the war and Varley subsequently married none other than Enid Firminger. Powell only learnt of this when Hodge's daughter wrote to him after reading about her mother and her stepmother in *Messengers*.

The career of William Chappell (1907-94), known to Powell as 'Billy', has striking parallels with that of Norman Chandler in *Dance*. Like his friends Frederick Ashton and Robert Helpman he was a very gifted all-rounder, who long before he hung up his dancing pumps had made a name for himself as a stage designer, writer and choreographer. He wrote one of the earliest studies of Margot Fonteyn, whom he partnered in her first starring role, as the Creole girl in the ballet version of Constant Lambert's *Rio Grande*. Later he produced a string of successful West End revues and musicals, worked with Orson Welles on his film of *The Trial* and did the choreography for the original production of Tom Stoppard's *Travesties*. His biographical links to the letters of Edward Burra, which he edited, are witty, pithy and instructive, particularly about the party scene in the Twenties. It's a shame he never completed his memoirs, since they would certainly have been a spicy read.

Chappell was called up in 1940 and commissioned in 1942. Trim and muscular, he must, like Chandler, have looked 'wonderful' in a Sam Browne belt. Since Powell is not generally thought of as being sympathetic towards homosexual men his liking for Chappell, very apparent from his Journals, deserves to be underlined. Again, although Chandler's role in *Dance* is minor, he is one of the few characters to emerge with a clean sheet.

For his part Chappell thought Powell was 'a nice man', but with a 'waspish' side to him. He could be 'very sharp with people' if he thought they were at all 'pretentious'. Recalling the holiday in Toulon (which he dates as 1928, a year or two earlier than Powell implies in *Messengers*) he said they only really saw Powell in the evenings, at a café by the harbour. 'He spent most of the day at the Station Hotel and its bar. I never once saw him at the beach, where we went every day.'[19]

*

In July 1933 Graham Greene wrote in his diary that he had an idea for a publisher. He proposed editing a symposium called 'The Old School', in which prominent young writers would dilate on the horrors of their public schools.[20] Greene's interest in this subject had been aroused by reading Robert Graves's *Goodbye to All That*, in which the author's experiences as an unpopular boy at Charterhouse serve as an appetiser for the horrors of trench warfare. But as the son of a former headmaster Greene would also have known that after a hundred years of unstinted applause the system was getting the bird – not just from radicals and Bolshies, but from Old Boys and Old Girls who felt that its worship of 'good form' was incompatible with the world that had emerged after 1919. A book of this sort would therefore be timely.

Powell was not on Greene's original list for the symposium. They had barely exchanged a word at Balliol and had not met since. Moreover Greene had been unimpressed by the one novel of Powell's he had read, *Venusberg*, describing it in his diary as 'a mildly amusing, rather tiresome book in the Evelyn Waugh manner – caricature and understatement without Waugh's narrative power'.[21] But for whatever reason Powell got the nod, joining an eclectic team under Greene's captaincy that included Harold Nicolson (Wellington), L.P. Hartley (Harrow), William Plomer (Rugby), W.H. Auden (Gresham's), Elizabeth Bowen (Downe House), Antonia White (Sacred Heart Convent, Roehampton), a token grammar school boy, H.E. Bates, and a token prole, William Greenwood, author of *Love on the Dole*.

Greene put down a marker in his preface: 'Whatever the political changes in this country during the next few years one thing is almost certain: the class distinctions will not remain unaltered and the public school, as it exists today, will disappear.'[22] There is no hint of this in Powell's piece, 'The Wat'ry Glade', which is, as I have said, a droll account of four pretty placid years in the 'worst' house at the 'best of schools'. By and large the tone is ironic, as in this comment about Pop:

> In the course of time, like the Royal Academy, it had grown into something a little different from what had been intended at the outset, and although the election of a boy undistinguished athletically was by no means unknown, an accumulation of the right colours (the simile still holds) was the surest means of getting there.[23]

Powell, as I have said, was not beaten at Eton. But neither does he admit to any Freudian bruises of the sort displayed by L.P. Hartley, whose 'ingrained habit of unpunctuality' is a grown-up reaction against five years of living 'in continual dread at being late for First School'.[24] He allows that fagging was a bore and that he would 'find it very irksome now to run errands or make toast for persons older and more prosperous than myself … like Mr J.B. Priestley or Mr Warwick Deeping' (a dig Greene would have appreciated, since Priestley had recently threatened to sue him over a supposed libel in *Stamboul Train*). 'But I do not think that at the age of thirteen or fourteen my life was soured by its equivalent.'[25]

What about sex? Powell chose to ignore this ever-interesting topic, presumably because, like scoring a century at Lord's or winning the Ladies' Plate at Henley, it was outside his experience at school. Other contributors were not so diffident, prompting Edward Garnett, in a *New Statesman* review, to identify sex as the system's Achilles heel. 'The "average public school man"', wrote Garnett, 'is rarely at ease with women; he is apt to idealise them, to avoid them or to tyrannise over them.'[26] Garnett might well have been talking about Jasper Fosdick, the cloddish elder son of Major Fosdick, who asks Zouch if he doesn't think that women are 'somehow different from men in a way?' But although, to judge from his Notebook, Powell shared some of Jasper's frustration, he later wrote, apropos P.G. Wodehouse, that it was preposterous to believe that 'nice men are ill at ease with the opposite sex'. This was why, despite his admiration for Wodehouse as 'a creator of phrases that bring an individual or a situation dazzlingly to life', he rarely finished one of his routine novels.[27]

Powell would, I imagine, have read Graham Greene's contribution, in which he quotes from a po-faced homily in the *Spectator* by P.H.B. Lyon, the headmaster of Rugby. Addressed to parents of new boys and entitled 'What you ought to tell Kenneth', it assures them at one point that 'Kenneth will, I believe, instinctively shy at the first suggestion of "smut"'.[28] Could this explain why Widmerpool is called Kenneth, the name lodging in Powell's memory as appropriate for someone who is indisputably a prig? One of the first things we learn about him is that he had someone sacked at school for sending a billet-doux to Templer, afterwards submitting Templer to a 'tremendous jaw on morals'. It is also worth noting that Mr Lyon's choice to expound the facts of life to 'Kenneth' is a mythical housemaster whose nickname is 'Fishface', the very epithet that could justly be applied to Widmerpool whose 'piscine countenance' gives the impression that 'he swam rather than walked through the rooms he inhabited'.

*

Powell was twenty-eight in December 1933. Though he claims to have been unaware of it, he was approaching a time when, as Nick Jenkins notes in *At*

Lady Molly's, 'the ice-floes of life's river are breaking up – as in that scene in *Resurrection* – to float down-stream, before the torrent freezes again in due course into new and deceptively durable shape'. Appropriately it was in the Spring of 1934 that this process began, its arrival heralded by a phone call from his future wife, Lady Violet Pakenham, posing as her sister Lady Pansy Lamb's parlourmaid. She was, she said, speaking for Lady Pansy, who wondered if Mr Anthony Powell could come to a party she was giving at Rutland Gate in a few days' time. Powell's diary was not as full as he would have liked, so despite the fact that he had barely set eyes on Lady Pansy since 1928, when she shared a flat with Evelyn Gardner, he accepted 'unhesitatingly'. It was only later that he learnt of the subterfuge, which was intended to shield his hostess from embarrassment lest the name in the telephone book proved not to be Anthony Powell, the novelist, but someone else of the same name.

When Nicholas Jenkins meets Isobel Tolland for the first time he knows instinctively that he has met his soulmate. Presumably she feels the same because not long after this their engagement is announced. The understanding between Anthony Powell and the twenty-two-year-old Violet Pakenham was not quite so immediate, but equally enduring. At the party, according to Lady Violet, 'no more words were exchanged than were needed for the offering and accepting of a gin and tonic'.[29] But Powell did impress Elizabeth Pakenham, who was married to Lady Violet's elder brother Frank, as a consequence of which he found himself exchanging his usual summer break in the south of France for a visit to Pakenham Hall in County Westmeath.

Powell says that Elizabeth Pakenham was very persuasive. She needed to be, because he was no fan of Ireland or the Irish, citing among other reasons his Welsh blood and the 'race memories' he inherited of 'Dark Ages raids'.[30] She was also careful not to brief him properly on his host and hostess, Edward and Mary Longford, concealing their total immersion in the affairs of the Gate Theatre, Dublin, which became their life's work. Powell, having only metropolitan gossip to dispense, soon felt superfluous. But after a week help came in the shape of the Lambs, Lady Pansy and her husband Henry, the painter, who brought with them not only their children, but also Lady Violet, seeking rest and recuperation after a summer of polo and parties.

It turned out that Henry Lamb, who was very much his own man, was as bored as Powell by endless talk of the Gate and its intrigues. One solution was to sneak off to local pubs, but Lamb also suggested painting a portrait of Powell, an exercise that involved three people rather than two, because he believed the presence of a third person, either reading aloud or chatting, helped to animate the sitter. Lady Violet fulfilled this role so well that Powell felt obliged to entertain her in turn, reading passages from his novel in progress, *Agents and Patients*. One thing led to another and by the time Powell's holiday was up he and Violet were in love. A few weeks later their engagement was announced, prompting a very belated paragraph in the *Bystander's* new gossip column, 'Listen':

> Two incredibly lucky young men are Mr Robert Laycock, who is in the Blues, and who is marrying Miss Angela Dudley Ward and Mr Anthony Powell, who is marrying Lady Violet Pakenham. Both these young men deserve their success as they have been making strong running for some time. Miss Dudley Ward has one of the most arresting faces we know, while Lady Violet is also quite lovely in a more orthodox way.[31]

Towards the end of her life Lady Violet told John Monagan that her friends thought she had 'done very well to marry Tony. He was considered quite a catch.'[32] Taking the long view this is unchallengeable. But at the time Powell must, in most people's eyes, have seemed the greater beneficiary. Titles counted for much in those days, so for a young novelist to marry the daughter of an Earl was a step up, notwithstanding his Eton and Balliol credentials. Nor were there any oppressive in-laws to contend with: Violet's father, a Brigadier-General, had been killed in August 1915 while her mother, after years of infirmity, had died the previous November. That left five siblings besides Violet: Edward, the sixth Earl, Pansy, Frank, Mary and Julia. From being someone with 'remarkably few relations', Powell now found himself joining a large extended family whose ramifications he must, as a budding genealogist, have looked forward to examining.* (Did he, one wonders, make a 'drill' of it, like Ted Jeavons with Lady Molly's family?)

On her mother's side Violet was descended from James I's favourite, George Villiers, First Duke of Buckingham. By contrast her father's family, the Pakenhams, owed their establishment in Ireland to Cromwell. Proud of the blood-soaked earth in which his own family tree was rooted, Powell was marrying someone whose pedigree was riddled with shot and shell. In the Napoleonic Wars the Pakenhams had supplied two generals and an admiral. Another admiral had commanded a battlecruiser squadron at the Battle of Jutland in 1916. In the Boer War Violet's father, commanding a company of the Imperial Yeomanry, had been one of the few to emerge with honour

---

* Deirdre Levi, Cyril Connolly's third wife, recalled an occasion when the Powells were staying with them in Firle and Connolly took them on a special 'scenic route' of the area, 'but Tony droned on relentlessly about Violet's heraldic "quarterings" and never once looked out of the car window!'

from the humiliating defeat at Lindley in 1900. His luck ran out fifteen years later at Gallipoli, when he was last seen leading his men in a suicidal charge up Scimitar Hill. One of Violet's earliest memories was of wearing forget-me-nots in her hat at his memorial service.

Both Violet's brothers had been to Eton and Oxford, where Frank was now installed as a don. She herself had had several governesses and then attended Queen's College, Harley Street, followed by St Margaret's, Bushey, where the daughters of indigent clergymen mixed with blue-blooded gels like Violet and the future Mrs John Betjeman, Penelope Chetwode. Violet's mother disapproved of young ladies like her taking a job once they had 'come out', but she was also against their doing 'good works'. Pansy and Mary, her two elder sisters, rebelled against this and left home, but Violet, to judge from her first volume of autobiography, *Five out of Six*, was in no particular hurry to earn her living. So what did she do? Her autobiography refers to hunting in the winter, polo in the summer and night-clubs all year round. There were Irish interludes and continental excursions and a desultory term or two at the London School of Economics which ended when she wrote a particularly inadequate essay in purple ink.

All of which reeks of privilege, and privileged Violet certainly was. She herself describes a moment when the gap between her situation and that of most other young people her age was encapsulated. The occasion was a fashionable wedding at St Margaret's, Westminster where the bridesmaids, among them Violet, 'were ... decked in wreaths and veils that would have been deemed adequate by many a bride'. Suddenly, in the crowd of spectators outside the church, she spied a fellow student of hers at the LSE, 'an earnest girl' who had tried to recruit her for a discussion group on the philosophy of H.G. Wells. 'Her face, as she looked at me, wore the expression of someone who dismisses as fantasy a resemblance belonging to a denizen of another world.'[33]

But Violet's privilege came at a price. Of her mother she writes: 'A passionate desire for privacy, and a phenomenal reticence about bodily functions, kept her growing family at arm's length.'[34] Or to put it more bluntly, their mother's love was not something Violet and her siblings took for granted. Edward, the eldest, received the lion's share. The rest had to fight for scraps, an early lesson, as Powell noted, in how competitive life can be. Nor was there that much money to spare, though whether because of death duties, primogeniture or mismanagement, or a combination of all three, is unclear. At any rate Violet's pearls came from Woolworth's, her hunters and polo ponies were hired or borrowed and when absent from home she relied heavily upon 'waves of hospitality' from friends and relations. Despite her loyal assertion that 'Tony ...was considered quite a catch', he cannot have been what she originally had in mind for a husband. He didn't hunt, he wasn't rich and his immediate prospects, for reasons that will become clear, were none too bright. But, reader, she married him, a union that lasted sixty-five years with no regrets on either side. And since both of them were tight-lipped about their innermost feelings, we shall probably never know what tripped the switch. All one can hazard is that marriage came at a mutually convenient time. Powell had spent seven years living alone, long enough to yearn for a mate; while Violet, with the lease on her late mother's house at Rutland Gate almost up, would have had to reorder her life come what may.

Powell proposed to Violet over the tea-table on 30 September 1934. Two months later, on 1 December 1934, they were married at All Saints, Ennismore Gardens, Knightsbridge. To judge from the notice in the *Times* it was not a big wedding, Powell's side of the aisle being particularly sparse. Adrian Daintrey, John Heygate and Gerald Reitlinger were there, as were Henry Green and Dig. Constant Lambert, who arranged the music, was too hungover from the pre-nuptial party the night before to attend. Powell's best man was Wyndham Lloyd, not to be confused with his brother John, known as 'the Widow', a stalwart of The Hypocrites. In *Faces* Powell simply describes Wyndham Lloyd as 'an old friend'. To learn more you have to read the Journals, where he is revealed as a doctor, a keen photographer and, like his brother, a homosexual.

The Powells spent their honeymoon in Greece, which neither had visited before, travelling there and back by the Orient Express. Travel was important to both of them; every year, wherever possible, they tried to go somewhere different. But unlike so many of his contemporaries Powell never went in for travel writing. This was partly because, having other jobs besides writing, his time was never his own. But it was also, I think, because he lacked that 'powerful strain of lawless eccentricity and flagrant individualism' that Paul Fussell identified, in *Abroad*, as the hallmark of those, like Robert Byron, Evelyn Waugh and Norman Douglas, who produced the 'highly personal' travel books that were such a feature of the genre between the wars.[35]

On their return the Powells had to come to terms with what was, for both of them, an entirely new way of life. Their first task was to find a larger flat than Brunswick Square. The one they chose was a little further east, the top two floors of No 47 Great Ormond Street, a mellow eighteenth-century terraced house facing the livid red brick of the Children's Hospital. It is still there, divided into four flats rather than three, part of what is now a rather trendy district whose hub is Lamb's Conduit Street, which Great Ormond

Street crosses. But a few yards away, in Barton Close, an alley named after a famous seventeenth-century developer, there is a redundant sign which must surely date from the Powell's era, if not earlier:

G. Bailey & Sons
Horse and Motor Contractors

Powell says that between them they had about £800 or £900 a year to live on. Nancy Mitford, who was married the year before, reckoned you could get by on £500 a year; but as her biographer pointed out, this did not leave anything to spare for treats or extravagances.[36] The Powells, who were not, by Mitford standards, extravagant, were therefore ahead of the game – which was fortunate, because at about the time that Powell was falling for Violet, Thomas Balston was falling out irrevocably with Gerald Duckworth, leaving Powell dangerously exposed. He had, as it happens, made himself too useful as an editorial dogsbody for Gerald to dismiss him; but with Balston gone, he could abandon any hope of a directorship.

Another worry was the difficulties he was experiencing with *Agents and Patients*. His first three novels had been written at a gallop; now he had to sit down and 'think the thing out pretty hard'. Sometimes he would sit in front of the typewriter for two or three days and nothing would come. He must also have been conscious that in writing a novel with no political message he was writing against the prevailing wind, which blew, so Harold Nicolson reckoned, all the way from Magnetogorsk, symbol of the 'New Civilisation' proclaimed by the Webbs and other credulous intellectuals. No doubt connubial bliss was a further distraction, though this took a nasty knock in the autumn when Violet suffered a miscarriage.

Writing of this 'disaster' in *Faces* Powell attributes it to the 'unfamiliarity with the condition of marriage' that was peculiar to his generation, a topic he had raised before. This is an example of what Clive James, in another context, called his 'irritating vagueness'.[37] It is almost as if he is proposing that pregnancy was something for which young married couples in the Thirties were totally unprepared. Perhaps this was the case, hence Moreland's comment to Jenkins in the nursing home that he is 'always hearing about miscarriages'. Sadly, Violet experienced the same trauma three years later, following which, according to Powell, she saw a specialist who improved her chances of having a baby. A further eighteen months later, in April 1940, their first son Tristram was born.

*

Agents and Patients was published in January 1936. Rereading it fifty years later, Powell thought the 'characters and situations brought back the period more vividly than I had expected', an impression predicted at the time by Francis Iles in the *Daily Telegraph*, who reviewed it in the same batch as the latest P.G. Wodehouse. The novel, he said, 'illuminates one small corner of the contemporary scene ... I feel the historian of the future may still feel gently grateful to Mr Powell, even after he has absorbed all Mr Wodehouse has to tell him'.[38] In 1988 Powell looked at the novel again and this time was struck by 'how astonishingly "like" were the "real people" there adumbrated',[39] an unusual admission for him to make given how cross he used to get at efforts to identify the 'real people' in *Dance* (possibly he remembered that he had once given a party in the Thirties to which all the 'real people' in his novels were invited).[40]

Powell's protagonists are, with one exception, superannuated Twenties types whose style has been severely cramped by the austerity of the new decade. The exception is Blore-Smith, a jug-eared, 'slightly Jewish-looking' simpleton just down from Oxford with time on his hands and money in his pockets. Blore-Smith falls into the clutches of Maltravers (John Heygate) and Chipchase (Powell), the one a raffish cinéaste, the other a supercilious art critic and amateur psychiatrist. Recognising a sucker when they see one, Maltravers and Chipchase persuade Blore-Smith to take a crash course in life enhancement, fees paid strictly in advance. What follows is a picaresque whose backdrops include an avant-garde art gallery, a *boîte* in the Latin Quarter and a queer night-club in Weimar Berlin. Among the 'real people' are the gallery owner Freddy Mayor (Reggie Frott), dubbed by Tom Driberg 'the Maecenas of the extreme Left in art'; Evelyn Gardner (Sarah Maltravers), identified by her taste for roadhouses and speedway riders, and Varda (Mrs Mendoza), a tall, glamorous and wilful blonde, once one of C.B. Cochran's young ladies, later the owner of a rackety bookshop, who cut a swathe through High Bohemia before coming to a sad end.

Blore-Smith soon discovers that experience does not come cheap, particularly when Mrs Mendoza decides that she will take him for a ride as well. Eventually he confronts his two chief exploiters, only to be told that since, when they took him on, he wouldn't say boo to a goose, the treatment must be working. And in any case, says Maltravers, why complain?

'When we met you your life was of a dullness so intolerable that you thought of suicide. You told me so. I repeat your very words. We take you in hand and in the space of a few months you are in the thick of everything. Love affairs. Business dealings of the most varied kind. Travel. Strange company.

Adventure ...I admit that it has cost you some money, but, after all, the money is no good unless you use it for something.'

Sensing that it's time to move on Maltravers and Chipchase present their final accounts, leaving Blore-Smith at the mercy of Colonel Teape, a spruce old queen who has been pursuing him for weeks. This ending prompted an avuncular letter from Harold Nicolson who, drawing on his own experience in such matters, opined that since Blore-Smith was not only ugly and slow-witted, but also unacquiescent, the Colonel's interest in him simply didn't ring true.[41] Nicolson had admired Powell's work from the start. When *Venusberg* was published he wrote to him out of the blue to say that he thought it was even better than *Afternoon Men*: 'Your deftness of composition makes all my fingers feel like thumbs ... I envy you your gifts and opportunity.'[42] Later, when Powell was in low water following his abortive trip to Hollywood, Nicolson arranged for him to review biographies for the *Spectator*. Grateful as he was for Nicolson's support and encouragement, Powell found him tricky in person: 'you never knew if he would be friendly or cut you dead.'[43] (He said the same about Kenneth Clark.) According to Nicolson's biographer, James Lees-Milne, the reason for this was that Nicolson 'did not feel cosy with hundred-per-cent heteros'.[44] If so, Nicolson's kindness to Powell was all the more praiseworthy.

In what must have been one of their first outings together as a married couple the Powells went to dinner with Cyril Connolly and his wife Jean. Powell asked Connolly for his opinion on him and Evelyn Waugh, to which Connolly replied that he thought Powell had more talent and Waugh more vocation. 'Tony,' he added in his journal, 'is likely to dry up and Evelyn to make mistakes, but you can learn from mistakes, you can't learn from drying up.'[45] Writing in the *New Statesman*, Connolly's close friend Peter Quennell also compared Powell and Waugh, though his departure point must have irritated Powell since he saw both writers as satirists. In Quennell's opinion Waugh packed a bigger punch because, as a true believer, he was bound to be angrier than someone like Powell who had 'no pity and very little indignation'. He found the satire in *Agents and Patients* 'curiously unfocused'. But, added Quennell, 'why complain of a book that makes one laugh? *Agents and Patients* has made me laugh aloud, at frequent intervals, from the first to the last page.' He recommended it to 'all readers who demand of a novel that it should be light, malicious and high-spirited'.[46]

Quennell was not to know it but laughs would soon be in short supply. In March Hitler re-occupied the Rhineland and the countdown to war began. In May the Left Book Club was founded and in July General Franco launched his putsch, the signal for all good men (and women) to come to the aid of the Party and agitate for a Popular Front. Oddly enough it was now that the Powells chose to visit the Soviet Union, not of course for ideological reasons, but in order to see the architecture and galleries, among them Moscow's Museum of Western Art which housed, so Powell reckoned, the finest accumulation in the world of Impressionist paintings. By chance I possess a dog-eared Intourist guide to Moscow dating from this period. Among the 'Classics of Marxism-Leninism' it recommends is one by Stalin which might well have appealed to Gypsy Jones: *Measures for Liquidating Trotskyite and Other Double-Dealers*.* These measures were well under way by then, triggered by the murder of Stalin's rival Kirov, which took place on the Powells' wedding day.

Powell would later claim that his experience, however superficial, of the 'sinister, lowering landscape of Russia' was an advantage when reading the great Russian writers, for many of whom he developed an enormous admiration. At that time the only one he was prepared to stand up for was Lermontov, whose *A Hero of Our Time* had already come to mean as much to him as Hemingway's *The Sun Also Rises*. Powell never quite puts his finger on what it was about Lermontov's story that so mesmerised him, possibly because by the time he came to write about it he was beyond recapturing the mood in which he first read it. But two of his comments are worth examining. The first concerns the rather brutal treatment meted out by Pechorin, Lermontov's caddish anti-hero, to the 'old captain' Maksim Maksimych, his grizzled former comrade-in-arms, when quite by chance they meet again after many years apart. Overcome by emotion the old captain tries to embrace Pechorin, who 'coolly, but with a friendly smile' stretches out his hand. Nor will he break his journey to dine with Maksim Maksimych and talk over old times, hurrying away after a brief exchange of pleasantries. In *Messengers*, Powell says that 'in European literature there is perhaps no more subtly moving episode to illuminate the brittleness of friendship'. In *Dance*, something similar occurs when Templer snubs Jenkins after a Cabinet Office conference during the war. It is by no means an exact parallel, since Jenkins, unlike the sentimental old captain, already knows to his cost how fragile friendship can be. But what he doesn't know is that he will never see Templer again, so that in retrospect the scene has a poignancy that is not apparent at the time.

The difficulty Powell had in conveying the essence of *A Hero of Our Time*

---

* In *Homage to Catalonia* Orwell says that when the Stalinist police searched his hotel room in Barcelona they were 'reassured' to discover a copy of this.

was underlined when, in 1958, he reviewed a new translation by two Americans. Most of his review was given over to the 'legitimate and illegitimate use of American English', about which there had just been a debate in the *TLS*. The book itself, he admitted, was 'strangely constructed' and ended with an anti-climax. However:

> The fact remains that one returns again and again to this short novel on account of the reality of its characters. There is no plot in the ordinary sense, but there is a perpetual feeling of tension and desire to know what is going to happen next. Pechorin himself, the old captain Maksim Maksimych, Grushnitsky (who is, it might be said, Pechorin seen from an unsympathetic angle), are all individuals we have actually met after reading the book.[47]

Substitute 'long' for 'short' in the first sentence and, let us say, Widmerpool, Stringham and Moreland for Lermontov's Russians, and you could well have an explanation for the enduring appeal of *Dance*.

Powell excepted Lermontov from his golden rule that the great Russian novelists were a far better guide to Soviet behaviour than revolutionary tracts, and as such ought to be read by all diplomats and politicians with an interest in the subject. He thought that Dostoevsky, in particular, was a must-read for Soviet specialists because he exemplified 'the power-worshipping provincialism of the Russian mind at its most sinister'.[48] This did not prevent him from being, in Powell's opinion, perhaps the greatest of all novelists, 'at once grotesque yet classical, funny and at the same time terrifying'.[49] Nor was there much a modern psychiatrist could teach him about the 'complication of human relationships'; he was a Freudian *avant la lettre*. Powell also approved of Dostoevsky's contempt for wishy-washy nineteenth-century Liberalism, the progenitor of so much twentieth-century violence and destruction. He thought it a nice irony that having been imprisoned by the *ancien régime* Dostoevsky should be denigrated by their successors.

One other insight Powell derived from his visit to the Soviet Union concerned Russian art. After traipsing through the massive Tretyakov Gallery in Moscow, where 'droves of factory workers and peasants' were instructed by their minders in the ideological lessons to be learnt from what they saw, he concluded that it had still to be proved that any Russian could paint a picture 'of anything approaching the first rank'.[50]

*

In 1931 P.G. Wodehouse blithely confessed to the American press that he had just spent a year in Hollywood being paid $2000 (£400) a week for doing virtually nothing. As a result of this – or so it was claimed – the Industry's Wall Street backers insisted that an end be made of such profligacy. But the myth of Hollywood as a sort of Eldorado for writers died hard, sustained in large part by the public's apparently insatiable appetite for films. Aware that it meant hard labour, Powell convinced himself that it would be worth it if you could make a quick killing and then move on. So in the autumn of 1936 he exchanged the Dickensian fustiness of Henrietta Street for the stark modernity of a whitewashed cell in Teddington, the riverside suburb where his new employers, Warner Bros, were renting a studio.

Powell had jokingly compared his duties at Duckworth to working on a chain gang. If he remembered this while working as a scriptwriter it can only have been with a wry smile. True, he was earning about three times as much: £15 a week, rising to £20. But for this the studio bosses expected assembly-line discipline and Stakhanovite targets: from Monday to Friday you clocked on at 10 a.m. and clocked off at 6 p.m.; on Saturdays, if you were lucky, you got the afternoon off, though this was at the bosses' discretion. Such a gruelling regime might just have been tolerable if it had resulted in a satisfactory end product. But Powell was writing for the 'quota', a Protectionist system that required British cinemas to show a proportion of home-produced films, be they never so tatty, which in most cases they were. Yoked together with two or three other writers he spent his first month at Teddington trying in vain to concoct a story about a messenger boy. Like every other assignment he undertook there it never got beyond the scenario-editor's desk, let alone reached the screen.

One of the other writers under contract to Warner Bros was Terence Rattigan, then on the brink of fame, whom Powell found acceptable enough as a colleague, if somewhat chilly in manner. Rather more to his taste was Nancy Astor's nephew, Tommy Phipps, the debonair younger brother of Joyce Grenfell, whose ambition it was to work in Hollywood. Although well connected, Phipps was far from well-off, with a wife and baby son to support; he did, however, manage to run an old banger in which Powell often accepted a lift. Returning home one evening they met some roadworks which reduced the highway to little more than a single lane. Suddenly, from the opposite direction, there appeared three large cars engaged in some sort of race. According to Powell, Phipps seized the handbrake and muttered to himself, 'This is just going to be a question of upbringing' – which observation Powell immediately filed away in his memory bank, where it lay undisturbed for the next fifteen years.

Although their acquaintance was brief, Powell reproduced aspects of Phipps – his love of family gossip, determination to get on – in the character of Chips Lovell. Phipps may also have been partially responsible for what seems, in retrospect, an uncharacteristically rash act of Powell's: his decision to go to Hollywood in the hope of working on the production of *A Yank at Oxford*. Phipps had visited Hollywood as an impressionable twenty-one-year-old in 1934, trading on the connections established there by his stepfather, a genial, hard-drinking hunk called Lefty Flynn who had starred in several silent movies. He liked what he saw, infecting David Niven, among others, with his enthusiasm. If Powell wanted encouragement Phipps would have supplied it. Within a couple of years he had become an American citizen and settled in Hollywood.

That said, Powell's decision was a strange one. Not only did he '*loathe*' scriptwriting, he was also no good at it, something he freely admitted.[51] Furthermore, he and Violet had just acquired the lease of No 1 Chester Gate, a small, semi-detached Regency house near Regent's Park. True, he was by April 1937 unemployed, since Warner Bros did not renew his six-month contract. But as he says in *Faces* there was no guarantee of a job in Hollywood, merely the vague assurance, given to his agent, that there was 'some hope of a deal' if he were 'on the spot'.

Perhaps, as the international situation worsened, the Powells decided that this might be their last chance to cast adrift. At any rate they sailed for Los Angeles early in May 1937, arriving about a month later to be greeted with the news that Powell's agent had died and, what was worse, her replacement was someone for whom he had no liking at all. After a few days of living it up at the Beverly Hills Hotel they decamped to 357 North Palm Drive, Beverly Hills, in those days an unfashionable district, hence the asking price of only $60 a month (say £12) for their three-roomed furnished apartment with all mod cons.* Powell afterwards wondered whether, had he found the lucrative work he sought, he would have had the nerve to go on living at North Palm Drive, thus risking professional opprobrium in return for financial gain. Since he didn't find a job the question never arose, but it was one that appealed to his taste for 'splitting the social atom'.

Powell was already aware that his inability to ham it up was a handicap when it came to putting his ideas across to unlettered studio executives for whom actions spoke louder than words. In Hollywood he was equally unsuccessful at selling himself, soon wearying of the potted life history he was obliged to give to the front-office types he was trying to impress. Nobody actually told him to get lost, but neither did they welcome him

---

* Scott Fitzgerald paid $400 a month for his apartment at the Garden of Allah Hotel on Sunset Boulevard.

aboard. A more profitable approach might have been to drop by at Musso and Frank's Grill on Hollywood Boulevard, the haunt of writers like William Faulkner, Dorothy Parker and Nathaniel West (whose *Miss Lonelyhearts* Powell had unsuccessfully recommended to Duckworth), but if Powell knew of this dive he doesn't mention it.

The one occasion when Powell must have brushed shoulders with writers en masse was at a showing of the Loyalist propaganda film, *Spanish Earth*, following which Hemingway, who had co-directed the film, was billed to speak. Powell wrote an account of this for London's chic new weekly, *Night and Day*, carefully maintaining the magazine's policy of political neutrality, though without managing to conceal his scepticism altogether.[52] His attitude to the Spanish Civil War was, as we shall see, markedly different from that of most English and American writers under forty. Also for *Night and Day*, under the heading 'ALL GOD'S CHILLUN GOT KILTS', he reviewed a US government-funded production of *Macbeth* given by a 'coloured' cast and set in Africa rather than Scotland. It was, he thought, an enjoyable evening, but he could not resist noting that 'in deference to the proximity of Hollywood', certain ingredients had been omitted from the witches' spell in the cauldron scene.[53]

One of the few genuinely friendly faces the Powells encountered in Hollywood was the English cabaret artist, Rex Evans, who together with his colleague Douglas Byng contributed something to Max Pilgrim. It was through a friend Evans had at MGM that Powell learnt, rather belatedly, that there already existed a script for *A Yank at Oxford* and that Scott Fitzgerald, with his Princeton background, had been assigned to polish it – the very job Powell himself had coveted! On learning how much Powell admired *The Great Gatsby* (which like *The Sun Also Rises* he would re-read about once a year), Evans's friend arranged for the Powells to have lunch with Fitzgerald at the MGM commissary.

Powell's account of this lunch has been widely publicised. Two things in particular about Fitzgerald struck him. His 'odd sort of unassuming dignity ... [with] no hint at all of the cantankerous temper that undoubtedly lurked beneath the surface' (Fitzgerald was temporarily on the wagon and drank only milk). Also his 'schoolmasterly streak', illustrated when he did a diagram showing the various channels by which culture had flowed into America. The meal went well. Fitzgerald was evidently heartened to meet an English fan, believing that his books didn't travel. Powell meanwhile could not get over Fitzgerald's eclipse, something he thought could never happen to an English writer of comparable stature. At the time this was attributed to a change in the zeitgeist, Fitzgerald written off as a tarnished relic of the Jazz

Age. But Powell later theorised that Fitzgerald became too good a writer to retain his mass appeal, hardly a compliment to his readers.

Fitzgerald questioned Powell about undergraduate slang but practically none of his dialogue survived the two further rewrites that the script underwent and he did not appear in the credits. The film was released in February 1938 and launched the Hollywood career of Vivien Leigh, of whom the *New York Times* wrote: '[She] is the sort of thing to make anyone want to go to Oxford.' By then Fitzgerald had begun living with his 'Beloved Infidel', Sheilah Graham, the London-born gossip columnist who became his last love. In *Faces* Powell quotes her as saying that their first date took place on the evening of 20 July 1937, the very day on which Fitzgerald had lunched with the Powells; but Matthew Bruccoli, in his life of Fitzgerald, refutes this, a point Powell overlooked when reviewing Bruccoli's book.[54]

At Teddington Powell had formed a low opinion of the Studio bosses, whose idea of a convivial lunch was to combine over-eating and drinking with the playing of a spelling game: 'A more barbarous form of disturbing the pleasures of eating and drinking ...while at the same time debasing the dignity of words, would be hard to conceive.' The little he saw of their Hollywood equivalents, while lunching with Fitzgerald, only confirmed his distaste for them as a species. They looked, he thought, like 'a picture by some Netherlands master of the moneychangers about to be expelled from the temple, or a group of appreciative onlookers at a martyrdom'. But what really struck him were the waves of disquiet that emanated from the bosses' table when it became apparent what a jolly time the Powells were having with Fitzgerald. 'The moguls looked puzzled; not so much angry as hurt.' This was because they must have sensed that shop talk, the staple fare at studio lunches, was the last thing on these boisterous interlopers' minds.

Powell was not, of course, the only pre-war writer to be appalled at the power wielded by the crass hucksters at the Industry's helm. In a novel called *Hollywood Cemetery*, published in 1935, one writer speaks for all his tribe when he asks another, 'Don't you think it's a shame that you and I, intelligent men with some talent, should be the pot-boys of the common ruffians that run this joint?'[55] But I think it's important to remember that this brief flirtation with the movies was to be Powell's only experience of Big Business, something that he, in common with most of his generation, had been schooled to regard with disdain. What he saw and heard in Teddington and Hollywood validated his prejudice. He came to believe that, at bottom, there was little to choose between a Soviet commissar and a typical grasping business boss.

By the time of the lunch with Fitzgerald the Powells had decided to cut their losses and return home via New York. They did, however, manage a brief visit to the Mexican resort of Ensenada, a boom town during Prohibition, staying at a 'sleazy establishment' where the security precautions involved a member of staff dossing down outside the bedroom door. A photo taken at the time shows Powell, in a jacket he seems to have slept in, scrutinising a bottle of Tequila. He took to this in a big way and regretted that it was unprocurable in Britain: 'It gives a "lift" of somewhat limited duration without later intoxication: just the thing for starting a luncheon party, for example.'[56]

In later life Powell would always refer to his six months as a scriptwriter as a season in Hell – 'I'm sure convicts were better treated!'[57] He claimed not to regret for one moment his failure to make a go of it, citing Aldous Huxley and Christopher Isherwood as examples of writers who were never the same again once they sold out to Hollywood. But perhaps there was also a slight element of sour grapes. Kingsley Amis, later a friend and admirer of Powell, once said that 'any proper writer ought to be able to write anything from an Easter Day sermon to a sheep-dip handout'.[58] Even if Powell did not go that far, he was aware that in the Thirties it was 'natural' for young novelists to work for a time in films, the implication being that most of them were equipped to do so. He thought he was and it turned out he wasn't, which can't have been good for his morale. Not that it was a total waste of time. He did learn something about narrative construction: the need to prepare early for what would come later, particularly important for anyone embarking on a long novel. He was not at that stage yet. But as is evident from *What's Become of Waring?*, his next novel, he had found the right sort of vehicle for a long haul.

7

Later Than We Thought

'Chamberlain played some of the worst poker in history. So Hitler raised him.'
John Gunther: *Inside Europe*

'And so an epoch, my epoch, came to an end.'
Evelyn Waugh: *Work Suspended*

On the boat to America there had been a party to celebrate the coronation of King George VI (who shared Powell's keen eye for military costume), following which Powell suffered one of his worst hangovers ever. By the time he and Violet returned to London in August the euphoria that had greeted the monarchy's rehabilitation had long since evaporated. Apprehension was now the order of the day, signalling the arrival of what Jenkins calls 'a decidedly eerie period' when war began to materialise 'in slow motion'.

Although resigned to the fact that 'sooner or later' there would be a war Powell had more immediate worries. Bereft of ideas for a novel he had no option but to try and find a job. Having washed his hands of publishing and failed as a scriptwriter it was probably inevitable that he should set his sights on advertising, in those days a church broad enough to accommodate Dorothy L. Sayers, Eric Ambler, Peter Quennell and John Betjeman, who was working in the publicity department of Shell Mex and BP. Powell went to see Betjeman who briefed him on the sort of campaigns Shell were running and suggested he send in some ideas, which he promised to lay before Jack Beddington, the publicity manager. Powell obliged, and on 17 October Betjeman wrote back to say that while most of his submissions were 'very good', they were not exactly original and he was sending them back. But he added that Beddington liked 'very much' three of Powell's suggestions for a campaign called 'Times Change ...' and was seeing what could be done with them.[1]

Powell later claimed that two of his suggestions were used by Shell and that he never received 'a halfpenny' in payment. He blamed Betjeman for this and never entirely forgave him. But he makes no mention of dunning

Shell, which suggests that his case may not have been as watertight as he made out. Still, it is a measure of how 'immensely hard-up' he was at the time that fifty years later he could still complain in his Journals at being cheated of the two guineas he felt Shell owed him.[2]

In between leaving Duckworth and going to work for Warner Bros Powell had a three-month stint of reviewing novels for the *Daily Telegraph*, work he found almost as dispiriting as scriptwriting and to which he had no inclination to return. Luckily it was now that Harold Nicolson recommended him to the *Spectator*, for whom he subsequently became a regular reviewer of autobiographies and memoirs. But before this, in December 1937, he wrote three of the magazine's 'Marginal Comments', one of them prompted by the *Left Review* pamphlet *Authors Take Sides on the Spanish War*. Powell does not reveal whether he was canvassed. Nor does he indicate which side, if any, he is on. His purpose is to mock the whole idea of writers and 'commitment', which he thought simply meant being committed to their own opinions.

There is, of course, as we are told early on, an overwhelming majority for the Left, though a sturdy little battalion consisting of Mr Evelyn Waugh, Mr Edmund Blunden, and Mr Arthur Machen, commanded by Major Geoffrey Moss and with Lady Eleanor Smith as a *vivandière*, declare themselves unequivocally for the Generalissimo. Mr H.G. Wells, Mr Bernard Shaw, who has a place to himself on the inside cover, and Mr Norman Douglas agree that there is a lot to be said against both sides. Mr T.S. Eliot remains aloof and has the support of Miss Ruby M. Ayres in this attitude. On the side of the Valencia government there are a whole lot of poets – twenty at least if you are not too severe about who has the right to such a designation – a number of novelists of whom the most distinguished are Mr Aldous Huxley and Mr Ford Madox Ford, some editors, a publisher or two, a deceased brigadier-general, and last but by no means least Mr Alastair [*sic*] Crowley, who introduces his measured reply with the essentially anti-fascist exordium: 'Do what thou wilt shall be the whole of the law.' It makes a notable list and scarcely thirty names cover the gloriously obscure.

But, pursued Powell, there were many notable omissions:

Where is Mr Maugham, for example, or the Sitwell family, Mr Roy Campbell, Mr Wyndham Lewis, Mr Peter Fleming, Mr Graham Greene, Mr Michael Arlen, Mr Gilbert Frankau and many more? Some who can forgive these absentees will find it harder to forgo two old favourites. There is no mention whatsoever of what Mr Beverley Nichols thinks, nor Mr Godfrey Winn. The whole enjoyment of the publication is marred by their truancy. Let us hope there will be a second instalment in which both will figure.

In fact, concluded Powell, his only quarrel with the list was that it was 'not nearly long enough'.

> After all two or three thousand novels alone are published every year, to say nothing of books of verse which in these days must seriously rival fiction. Besides we should like to read not only what writers think about the Spanish war, but also a few words about what they like to eat, where they are going for their holidays, who is their favourite film star, etc, etc. All this would make a background for weighing their political opinions, which, of course, it would be unfair sometimes to judge from the quality of their published works.[3]

Powell is careful to avoid putting Jenkins on the spot over Spain. But it's fairly clear from a passage like this in *Casanova's Chinese Restaurant* that his narrator will not be clenching his fist with St John Clarke, the clapped-out Edwardian novelist whose belated conversion to Communism, like so much else at the time, strikes Jenkins as at once ludicrous and alarming:

> 'People like myself look forward to a social revolution in a country that has remained feudal far too long,' said St John Clarke, speaking now almost benignly, as if the war in Spain was being carried on just to please him personally, and he himself could not help being flattered by the fact.

St John Clarke says this at a Tolland family lunch that takes place immediately after the relief of the Alcazar on 27 September 1936, to which reference is made by Robert Tolland, one of Jenkins's numerous new in-laws. At that point the decision to raise the International Brigades had only just been taken by the Comintern, so Jenkins is previous in supposing (erroneously as it turns out) that his left-wing brother-in-law Erridge will be enlisting in their ranks. Moreland is equally premature when, later the same day, he cracks a joke about Franco's German and Italian 'volunteers', who had yet to arrive in any numbers. But there is nothing in the least anachronistic about Maclintick's riposte to his shrewish wife's declaration that she would rather have the Communists than the Fascists:

> 'Only because you think it is the done thing to be on the Left,' said Maclintick, with an enraging smile. 'There isn't a middle-brow in the country who isn't expressing the same sentiment.'

People like Powell had been saying things like this for years. In his case the distaste he felt for Communism was quickened by the belief that professionally speaking its hold on the literary world had harmed him. But this did not make him a Fascist sympathiser, something that needs to be written on the wall. As he explained to John Monagan, he saw Franco as, at best, the lesser of two evils:

> My position on the Spanish War was that people should mind their own busi-
> ness. Much against my taste I should have been for Franco in preference to a
> Left [government] dominated by Communists. It seems now clear that had
> Franco not won, the Communists *would* have dominated Spain, there would
> have been a Europe 'Red at each end', [in 1939] Spain, like Russia, would have
> come in on the Nazi side and we should have been in a very ticklish situation.
> Unpleasant man as he was, at least Franco did not muck in with Germany. I
> once said to George Orwell that if it came to a showdown I should have
> supported Franco and George said, 'Well, I think it depended very much on
> what part of Spain one lived in.'[4]

Powell's hypothesis that a Communist Spain would have joined the Nazi-Soviet pact and perhaps threatened France is debatable. I have not seen it advanced before. But at the time his position was almost identical to Evelyn Waugh's. In reply to the *Left Review's* questionnaire Waugh said that if he were a Spaniard he would be fighting for Franco. But he added an important rider:

> As an Englishman I am not in the predicament of choosing between two evils.
> I am not a Fascist nor shall I become one unless it were the only alternative to
> Marxism. It is mischievous to suggest that such a choice is imminent.[5]

This, I think, is the moment to answer an objection to *Dance* raised by Christopher Hitchens in 'Powell's Way', a retrospective piece for the *New York Review of Books*. Assuming, says Hitchens, that Powell's fiction is 'an echo or mirror or madeleine of the period', how come 'the Fascist and crypto-Fascist element in upper-class British society makes no appearance at all ...Think of it – a lovingly etched social portrait, with background, of the British upper classes in the 1930s, and there isn't a Unity Mitford or a "Chips" Channon or a Lord Halifax among the lot of them.'[6]

Hitchens implies that Powell, a High Tory, was unwilling to face the fact that there were people like him who sucked up to Hitler and Mussolini and even joined Mosley's Blackshirts. I disagree. Powell wrote about the world he knew. If there are no upper-class Fascists or crypto-Fascists in *Dance* this is because, with the possible exception of John Heygate, he didn't know any well enough to include them. Absent from his Memoirs are any impressions of Lady Astor or Mrs Ronnie Greville, the 'silly, selfish' right-wing host-esses whose influence was deplored by Harold Nicolson.[7] Nor will you find any mention of Powell himself in 'Chips' Channon's *Diaries*. He didn't move in such exalted circles; and even if he had, I believe he would have shared Robert Byron's disgust at Channon's willingness to be courted by the Nazi brass.*

But if you agree with Hitchens that *Dance* is 'an echo or mirror or madeleine of the period', then a far more significant omission, in my opinion, is that of sport, under which umbrella I include ball games, field sports, motor racing, yachting, rowing and the Turf. Anyone who doubts the part these activities played in upper-class life between the wars should leaf through contemporary issues of *The Tatler* or *The Sketch*. Why then are they virtually absent from Powell's canvas? Because having not the slightest interest in sport, he could not have written about it in a convincing way. He elaborated on this in an interview with the *Times*, saying he thought it was 'a tremendous mistake' on the part of critics to assume you could do the thing 'from the outside'. For instance,

> Walter Allen on one, if not more, occasions has said there's nobody in the book who's becoming a Catholic convert. Considering Evelyn Waugh and so on. But like Hollywood and sport, it just doesn't happen to appeal to me to write about. No doubt there are now [1970] people who think one should introduce a character who will make remarks apropos the Common Market. An enormous number of bad novels are written that way.[8]

Oddly enough, given his loathing for cricket, Powell was for many years a member of the Marylebone Cricket Club (MCC) – or so it would seem from his early *Who's Who* entries. I say 'so it would seem' because the membership office of MCC at Lord's, not a particularly obliging crew, had no record of Powell in their files. I am sure this was an oversight. And indeed after Powell's death Lady Violet confirmed that he had been a member for thirty years, from 1935 until about 1966.[9] She said he had been put down at birth, presumably at the same time that he was entered for Eton and perhaps from the same vaguely snobbish motives. No doubt he went to the Eton v Harrow match, but I can't imagine him taking his place in the Pavilion on a regular basis. His friend Alan Ross, the poet and cricket writer, could not recall ever seeing him there, and neither could another cricket fan, the novelist Simon Raven. When, in 1954, he was arranging for his elder son Tristram to go on the MCC waiting list he admitted to Alan Pryce-Jones, who had agreed to propose Tristram, that he could not 'think of anyone to second him'.[10]

---

* Channon, an American *arriviste* married to a Guinness heiress, was told by Byron: 'I suppose I should not be surprised to learn that you are prepared to sacrifice the interests of your adopted country in the supposed interests of your adopted class.'

*

Having failed to break into advertising Powell gritted his teeth and began work on a new novel, *What's Become of Waring*, although there would be days when he sat at the typewriter and managed not a single word. Rereading it years later he claimed that beneath its apparent frivolity he could detect 'an extraordinary feeling of nervous tension ... of the war coming, in a rather indefinable way'.[11] I am not aware of this myself. But I do think it rather eerie that he should begin by evoking a building, the Guards' Chapel, that would be flattened by a flying bomb a few years later with the loss of 121 lives:

> I was sitting in the Guards' Chapel under the terra-cotta lunette which contains the Centurion saying to one, Go, and he goeth; and to another, Come, and he cometh; and to his servant, Do this, and he doeth it. The occasion was the wedding of a girl called Fitzgibbon who was marrying a young man in the Coldstream ...There was a wait while the photographers did their business; and the crowd began to struggle towards the doors of that extravagant Lombardian interior, which always seems like a place you are shown round after the revolution, the guide pointing out celebrities among the carved names, rather than a church in regular use. The congregation hung about for a while among the sad, tattered colours and glittering Victorian blazonry, until they were disgorged at last from under the massive pediment on to the barrack square.

We never learn the narrator's name but his tone of voice, at once measured, precise and slightly ironic, is reminiscent of Nick Jenkins's. Almost immediately there is another link with *Dance* in the person of Eustace Bromwich, a raffish ex-Guards officer who surreptitiously flicks a note to the narrator from two pews behind. Bromwich, known for his 'enormous histrionic gifts', is the prototype of Dicky Umfraville, the much-married gentleman rider and self-styled 'professional cad'. Both have suffered from slow horses and fast women. And both, when attending weddings, make the same joke about being the real father of the bride.

Powell's plot hinges on the enigmatic life and death of T.T. Waring, the bestselling young travel writer who accounts for a large slice of the turnover of Judkins and Judkins, the small family publisher for whom the narrator works. Like B. Traven, the author of *The Treasure of Sierra Madre*, Waring is a mystery man whom no one has ever met. Naturally this adds to his *réclame*, so that when the news arrives of his death in the south of France, his publishers are anxious to commission a biography. This backfires because their shadowy bestseller turns out to be a fraud who has cribbed most of his

114

material from obscure nineteenth-century tomes. Now hitched to a wealthy widow he has no need to continue his deception, hence the announcement of T.T. Waring's 'death'.

As noted above Powell used Duckworth as a model for the firm of Judkins and Judkins, depicting Gerald Duckworth as Bernard, the obstructive elder brother, and borrowing Thomas Balston's manner, but not his appearance, for Bernard's younger brother Hugh. Bernard's is not a flattering portrait: his life is described as 'one long crusade against the printed word'. But by then Gerald Duckworth was not in a position to protest, having died in May 1937. Hugh is depicted more sympathetically until the final chapters, when he gets a bad attack of religious mania after being duped by an adventuress. Balston, who read the manuscript, does not seem to have recognised himself, since he praised Powell's ingenuity with regard to the plot and hoped that the book would 'sell like hot cakes'. Duckworth, to whom *Waring* was first submitted, made no complaint about the content, but would not pay the asking price, so the book went to Cassell, Powell's only appearance in their list.

Roberta Payne, the girl who bewitches Hugh, is based on the writer Inez Holden, who in Powell's words 'made hay'[12] of Balston, persuading him to accept a novel of hers that Powell, professionally speaking, had doubts about. Not that Powell had doubts about Inez herself, whom he first met in 1927 when she was about twenty-four. In the beginning she intrigued him, for much the same reasons that Roberta Payne intrigues the narrator of *Waring*: she was pretty, witty and at home in a variety of London circles, some quite exalted, yet without any visible means of support except her writing, which could not have brought in much. People supposed she must have an unpresentable 'Sugar Daddy', but according to her cousin, Celia Goodman, she received an allowance of two pounds a week from a rich uncle – 'the only money she ever got from her family'.[13] Later, after she lost her looks following a botched operation, Powell admired the guts with which she confronted periods of extreme poverty and a succession of disappointments in her private life. She was also responsible for introducing him to George Orwell.

Hugh Judkins is not the only character in *Waring* to fall for Roberta Payne. She also bowls over T.T. Waring's would-be biographer, Captain 'Tiger' Hudson, thus imperilling his future marriage to the eminently suitable Beryl Pimley, a major-general's daughter. While not in the same league as Major Fosdick, Hudson – based, I guess, on the rather blinkered young subalterns Powell met as a boy – is another example of the eccentric soldiers he specialised in. On the face of it no one could be more conventional, yet we soon learn that his life is regulated by a 'profound romanticism'. This is why he so admires T.T. Waring, hacking his way through the jungle or marching across the steppes 'while we potter about here trying to earn a living'. It is also why, despite holding 'strong views on the subjects of cosmetics, painted finger-nails and equivocal conversation in women' he is smitten by Roberta, who is such a contrast to his wholesome fiancée.

Despite his rather limited view of the world Hudson is a sympathetic character and it is fitting that he and Beryl should eventually make it up. But just occasionally I detect traces of Widmerpool in him. For instance when the narrator remarks that writing T.T.'s life will be 'an awful sweat with all your other work' (he is a Territorial adjutant, Philip Powell's old job), Hudson replies, 'I like work.' Then there is this exchange, which anticipates the sort of mutual incomprehension that often exists between Jenkins and Widmerpool. Hudson is asking a favour of the narrator:

> 'I've found an iron Beryl lent me. I don't exactly like to send it back without saying anything. Equally I don't want to have to write to her. I wondered whether you could take charge of it and hand it back when you get the chance.'
> 'A flat-iron?'
> 'A golf-club, you bloody fool.'

In a radio discussion Powell had with Kingsley Amis he said at one point that 'slickness' was something novelists needed to be wary of – 'one should always prefer to leave loose ends and bits of irrelevance'.[14] By this yardstick *Waring* is Powell's slickest book, since there is not a loose end in sight. But it happens to be one of my favourites, not least because of a passage like this, which is not only very evocative, but also a reminder that as a boy, Powell thought he might become a painter of huge 'subject' pictures in the manner of Frith:

> At Toulon there was a lot of sun and a breeze from the sea. The interior of the railway station appeared neatly arranged as for the opening act of a musical comedy. Sailors with white trousers and red pom-poms in their caps wandered about pointing at Cocteau's latest on the bookstalls, or watched the engines puffing up and down the line. Some Tonquinese infantrymen in khaki were entraining for the Buddhist temple at Frejus. Overgrown blacks from Senegal, with their waists pinched in by red cummerbunds and wearing high tarbooshes on their tiny heads, leant against the wall, finding perpetual amusement in the antics of the French. A captain of Spahis in a scarlet tunic, baggy trousers, and a long cloak strode up and down as if he were about to sing the first number of the show.

The chapter Powell devotes to Toulon, where Hudson and the narrator join Bromwich for a holiday, and where T.T. Waring is unmasked, strikes me as quite unlike anything else he ever wrote. Just as Hudson is ordered by Bromwich to dress like a matelot and not a country gentleman, so Powell loosens his collar and even bares his chest. Perhaps he was unconsciously aware that places like Toulon – 'our dream town, naughty and cheap' according to Billy Chappell[15] – were living on borrowed time, like the Third Republic itself.

A final point concerns the origin of Powell's title. The automatic assumption must be that he borrowed it from Browning, whose lines he quotes on the frontispiece. But as is apparent from a draft of the novel in the Eton College Library, it was originally called *What's Become of Stokes*. This lends weight to a theory I heard some years ago. Unfortunately I've forgotten who told me, but the gist of it was that he – or someone he knew – inherited Powell's desk at Duckworth, on which the 'Waring' was missing from the 'Waring and Gillow' trademark. Since the novel implies that publishing is, at best, a pretty ramshackle trade, I like to think that Powell's desk deserves the credit rather than Browning.

What's Become of Waring was published inauspiciously at the end of January 1939, by which time it was becoming clear to many people that the Munich agreement had been merely a stay of execution and not a reprieve. The novel got a good write-up in the *TLS*, whose reviewer was particularly struck by Hudson, 'a superb portrayal of a competent, wooden-headed professional soldier', and also by 'the innumerable and polished vignettes, both of character and of incident, for which Mr Powell's astringent wit and sharp perspective make him so admirably qualified'.[16] In the *Spectator* Kate O'Brien described Powell's irony as 'a very frequent pleasure', but she wondered if his manner had not become 'too dry'. Nobody saw the book as a 'genuine and at the same time tongue-in-cheek' requiem for 'when the going was good', which is how it struck Paul Fussell forty years on.[17] And Balston's hopes went unrealised: sales were far from brisk and by the time Cassell's warehouse was bombed in 1940, only 999 copies were in circulation.

It would be twelve years almost to the day before Powell published another novel, an unusually long interregnum for a writer who was far from being a household name. But during the barren years ahead he could console himself with the knowledge that in *Twilight on Parnassus*, a survey of post (first) war fiction published the same month as *Waring*, he was placed near the top of the class. The author of this survey, G.U. Ellis, is forgotten now, along with the novels that he wrote in his spare time while working for Lloyd's Bank. But *Twilight on Parnassus*, although heavy going in parts and over-long, must be one of the first books of its kind to try and explain why writers like Powell were so hostile to the

Edwardians. Ellis blamed the war, saying it had artificially prolonged the shelf life of writers like Galsworthy, Wells and Bennett, a phenomenon he called 'the survival of the unfittest'.[18] The public's appetite for their books might be undiminished, but to young writers like Powell they were dinosaurs whose extinction was long overdue.

Ellis saw Powell's work as 'the final development of the revolt against the Victorian and Edwardian presentation of life in fiction'.[19] Obsessed with story, structure and denouement, the old order had tried to impose a pattern on life that simply wasn't there. For Powell and his coevals life was a messy business with precious little structure and no neat endings. Experience, far from being the name that everyone gave to their mistakes, was something from which no conclusions could be drawn. Things happened to people: that was all. It was up to the writer to try and show, as faithfully and objectively as possible, how they coped.

Ellis was writing in 1938, before the appearance of *Waring*, so we shall never know whether he would have amended his remarks about Powell in the light of such a traditional piece of storytelling. It is also undeniable that by the time he came to write *Dance*, Powell had concluded that there *was* a pattern to life, determined by 'the inexorable law of coincidence'. But Powell was grateful for the recognition he received from Ellis. More than twenty years would elapse before anyone else paid him a similar compliment.

*

Some writers thrive on tension; Powell was not one of them. This explains why he shut up shop as a novelist in 1938 and only reopened for business after the war. He was, however, determined to keep his hand in somehow, whatever exigencies lay ahead. So having handed over *Waring* he began some preliminary research on the life of John Aubrey (1626-97), the biographer, antiquary and dilettante, with a view to writing his biography if he survived.

Why Aubrey? Because, as Powell says, he was one of the most arresting figures of the seventeenth century and also, at that date, one of the most obscure. For this reason alone a biography of him was long overdue. But for Powell, at any rate, commercial considerations were of secondary importance: he did not sign a contract until the book was finished. What really mattered was reaching back in time to someone who shared his preoccupation with 'the vast extent of human oddness'. Aubrey, he thought, was the first writer in whom this particular sensibility was apparent; hence the appeal of his *Brief Lives*, 'that extraordinary jumble of biography from which later historians have plundered so much of their picturesque detail'.[20] But when it came to writing about himself Aubrey was curiously inhibited. The few scraps of auto-biography he completed were prefaced by the instruction that they should be interposed 'as a sheet of wast [*sic*] paper only in the binding of a book'.[21] So Powell was starting almost from scratch, a daunting prospect at the best of times, without the dislocations that war would bring. Fortunately the genealogical research he had been intermittently engaged upon since leaving Oxford was a good training for the sort of detective work necessary. He didn't mind getting his hands dirty; and, as he later recalled, it was amazing how soothing seventeenth-century prose could be when there was an air-raid on.

Powell and Aubrey had more in common than their intense curiosity about other people. Both their families hailed from the Welsh Marches. Both, in Aubrey's words, were 'very weake and like to dye'[22] as infants. Both experienced a lonely childhood in which drawing was a particular solace and both had to put up with irascible fathers. Both were gregarious, with a taste for high bohemian society, and both loathed Puritans. Aubrey was intrigued by the occult, as was Powell, and like Powell he had a powerful visual imagination. And what Powell says here about Aubrey could well be said of himself: 'He was there to watch and to record, and the present must become the past, even though only the immediate past, before it could wholly command his attention.'[23]

For Powell, the immediate past had already begun to crystallise during the last months of peace, a process that accelerated once war was declared. In one of the last reviews he wrote before going into the Army he had this to say about the intellectual life of the *entre deux guerres*:

> The period of which Monsieur Blanche writes in these memoirs has been lopped off and sealed up in a glass case; a cultural interlude between two combats, dividing itself crudely into the Twenties, with the artists and good timers, followed by the Thirties with the politicians and the prigs.[24]

This might serve as a framework for the first six volumes of *Dance*. So had he, in 1939, begun to think of writing a long novel about the last twenty years? He said as much to the *New Yorker* in 1965. But since, in the same interview, he is quoted as saying that he was writing *Afternoon Men* in Toulon in 1931, the year it was published, there may have been some misunderstanding about dates. Probably he knew now that he would always struggle with plots, but that was all. If any design did take shape during the next six or seven years it was in his subconscious.

*

In *The Kindly Ones*, which contrasts the sudden arrival of the first war with the long drawn-out, yet inexorable, coming of the second, the following passage occurs: 'To explain why you see less of a friend, though there has been no quarrel, no gradual feeling of coldness, is not always easy.' Jenkins is speaking of Moreland, but it could equally well have been Powell speaking of Constant Lambert, the companion of his youth. In 1931 Lambert had surprised everyone by marrying Flo Chuter, a sixteen-year-old orphan he had been secretly courting for two years. To begin with all went well. Flo, the product of a brief liaison between a Javanese sailor and an Englishwoman from the London docks, had the sort of looks that appealed to Lambert's Baudelairean side: pale olive skin, high cheekbones, almond-shaped eyes. Though uneducated she was intelligent, and responded well to the coaching in the arts that Lambert gave her, impressing Powell with her 'quite remarkable appreciation of such things'. But from the moment their son Kit was born in 1935 the marriage deteriorated. As Andrew Motion explains, 'Kit distracted [Lambert] from composing, made it difficult for him to have as much sex with Flo as he liked, and continually interrupted their conversations.'[25] Lambert, who disliked drinking at home, began to spend more and more time at the pub. And since, in addition to composing, he was also conducting at Sadler's Wells, which involved late hours, he became a largely absentee husband. But what finally killed the marriage was Lambert's involvement with the young Margot Fonteyn, then at the start of her phenomenal career. This affair, which lasted for several years, was not common knowledge until Andrew Motion's book appeared in 1987. Powell knew about it of course: he and Violet saw 'a good deal of Margot'[26] before the war. But like everyone else he kept mum, omitting any reference to it from his Memoirs.

The Powells were not prudes. Although a regular churchgoer Violet took a liberal attitude towards sex, the wilder shores of which intrigued her as much as her husband. They both knew people who habitually 'stepped aside', Powell's phrase for sexual infidelity. Even so there is always an element of awkwardness when the marriage of someone you know breaks up, particularly if they are largely responsible, as Lambert was. At the very least readjustments have to be made, which takes time. Then there was Lambert's neglect of Kit, which must have been distressing to a couple whose own efforts to have children had so far come to naught. I am not suggesting that the rapport between Powell and Lambert was extinguished; their friendship revived after the war when Lambert and his second wife, Isabel, lived just round the corner in Albany Street. But, quite coincidentally, at about the time that Powell began to see less of Lambert he met Malcolm Muggeridge, who would become the companion of his middle years.

Of the many dazzling portraits to be found in *Faces* that of Muggeridge is the only one to be omitted from the index, a lacuna that some may find symbolic given their estrangement after twenty-five years of friendship. More of this later. How did their friendship begin? Muggeridge dated it from a house-party like the one Sir Magnus Donners gives in *The Kindly Ones*, 'though in decidedly less grand circumstances'.[27] Powell was more specific. He identified the host as Gerald Reitlinger, mentioned earlier as the model for Pringle in *Afternoon Men*, a Groucho Marx lookalike (to judge from photos of him) who wrote one of the earliest accounts of the Final Solution and later bequeathed his magnificent collection of oriental ceramics to the Ashmolean. Known to his friends as 'the Squire', Reitlinger owned a country house called Woodgate at Beckley in Sussex, not far from Whatlington, the village where Muggeridge and his family lived. In the spring of 1938 he asked the Powells down for a weekend, and having picked them up from the local station (they had not owned a car since returning from Hollywood), suggested paying a call on Muggeridge *en route* to Woodgate.

Reitlinger's proposal could not have been better timed. A few weeks before, Powell had read an article by Muggeridge in the *Daily Telegraph* which was unusually scathing about the Moscow show trials, the latest of which involved old Bolsheviks like Bukharin and Radik and the former boss of the secret police, Yagoda. Such criticism was rare, even in conservative broadsheets like the *Telegraph*, causing Powell to wonder who Muggeridge was. Nobody he spoke to seemed to know, which seemed odd at the time and extraordinary forty years later, so famous had Muggeridge become thanks to television. After meeting Muggeridge, whom he took to immediately, Powell concluded that the reason such a 'manifestly gifted and unusual man' was not better known was that he preferred it that way. 'Getting on' held none of the mystique for him that it did for Powell and his gang. He had thrown up a well-paid and undemanding job on the *Evening Standard*'s 'Londoner's Diary' in order to live in the country and write books, doing what freelance journalism he could to make ends meet.

In fact, as Powell later acknowledged, his ignorance of Muggeridge reflected on him as much as on Muggeridge. In Fleet Street, where he had earned his bread in one way or another for several years, Muggeridge was known for his strong views. He had written a libellous novel based on his experiences as a leader-writer on the *Manchester Guardian* and an irreverent life of Samuel Butler that enraged Butler's many admirers in the literary Establishment. In left-wing circles he was reviled as an apostate because he had dared to proclaim that Soviet communism, in which he had once reposed so much faith that he went to live under it, was an experiment that had gone horribly wrong. Powell might have lost some readers through his refusal to espouse progressive causes; Muggeridge, with a wife and four children to support, had lost a great deal more through his cussedness. At the time when he and Powell met, his only regular employment was reviewing novels for the *Telegraph* at £5 a week, the thankless task Powell had briefly undertaken a few years before. It left him with a horror of dust jackets, a phobia Powell shared.

Although in thrall to words and the 'wonderful things' that could be done with them, Muggeridge was indifferent to the arts. In days gone by this would certainly have put Powell off. But I think it is safe to assume that like Jenkins on his second visit to Stourwater, he no longer felt bound by the 'uninstructed severity' of his early twenties, and 'could now recognise that individuals live in different ways'. It is, says Jenkins just before the war, a failing of Moreland's that he cannot accustom himself to 'complete aesthetic indifference' and sometimes underestimates people like Peter Templer as a consequence. Powell did not always see eye to eye with Muggeridge, but he never underestimated him.

Just as soldiering had seemed the natural profession to Powell as a boy, so it was politics that shaped Muggeridge's early years. His father, who began life as an office boy, was a local Labour Alderman and, briefly, a Labour MP. In his autobiography Muggeridge describes how, as a ten-year-old in Croydon, he would stand beneath his father's soapbox on Saturday evenings listening to him denounce capitalism and laud the brotherhood of man; afterwards he and the rest of the tiny audience would sing *The Red Flag*. Muggeridge went from the local grammar school to Cambridge, as melancholic an interlude for him as Oxford had been for Powell, but with one important consequence: a friend he made there, Leonard Dobbs, had a sister called Kitty whom Muggeridge married in 1927. It was, he said, the one act he never regretted.

Kitty Dobbs was, in socialist terms, very well connected. She was the niece of Sydney and Beatrice Webb, the Fabian elders whose *History of Trade Unionism* adorned Muggeridge Senior's bookshelves. Muggeridge had some savage fun at the expense of this well-meaning but deluded couple whose ashes were interred in Westminster Abbey and not, as they might have hoped, in the Kremlin. But their name opened many doors for Muggeridge as a young man, particularly in the Soviet Union, where he and Kitty went to live in 1932. They went in the wake of the Labour Party's collapse at the 1931 general election, which convinced them both that nothing short of revolution could save Britain from terminal decline. As Muggeridge later wrote: 'I had resolved to go where I thought a new age was coming to pass; to Moscow and the future of mankind.'[28]

Nine months later they were back. The new age, Muggeridge now knew, was a dark age, and, what was worse, a dark age which Soviet apologists in the West were at pains to deny. For years to come he would 'boil over with rage' at the 'corruption' of intellectuals like Bernard Shaw and Harold Laski who insisted that the Soviet Union represented progress and freedom.[29] Although he was there before the purges began he was the only foreign correspondent to see for himself the hideous consequences of forced collectivisation: a famine in the Ukraine, Russia's breadbasket, that killed literally millions of peasants and small farmers. The *Manchester Guardian*, for whom he was working as a free-lance, took the sting out of his despatches; even so many of its readers were convinced he was lying. When the paper bowdlerised his account of the Metro-Vickers trial* he resigned. 'You don't want to know what's going on in Russia, or let your readers know,'[30] he told the editor.

Detractors of Muggeridge have argued that he was not, as he sometimes implied, the first fellow-traveller to break ranks. The fact remains that it took guts for someone in his position to take the stand he did. Powell applauded this, just as he relished Muggeridge's endlessly quotable contempt for those engaged in the pursuit of power, which they both saw as a manifestation of the will. Persuaded by his friend Hugh Kingsmill, Muggeridge had come to see life as a titanic struggle between the Imagination, from which all good things flowed, and the Will, the source of everything bad. A typical entry in his diaries runs: 'The will in full cry is the most terrible thing life holds.'[31] Since *Dance* pits those who live by the will against those who live by the imagination, the reader is entitled to wonder at the extent of Muggeridge's contribution. This I shall consider when we reach the immediate post-war years, when the friendship between Powell and Muggeridge really blossomed. For now it is enough to note that despite their living some distance apart they soon, in Powell's words, 'began to see a good deal of each other'.

*

Writers as different as Geoffrey Household, Christopher Isherwood and George Orwell all confessed to feeling guilty at having been too young to take part in the First War. 'You felt yourself a little less than a man, because you had missed it,'[32] wrote Orwell, a view echoed by Household, who compared being shot at to sleeping with a woman – 'something you had to experience at first hand'.[33] For Isherwood it all added up to 'The Test. The

---

* This was a show trial of six British engineers on trumped-up charges of espionage and sabotage.

Test of your courage, your maturity and your sexual prowess: "Are you really a Man?"'[34]

Powell did not share this guilt, however conscious he might be of the debt that was owed to the previous generation. But it was always his intention to get into uniform, partly out of duty, but also because it seemed the most fruitful option for a writer like him who was interested in human behaviour. Naturally he hoped for a commission, preferably without having to serve in the ranks first. He could expect no help from his father, whose only thought was to obtain re-employment for himself. The most sensible course, once it became apparent that another war was inevitable, would have been to join the Territorials (the step Widmerpool rebukes Jenkins for failing to take). But throughout 1938 Powell was too busy writing *Waring* to be bothered with this. Probably he thought that having been a sergeant in the school OTC, he would be offered a commission anyway, as had certainly been the case in the Great War. But when, in March 1939, having cleared his desk, he applied to join the Territorials, he learnt that at thirty-three he was a few months too old. The War Office was, however, prepared to accept him for the Army Officers' Emergency Reserve, a huge pool of men in their thirties and forties who had to sit tight until their number came up.

A writer in a similar position to Powell was Evelyn Waugh, who later confided in his Diary that he had always suspected that the 'chief use' of the war 'would be to cure artists of the illusion that they were men of action'.[35] Waugh learnt this lesson the hard way; eventually he became so unpopular in the Army as to be virtually unemployable. Powell was better prepared. As a schoolboy he had concluded, albeit reluctantly, that he was not cut out for a life of action. At the same time, with his military background, he knew that, finally, soldiering was a job like any other. This is why Nick Jenkins's knapsack contains the works of Alfred de Vigny, who emphasised the tedium of army life and the need for abnegation, two things Waugh never really came to terms with. But despite their very different expectations and experiences, both writers found the war of great benefit to them professionally. What Waugh says here could equally well have been said by Powell: '[I]n an age of scant opportunity for adventure [Army life] serves to dissipate literary vapours.'[36]

*

In August 1939 the Powells visited Burgundy, their last holiday together abroad for more than a decade. At one point on this trip Powell twice failed to recognise Violet's elder sister Mary, who quite by chance was staying in the same hotel, and who he says 'stared rather hard at him and then looked quickly away'. It was left to Violet to establish contact. I mention this incident, trivial enough at the best of times, which these certainly weren't, because it is another example of deliberate obscurity on Powell's part. Did he and Mary fail to recognise each other (if indeed she did fail to recognise him) because they were out of context? Or are we to assume that they saw so little of each other that neither could be sure who the other was? Perhaps, on second thoughts, the point of the story is Powell's hobby-horse, coincidence. But if so he makes very little of it.

Soon after the meeting with Mary came news of the Nazi Soviet pact, prelude to the partition of Poland between Hitler and Stalin. Unsure how immediate the British government's response would be, the Powells decided not to cut short their holiday unless Parliament was recalled. On 24 August it was recalled and they immediately packed their bags.

Throughout the Thirties people had been told that the bomber would always get through. Many feared that when the next war started there would be no formal declaration, just the sound of sirens closely followed by the crash of exploding bombs. If this had come to pass then Violet would have been in the thick of things immediately. She was a volunteer nurse with the Port of London Authority River Emergency Service, a sort of amphibious ambulance unit. But the long prophesied rain of bombs was deferred for a year, by which time Violet had given birth to a son, Tristram. The news that she was pregnant came late in the evening of the day war was declared, Sunday 3 September, so what ought to have been a cause for celebration became a cause for anxiety instead.

Violet was advised that to minimise the risk of a third miscarriage she must lie up throughout any future pregnancy. Since Powell expected to be called up any minute this meant finding somewhere safe and comfortable to stay outside London. Luckily Violet's aunt, Lady Dynevor, was happy to accommodate her in Carmarthenshire, but this meant that she and Powell would be separated during what promised to be an unusually nerve-racking nine months. The morning after learning that she was 'with child' (Powell's description – and that of Jenkins), Violet was seen off at Paddington by Powell. An unapologetic enthusiast of the stiff upper lip, he does permit himself a slight tremble when recording the 'sad and upsetting moment' the train steamed out of sight.

*

Powell had been wrong in supposing that he would soon be called up. The army was in no greater hurry to avail itself of his services than those of Evelyn

Waugh's hero, Guy Crouchback, who is told by an acquaintance that it's proving to be a 'very exclusive war'.[37] Then fate took a hand, just as it does for Crouchback (and Jenkins). The instrument was a Captain Perkins, whose wife ran the cattery to which the Powells' two Siamese, Bosola and Paris, had been despatched for the duration. Captain Perkins was in the War Office department that dealt with reservists. Sometime that autumn he rang Powell to assure him that all was well with the cats, then added that Powell's details had crossed his desk. On learning that Powell was anxious to be drafted he asked what regiment he hoped to join. Powell had not given this any thought, supposing he would have no say in the matter. Off the top of his head he named his father's regiment, The Welch, which was not the answer Captain Perkins had expected. 'Easily get you into a funny regiment like that,' he said, a comment Powell did not pass on to his father, who had by now given up all hope of re-employment himself. Somewhat grudgingly Philip Powell handed over various items of equipment, including a suit of ancient blue patrols that strapped under the foot, a detail that helped to break the ice between Powell and George Orwell when they met for the first time in 1941. Three weeks after talking to Captain Perkins Powell got his marching orders. In the days that remained to him before reporting for duty he wrote a few reviews and composed this mordant stanza on the 'lost leaders', W.H. Auden and Christopher Isherwood, who had recently emigrated to America. After circulating in Grub Street, it was published by Raymond Mortimer in the *New Statesman*,[38] the only occasion, Powell later recalled, he ever appeared in 'that nauseous rag'.[39]

> A literary (or left wing) erstwhile well-wisher would
> Seek vainly now for Auden or for Isherwood
> The Dog-beneath-the-skin has had the brains
> To save it, Norris-like, by changing trains.*

On 11 December 1939 Powell himself caught a train which took him, he said, into a new life and, much more important, out of an old one to which there was no return. 'Suddenly the gate came down. The whole of one's life was totally cut off.'[40]

---

* Tom Driberg obligingly quoted this in a letter to Isherwood, who admitted that the reason it stung him so was because it was 'really clever'.

The Natural Profession

'What I really couldn't stand in the Army was the intellectual strain – you couldn't moon about.'

Anthony Powell

'If it moves, salute it. If it doesn't, paint it.'

Old Army adage

Powell's destination was Haverfordwest in Pembrokeshire, not far from St Bride's Bay where his improvident ancestor Philip had fetched up. The unit he was joining was the 1/5th Welch, a Territorial battalion whose men were mostly miners from the Valleys under the command of bank staff from Cardiff (shades of Captain Mainwaring). Proud of his Welsh roots, but conscious that they were far from apparent, Powell was understandably nervous about the welcome he would get. In the event he was received with great cordiality, his arrival the excuse for a long session at the bar of the hotel where his brother officers were billeted. Although the men's billets were primitive and the training areas were bad, it was expected that they would remain at Haverfordwest until at least Christmas, arrangements for which had already been made. But, as a foretaste of the 'buggering about' endemic to army life, they were ordered to move to Portadown in Northern Ireland on 19 December, the beginning of one of the longest and coldest winters for years.

Powell insisted, time and again, that he never worked harder than during the war. It was a mystery to him how so many of his contemporaries, while serving in the forces, found time to do all sorts of other things besides war work – 'I was at it absolutely the whole bloody day.'[1] To begin with the problem was that at thirty-four he was 'decidedly ancient' for an untrained subaltern. Although graded A1 in his medical he had taken no exercise since leaving Eton and could have done without all the running around. There was also, he claimed, a surprising amount of intellectual strain, giving rise to anxiety of the sort he had previously associated with love affairs. Still, in his experience you were 'never asked to do anything unreasonable',[2] and I am sure that this exchange, between

Jenkins and Jimmy Brent, who he meets on a course, sums up the author's feelings as well:

> 'How do you like the army?'
> 'Bloody awful,' he said, 'but I'd rather be in than out.'
> 'Me, too'

Brent, incidentally, is a good example of the dispensation accorded by Jenkins to anyone, however unappealing, who 'does his bit'. He has no cause to love this 'fat swab' who Jean unaccountably threw him over for. Yet on learning that Brent, now in his late thirties, left a cushy job in South America in order to join up, he immediately thinks better of him. The contrast with Jimmy Stripling, another of Jean's awful lovers, is inescapable. Stripling did not serve in the Great War owing to ill health. Yet you sense that in Jenkins's opinion anyone fit enough to take up motor racing could, and should, have reached the trenches. (By the same token Powell, although well disposed in general towards P.G. Wodehouse, did not think he deserved a memorial in Westminster Abbey because his conduct was 'something less than distinguished in both wars ... If Death is to be pompously commemorated, Life must have produced the right credentials.'[3])

Understandably, since they did not see any action until after D-Day, the activities of the 1/5th Welch during the Second World War receive scant attention in the regimental history. For the first few weeks in Northern Ireland they did not even have any small-arms ammunition and it was not until April, under a new Commanding Officer, that training began in earnest and 'toughening up exercises' were carried out. By this time, having been on a course like the one on which Jenkins meets Brent, Powell suspected that he was scarcely up to commanding a platoon, let alone a company, the first real challenge for an infantry officer. In his Notebook is the entry: 'Here was I with a platoon, but the power had come too late, thirty men were only a bore, a responsibility.'[4] Although this is probably supposed to be Jenkins speaking, since he says something very similar in the novel, Powell, to judge by *Faces*, must have felt the same. He and Jenkins are never closer in thought, word and deed than on active service, so that when, forty years later, Jenkins is guiltily reminded of his shortcomings in the field, I assume that Powell, with his painter's vision, was similarly handicapped:

> My own guilty feelings, on such occasions, came back to me, those sudden awarenesses at military exercises of the kind that, instead of properly concentrating on tactical features, I was musing on pictorial or historical aspects of the

landscape; what the place had seen in the past; how certain painters would deal with its physical features.

After a brief spell with his company at the Divisional Tactical School based at Gosford Castle (Castlemallock, where Jenkins 'knew despair'), Powell left the battalion for good, having been appointed an assistant Camp Commandant at the Divisional Headquarters in Belfast. He had served with the 1/5th for about seven months, long enough to take the measure of basic regimental soldiering and long enough also to appreciate the distinctive character of the battalion's south Welsh troops, in particular their delight in song and their habitual use of irony, both deployed to good effect in *The Valley of Bones*. Fifty years later, in a letter to John Monagan, he said he was sorry he was too frail to meet the Labour leader, Neil Kinnock, at a degree ceremony because he thought he 'might well have been like the chaps in my platoon at the beginning of the war'.[5] It would be interesting to know what they made of him, no clues to which are given in the novel. But in *Faces* he does say that relations between officers and men were good, resulting from an instinctive rapport that was not, however, prejudicial to discipline. Rather to his embarrassment his batman always gave him a friendly smile as he prepared to inspect the platoon.

In *Dance*, it is Widmerpool who is behind Jenkins's transfer to Divisional HQ. Powell's appointment seems to have stemmed from his being 'less than utterly uncouth in habits', an ironic reference to the fact that while on exercise the assistant Camp Commandant occupied a place, albeit far below the salt, at the Divisional Commander's Mess. Powell was impressed by the Divisional Commander, Major-General Ridley Pakenham-Walsh, whom he describes as 'not at all unenlightened.' His Staff, by contrast, were in Powell's opinion peevish mediocrities, a verdict endorsed by his depiction of them in *The Soldier's Art*. I think Powell's year at Divisional HQ also explains something he said after the war in a letter to Christopher Sykes. Congratulating Sykes on *The Song of a Shirt*, his novel about intrigue on the Staff, he wrote, 'I think it is far the best account of life in the Army during the war that I have read to date. The way you put over the indescribable commonness of almost everybody is so good.'[6]

The London Blitz, which began in earnest in September 1940, precluded any thoughts of Violet returning to Chester Gate with Tristram. For a time they lived in Sussex, but since this was under the Luftwaffe's flight path Powell decided they would be safer in Belfast, which had not, as yet, suffered any raids. Finding suitable accommodation was not easy in a strange city in wartime and to begin with Violet and her baby boy were parked in a cheerless boarding house. Quick to discern a pattern in life Powell cannot have failed to notice that his son was experiencing the same dislocations in infancy as he had, the difference being that Violet was on her own. Eventually they found a small house they could afford to rent. But soon after this, in January 1941, Powell was ordered to attend a two-month politico-military intelligence course at Cambridge, thus conforming to another pattern, because in 1917 he and his mother had lived in Cambridge while Philip Powell was an instructor at the Staff College, then quartered there.

Powell never knew for certain who recommended him for this course, but at least it proved that he had not sunk without all trace in the military morass. He was also cheered by the nerve of those whose confidence in ultimate victory was such that they could devise a course that addressed the problems of governing Europe in the wake of a Nazi defeat. The man chiefly responsible was Colonel Barker-Benfield, the Commandant of the Intelligence Training Centre, whose high opinion of Powell I have already noted. It was he who subsequently made the civilised remark attributed to Major-General Liddament in *The Soldier's Art*: 'One's in this world for such a short time that it seems best so far as possible to do the work to which one's best suited.'

Since joining up Powell had been among people for whom all books were closed books, so it must have been refreshing to mingle with highbrows again. The course itself was useful in all sorts of ways. He received a thorough grounding in modern European history, the key, it was thought, to understanding the ethnic tensions that the Treaty of Versailles had brushed aside. This was invaluable when he became a liaison officer. He also – though he may not have realised it at the time – acquired some nuggets of raw material for *Dance*. For instance he was exposed to the exuberant egotism of the philosopher-historian Professor Sir Ernest Barker, a scholarship boy and proud of it, who was in charge of the teaching on the course. It was Barker, said Powell, not Bowra or Urquhart, who suggested Sillery to him, though the resemblance was not close. (Another famous Cambridge figure to whom Sillery has been compared is Sir John Sheppard, the venerable Provost of King's, whose Sunday evening gatherings were as popular with undergraduates as Sillery's tea-parties, despite there being no refreshments on offer at all. Like Sillery, Provost Sheppard had relatively humble origins; like Sillery, he played old, a masquerade assisted by his hair, which he wore long, having gone white at an early age. He also liked handsome young men. If Powell met Sir John he doesn't say so; but King's is almost next door to Trinity, where the course was billeted, close enough for the Provost's aura to be experienced.)

Powell's colleagues included at least two published writers, both of whom contributed to *Dance*. One he identifies as Captain Geoffrey Dennis, author of two experimental novels in the Twenties, a highly-strung individual who became the victim of an end-of-course prank like the one played on Bithel in *The Valley of Bones*, involving a dummy in his bed. Perhaps he was used to being ragged. At any rate his reaction to the dummy was the same as Bithel's, and equally disconcerting to the perpetrators, who did not know where to look. Powell's other contributor, whom he failed to name, was a pre-war thriller writer who oversaw the illegal extraction from a British military prison of a Polish desperado earmarked by SOE for skulduggery in the Balkans. In *Dance*, it is Sunny Farebrother and Odo Stevens who pull off a similar stunt, deprecated by Jenkins as 'military bohemianism of the most raffish sort'. Intrigued by this affair, which Powell said caused a 'tremendous rumpus', I wrote and asked M.R.D. Foot, an authority on SOE, if he knew who the real culprit was. He replied that there was no mention of the incident in 'the obvious sources', and he hadn't a clue as to who had been responsible. In a postscript he mentioned Geoffrey Household, author of *Rogue Male*, as 'an outside possibility', adding that he was 'probably abroad' when the course took place (he was). I then discovered that there was a Foreign Office file on politico-military courses in the Public Record Office, but this too was of no use because the list of those on Powell's course was missing. A call to the Foreign Office archives confirmed, first, that the list ought to have been there, and secondly, that there was no duplicate.

Powell went back to Belfast a few weeks before it suffered its first serious air raid. To read *The Soldier's Art* you might suppose that the city housing the Divisional Headquarters to which Jenkins is attached was regularly bombed. But Violet and Tristram would never have come to Belfast when they did had that been the case. The absence of raids made the authorities complacent so that when, on 15 April 1941, the Luftwaffe arrived in force, there were practically no shelters or effective anti-aircraft defence, and 745 people were killed, more than in the notorious raid on Coventry, with thousands fleeing to the countryside. In May the docks were bombed, resulting in the gaudy *son et lumière* witnessed by Jenkins and Bithel from the requisitioned playing field near the Divisional HQ. Like Jenkins, Powell had to muster the Defence Platoon whenever a raid was in progress, their Bren guns at the ready in the unlikely event of some dive-bombing. This, he told John Monagan, was the nearest he came to being in action, an experience he was very sorry to have missed.[7]

Powell had returned to his unit from Cambridge buoyed by the knowledge that provided a niche could be found for him he was destined for the

Intelligence Corps. In June he would also, after eighteen months' service, automatically move up one rank to Lieutenant. This meant a slight advance in pay, from eleven shillings a day to thirteen shillings a day. Meanwhile Divisional HQ was on the move, from Belfast to Castlewellan in County Down, with Violet and Tristram in their train. No sooner had lodgings been arranged for them nearby than Powell's transfer from The Welch Regiment to the Intelligence Corps was confirmed, and he was sent on a six-week War Intelligence course at Matlock in Derbyshire. After that he was posted to the Intelligence Corps depot in Oxford until such time as a suitable vacancy occurred. It was now that he interviewed unsuccessfully for the job of liaison officer with the Free French, as described in *The Soldier's Art*. Then, a little later, he was posted, on probation, to Military Intelligence (Liaison) – MIL – at the War Office. Here he remained for the next four years.

*

In his official history of the Intelligence Corps, *Forearmed*, Anthony Clayton devotes a mere eight lines to MIL (or MI 11 as it subsequently became). This is not altogether surprising. To begin with it was a small unit, about a dozen strong. Secondly, it was neither glamorous nor, in terms of the war effort, of particular importance. It played no part in the stupendous programme of strategic deception, Churchill's 'bodyguard of lies'; and it had as little to do as possible with either the Secret Service (MI6) or SOE. Its remit was liaison with foreign military attachés in London, some Allied, others neutral, but excluding the Americans, the Russians and the Free French, all of whom required separate missions.

Luckily for Powell, who could only offer 'a scrap of French', the gift of tongues was no longer considered essential for someone doing his job. Application, intelligence, flexibility and tact – these were what was required; also, perhaps, the imagination necessary to put yourself in another person's shoes, so vital to the novelist as well. After a short probationary period doing odd jobs for all and sundry he was appointed a General Staff Officer 3 (GSO 3), promoted to Captain, and assigned to the Polish desk as assistant to Captain Alick Dru. It was now that Powell had reason to be grateful for what he had learnt on the politico-military course, because without some knowledge of Poland's immediate past, in particular the recriminations that resulted from Marshal Pilsudski's coup in 1926, his job would have been very difficult to carry out.

When they became Powell's responsibility the Poles mustered some 17,000 fighting men, making them the largest Allied contingent in exile after the Free French. Most of these troops had witnessed the fall of France as well as the brutal suppression of their own country; they were angry, and wanted a chance to even the score. But however patriotic, few of the exiled Poles wished to restore a military dictatorship of the kind imposed by Pilsudski and preserved by his successors. Like their leader General Sikorski, who fell out with Pilsudski in 1926, they were from western Poland, whereas Pilsudski drew most of his support from the east. The situation was complicated by another important consideration, wryly alluded to in *The Military Philosophers*: 'these troops held by our Russian Allies since their invasion of our Polish Allies in 1939.'

When Poland was partitioned by Hitler and Stalin the Russians deported about 1.5 million Polish citizens, including 200,000 troops. Most of the troops were sent to prisoner-of-war camps, but up to 15,000 officers simply disappeared without trace. While the Nazi-Soviet pact was in force the British were in no position to concern themselves with either the POWs or the missing officers. But once the Russians became our allies and Stalin had agreed to the formation of a Polish army consisting of former POWs, the whereabouts of the missing officers became of interest to the British, particularly after the Polish commander, Anders, had extricated his men from Russia and put them under British command. As we now know these officers had been shot by the Russians, a crime whose enormity is underlined by this exchange in *Dance*:

'What are the actual figures?' asked the sailor.

'Been put as high as nine or ten thousand,' said the airman ...

'How would that compare with our own pre-war army establishment?' asked the sailor. 'Let me see, about ...'

'Say every third officer,' said the soldier. 'Quite a crowd, as I remarked. Say every third officer in our pre-war army.'

But for the most part Powell's preoccupations, like Jenkins's, were infinitely more banal, as it might be the provision of soap for the Polish Women's Corps or finding civilian jobs for redundant Polish officers, of which there were a great many. There was a lot of paperwork. Powell arrived at his desk at 9.30 a.m. and left at about 7 p.m. He usually took a bus home to Chelsea, eating supper at his local pub and then, unless required to fire-watch, tucking up with some Aubrey material at his one-room flat in the King's Road.[8] He had one day off a week which he would save up so as to have a weekend off every fortnight. This he would try and spend with Violet and Tristram, who were living at Shoreham in Kent, in a house owned by Violet's uncle, Lord Dunsany.

Powell admitted that *The Military Philosophers* was the most autobiographical volume of *Dance*. For instance the CIGS (Field-Marshal Alanbrooke) and the wiry Field-Marshal (Montgomery) are drawn from life; so too are some of the military attachés like the Pole, Major-General Bobrowski and the Czech, Colonel Hlava. Powell also identifies his brother-officer Alick Dru, who married a sister of Evelyn Waugh's second wife Laura, as the model for Pennistone, the authority on Kierkegaard. However he is at pains to explain that for technical reasons to do with the balance of the novel he based the character of Finn, the Commanding Officer of MIL, on the second-in-command, Major Ker, rather than the actual CO, Lieutenant-Colonel Carlisle.

Powell says that much to his relief Carlisle was taken in by this sleight of hand, his only objection being to the award of a VC, which Ker held. But I wonder what Carlisle made of that 'downy old bird' Sunny Farebrother, since it seems to me that they have enough in common for the resemblance to be more than coincidental. Powell says that in peacetime Carlisle was a City banker and businessman who had served with distinction (DSO, MC) with a London Territorial unit in the Great War. This is almost identical to Farebrother's CV. Powell describes Carlisle as tall, slim and well preserved for his age, with 'candid blue eyes' and immense charm 'of which he was not at all unaware'. He was hard-working, devious and resilient, but obsequious beyond the call of duty to his superiors. He would also, when appropriate, assume his 'religious face'. Sound familiar? Of course there are other things about Farebrother that may owe nothing to Carlisle. His parsimony, for instance, and his wish to put women on a pedestal. But all fictional characters are composites and I am sure from the evidence that without Colonel Carlisle there would have been no Sunny Farebrother.

*

In September 1941, shortly before Powell joined MIL, he and Violet had an evening out at the Café Royal. As this was something they had not done since before the war Powell decided to deck himself out in his father's blue patrols. It so happened that Inez Holden was there too, with George Orwell and his wife Eileen. Knowing that Powell was a great admirer of Orwell, she came across to their table and asked if they would like to join her. Powell was hesitant. He thought Orwell would disapprove of his Junkerish get-up. But between them Inez and Violet persuaded him to take the risk. Orwell wasted no time on preliminaries. 'Do your trousers strap under the boot?' he asked. On being assured that they did, Orwell announced that he too had worn trousers like that when in the Burma Police. 'Those straps under the feet give you a feeling like nothing else in life.'[9] So began a friendship that lasted until Orwell's tragically early death in 1950.

Eric Blair, to call Orwell by his real name, was two years senior to Powell at Eton, having won a scholarship there from St Cyprian's, the pushy prep school that also housed Cyril Connolly, who followed him into College. Powell had no memory of Blair at Eton and no idea that he was 'George Orwell', author of *Down and Out in Paris and London*. He had read this on Adrian Daintrey's recommendation and was impressed by its 'savagery and gloom'. He marked Orwell down as an authentic voice, albeit a cranky one, and read his third novel, *Keep the Aspidistra Flying*, within a week or two of its publication. Shortly after this, in May 1936, he and Violet went to dinner with the Cyril Connollys, where Powell learnt that 'George Orwell' was Connolly's old College chum, Eric Blair. Connolly urged him to write a fan letter, which he did. Addressing Orwell as 'Dear Sir', he says he enjoyed his new novel so much, particularly the remarks about the 'scotchification of England', that he hopes Orwell won't think it 'a great impertinence' if he encloses a copy of his anti-Scotch satire, *Caledonia,* written during a bout of insomnia* just before his marriage. 'I should also like to condole with you,' he adds, 'on the extraordinary imbecility of most of the reviews I have seen of your book.'[10]

Connolly had told Orwell to expect a fan letter from Powell. As is apparent from his *Collected Essays, Journalism and Letters*, Orwell wrote a perfectly courteous reply, applauding Powell's mockery of 'Scotchmen' in *Caledonia* and agreeing with him about the 'awfulness' of reviewers.[11] But for some reason Powell detected a slight chill and decided that Orwell was not for him.

Shortly afterwards the Spanish Civil War began. As I have said, Powell thought this was none of our business. But he admired courage, whether physical or moral, and applauded Orwell's determination to 'spill the Spanish beans' in *Homage to Catalonia*, a dish that many orthodox left-wingers simply couldn't swallow – Quiggin among them. Powell has him complain at Erridge's failure, while in Republican Barcelona, to distinguish between POUM, FAL, CNT and UGT, which surely arises from Orwell's admission that all those initials 'exasperated' him.[12] There are other similarities between Erridge and Orwell, but only superficial ones. Erridge is an unsympathetic figure, not least because of his frugality, a characteristic

---

* Powell slept badly for years, as indeed did his two close friends Constant Lambert and Malcolm Muggeridge.

Powell deplored. Orwell, despite his 'wintery conscience', was someone for whom he had the greatest respect.

By the time Powell met him at the Café Royal Orwell was becoming quite well known, something Inez Holden reflected on in her journal:

> Tony had told me he wanted to meet Orwell of whom he is a great admirer. It's strange the way a writer's fame begins slowly creeping up to him and then racing so that after a while he seems to be a poor relation of his own fame. People of taste and sensitiveness, writers, political workers and actors (who now show signs of being extremely left wing), socialist doctors, factory workers and technical instructors in touch with their labour organisations are all well aware of Orwell.[13]

Powell later wrote that Orwell was somebody 'for whom it was impossible not to feel a deep affection'.[14] Orwell returned the compliment: 'Tony is the only Tory I have ever liked,'[15] he told Julian Symons, who after the war made up a regular four for lunch with Orwell, Powell and Malcolm Muggeridge. Powell was irritated when people wondered how on earth he and Orwell made friends, given that they were poles apart politically. But perhaps, deep down, they weren't so far apart after all. This was what Muggeridge concluded, to judge from some notes he made for his unfinished third volume of autobiography:

> Orwell's politics and general view of life were curiously confused, and sometimes seemingly contradictory. In principle, he was a Socialist with left-wing leanings ...Actually, many of his views and attitudes were strongly, almost pathologically conservative; more so than Tony's, a card-carrying member of the Conservative party, or than mine, a hater of the Left with no Rightist doctrinaire affiliation, and certainly not with the Conservatives.

Muggeridge added that 'another point in Orwell's favour, as far as Tony was concerned, was that he had been at Eton'.[16] I am sure that Muggeridge was right; indeed Powell insisted that despite the efforts he made to disguise the fact – rolling his own cigarettes, drinking pints of mild and bitter – Orwell was a typical Etonian. He thought that what threw people off the scent was that Orwell did not go to Oxford. This was why he turned out so differently from contemporaries of his who did, like Cyril Connolly, Henry Green, Brian Howard and Powell himself. But as Orwell's biographer Bernard Crick asked: What is a typical Etonian?[17] Perhaps that is a question only someone who didn't go to Eton would ask. Even so it is difficult to deduce from Powell's recollections of Orwell what marked him out as a typical Etonian, except perhaps his determination to give his eccentricities 'full scope', a comment Powell made in respect of the writer Sir Lawrence Jones, who was at Eton in Edwardian times.[18] Orwell certainly didn't strike Muggeridge as typical. Recalling his friend's fear that however thick the layer of proletarian camouflage he applied he would 'stand revealed as an Eton product', Muggeridge wrote:

> In point of fact with his lean features, thin strip of 'tache above the upper lip and general air of shabbiness, if not seediness, he was less like the popular notion of an Etonian and less likely to be taken for one, than anyone else I have known.[19]

Powell would have jibbed at 'seediness'. He thought Orwell wore his shabby clothes with style, hinting at the latent dandyism revealed by his comment about the boot straps. There is support for this in a photo of Orwell taken at Eton after a swim in the Thames. He stands nonchalantly on the bank with his hands in his pockets, a rolled towel under one arm, wearing a floppy sun hat and with an illicit cigarette stuck between his lips. Here, one feels, is another example of the debonair insouciance that made such an impression on Powell when he glanced out of his study window on his second day at Goodhart's.

Powell's duties meant that he did not see much of Orwell until after the war, when Orwell's life was transformed by the huge success of *Animal Farm* and *Nineteen Eighty Four*. He preferred Orwell the bibliophile to Orwell the visionary ('Never much cared for people who want to put the world to rights').[20] But, as we shall see, Orwell's theories about power and the attraction it held for certain sorts of people contributed significantly to *Dance*.

Gall and Wormwood

'We are moving Left with the troops.'

Army Bureau of Current Affairs

'Work and bed. Might as well be dead.'

Wartime factory workers' complaint

One of Powell's most attractive qualities was his honesty about his, and Jenkins's, reverses, whether they involved women or the world. A case in point is the unhappy interval he spent as a Military Assistant Secretary at the Cabinet Office, the job Widmerpool holds at the beginning of *The Military Philosophers*. Unlike the duties of a Company Commander, the duties of a Military Assistant Secretary must have seemed well within his compass. You were the scribe whose job it was to summarise, at close of play, the deliberations and conclusions of the Joint Intelligence Staff committee to which you were assigned. What you wrote would then be read through by the other members of the committee and, if necessary, amended, following which it would be submitted to a higher authority for consideration. It was hard work, often involving a fourteen-hour day. But the pay-off was substantial: promotion, plus the satisfaction of knowing that you could, if you played your hand well, influence the course of the war. This, naturally, is what appeals to Widmerpool; and even Powell himself was excited by the possibilities. The difference was that unlike Widmerpool, he had not intrigued for the job: it came out of the blue.

Powell was posted to the Cabinet Office in March 1943 at the request of Lieutenant-Colonel Denis Capel-Dunn, Secretary of the Joint Intelligence Committee since its inception in 1941. A barrister by training who had, like Widmerpool, held a Territorial Army commission before the war, Capel-Dunn was rated very highly for his skill in drafting. Noel Annan, a member of the Joint Intelligence Staff, called him 'elusive and secretive'.[1] Others were less complimentary. Bloated in appearance, bombastic in manner, he was known in his club, the St James's, as 'Young Bloody'. Powell had met Capel-Dunn a few times through Alick Dru, who had been at Downside and Cambridge with him. Dru was amused by 'The Papal Bun', as he called him. Powell, most definitely, was not. Nevertheless when, to his astonishment, Capel-Dunn announced that he needed an assistant and that Powell would fit the bill, he did not demur. Congenial though his colleagues were at MIL, the job itself was a bit of a dead end. He was frankly envious of Malcolm Muggeridge, who had wangled his way into MI6 and was now, after several weeks sampling the bright lights of Lisbon, Our Man in Lourenço Marques. 'When I think of your travels,' he told Muggeridge in August 1942, 'I get a slight twinge like being told of someone else's successes in love which one would really rather not hear about. It must be extraordinarily interesting.'[2]

Powell lasted nine weeks as a Military Assistant Secretary. He admits he wasn't up to it but says that Capel-Dunn, having hand-picked him, went out of his way to be as inconsiderate as possible – and then has second thoughts: 'Perhaps ... I am being unjust ... [P]robably no job is done well unless done instinctively.' I take this to mean that, as with screenwriting, he lacked the flair. Powell adds, quite legitimately, that it was a job that made great demands on stamina, 'particularly if the blitz had extinguished sleep the night before'. He may have been wanting in this as well. One other disqualification suggests itself when he describes, in *The Military Philosophers*, how Jenkins's attention wanders when listening to Montgomery addressing the military attachés at his Tactical Headquarters. Conscious that the Field-Marshal's map shows the cockpit of Europe, Jenkins muses on battles long ago and the characters they bring to mind, like Sir Philip Sidney, wounded at Zutphen, and D'Artagnan – 'rather a non-Vigny figure', unlikely to take on 'disagreeable and unglamorous army jobs'. Such reveries are meat and drink to the novelist but best avoided by a conscientious secretary.

Powell's pocket suffered as well as his pride. On losing his job he was reduced from Acting Major to Lieutenant, forfeiting more than half of his pay. His future was at best uncertain, but luckily a vacancy soon occurred in his old Section, as Liaison Officer to the Belgians and Czechs. When Colonel Carlisle learnt that he was available, he took steps to re-employ him. He had been reluctant to let him go in the first place and was relieved that he had not, after all, lost the services of an officer on whom he could rely. Powell was fatalistic: there were worse fates than liaison duties, however humdrum. As for the egregious Capel-Dunn, his secretarial skills cost him his life. A member of the Cabinet Office team at the signing of the United Nations Charter in June 1945, he was one of nine passengers presumed killed when their Liberator disappeared over the Atlantic on the flight home.

Powell wondered whether, had he made the grade, he too might have been on that flight. I rather doubt it, since besides Capel-Dunn the only males lost were a Foreign Office lawyer and someone from the India Office; the other victims were female members of the Secretariat.

Given that *The Military Philosophers* is autobiographical I can think of another reason why, in the long run, Powell was better off in MIL: he was not too constrained by the Official Secrets' Act, which would certainly have been the case had he wanted to depict, in any detail, the workings of the inter-services committees whose minutes he took. We get two brief glimpses of such a body, presided over by Widmerpool, but that is all. In *Faces* Powell says that 'secrets', e.g. the date of an offensive, were of less moment than more mundane matters like manpower, logistics, the German order of battle and, crucially, German morale. Even so, once confirmed in his appointment, he could not have failed to be 'in the know', the phrase used to describe personnel cleared for top-secret Ultra intelligence. Consequently after the war he might well have faced a similar dilemma to that of the thriller-writer Dennis Wheatley (1897-1977), who had served as a member of the strategic deception team attached to the Joint Planning Staff. Wheatley was, in his own words, 'so stuffed full of secrets'[3] that he dared not write any more contemporary blood-and-thunder lest he give something away. Instead he began a historical series, the very successful Roger Brook stories set during the Napoleonic wars.

Wheatley and Powell briefly worked in the same building, but there is no evidence that they met until long after the war, when Powell, as we shall see, consulted Wheatley about *Dance*. But in his memoirs Wheatley reveals that he too fell foul of Capel-Dunn, whose responsibilities included allocation of space in the bomb-proof basement that housed the Joint Intelligence Staff and the War Cabinet. Wheatley thought his section deserved more than the two rooms they had been allotted by Capel-Dunn. He did not mince his words. Capel-Dunn was equally forthright. He told Wheatley, who was junior to him in rank,* that he was being impertinent. Unabashed, Wheatley appealed to a Higher Authority with whom, as it happened, he used often to dine. Capel-Dunn was overruled and the deception planners got the extra rooms they needed. Characteristically – for he was a generous man – Wheatley then invited Capel-Dunn to lunch. Not only did he accept, but, like Wheatley, he proved to be a lover of fine hock. From then on, said Wheatley, they became firm friends.

---

* On joining the deception team Wheatley had been rapidly promoted to Wing Commander, the equivalent of a Major in the Army. In the first war he had been a Gunner subaltern.

*

In *Dance*, when Jenkins takes over the Czechs and Belgians, his predecessor, with some reputation as a ladies' man, gives him this tip: '"By the way, when you're dealing with two Allies at once, it's wiser never to mention one to the other. They can't bear the thought of your being unfaithful to them."' Sound advice, which Powell himself probably received. He found the Czechs quite a contrast to the Poles since they had, as yet, no reason to distrust the Russians, and could be forgiven for feeling that Britain and France had betrayed them at Munich. Nevertheless, Czech pilots had fought with great distinction in the Battle of Britain and they had enough troops over here to form an armoured brigade. Lacking the panache of the Poles, the Czechs were considered rather dour, an exception being the military attaché Colonel Kalla (Hlava in *Dance*), whom Powell describes as 'a delightful man'. Despite having fought against them in the First World War, Kalla was pro-Russian. But tainted by his association with the Western Allies he was placed under house arrest on his return to Czechoslovakia after the war and died, it was said, of heart failure.

The Belgians, though a smaller contingent than the Czechs, were potentially more of a handful owing to their relish for fratricidal conflict. Not only did the country consist – as indeed it still does – of two mutually hostile ethnic groups, the French-speaking Walloons and the Dutch-speaking Flemings, it was also at loggerheads over the conduct of King Leopold III, who in 1940 chose to remain in Belgium rather than join the government-in-exile. Leopold, born 1901, had overlapped with Powell at Eton (the sight of his address on the School List, c/o 'H.M. King of the Belgians', gave Cyril Connolly snobbish palpitations). Despite being an Old Etonian he was not regarded as particularly Anglophile, having barred Allied entry to Belgium until the Germans invaded, by which time it was too late.

Powell was of the opinion that the Belgians were 'a race with strong opinions about social distinctions'. In support of this Jenkins's predecessor relays an anecdote from the Great War,

'[O]f an English officer, French officer, and Belgian officer when a woman rides by on a horse. The Englishman said, "What a fine horse"; the Frenchman, "What a fine woman"; the Belgian, "I wonder what she was *née*". Of course I don't suggest that would happen today.'

To which Jenkins replies, 'One can't make the classless society retroactive', a maxim to be found in Powell's notebook.

When Powell took over the Belgians in the spring of 1943 a row that had been simmering since the previous autumn was coming to the boil. At issue were the credentials of Major, later Baron, Paul Kronacker, in civilian life a very big cheese indeed. There is a passing reference to this in *Dance*, where Kronacker appears as Kucherman, and a page or two in *Faces*, neither of which does justice to the passions aroused. Both sides thought there was an important principle at stake and acted accordingly. In a curious way it is reminiscent of the quarrel between Messrs Orn and Lundquist at La Grenadière.

The son of a German Jew who became a Belgian citizen, Paul Kronacker (1898-1994) was a distinguished chemist, a Senator in the Belgian Parliament and the boss of a large sugar refinery. He spoke several languages, was (then) married to an Austrian Countess and had business interests all over Europe and in Britain and the United States. Decorated in the Great War he served briefly as a staff-officer in 1940. When Belgium surrendered he refused to collaborate with the Germans and found his way to the United States via Spain. Understandably his compatriots in London wanted him on board and to judge from his Memoirs he spent a year or more as an emissary of the Belgian government-in-exile, a job over which the British government had no jurisdiction. Then the Belgians made him their assistant Military Attaché, whereupon alarm bells rang in Whitehall.

Powell says the trouble arose because the Belgians couldn't be bothered to write a formal letter announcing Kronacker's appointment. The file in the Public Record Office tells a different story.[5] From this it is clear that MI5 cast the first stone, their explanation being that 'reliable sources' had informed them that Kronacker and his wife were pro-German. The Foreign Office concurred, saying they had 'no confidence in that gentleman'. They accused the Belgians of playing politics and perpetrating 'a ramp of the worst sort'. What followed was a stand-off. The British did not exactly hinder Kronacker, whose duties included liaison with the Dutch and the Americans: they ignored him. If he wrote a letter to MIL, the reply was addressed to his superior, who had privately told Colonel Carlisle that he shared British misgivings about Kronacker. Then Paul Spaak, the Belgian foreign minister-in-exile, wrote a formal letter of complaint to Anthony Eden, the Secretary of State for War, initiating a flurry of letters, minutes and memos. Both sides dug their heels in. At one point Eden's private secretary was moved to comment that 'the Belgians are indeed among the most unsatisfactory of our allies', a verdict endorsed by Colonel Carlisle who accused the Belgians of sacking any attaché who was thought to be pro-British. Then, to the embarrassment of the British, MI5 did an about turn and gave

Kronacker a clean bill of health. 'We have made a "blob",' admitted one of the mandarins.

Kronacker ignores this unpleasantness in his Memoirs. He describes being an attaché as 'l'une des periodes les plus intéressantes de ma vie'.[6] But according to Powell Kronacker was justifiably furious at the doubts cast on his loyalty, which may well have been planted on MI5 by enemies of his within the Belgian *Sûreté*. Even after he had been vindicated there was still reluctance on the part of the Foreign Office to add him to the Diplomatic List, though in September 1943 Carlisle reported that he was 'carrying out his duties efficiently and co-operatively'. Powell thought highly of him: 'Of all the Allied officers with whom I came into contact during the war Paul Kronacker was certainly the outstanding figure.'

MIL had a Yugoslav section whose job was not made any easier by the Allies' decision to switch their support from Mihailovic's Royalist Chetniks to Tito's Communist Partisans. To his relief Powell was not personally involved in this betrayal, as he saw it. But novelists cannot afford to be too choosy about their material, or the uses to which they put it. Hence the demise of Peter Templer, whose misfortune it is to be picked for what Odo Stevens calls the squire's team when the smart money is on the village boys. But what was Templer doing in the Balkans in the first place? I cannot be the only reader to find implausible his translation from stockbroker-turned-bureaucrat to guerrilla fighter, however many strings he pulled to bring it off. He's at least forty, 'slowing up' and with no previous military experience, hardly the ideal background for a life on the run in the mountains. It could, I suppose, be argued that if Evelyn Waugh could be sent to the Balkans, why not Templer? But Waugh had served with the Commandos and seen action in Crete. Templer's only qualification is that he had done a bit of business in the area before the war.

In *Dance*, Widmerpool is blamed for the decision to abandon Templer to his fate. In real life, the person largely responsible for Allied disengagement from Mihailovic was Brigadier Fitzroy Maclean, a deceptively languid Old Etonian who persuaded Churchill that from what he had seen the Partisans posed a far greater threat to the Germans than the Chetniks. This so antagonised the pro-Mihailovic faction in SOE Cairo that Maclean feared for his life. Powell shared SOE Cairo's low opinion of Maclean. Forty years later, writing in his Journals, he wondered why he was 'allowed to travel more or less where he likes in the Soviet Union'.[7]

*

9. Gall and Wormwood

Two old favourites consigned to the wings during the war volumes of *Dance* are Quiggin and Members, both in 'reserved' occupations. Their absence reflects how detached Powell was from literary London in wartime. For instance he scarcely read *Horizon*, let alone contributed to it, despite repeated requests to do so by the editor, Cyril Connolly. There was a perfectly valid reason for this: pressure of work. But I also suspect that Connolly was one of those sacred monsters, John Betjeman being another, whom Powell preferred to keep at arm's length, the better to see them plain.

Like Evelyn Waugh, Maurice Bowra and many others, Powell was fascinated by Connolly. As he explained in *Infants*:

> He was one of those individuals – a recognised genius – who seem to have been sent into the world to be talked about ... Connolly's behaviour, love affairs, financial difficulties, employments or lack of them, all seemed matters of burning interest ... [H]e was the subject of profuse anecdote; his interest in himself somehow communicating its force to other people.

But like all such forces Connolly's egotism could repel as firmly as it attracted. 'Ugh!' was all that the publisher Rupert Hart-Davis could bring himself to say about Connolly in one of his letters to George Lyttelton, who had taught them both at Eton. Powell, in certain moods, would have echoed Hart-Davis. In response to a letter from Christopher Sykes, who referred to some 'horrible truths' that had emerged about Connolly after his death, Powell wrote, 'I feel sure, incidentally, that we have not heard the *half* yet.'[8] But he later admitted that when Connolly was alive he would 'always take steps to get hold of him' if he was in the vicinity. He thought that those 'who refused to be drawn into the net of Connolly gossip ... perhaps missed something in life'.

An only child like Powell, Connolly had a similar background. His mother's family, the Vernons, were Anglo-Irish gentry. The Connollys were from Ireland too, but for a century or more they'd been settled in Bath, serving the Crown as soldiers and sailors. Connolly's grandfather was an Admiral; his father, who became an eminent conchologist ('the Berenson of the South African non-marine mollusca'), retired from the Army in the rank of Major. Like Powell, Connolly had a peripatetic childhood, which left him yearning to own the perfect house, something he never achieved. As already noted he went from St Cyprian's to College at Eton, where to everyone's amazement – 'so *plain*, and no good at games'[9] – he charmed his way into Pop.

Powell's first conscious impression of Connolly, shortly after he'd been elected to Pop, is an early indication of how conformist he could be in matters of dress. Connolly, now above the law, decided that when not required to wear tails he would exchange the traditional tweed jacket or blazer, worn with grey flannels, for a dinner jacket. Seeing him thus attired, Powell felt 'conventional misgiving at the dinner jacket as an innovation in school dress'. At Balliol, where they met once or twice, Powell probably had conventional misgivings again, this time about Connolly's homosexuality, details of which were 'widely ventilated' by Maurice Bowra, who had fallen out with Connolly over Pierce Synnott. He was, in any case, still slightly in awe of Connolly, who was not only two years older, but regarded by his peers as the most extraordinary undergraduate of their generation.

Connolly went down in 1925, and they did not meet again until 1927 when Powell, wearing his Duckworth hat, rejected a guide to the Balkans that Connolly had written. At only 25,000 words it was, he said, too short; but if Connolly were ever to produce a book of essays he would like first refusal. Did Powell suspect, even then, that despite his extraordinary way with words Connolly lacked the temperament to become a novelist? Probably not. But it is interesting to see that only two years later Connolly admitted to David Garnett that he would never get beyond the first chapter of a novel unless there was somebody standing over him.

In 1930 Connolly married Jean Bakewell, a good-natured American brunette with £1000 a year or so of her own. Consequently he was, like Quiggin, even less inclined to 'rush into print'. His Mediterranean novella, *The Rock Pool*, completed in 1935, fell foul of Mrs Grundy and had to be published in Paris. It was not until 1938 that his immortal work, *Enemies of Promise*, appeared, by which time it was clear to many that if, as he later proposed, the true function of a writer was to create a masterpiece, his own masterpiece was himself.

Powell did not see much of Connolly in the Thirties. One reason for this was that Connolly and his wife spent about half the year abroad, usually in Provence. It was also the case that two of Powell's closest friends, John Heygate and Constant Lambert, were actively disliked by Connolly. Connolly's rather unconvincing flirtation with the Left cannot have helped either. In Powell's opinion it detracted from his criticism, blinding him to the faults of the renegade public schoolboys who made up the Auden group.

The Spanish Civil War, which he briefly covered for the *New Statesman*, was a turning point for Connolly. Although he never wavered in his support for the Republic he was, like Orwell, sickened by the brutality of the Stalinists towards their own side. When, in *Enemies of Promise*, he wrote that 'the writer whose stomach cannot assimilate with genius the starch and acid of contemporary politics had better turn down his plate',[10] he was speaking for himself. From now on, whenever he heard the word 'politics', Connolly would reach for his culture. This was the rationale behind *Horizon*, which was launched, audaciously, in January 1940. Convinced that in official eyes art and literature were surplus to requirements, Connolly was determined to ensure that they came 'up with the rations' after all. And so they did. Although a 'little magazine', *Horizon* punched far above its weight, replacing the proverbial field-marshal's baton in thousands of serviceman's knapsacks. Naturally there were those who disapproved, who thought that to concern yourself with the arts in wartime was at best unhealthy, at worst downright subversive. But to judge from the number of other little magazines that bobbed up in *Horizon's* wake, many of them run by and for servicemen, the hunger for cultural stimulation was real enough.

Whereas Connolly himself was obsessed by what Powell calls his 'myth', specifically the way in which a cruel Fate had inhibited his genius, gossip about him had mostly to do with money and sex, both of which, despite protestations to the contrary, he was remarkably adept at obtaining. Women liked him because he had what Peter Quennell called 'the dangerous gift of intimacy',[11] which more than made up for his absence of good looks. 'If Cyril was sitting beside someone at dinner and he took a fancy to them he knew how to make a favourable impression. He had great conversational skills,' said Quennell. At *Horizon* much of the donkey-work was done by three or four young women whose devotion to Connolly was demonstrated again and again. It was commonplace for them to pool their ration books so that he could have a blow-out, which they of course would cook. One of them, Lys Lubbock, who became his mistress, was the daughter-in-law of the pianist Irene Scharrer whom Powell's housemaster Goodhart was supposed to have pursued. She was known behind her back as 'Mrs Connolly-by-deed-poll' because she changed her name to Connolly. Another of the handmaidens was Sonia Brownell, aka 'The Euston Road Venus' and 'Buttocks Brownell', who became the second Mrs George Orwell – on Connolly's orders, so Powell maintained.

Connolly had no money of his own. But as Peter Quennell remarked, 'Cyril usually managed to fall on his feet or, failing that, somebody else's.' When his first wife left him her mother, a wealthy woman, continued to give him an allowance for several years. Meanwhile in Peter Watson, heir to a fortune made from margarine, he found the perfect patron: generous, cultivated, discriminating (particularly about modern art, of which he had a magnificent collection), calm, and above all, hands-off. Complain as he might – for he was, as Powell once said, one of world's great grumblers – Connolly knew he was on to a cushy number. 'If we're all back at school one must be a prefect,'[12] he declared in 1939. And since editing a magazine was a reserved occupation, absolving him from National Service of any kind, a prefect he became. Only if the magazine failed to appear was there any risk of his being called up and thus compelled to 'fag' for the government.

By chance, the contrast between Powell's war and Connolly's is captured by two drawings Osbert Lancaster did for *Horizon*, part of a series called 'Landscape With Figures' depicting the London scene in wartime. In one he shows a crowd of middle- to high-ranking officers, Army and Navy, British and Allied, coming and going outside the old United Service club on the corner of Waterloo Place and Pall Mall. Some are saluting, most carry their gas masks, all have bags of swank. It is immediately apparent what Chips Lovell meant when he said it was 'a tailor's war'. This was Powell's milieu – though not as it happens his club: he belonged to the Travellers, just down the road. Lancaster's other drawing, which ought to have a key, is of the Café Royal during the Blitz. On the balcony is Lancaster himself, with Brian Howard, recognisable by his lips and eyelashes, round the corner to his right. Down below a haggard Stephen Spender in his fireman's uniform is sandwiched between the cashier and Tom Driberg, who may have spotted John Lehmann tête-à-tête with a precious-looking matelot. Meanwhile Connolly, pouchy and unshaven, with Lys Lubbock in tow, has just arrived at the banquette where Peter Quennell sits beside a pretty girl with high cheekbones and a poodle hair cut. What makes this tableau so piquant is the girl's identity. She is Barbara Skelton, alias 'Skelters' or 'Babs' or 'Baby', then stepping out with Quennell (among others) but later the second Mrs Connolly and also, in word and deed if not in appearance, the model for Pamela Flitton.

That Lancaster should have brought Connolly face to face with his future wife was, of course, an accident. But it was the sort of accident that would have intrigued Powell and it would be interesting to know if he ever saw the drawing. As for Skelters, 'the most sinister person ever to have stayed under [our] roof'[13] according to Violet, she raised as much hell as her fictional counterpart. In *The Wanton Chase*, where she appears as 'Julia', Quennell says he asked her why she often made their life so difficult. 'I *like* things to be difficult,' she replied. Quennell thought 'she needed love, yet resented being loved; and her resentment was apt to assume an unexpectedly aggressive guise'. She also, despite her youth, had the annoying knack of detecting her lovers' limitations and exposing their pretensions, 'holding up a glass where one saw one's silliest face reflected'.[14] Quennell blamed her character on her stormy childhood, in which love had played little part.

The daughter of a Gaiety Girl and her stage-door Johnny, a rather inef-fectual Army officer, Skelters was expelled from one school after another and at the age of fifteen went to work for Gooch's, a Knightsbridge store that numbered her father's best friend among its directors. Soon she became his mistress and lived the life of a *poule de luxe*. But following an abortion she decided to cut loose, grabbing at the chance to visit her uncle, a General, in India. There she met a young officer who was so smitten he deserted in order to sail back to England with her. Arrested at Aden he was not cashiered but sent to redeem himself on the North-West Frontier, which he did soon after-wards, dying in an ambush. Skelters then modelled for Schiaparelli until the Blitz halted *haute couture*, after which she spent two years avoiding being called up and coping with what she calls in *Tears Before Bedtime* 'the inevitable amorous complications'. Eventually she was sent to Egypt as a cipherine where she caught the eye of King Farouk, who may not have been much of a monarch, but who knew how to keep his girls in line: he once flogged her on the steps of his palace with a dressing gown cord. When her association with Farouk became too blatant she was sent to Athens, then in the throes of a civil war, which is where, for the moment, we shall leave her.

*

Shortly after D-Day, when at last there seemed a light at the end of the tunnel, the Germans launched the first of their secret weapons, the V1 flying bomb. The sound of these proved as unnerving as the sirens attached to Stuka dive-bombers, the difference being that it was when the noise stopped that you dived for cover. It was these 'doodlebugs' and the danger they posed that produced one of Cyril Connolly's most famous quips. Reminded by Harold Nicolson that his 'dear ones at the front' were in far greater danger than he was, Connolly replied: 'That wouldn't work with me at all, Harold. In the first place, I have no dear ones at the front. And in the second place, I have observed with me perfect fear casteth out love.'[15]

Powell admitted that after four years or more of total war, V-bombs were the last straw. 'One was so *bored* by it all. You couldn't sleep – not feeling afraid so much as frankly embarrassed,'[16] a view echoed by Moreland. In *The Military Philosophers* Jenkins, accompanied by his erudite clerk, Curtis, has a panoramic view of a V1 raid from one of the pepperpot domes on the roof of the War Office:

[T]hree rapidly moving lights appeared in the southern sky, two more or less side by side, the third following a short way behind, as if lacking acceleration or will power to keep up. They travelled with that curious shuddering jerky movement characteristic of such bodies, a style of locomotion that seemed to suggest the engine was not working properly, might break down at any moment, which indeed it would. The impression that something was badly wrong with the internal machinery was increased by a shower of sparks emitted from the tail. A more exciting possibility was that dragons were flying through the air in a fabulous tale, and climbing into the turret with Curtis had been done in a dream. The raucous buzz could now be plainly heard. In imagination one smelt brimstone...

The first two cut out. It was almost simultaneous. The noisy ticking of the third continued briefly, then also stopped abruptly. The interval between cutting out and exploding always seemed interminable. At last it came; again two at once, the third a few seconds later. All three swooped to the ground, their flaming tails pointing upwards, certainly dragons now, darting earthward to consume their prey of maidens chained to rocks.

'Southwark, do you think?'

'Lambeth, sir – having regard to the incurvations of the river.'

'Sweet Thames run softly ...'

'I was thinking the same, sir.'

(For once Jenkins makes an allusion that is not lost on his *vis-à-vis*. Normally it falls on deaf ears, as in this exchange with a 'brisk little cocksparrow of a captain' in Brussels:

'We had a hell of a party here the other night,' he said. 'A crowd of senior officers as drunk as monkeys, brigadiers rooting the palms out of pots.'

His words conjured up the scene in *Antony and Cleopatra*, when arm-in-arm the generals dance on Pompey's galley, a sequence of the play that makes it scarcely possible to disbelieve that Shakespeare himself served for at least a period of his life in the army.

'With thy grapes our hairs be crowned?'

'Took some cleaning up after, I can tell you.')

One of the flight paths of the V1s was over Shoreham in Kent, where Violet and Tristram were living. Being not far from Biggin Hill aerodrome, Shoreham had already been singled out for attention by the Luftwaffe, one direct hit on a farm wiping out a mother and her children who were known to the Powells. Violet, normally imperturbable, had been 'nervously reduced'[17] by this tragedy, so when the V1s arrived she and Tristram went walkabout until December, when it was decided to reoccupy No 1 Chester Gate.

The Powells had been lucky. The house next door had been gutted by a bomb, but No 1, which contained all their worldly goods, was relatively unscathed. Nor had it been burgled, which given how long it had been unoccupied was little short of a miracle. Alick Dru and his wife, who was expecting her second child, joined them there; and a spare bed was kept available for Malcolm Muggeridge, now liaising with French military intelligence, who must have found it quite a contrast to the Rothschild mansion he shared in Paris with Victor Rothschild.

Powell had also begun to deal with the French, an added responsibility that brought promotion to Major and two subordinates to assist with the increase in paperwork (he refers in his Journals to the 'ten thousand letters' that passed between him and his French colleague). Like most of his generation he was Francophile, though by no means as starry-eyed as some. For instance he disagreed with Nancy Mitford's notion that the French were always practical and hard-headed about love, saying he knew many exceptions to that rule. But France provides a defining moment in the war trilogy, as one supposes it did in real life. Bowling along through the war-scarred *bocage* with a bus full of chattering attachés Jenkins glimpses an old Frenchman, complete with beret, who waves a greeting. All at once the point of fighting the war, and winning it, strikes home. For the first and last time in our presence Jenkins is in tears.

Powell was Colonel Carlisle's number two on this cross-channel jaunt, the climax of which was a visit to Montgomery's Tactical Headquarters on the Dutch-German border. The first night they stayed at Cabourg, 'Balbec' in *A la recherche du temps perdu*. Powell was struck by the resort's charm, even in November, but failed to grasp its significance, possibly because he was distracted by the row over the bath, which really happened, involving a Nepalese Major and a Norwegian (rather than Swedish) General. Only on his return to England did the penny drop. A less disciplined novelist might have made more of this numinous episode, arranging for Jenkins to spend the night in the Grand Hotel, where Proust stayed, instead of the unremarkable Petite Auberge. As it is, Jenkins consoles himself with the thought that his disappointment 'was in its way suitably Proustian too: a reminder of the eternal failure of human life to respond a hundred per cent'.

Powell had spent four years in Whitehall. He was out of touch with the Army in the field, almost all of it made up of conscripts who took a justifiable pride in what they had achieved but were impatient with too much formality. This, I think, accounts for his rather snooty description of the mood at Main Headquarters, which he compares to that of 'a minor public school which had just defeated its chief rival on the football field. Everyone seemed young, aggressive, enormously pleased with himself, so much that normal army courtesies were sometimes forgotten.' Jenkins gives what I take to be an example of this when he reports a junior staff officer ticking off Colonel Finn for parking his vehicles in the wrong place: '"Get 'em out of the way at once and look sharp about it."'

151

Headquarters took its cocky mood from the Commander-in-Chief, Montgomery (as a schoolboy, captain of rugby at St Paul's). Being a connoisseur of generals and their individual styles Powell welcomed the chance to examine him before, as he later put it, 'he hardened into an exhibit'. What he saw aroused respect rather than admiration. Montgomery did not give off waves of energy like the CIGS, Alanbrooke. His will was steely rather than effervescent. 'It was an immense, wiry, calculated, insistent hardness, rather than a force like champagne bursting from a bottle ... One felt that a great deal of time and trouble, even intellectual effort of its own sort, had gone into producing this final result.' Montgomery's features, in particular his 'deepset and icy cold' eyes, belonged, Powell thought, to a mythical beast like one of those in *Alice in Wonderland*, 'full of awkward questions and downright statements'. His voice was 'an army voice, but precise, controlled, almost mincing ... [with] a faint and faraway reminder of the clergy, too' (Montgomery's father was a Bishop). Alert to military dress and its symbolism, Powell noted that while Montgomery had abandoned the 'conscious informality of ready-to-hand garments appropriate to desert warfare', his new turn-out, a 'neatly-tailored' battledress of smooth service-dress material, peculiar to himself, 'was clearly conceived at the same time to avoid any resemblance to the buttoned-up army officer of caricature. It lacked too, probably also deliberately, the lounging smartness of which, for example, Dicky Umfraville, or even in his own fashion, Sunny Farebrother, knew the secret.'

'Correct: neat: practical: unpompous', Montgomery was a horse of a different colour from his elegant comrade-in-arms Alexander (another exemplar of 'lounging smartness'); but, as Powell conceded, he was probably right for the course he had to run. One wonders how, in his exposition to the attachés, Montgomery explained the débacle at Arnhem, for which he was largely to blame. Jenkins, musing on D'Artagnan and Co, offers no clues.

With his eye for the incongruous Powell concludes his impressions of Montgomery with a post-war anecdote of Nancy Mitford's: '[She] told me that Montgomery had expressed a wish to meet her at dinner in Paris, when he had revealed a perfectly competent knowledge of her novels.' This is as unexpected as the revelation in his Journals that Mrs Thatcher had enjoyed Dame Helen Gardner's book on Eliot's *Four Quartets*.

*

Nazi Germany surrendered on 8 May 1945. Powell spent VE Night in bed reading *The Cambridge History of English Literature*, the only person so occupied thought Violet, a pretty safe assumption in the circumstances. By then he would have known, like Pennistone, that '[N]ot all the fruits of victory are appetising to the palate … An issue of gall and wormwood has been laid on.' Poland was about to go Communist, Tito was threatening Trieste and there was a real fear that the Russians might cross the Elbe and keep going until they reached the Channel. What Powell cannot have foreseen, being ignorant of rank-and-file opinion, was Labour's crushing victory in the General Election, which they won by almost 150 seats. Two years later he was still trying to explain this away: 'The great thing to remember … is that 12 million votes were given for Labour; nearly 10 million for the Conservatives; and more than 2,200,000 for the Liberals – so much for "a resounding Labour victory".'[18]

Powell's mixture of astonishment and dismay at the size of Labour's victory was shared by many, including the historian of the Conservative party, Robert Blake, a prisoner of war from 1941 until 1944. Although their circumstances were different, much of what Blake says here, in a review of Paul Addison's book *The Road to 1945*, could well have been written by Powell:

Although I was in England till May 1941, the world of the OCTU and Officers' Mess tended to insulate one from current political movements. In any case the significant developments towards the Attlee consensus occurred later. I was not back in England till early in 1944. I then realised that a vast change had taken place in the climate of opinion, and I cannot pretend that I found it at all congenial.

There was, for example, much toadying to Russia, which seemed repugnant at the time and in retrospect appears positively nauseous. Dr Addison has some good examples: the rejection by T.S. Eliot, as adviser to Faber & Faber, of George Orwell's *Animal Farm* on the grounds that it implicitly criticised our gallant ally; a book by Lionel Barnes, a Fabian colonial expert, showing that British colonial servants in tropical Africa had much to learn from Soviet rule in central Asia …most absurd of all, the dozen government-sponsored demonstrations in big cities, each addressed by a minister, to celebrate the twenty-fifth anniversary of the Red Army in February 23, 1943. 'Nothing like this', Dr Addison writes, 'had been seen since the coronation of George VI.'

Adulation of Russia was very far from being the only change between 1940 and 1944. There was a new egalitarianism, an almost masochistic acceptance of rationing, austerity, fair shares, equal sacrifice etc. This was no doubt commendable, even if it was somewhat tedious for an escaped prisoner of war whose rosy-coloured vision of England soon vanished with the greyness of its reality. What seemed to me more disturbing was the way in which articulate opinion regarded the future. The talk was all of planning, controls and 'social justice', along with what was called 'privilege', 'vested interests' or the 'old gang'. The Beveridge Report, production of one of the most conceited of men that ever lived, had become scarcely distinguishable from Holy Writ …

153

I cannot have been alone in feeling that, whatever I was fighting for, it was not socialism or equality. Like most of my Oxford friends, I hoped that post-war Britain would be a better place than pre-war Britain, but – again like most of them – I did not feel that I was actually fighting to make it better, rather to prevent it from being much worse. We took the King's shilling to stop the swastika from flying on Buckingham Palace, not to implement the Beveridge Report.[19]

Some of these discontents are explicit in Powell's treatment, in *Dance*, of the Thanksgiving Service for Victory at St Paul's, with its 'fashionably egalitarian' congregation, 'forward-looking' ritual and conciliatory mood towards 'our enemies in defeat'. Soon, foresees Jenkins, 'people would, in any case, begin to say that the war was pointless, particularly those, and their associates, moral and actual, who had chalked on walls, "Strike now in the West" or "Bomb Rome".' Expediency is now the order of the day, as witness the gratuitous award of a CBE to a newly-arrived South American attaché whose country, says Finn, the Foreign Office are 'anxious to keep in with'.

This attaché is Colonel Flores, for some years now the husband of Jenkins's old flame Jean. His failure to recognise her outside the cathedral demonstrates how foreign a country the immediate past has become to Jenkins after six years of living either in the present, or, when mugging up Robert Burton, the seventeenth century. For instance only a minute or two before this lapse Flores had told him something that in days gone by would surely have brought Jean to mind. Asked whether this was his first visit to London, Flores reveals that he and his family – 'an absolute tribe of us' – had stayed at the Ritz about fifteen years before. Immediately the reader recalls that on the night Jenkins unexpectedly became Jean's lover he had arranged to meet Mark Members at the Ritz, where there was a large family of South Americans spread across the lounge. That was in December 1932. Could Colonel Flores be mistaken, and he was here thirteen years before, not fifteen? Such a coincidence would be truly Nietzschean, but Jenkins is so overwhelmed by Jean's transformation into a chic South American lady that he overlooks it.

Talking of coincidences, I remember that about the time I first read *The Military Philosophers* I also read Alison Lurie's Los Angeles novel, *The Nowhere City*, the denouement of which also turns on a woman reinventing herself, in this case so successfully that her errant husband doesn't recognise her on his return from a few months in New England. I did not know then – it must have been about 1968 – that Powell and Miss Lurie were friends, or that *The Nowhere City*, published in 1965, was his favourite among her novels. Whether this is significant I cannot pretend to know. But it is the sort of detail that appealed to Powell, which is why I mention it here.

*

Powell was indignant when a reviewer complained that it was unrealistic for so many of his characters to die in the war. He pointed out that of the 750 Old Etonians who fell, forty were known to him by sight. One of these was John Spencer, whom Powell identified as the prototype for Peter Templer. A raffish type, sacked from the OTC for drunkenness, fond of fast cars and night-clubs, Spencer, in civilian life a Lloyd's underwriter, sounds just the sort of well-heeled man about town who might have played golf with Ian Fleming. He must also, I think, have been one of the 'unmilitary' figures Powell said he knew who met exemplary deaths, in Spencer's case while serving with the Welsh Guards in North Africa. Spencer's widow, whom he had divorced and then remarried, then married a tycoon called Renwick who inspired a character in a detective story by Roy Fuller. While insisting that Mrs Spencer/Renwick had no resemblance to 'Betty Taylor or Porter', Templer's dotty second wife, Powell remarked that it still showed 'how few people there are to go round for the use of novelists'[20] – which brings me to another casualty, Hubert Duggan, the inspiration for Stringham as a schoolboy.

Like most of Powell's contemporaries Duggan was a man of the Twenties who found little to rejoice over during the Thirties, throughout which he was Tory MP for Acton. In 1930 his marriage broke up. In 1931 his feckless mother, Lord Curzon's widow, had the duns in at No 1 Carlton House Terrace (which became the German Embassy) and Hackwood, her country seat. It cost Duggan £50,000 to bail her out. Another worry was his elder brother Alfred, who spent the decade battling with drink. In 1940 Duggan rejoined his old regiment, the Life Guards. Three years later his mistress, the beguiling Phyllis de Janzé, died suddenly, whereupon he went into a decline. His health had never been good and one wonders how he managed to pass his Army medical. A witness to his last days was Evelyn Waugh, then at a loose end of his own making, who sought to relieve his *cafard* by saving Duggan's soul. Against the wishes of Duggan's sister Marcella, he brought a priest to the death bed and had the satisfaction of hearing his friend accept absolution. But that was not the end of it, as he later explained to Ronald Knox:

> I am delighted you became reconciled to B[rideshead] R[evisited] in the end. It was, of course, all about the death bed. I was present at almost exactly that scene … when a friend of mine whom we thought in his final coma and stub-

bornly impenitent, whose womenfolk would only let the priest in because they thought him unconscious, did exactly that, making the sign of the cross. It was profoundly affecting and I wrote the book about that scene.[21]

Waugh never seems to have associated Duggan with Stringham. Reviewing *The Kindly Ones* he declared:

I have known Mr Powell for forty years and we have countless friends and acquaintances in common. In this sextet, as distinct from the books that captivated us before the war, I have recognised no character or incident 'taken from life'.[22]

Waugh's admission indicates what very different lives he and Powell led, despite their having people in common. His *Letters* and *Diaries* confirm this, as indeed does Christopher Sykes's biography, in which Powell is mentioned only twice. Powell, for his part, makes no reference to Duggan in connection with *Brideshead*, a novel he thought irredeemably flawed. But flawed or not it became an international bestseller at a time when Powell did not have a single word in print. All he had to show for six years in uniform were the notes he had made for his projected biography of John Aubrey. His conscience, however, was clear. He had submitted to the Rules and Discipline of War with better grace and to more effect than Waugh, who ended the war as a Captain, the same rank as his immortal scapegrace, Grimes. Powell was demobbed in the rank of Major, with a cluster of foreign decorations to mark his labours at MIL. Like everyone else he knew, he had been 'shaken up' by his experiences and it would be some years yet before he achieved the inner calm necessary to begin another work of fiction.

10

The World Turned Upside Down

Writing is governed more than anything else by the spirit of the age.

Malcolm Muggeridge

Don't expect too much of us. We're batting on a very sticky wicket.

Clement Attlee

Tristram, the Powells' elder son, was conceived about five or six weeks before the war in Europe began. Their younger son John, born 11 January 1946, must therefore have been conceived about the same period before VE Day, another of those recurring patterns in which Powell delighted. He had learnt about Tristram's birth while crossing the parade ground at Newry. The news that John had been born was relayed to him at Balliol, his base while working up Aubrey material in the Bodleian. This task he began after the statutory three months' leave pending final demobilisation, most of it spent with Violet and Tristram at the North Devon resort of Lee.

Like everyone else who had been on active service Powell needed time to readjust, not just to being out of uniform – the newly-demobbed Jenkins almost salutes a French general looming up out of the London fog – but also to the vastly different post-war landscape. It wasn't just that the contours had changed; so had his perspective: 'You went into the war as a young man and emerged middle-aged.'[1] Nor was the landscape so full of familiar faces as before.

As the forlorn purlieus of the railway-station end of the town gave place to colleges, reverie, banal if you like, though eminently Burtonesque, turned towards the relatively high proportion of persons known pretty well at an earlier stage of life, both here and elsewhere, now dead, gone off their rocker, withdrawn into states of existence they – or I – had no wish to share. The probability was that even without cosmic upheaval some kind of reshuffle has to take place halfway through life.

In Devon Powell saw something of T.S. Eliot, whose belief that '[a]ny writer who discusses his art suffers in public opinion' he would sometimes invoke when an interviewer tried to pin him down.[2] Powell also shared some of Eliot's forebodings about European civilisation in a world dominated by America and Russia. But unlike Eliot he was not a Christian, believing that '[e]xtreme scepticism is the only possible terms to accept religion'.[3] So when, in 1984, he learnt that he had been nominated for the T.S. Eliot Award for Creative Writing, from an American foundation whose charter emphasised Judaeo-Christian values and the Ten Commandments, he made it a condition of acceptance that he could not publicly endorse either of these. The most he would allow was that as a traditional Tory he was 'broadly speaking sympathetic' to them.[4]

Balliol was not the most congenial billet for a traditional Tory in early 1946. High-minded and austere, it was a microcosm of the society held up for admiration by the new government. Luckily Powell found the seventeenth century a good opiate. Always fascinated by other people and their idiosyncrasies, he soon became immersed in his subject's raw material, the 'writers, clerics, statesmen, soldiers, lawyers, scientists, astrologers, schoolmasters, rakes, ladies of the town and obscure old friends'[5] whose lives Aubrey had recorded. He may also have derived some comfort from the knowledge that, in Aubrey's day, the world had turned upside-down, only to right itself in due course.

Powell finished *John Aubrey and His Friends* in May 1946, which given its length – 300 pages – and the fact that he had also begun to do some reviewing, was unusually fast going. Why then did it take two and a half years to appear in print? One reason was that paper, like almost everything else at that date, was in very short supply. But Powell probably chose the wrong publisher as well. Piqued at the small advance offered by his first choice, the Oxford University Press, he took Malcolm Muggeridge's advice and gave it to Graham Greene, then the deputy managing director of Eyre and Spottiswoode. Greene made a better offer, which included an option on any fiction that Powell might write, probably what he was really after. He then sat on the manuscript for two years, doubtless considering that more immediately marketable material must take precedence. OUP, an academic publisher with different priorities, would surely not have acted in this way.

Although peeved at the delay, Powell had good reason not to fall out with his publisher. He had begun to review about twenty books a month for the *New English Review*, a quirky right-wing periodical owned by Eyre and Spottiswoode whose chairman, Douglas Jerrold, was the editor. Powell was not paid much for digging these 'mass graves' – no more than a few guineas a time. But his haul of review copies, flogged at half price to the Library suppliers, Thomas Gaston, were a regular source of tax-free cash he could ill afford to lose. (In fifty years or more of reviewing Powell must have collected a tidy sum from Gaston's till.)

Powell ceased to review for the *New English Review* in February 1948, having been appointed fiction editor of the *TLS*. So he could afford to remonstrate when, several months later, Greene told him that his book, scheduled for publication in late autumn, would once again be delayed. 'A brisk exchange' (later amended to 'a colossal row') followed, with Greene saying that it was 'a bloody boring book, anyway'. Powell said he took this to mean that he was released from any obligation to offer further books to Eyre and Spottiswoode, which Greene confirmed. Douglas Jerrold, however, insisted that Greene could not release him from his contract and a three-sided tussle ensued. After further angry words, Greene, who was tired of trying to juggle publishing with novel-writing, resigned. Jerrold, under pressure from Powell and his agent, agreed to tear up the contract. And *John Aubrey and His Friends* was, after all, published in late autumn, selling so well that a second edition appeared just before Christmas.

Powell implies that it was Greene's love of conflict that impelled him to say what he did, something he would never have done himself in such circumstances. But there may have been more to it than that. On 16 April 1948 Malcolm Muggeridge noted in his Diary that Powell had been reading Greene's new novel *The Heart of the Matter*, 'which he said was excellent in parts but, of course, to him not really congenial. He said Greene always seemed to him like a scholarship boy who was putting up a really wonderful performance.'[6] When Powell showed Muggeridge what he had written about *The Heart of the Matter* for the *TLS*, Muggeridge commented: 'quite good, but, as I pointed out to him, it is very difficult to be deceitful in the written word, and his feeling that the novel is [largely drivel] shows through his ostensible praise of it.'[7] Soon afterwards Muggeridge implied that Greene had indeed seen through Powell's review. If so, Greene probably felt justified in evening the score when he had the chance.

In later life Powell used to say that one of the few advantages of growing old was that you 'saw the end of a few stories'– a polite way of saying that you had the last laugh. Greene, who died in 1991, was a case in point. Powell thought him absurdly overrated as a novelist: 'vulgarised Conrad, to which tedious Roman Catholic propaganda is added'; and deeply flawed as a man – 'completely cynical, really only liking sex and money and his own particular brand of publicity'.[8] But while Greene was alive he was careful not to let on, treating him as a '*cher confrère*'. This was partly because he thought literary vendettas and offensive exchanges were an 'utter waste of time';[9] but also because to have attacked Greene, or his novels, would have exposed him to charges of jealousy which might have been difficult to refute. Ironically, it was Greene's excursion into seventeenth-century biography that provided Powell with what he thought were justifiable grounds for jealousy. In 1934 Greene's biography of Rochester, *Lord Rochester's Monkey*, was rejected by his publisher Heinemann, almost certainly because the gamy Restoration poet was then considered too pornographic a subject for the general reader. Forty years later, when obscenity was no longer an issue and Greene's name guaranteed a large print run, the biography was published in a coffee-table edition and not only became a bestseller but also received gushing reviews. This aggrieved Powell, who complained in his Journals that whereas his book on Aubrey was the product of original research – 'getting one's hands dirty' – Greene's biography was cobbled together from secondary sources.[10] He felt he never received sufficient credit for rescuing Aubrey from the shadows. Almost the last review he wrote, of a new life of Aubrey, pursued the same theme. Under the heading, 'Thou shalt not covet thy neighbour's life', he rebuked the author for doing 'little, if any, original research' and said that it was 'almost within hail of being actionable'[11] for his publisher to use a cover identical to that of the paperback edition of *John Aubrey and His Friends*.

*

As liaison officer to the Belgians Powell also looked after a small contingent of troops from Luxembourg, in the course of which he became friendly with the Luxembourg Minister, André Clasen, later their Ambassador. This probably explains how, in May 1946, Powell became the London correspondent of *Luxemburger Wort*, the Duchy's daily paper. I say 'probably' because Powell is silent on this subject. He never refers to it in interviews, nor is it mentioned in his Memoirs or Journals. Without the publication of George Lilley's comprehensive Bibliography it would not have come to light.

Under the headline 'England In Transition' Powell was introduced to his readers as an 'important English publicist' who would give them an insight into English life and politics at a significant moment in the country's history. In practice, Powell contributed a chatty London letter every two or three weeks, covering politics, society and the arts, with occasional articles on more weighty matters like the partition of India after Independence and the strength of the British Communist Party. Probably it made a change from reviewing, which he had begun to do for the *Telegraph* as well, and helped to pay the bills; but it is strange that he chose to ignore it afterwards since he was usually prepared to comment on all aspects of writing, creative or not.

As Powell pointed out in *Faces*, Luxembourg fared no better than other states during the Nazi Occupation, so it would have been tactless of him to dilate on the bleakness of life under Labour. And life would get worse before it got better, courtesy of one of the longest and hardest winters ever recorded. For two months snow lay where it fell, turning to ice underfoot. Coal was in desperately short supply; there were frequent power cuts; everybody shivered. Powell described it as 'a frightfully grisly period, almost grislier than the war in certain respects because there was no common cause to unite people. London really was frightfully bleak. Everybody was tremendously tired and there was nothing to eat and jolly little to drink and then the pipes froze and we had to beg a bath off our neighbours.'[12] A lucky few, the Powells among them, received food parcels from abroad. 'I cannot tell you how good it is,' wrote Powell of the ham Muggeridge had sent him from America.* But nothing could compensate for the absence of wine, a consequence of the 'prim austerity' imposed by the Labour Chancellor, Hugh Dalton. 'Reading about wine is so depressing nowadays,' complained Powell in a review, 'when it is impossible to obtain and the government cannot make up their mind whether or not they are going to allow its importation by private enterprise ...'[13]

But in one important respect life was better for Powell in 1947 than in 1937. Literature had turned its back on the Left. The hierarchy was upper middle-class, upper middle-aged and upper middle-brow. Evelyn Waugh might complain that the sergeants were taking over; he forgot about the ivory tower. This remained off-limits to NCOs and other ranks even under a Labour Government. Mandarins like Harold Nicolson, Desmond MacCarthy and Raymond Mortimer dominated the review pages, while the most powerful literary editors were three cultivated Old Etonians, Cyril Connolly, John Lehmann and Alan Pryce-Jones. This led to back-scratching of the sort described by Doris Lessing at the beginning of her novel, *The Four-Gated City*. Her heroine, Martha Quest, newly arrived from Rhodesia, has landed a job as secretary to Mark Coldridge, author of a bestselling war novel. Mark is a thoroughbred, with brothers who went to Eton and a mother, Margaret, who knows simply everybody. Hence, Martha learns, the successful launch of his novel:

> The book had been, as they say, widely noticed. This was because, Mark said, giving the fact without emphasis, he was a Coldridge. Exploring this it became clear that the literary editors, the reviewers, the people who ran the arts in England at that time, had been at school, or at university with – not Mark, but

---

* Muggeridge was spending eighteen months in America as the *Daily Telegraph's* Washington correspondent. He was much missed by Powell.

his brothers, and 'knew' Margaret, or at least all knew each other. No litera-ture-fed person comes from outside Britain without expecting to find some marvellous free market-place of the arts, internationally fed, high-minded, maintained by disinterested devotees drawn from wherever they can be found. All that excellence, the high standards – surely they were not sustained by Tom and Dick and Harry who had gone to school with Mark's brothers and who 'knew' Margaret? Well, why not? Mark demanded, when he finally saw that what he took for granted, she took with incredulity. Why not? If it works?[14]

The reissue of *From a View to a Death* was evidence of this shift in direc-tion. Here was a novel with no redeeming social features, about the sort of people some Labour MPs considered vermin. The publisher was not Duckworth but John Lehmann, who for more than a decade had been at the helm of the magazines *New Writing* and *Penguin New Writing*. If anyone knew which way the wind was blowing Lehmann did. An ardent left-winger in the Thirties, he had become increasingly impatient with austerity for austerity's sake. How Powell must have been tempted to say 'I told you so', since Lehmann, a year or so behind him at Eton, was one of the *clercs* – like Quiggin – whose reluctance to apologise for their *trahison* he deplored.

Another augury was the appointment of Alan Pryce-Jones as editor of the *TLS*. Wealthy, well-preserved and very well-connected, Pryce-Jones was one of those lucky people who manage to have their cake and eat it – by no means a recommendation at a time of 'fair shares for all'. Not yet twenty-one when Wall Street crashed he had already been pronounced 'amusing' by Bloomsbury and the Sitwells despite leaving Oxford under a cloud after only two terms. For the next few years he lived comfortably enough on his wits, wrote a travel book or two, and then in 1934 had the good fortune to marry into a family of rich, cosmopolitan Austrian Jews. During the war he divided his time between Bletchley Park and the War Office, in the bowels of which he sometimes ran into Powell. Despite having many friends in common they did not, so Powell said, know each other 'at all well'. He assumed, reasonably enough, that Pryce-Jones was a dilettante, so it was with some surprise, shortly after the war, that he learnt of his ambition to edit the *TLS*.

Whether, as Powell thought, Pryce-Jones's appointment was a tribute to his willpower; or whether, as others have alleged, it resulted from his kinship with the Astors, who then owned *The Times*, the result was benefi-cial to Powell. While he was still editor-designate Pryce-Jones offered him the job of chief novel reviewer. On taking over the chair he invited him to become fiction reviews editor as well, at a retainer of £350 a year. Although an important position on the paper, this made few demands on Powell's

1. Maud Mary
Wells-Dymoke.

2. Lieutenant-Colonel Philip Powell.

3. The 'little pixie'. Powell, front row left, as a fag at Eton.

4. Detail from group photo at Old Boys' match to mark the retirement of
A.M. Goodhart in 1924. The dapper figure on Powell's left is Bill Allen.

Spring

Summer

Autumn

Winter

5. Drawing by Powell for *Cherwell*.

6. 'One is said, for some reason, to
"have a good time in The Tins".'
Hubert Duggan as a subaltern
in the Life Guards.

7. Constant Lambert.

8. Nina Hamnett.

9. John Heygate on the ski slopes.

"A nip in time saves nine".

10.   Henry Lamb's portrait of Powell, now in the National Portrait Gallery.

11. Powell with Tequila
bottle 'down Mexico way'.

12. Violet in her uniform as a
volunteer nurse.

13. 'It's a tailor's war.' Osbert Lancaster's drawing of the United Service club in 1941.

14. The Café Royal in wartime. Those present include Cyril Connolly, Lys Lubbock, Peter Quennell, Barbara Skelton, Tom Driberg, Stephen Spender, Brian Howard and Osbert Lancaster, who did the drawing.

15. Monty putting the attachés in the picture. Colonel Carlisle is behind the French General. Powell, wearing beret, is in the background.

16. Powell and Malcolm Muggeridge outside the National Gallery. People sometimes thought they were brothers.

17. The Chantry seen from the rear.

18. Barbara Skelton and Cyril Connolly at Oak Cottage.

19. 'We might go straight into lunch.'
Widmerpool as seen by Mark Boxer.

20. 'Human beings aren't subtle enough to play
their part.' X. Trapnel as seen by Mark Boxer.

21. The Powells at a Cairo nightclub.

22. Powell on the sofa at
The Chantry's library.
Photograph by Chris
Ridley.

23. Powell at his desk.
Photograph by John
Monagan.

time. In the words of Pryce-Jones's deputy, Arthur Crook, 'Tony would turn up at the office on Thursday morning, sift through the novels and assign reviewers, inquire about the latest gossip and then go off to lunch with Alan Pryce-Jones at the Travellers. He never attended editorial conferences or anything like that.'[15] Since Powell was also paid a minimum of three guineas for his weekly novel review, and had his pick of unwanted review copies to flog to Gaston's, he could contemplate the future with more confidence than at any time since his return from America ten years before.

As a young man Powell had proposed that one way of ending controversy over who should be buried in Poets' Corner would be to inter an Unknown Author there and have done with it. In much the same vein he and Malcolm Muggeridge agreed that ribbons should be awarded for reviewing certain books, as for military campaigns – the Priestley Star, the Galsworthy Cross and so on. Powell gave a lot of thought to the business of reviewing, though some of what he said was contradictory. For instance in a letter to the novelist Jocelyn Brooke he complained about 'the sheer incompetence of reviewers – favourable as well as unfavourable, so far as one's own notices are concerned – in the way that they never give a thought to the technical problems that any novelist has to face. It is like someone saying, "This is a nice plum-pudding, but there is no taste of salmon" and never pausing to think that if there were a taste of salmon, it would not be the same dish, indeed the plum-pudding aspect might be seriously prejudiced.'[16] He thought non-novelists made this mistake all the time because they were incapable of seeing things from the novelist's point of view. 'The books people write are the books they write,' he told an interviewer. 'It's no good reviewers trying to rewrite them or address them in terms that are very different from how they actually are.'[17] Yet he also admitted that one of the hazards of reviewing fiction for a novelist was that you were always conscious that you would have tackled the story in a different way.

At that time all reviews in the *TLS* were unsigned. Before he became editor Pryce-Jones told his friend James Lees-Milne that he intended to change this, but it was not to be, and he ended up defending the practice when it came under attack during his last years as editor. Still, anonymity when added to the rather modest fees the paper paid was a deterrent to famous names like Evelyn Waugh or Cyril Connolly becoming contributors, so Powell had to recruit his team of reviewers from the ranks of the second eleven and below. He chose well, as Arthur Crook, who did not care for him personally, admitted. Crook, who began work on the paper as a fourteen-year-old messenger boy and succeeded Pryce-Jones as editor, never warmed to Powell because he was 'such a snob. He admitted it himself. He was always dropping names and used to glory in the fact that his favourite bedside reading was *Burke* and *Debrett*.'[18] But Crook acknowledged Powell's skill as a talent-spotter. 'He brought in people like Malcolm Muggeridge, Julian Symons, Francis Wyndham and Alan Ross. Another of his finds was [Julian] Maclaren-Ross. He was a very tricky customer because you had to try and get copy out of him before he flogged the books he was supposed to review. Tony usually managed to do this.'[19] (Crook may be doing Maclaren-Ross an injustice. Others assert that however desperate his situation, his journalism was almost always on time. Novels were another matter. He took the advance and ran, believing that it was permissible to extort every penny possible from a publisher because '[h]e'll have a country house and polo ponies when you are still borrowing the price of a drink in Fitzrovia'.[20])

Of no fixed abode, his few possessions in and out of hock, Maclaren-Ross was a victim of what Dylan Thomas, with whom he'd worked during the war on documentary films, called 'the capital punishment' – life in London for those whose means never matched their ends. This is apparent from the answer he gave to a *Horizon* questionnaire, in which writers were asked, among other things, how much they needed to live on. 'A writer needs all he can lay his hands on in order to keep alive,' he replied,

> How much he should actually have depends on the writer himself: his tastes and habits ...If he is a drinker he shouldn't have to worry whether he drinks beer, or spirits or wine, though he shouldn't necessarily have enough to get sozzled every night. If he is a smoker he shouldn't have to buy Woodbines if he prefers Perfectos. If he wants to buy a book he should be able to buy it, not wait until it is sent to him for review or lent to him by a friend. If he doesn't drink, smoke, read books or go to the cinema, then he almost certainly has other vices, or else a wife or mistress to spend money on; well, he should have enough to spend. A writer's standard of living should be at least as high as that of a solicitor, or any other professional man. I am a metropolitan man and I need a minimum of £20 a week to live on, given the present cost of living, and that's not including rent.

Characteristically, Maclaren-Ross concluded with this appeal: '[P]lease pay promptly for this contribution, because I am broke.'[21]

Powell had met Maclaren-Ross through Bobbie Roberts, a disreputable old friend of his, said literally to bore the pants off women, who contributed to Lushington in *Afternoon Men* and Bagshaw in *Books Do Furnish a Room*. Like Roberts, Maclaren-Ross was a great pub man, though he valued the company as much as the drink, being always in need of an audience; and since pubs were oases of cheer in the dingy post-war London landscape Powell saw rather more of him at this period than might otherwise have been the case. As a talker Maclaren-Ross was in the Ancient Mariner class, mesmerising his audience with his esoteric monologues on pre-war novels and films, the plots of which he had by heart. Malcolm Muggeridge recorded his impressions of him in his Diary:

> [Tony and I] discussed a writer named Maclaren-Ross, at whose hands Tony suffers a good deal of boredom. The trouble with him, we agreed, was his egotism, which acts on conversation like the Sirocco. When his wife was present, I said, his egotism was worse. Tony agreed and said she collaborated with, or acted, like a Quisling towards his egotism ...Every man, I said, gets the bores he deserves, and types like Maclaren-Ross are his speciality.[22]

Muggeridge was wrong in one particular: the 'Quisling' was not Maclaren-Ross's wife, but the latest in a succession of girlfriends who, for a season, would love and succour him. But he was right in other respects. Powell was quite capable of disengaging himself from bores – or other disagreeable persons – if he chose. But his curiosity about people was such that he was prepared to suffer a good deal of tedium, discomfort and even offence in order to satisfy it. As with Powell, so with Jenkins, who finds Ted Jeavons 'oddly interesting' despite his reputation as 'a dull dog'.

When he wasn't holding forth at the bar Maclaren-Ross wrote with sufficient dash and originality for well-wishers to suppose that if only he were a little less rackety he might earn a decent living by his pen (*le mot juste*: he wrote in longhand, minutely but legibly, with no corrections). He was versatile and prolific, turning out novels, short stories, radio plays and film scripts in addition to literary journalism. Evelyn Waugh thought his Army stories, *The Stuff To Give The Troops*, 'deliciously funny' despite their heroes' reluctance 'to do their bit'. He was also acknowledged as a very skilful parodist, in which capacity Powell regularly employed him when editing the book pages at *Punch*. And Powell would certainly not have chosen him to write a *TLS* 'middle' on *A Question of Upbringing* unless he had complete confidence in him as a reviewer.

Maclaren-Ross was a fan of Powell's early novels, but this cannot explain the trouble Powell went to on his behalf. What Mrs Erdleigh says about Jenkins comes to mind: 'You are thought cold, but you possess deep affections, sometimes for people worthless in themselves.' Maclaren-Ross was certainly not worthless, but neither was he the sort of character you would expect Powell to put himself out for. Yet this is what he did. In January 1947, only a few months after meeting him, Powell wrote in support of his appeal to the Royal Literary Fund for a grant, stressing his 'extremely straitened circumstances'.[23] Maclaren-Ross received £100. Two and a half years later he again wrote to the

Fund on Maclaren-Ross's behalf. He also arranged that he be paid in cash, on the nail, for his contributions to the *TLS* – no mean feat. Later, at *Punch*, a problem arose when some duns traced Maclaren-Ross to the magazine and camped on the doorstep, alarming the proprietor. Aware that without his income from *Punch* Maclaren-Ross would probably go under, Powell refused to sack him unless ordered to do so; instead, he would hand over the money in a pub, either to Maclaren-Ross himself or his current girlfriend. He tried to find other work for him as well. In a letter dated 2 May 1956, he asked Maclaren-Ross if he fancied reviewing for the *Daily Telegraph*, because someone he'd known at Oxford, H.D. Ziman, 'commonly known as "Z"', was now the Literary Editor: 'If you do [want to review for them], I should make it clear that you don't *expect anything*, but are just doing it in case anything should turn up which he might find convenient to send you.'[24]

A year later Powell performed another service for Maclaren-Ross, appearing as a character witness when he was hauled up before the beak at Bow Street Magistrates' Court under the Debtors' Act. Whatever he said must have helped, because instead of being made bankrupt Maclaren-Ross was merely put on probation and ordered to settle his debt by instalments. A few months after this Muggeridge gave up the editorship of *Punch*, and the following January Powell was sacked as Literary Editor. In the absence of professional incentives, contact between Powell and Maclaren-Ross then ceased. Six years later, aged fifty-two, Maclaren-Ross died suddenly of a heart attack. But by what Powell called 'one of those unforeseen turns of the wheel' he had just appeared in a television programme called *Writers during the War* which was produced by Powell's elder son Tristram.

Powell was heard to say, 'You have to bear certain crosses in life. Once you've chosen yours, you have to bear them without complaining.' Perhaps this is how one should interpret his relationship with Julian Maclaren-Ross. Nor did his loyalty go unrewarded, because by quitting the stage when he did Maclaren-Ross more than repaid him for all his support, since it was now possible for Powell to depict him, with knobs on, as X. Trapnel, a liberty inconceivable while Maclaren-Ross was still alive. Powell gave Trapnel a beard, whereas Maclaren-Ross was clean-shaven, and exchanged the latter's teddy-bear overcoat for a dyed RAF greatcoat. But no one who had met Maclaren-Ross, and many who only knew him by reputation, could have failed to penetrate the disguise:

> He looked about thirty, tall, dark, with a beard ...Although the spring weather was still decidedly chilly, he was dressed in a pale ochre-coloured tropical suit, almost transparent in texture, on top of which he wore an overcoat, black and

belted like Quiggin's Partisan number, but of cloth, for some reason familiarly official in cut …The walking stick struck a completely different note. Its wood unremarkable, but the knob, ivory, more likely bone, crudely carved in the shape of a skull, was rather like old Skerrett's head at Erridge's funeral. This stick clearly bulked large in Trapnel equipment. It set the tone far more than the RAF greatcoat or tropical suit. For the rest, he was hatless, wore a dark blue sports shirt frayed at the collar, an emerald green tie patterned with naked women, was shod in grey suede brothel-creepers.

The general effect, chiefly caused by the stick, was of the Eighteen-Nineties, the *décadence*; putting things at their least eclectic, a contemptuous rejection of currently popular male modes in grey flannel demob suits with porkpie hats, bowler-crowned British Warms, hooded duffels, or even those varied outfits like Quiggin's, to be seen here and there, that suggested recent service in the *maquis*. All such were rejected.

Two points are worth making here. Powell used Trapnel as a mouthpiece for some of his theories on the novel, notably this riposte to those who accused him of drawing too many characters and situations from life. 'People can't get it right about Naturalism,' says Trapnel:

> They think if a writer like me writes the sort of books I do, it's because that's easier, or necessary nowadays. You just look round at what's happening and shove it all down. They can't understand that's not in the least the case. It's just as selective, just as artificial, as if the characters were kings and queens speaking in blank verse … [I]f you took a tape-recording* of two people having a grind it might truly be called Naturalism, it might be funny, it might be sexually exciting, it might even be beautiful, it wouldn't be art. It would just be two people having a grind … Human beings aren't subtle enough to play their part. That's where art comes in.

All of which is fair enough; indeed Norman Douglas made the same point when he said that 'a human character, however convincing and true to itself, must be licked into shape'. But it strikes me as paradoxical that we should hear it from someone whose antecedents Powell freely acknowledged – unless of course Powell expects his readers to see 'where art comes in', a tall order unless you knew Maclaren-Ross well enough to distinguish between him and Trapnel.

Which brings me to my second point. Powell was asked point-blank by Maurice Cranston whether Trapnel was based on Maclaren-Ross during a recorded discussion they had before an audience in 1971, the year *Books Do Furnish a Room* was published. Powell admitted the resemblance, but

---

* Surely an anachronism. Tape-recorders weren't around in 1948, when Trapnel says this.

insisted that too much should not be read into this. He cited the example of Proust, who used 'great chunks' of Comte Robert de Montesquiou in fashioning Monsieur de Charlus, 'yet Charlus is a very different person from Montesquiou.' Powell then added that unlike Trapnel, Maclaren-Ross didn't have a sword-stick. 'But he did,' came a voice from the audience. 'Well, I never knew that,' said Powell, who sounded genuinely surprised.[25] Unfortunately the recording ends there, so we don't know whether Powell went on to say that of course he knew Maclaren-Ross carried a silver-knobbed stick – like dark glasses it was an essential prop – but he'd no reason to suppose it was a sword-stick. The question is addressed here by Maclaren-Ross's biographer, Paul Willetts:

> In the late 1940s Maclaren-Ross used to tease Walter Allen by saying that his cane was really a sword-stick that he carried in case his burly friend John Davenport attacked him. By about late 1953 he had, however, acquired the real thing. How long he retained it is another matter, though, as he frequently lost or pawned his various canes.[26]

*

Throughout this depressing epoch of iron curtains and iron rations Powell had been meditating on what sort of novel he might write when the Muse rejoined him. Even before the war it had become apparent to him that he would always struggle with plots and that there was a limit to the number of times he could recycle the sort of characters who interested him. The solution he hit on – to write a long novel consisting of at least six volumes – would allow him to operate on a much broader front than he could hope to cover in 80,000 words. This had obvious advantages for him as a writer, but what would a reader make of it? For unlike C.P. Snow or, later, Simon Raven, Powell was not proposing to write a sequence whose individual volumes could stand on their own. He was planning a serial novel whose instalments would arrive at two- or three-yearly intervals. The disadvantages of such an approach are succinctly expressed in A.N. Wilson's novel, *Daughters of Albion*, itself part of a sequence called *The Lampitt Papers*.

> The *fleuve* novels have to be bloody lucky to make sense. You pick up Volume Five or Volume Seven and ask yourself, 'Who the f-ing hell *are* all these people?' It's like arriving at a dinner party a couple of hours late and not being introduced to the other guests and spending the whole evening picking up the fag-end of their conversations.[27]

The person who says this is a publisher, and having been a publisher himself Powell would have understood his point of view, even if he didn't share it. There was also the risk that he would run out of steam, like Richard Hughes or, more recently, Andrew Motion, both of whom were unable to finish multi-volumed projects. But as Powell said on more than one occasion, 'You'll never get anywhere unless you have a certain confidence in yourself, and it wasn't as if I hadn't written a novel before.' In his interview with Paul Gaston he compared himself to Queen Victoria: 'It was always said, you know, that [she] never looked round when she sat down because she knew that someone would push a chair there. I think you have really got to behave like that.'[28]

Although the entries are undated, the chronology of Powell's Notebook is not indecipherable and you can see that well before he ever embarked on *Dance* he had begun to amass material. For instance opposite the page on which the name of Widmerpool is noted there is this quip from *Books Do Furnish a Room*: 'The only positive thing about him was his Wasserman test.'[29] A page or two later there is a reference to 'Blackhead, a civil servant', being 'German some generations back' and two pages after that these titles: *A Question of Upbringing* and *The Valley of Bones*. What you might expect to find, but don't, is any mention of *A Dance to the Music of Time*, either as a title or a painting.

Powell is vague about when he experienced his epiphany in the Wallace Collection; it was, he writes, 'at a fairly early stage'. But he is clear about the impact Poussin's 'curiously hypnotic' painting had on him. Whoever the four figures might be – the Seasons, as he thought, or Man's destiny, as the Catalogue Raisonné has it – they were dancing to Time's tune. 'I knew all at once that Poussin had expressed at least one important aspect of what the novel must be.'

> The image of Time brought thoughts of mortality: of human beings, facing outwards like the Seasons, moving hand in hand in intricate measure: stepping slowly, methodically, sometimes a trifle awkwardly, in evolutions that take recognisable shape: or breaking into seemingly meaningless gyrations, while partners disappear only to reappear again, once more giving pattern to the spectacle: unable to control the melody, unable, perhaps, to control the dance.

Powell found the figure of Time 'extraordinarily sinister'.[30] Myself, I am struck by the contrast between his aged head and muscular torso. No doubt this was a convention of the period; but given his reservations about Perugino's Saint Sebastian – too young and handsome to be a hardboiled Roman NCO – one would like to hear Mr Deacon's thoughts on the subject. The other thing that surprised me about the painting when I saw it for the first time was its size. Reproductions suggest a large canvas. In fact it measures only 2ft 6in by 4ft.

Another important decision Powell had to make was how to tell the story. Like Proust, he opted for a narrator. But unlike Proust's Marcel, Nick Jenkins is more of an observer than a participant. His trip down memory lane is not activated by anything so subjective as the taste of a *madeleine* dunked in tea but by what he sees through a window. The argument in favour of a narrator like Jenkins was given by Scott Fitzgerald's editor, Maxwell Perkins. Applauding Fitzgerald's employment, in *The Great Gatsby*, of a narrator who is 'more of a spectator than an actor', he wrote:

> [T]his puts the reader upon a point of observation on a higher level than that on which the characters stand and at a distance that gives perspective. In no other way could your irony have been so immensely effective, nor the reader feel so strongly at times the strangeness of human circumstances in a vast heedless universe.[31]

Perkins could just as easily have said this to Powell. After all, irony is one of Jenkins's hallmarks. And 'a vast heedless universe' is how life sometimes seems to him. As Powell remarked to Jocelyn Brooke, 'One of the difficult things in a book is to deal with the absolute lack of interest human beings do in fact feel for each other in daily life.'[32]

When people drew attention to the similarities between Jenkins and his creator Powell would agree that they had lived similar sorts of lives,

> because it's much easier that way. Supposing, for the sake of argument, I wrote from the point of view of a surgeon. Well, I don't really know what a surgeon's life is like. And although I could read it up, I'd probably make some fearful howler about what it *feels* like. So having decided to do the thing in the first person, which in itself is a decision – one might have done it in other ways – I came to the conclusion that if you try and avoid what is roughly speaking your own point of view, it simply comes out another way. And so it's much simpler to write about someone who is roughly speaking the same sort of person, has roughly speaking had the same sort of life ... but that doesn't necessarily mean that all the things that happen to him have happened to me.[33]

But Powell knew how difficult it was for readers to make that distinction. When, in 1962, his American publishers Little, Brown published an omnibus edition of the first three volumes of *Dance*, he declined to write an introduction, 'because in a book told in the first person there is always particular delicacy about the intrusion of the personality of the author. I should be very unwilling to sign anything like an introduction even with initials for that reason, as I think it compromises the theoretically autobiographical nature of the narrative.'[34]

Jenkins, like Powell, is an essentially conventional person – priggish, even, as he sometimes admits – whose blinkers come off when curiosity – 'which makes the world go round' – gets the better of him. He wants to know what makes people tick – other people, that is, since he is no keener on self-analysis than was Powell. But by analysing other people and their motives he does, of course, discover a few things about himself. 'You must try to understand life,' Mrs Erdleigh tells him, an injunction that recalls the novel's opening, with its sombre allusion to the forces that shape our lives. Considered from this angle, and remembering the high regard in which Powell held *The Autobiography of Henry Adams*, 'The Education of Nicholas Jenkins' does not seem too far-fetched as an alternative title – were it not that Jenkins, like Powell, was clearly brought up to believe that it was ill-mannered to draw attention to oneself. He holds up a mirror to other people, but only rarely to himself – and then obliquely. We never see him plain. This is why, when Mark Boxer designed the covers for the Fontana paperback edition of *Dance*, he omitted Jenkins from his gallery of protagonists.

What is distinctive about Jenkins is his aloof yet tolerant tone of voice, pungently evoked here by Simon Raven, who admired Powell's novels, but deprecated his syntax:

> It's the tone of a gentleman's club, really, with a slight breath – not exactly of the *slums* creeping in – but a breath of corruption. It's a bit like sitting in, say, White's or Brooks's, and every now and then somebody opens the window and a rather nasty smell – not exactly of shit – well, yes, of shit, but also of corpses – comes into the room. And somebody makes a polite observation as to the nature, respectively, of shit and corpses and closes the window for the time being. That's how it strikes me.[35]

This also illustrates the crucial difference in approach between Raven and Powell. Raven is explicit. Powell is implicit. In Raven's fiction the source of the nasty smell – a steaming turd, a festering cadaver or whatever – is there on the carpet for all to see. In Powell's fiction we never really establish what it is or where it comes from, only that it stinks. Raven's characters simply ring for a servant to clear up the mess, following which they settle back in their armchairs as before. He is, for all his lurid effects, a cosy writer. Powell, most emphatically, is not. His characters will probably have to live with that smell whether the window is open or not because it may, after all, be the drains (but try telling that to the club secretary). 'The world is never a very nice place,' he said more than once. 'Tony's far more melancholy and serious than I am,' was Raven's comment.

Powell's own take on his narrative was that he was 'telling the story over the dinner table',[36] which as Jocelyn Brooke observed was also what Norman Douglas set out to do. Powell met Douglas from time to time in the Forties, praised his 'powerful and insatiable intelligence' and 'no-nonsense' approach to life, and hoped that the government would see fit to grant him a Civil List pension (which it didn't).[37] But if Douglas was an influence he doesn't say so. It was Aubrey, with his tremendous 'grasp of character' and delight in anecdote, he wanted to emulate. In his Introduction to *John Aubrey and His Friends* he writes, '[T]o the question: "What are the English like?" worse answers might be given than: "Read *Aubrey's Lives* and you will see".'[38] Many, myself included, would say the same about *Dance*.

Powell thought the English presented special problems for a novelist. Whereas the Russians and Americans – and to a certain extent the French – could 'throw somebody onto the canvas, so to speak, and everybody knows what they're talking about ... I think here everybody has to be described much more. You do get these extraordinary variations.'[39] Jenkins wrestles with the implications of this while waiting in vain for Mark Members at the Ritz:

> I began to brood on the complexity of writing a novel about English life, a subject difficult enough to handle with authenticity even of a crudely natural-istic sort, even more to convey the inner truth of the things observed ... Intricacies of social life make English habits unyielding to simplification, while understatement and irony – in which all classes of the island converse – upset the normal emphasis of reported speech.
>
> How, I asked myself, could a writer attempt to describe in a novel such a young man as Mark Members, for example, possessing so much in common with myself, yet so different?

There was, however, one English habit that worked to his advantage: boarding school. Faced with the problem of explaining how four such disparate characters as Jenkins, Stringham, Templer and Widmerpool should know each other, he had only to arrange for them to be in the same house at school. And of these four it is Widmerpool, the embodiment of the 'black Misfortune' Thomas Gray alludes to in his *Ode*,* who engages the reader's attention throughout. Later, when Widmerpool's machinations had

---

*'Alas, regardless of their doom/The little victims play/No sense have they of ills to come/Nor care beyond today/Yet see how all around 'em wait/The Ministers of human fate/And black Misfortune's baleful train!'

become the talk of the town, Powell appeared to take against him. 'Now I know how Frankenstein felt,' he's supposed to have groaned after yet another fan buttonholed him about his monster. But as he admitted to Evelyn Waugh, 'Widmerpool was planned from the start to be the main character.'[40]

Waugh was one of those – the majority, I guess – who could not get enough of Widmerpool. In a letter to Ann Fleming he pronounced *Casanova's Chinese Restaurant* 'a sad disappointment' because there were 'only three pages of Widmerpool'.[41] The contrary view was put by another admirer of Powell, Julian Symons. Reviewing *The Kindly Ones* in the *TLS* he said that the danger in writing a series of books was that they would appeal to the wrong sort of readers – '[those] who are not concerned in the least with artistic values' – for the wrong sort of reasons, e.g. who's marrying who and what's old so-and-so up to now. 'It is difficult, however,' argued Symons, 'to think of any of these six books in terms of: "Is Widmerpool in this one?" Their structure is so intricate that such a question is almost meaningless.'[42] Two weeks later there were letters in the *TLS* saying how wrong he was. So Symons wrote back saying that if people did go about asking each other, 'Is Widmerpool in this one?', this underlined 'the terrible dangers to which any novelist who embarked on a series exposed himself'.[43]

There was one other question people asked about Widmerpool: Who is he? I propose to try and answer this by following Powell's example and shaking the branches of his family tree. The ancestor who falls to earth is Major Joseph Widmerpoole (*sic*), a Cromwellian Captain of Horse who served under Colonel Hutchinson, commander of the Nottingham garrison during the Civil War. Hutchinson's wife Lucy kept a diary that Powell read while researching Aubrey. This is the entry that caught his eye:

> A man of good extraction, but reduced to a small fortune, in whom had declined all the splendour of an old house … he had a good discretion and tho' he were older than all the rest, yet was so humble as to be content to come in the rear of them, as having through the declining of his family, the slenderness of his estate and the parsimony of his nature, less interest in the country.[44]

Time has not revived the Widmerpool fortunes. The Widmerpool estate, on the Notts and Leicester border, is now owned by the AA, and there are no Widmerpools in the local phonebook. There was, it is true, a race run at Leicester some thirty years ago for the Widmerpool plate; but it was a one-off, named after the village of Widmerpool, not the character. All in all I think I might feel a bit aggrieved if I were the spirit of Major Widmerpoole. He must rue the day that Widmerpool's grandfather changed his name from Geddes. We, on the other hand, should be grateful to that upwardly-mobile Scot. Widmerpool by any other name would smell not half so fishy.

But Widmerpool owes more to the seventeenth century than his name. Jenkins says somewhere that Widmerpool reminds him of Pepys without his wig, both of them wearing the same 'obdurate, put-upon, bad-tempered expression'. And surely this could be Widmerpool at his most insufferable:

> A better instance of a squeamish and disobligeing, slighting, insolent prowd fellow, perhaps cant be found ... No reason satisfies him. But he overweens and cuts some sower faces that would turn the milk in a faire ladie's breast.[45]

That was Gwyn, Lord Oxford's secretary, an old enemy of Aubrey who is the model for a character called Sir Fastidious Overween in his unfinished play, *Country Revell*. Powell singles him out, saying that his 'disagreeable demeanour is conveyed over the years as keenly as if we had encountered him only a few hours ago'.[46]

Most people, however, were convinced that Widmerpool was drawn from life, a theory endorsed by Powell's brother-in-law, Lord Longford, who said that he was the model.* Powell denied this as he did all the other suggestions put forward, and the secret of Widmerpool's identity – if he *had* an identity – seemed likely to perish with him. Then in 1991 Desmond Seward, in his social history of Brooks's, identified Denis Capel-Dunn as both Alick Dru's Papal Bun *and* Widmerpool. Powell conceded that he might be on to something without, however, acknowledging that this put another promising candidate, Sir Reginald Manningham-Buller (later Lord Dilhorne), in the clear. The latter, variously nicknamed 'Bullyingham-Manner' and 'Bullying-Manner', was said by Powell to have cut a distinctly unappealing figure at Eton, where he got a master sacked for sending an indiscreet note to a junior boy.

Myself, I think the urge to unmask Widmerpool misses the point. He is better understood as 'a hero of our time', like Lermontov's character Pechorin. Pechorin is the product of his age, an age of nihilism when the golden lads of Russia lived fast and often died young, as does Pechorin – and as did Lermontov himself. Widmerpool is also the product of his age. Not the age when we first meet him, the Twenties, but the age when Powell conceived him: the age of austerity, of planning and controls, when it

---

* Lord Longford also claimed to be Erridge, prompting Powell to protest: 'Come off it, Frank. How many characters do you want to be – the whole bloody lot?!'

seemed to High Tories like Powell that Widmerpool and his sort really were, as Hartley Shawcross boasted, 'the masters now'. And who were Widmerpool's sort? Powell gave the answer in a review he wrote in June 1946:

> Capitalism is said to be declining and its heir, instead of being Socialism, is to be the 'managerial' caste; and it is certainly true that the typical Russophil of today is now no longer the Left-Wing intellectual so much as the businessman or power-politician.[47]

Powell was referring to a long piece by George Orwell, who explained that this new breed of Russophils were

> not managers in the narrow sense, but scientists, technicians, teachers, journalists, broadcasters, bureaucrats, professional politicians: in general middling people who feel themselves cramped by a system that is still partly aristocratic, and are hungry for more power and more prestige.[48]

C.P. Snow called such people 'New Men', and reading some of Widmerpool's more turgid pronouncements I've sometimes wondered if by chance he had escaped from one of Snow's novels. But in fact Orwell's piece was about James Burnham's book, *The Managerial Revolution*, an apocalyptic tract whose totalitarian world-view Orwell would extrapolate in *Nineteen Eighty Four*. Burnham's book is largely forgotten now, but in the early Forties it had the same sort of impact as Francis Fukuyama's *The End of History* had in the 1990s. His thesis was that the future belonged to managers; so a state like Nazi Germany, which had harnessed this new social force, would come out on top. Later, when it became apparent that the Nazis would lose the war, he plumped for the USSR instead, precisely the course charted by Widmerpool. In both cases the motive is power-worship, the virus that Orwell detected in the bloodstream of all absolutist intellectuals like Burnham (who starting out as a Trot, subsequently became a rabid right-winger).

Of course Powell could have ended all speculation about Widmerpool by taking a leaf out of Flaubert's book. When people asked him who Madame Bovary was, he replied: 'Madame Bovary, c'est moi.' But for some reason Powell could not bring himself to follow suit.

11

Invitation to the Dance

'I decided that the thing to do was to produce a really large work about all the things I was interested in – the whole of one's life in fact ...'

Anthony Powell

'The writer whose direct experience gives him one satisfactory novel ... in fifty years is very lucky.'

Kingsley Amis

In January 1948, to Powell's delight, Malcolm Muggeridge returned to London from Washington and resumed his old job as a leader-writer on the *Daily Telegraph*. He and his family took a large flat at Cambridge Gate, just round the corner from the Powells, and it is clear from his Diaries that for the next three years barely a day went by when he and Powell did not speak. A favourite activity for them both was to walk round Regent's Park discussing *Dance* and, in particular, what lay in store for the characters, an exercise that reminded Muggeridge of his days as a spymaster in Lourenço Marques:

Had the time come for A to seduce B? And if C got to know, how would he react? And D – what, if anything, would she feel if C, as he was bound to, told her about it? By the time our walk was over, I had to jerk myself back into my own identity, so absorbed had I become in these fictional beings.[1]

'I want readers to react to my characters as people,' Powell used to say. Muggeridge was probably the first to do so.

When they were introduced in 1938 Muggeridge had surprised Powell by his apparent lack of ambition. There could now be no question that he wanted to 'get on'. He had had a good war, emerging with the Légion d'honneur and the Croix de Guerre, and was already being spoken of as a future Fleet Street editor. He was also literary advisor to Heinemann and, significantly, had begun to take an interest in broadcasting, whose technique, he noted, was 'entirely different from journalism or public speaking'.[2] Only as a novelist had he failed to make the grade; and while

177

this may have come between him and Powell later on, immediately after the war it didn't signify: they were as close as it's possible for married men in their forties to be.

Discussing Powell with his other great friend, Hugh Kingsmill, Muggeridge said that 'part of his extraordinary charm lay in the fact that all his tastes and opinions, even his conduct, are all defined. This makes him something of a sport in this age.'[3] For instance when a rather flatulent illustrated survey of modern British poets was published Muggeridge wrote, 'Tony gave me a brief paragraph, in his inimitable way, on all the characters concerned.'[4] Elsewhere in his Diaries he refers to a call Powell had paid on his parents: 'Tony gave one of his vivid descriptions of life in the Weybridge private hotel where his parents and other elderly, fairly well off people live.'[5] And on another occasion he writes that he was 'much amused by a remark of Tony's that some people he'd met at a cocktail party were "gaffer's luck", after the opening of *Our Mutual Friend*, when the discovery of a corpse in the river is described as "gaffer's luck"'.[6]

Muggeridge shared Powell's love of gossip and, being in Fleet Street, had plenty to offer himself, particularly about the misdeeds of 'those set in authority over us', a favourite phrase of his. 'The only fun of journalism,' he said, 'is that it puts you in contact with the eminent without being under the necessity to admire them or take them seriously. It is the ideal profession for those who find power fascinating and its exercise abhorrent.'[7] In much the same way that Moreland and Maclintick compare Don Juan and Casanova, he and Powell used to discuss the difference between rank and power. Those who think of Muggeridge as an impish iconoclast may be surprised to learn that at this period he agreed with Powell that it was 'far less pernicious socially that people should be snobbish in a hierarchical sense than in an egotistical sense'.[8] He endorsed 'Tony's general position' that the old order imposed obligations on those at the top that egalitarian societies didn't recognise and quoted, with approval, his dictum that Liberalism** was 'a force unconsciously seeking anarchy'.[9]

Both of them soon had a chance to stand up and be counted – literally. It so happened that the Central London branch of the National Union of Journalists, to which they belonged, had through the apathy of its members been taken over by a small Communist clique. Determined to spike their

---

* Hugh Kingsmill's description of such people was 'Excrement living off increment'.

** Although unsympathetic to Liberalism, Powell was not, he used to stress, a totalitarian. In a review of Curzio Malaparte's *The Skin* (TLS, 9 January 1953) he quoted approvingly Malaparte's definition of a totalitarian State: 'a State in which everything that is not forbidden is compulsory'.

guns, Muggeridge persuaded Powell to accompany him to the branch meetings. Although on record as saying, after one particularly long-winded session, that 'outside Broadmoor, it would difficult to imagine any more fatuous proceedings',[10] Powell did his bit. Another insurgent, H.D. Ziman, paid him this tribute in 1971:

> To fume through a union meeting lasting anything from two to five hours, simply in order to vote down some nefarious motion must have meant to a creative writer, who also had administrative duties, a gross sacrifice of his time to the public good. He did not flinch, and has not yet recouped himself by any trade union conversation piece in *The Music of Time*.[11]

In *God's Apology*, his story of the friendship between Muggeridge, Hugh Kingsmill and Hesketh Pearson, Richard Ingrams writes that so influenced by some of Kingsmill's ideas did Muggeridge become 'that afterwards he could never be sure when he was quoting Kingsmill and when speaking for himself'.[12] I think something similar happened with Powell and Muggeridge, though who influenced whom is not always apparent because they were generally in accord. The phrase 'We agreed that' occurs all the time in Muggeridge's Diaries with regard to Powell: 'We agreed that the only thing one wanted to do as a writer was to succeed in conveying a sense of reality' (4 July 1948). And: 'We agreed that the essence of a bore is that he takes the greatest pleasure in telling you at great lengths what you know already' (1 September 1948). Discussing Scott Fitzgerald, whom Powell was doing for the *TLS*, they 'agreed that there was no complete English equivalent to *The Great Gatsby* because in this country the money mystique was mixed up with other things like politics and snobbishness etc ...whereas in America it was pure and undefiled' (29 January 1948). And when there was talk of who could edit a successor to *Horizon*, they 'agreed that it would have to be someone who belonged to that nonsensical world' (26 November 1949).

They took particular pleasure in recording the physiognomy of power-addicts. Muggeridge thought that 'power appears to make people bloated physically as well as morally' (12 February 1948), while Powell, he reports, thought love of power gave people 'a grey putty look' (27 March 1948). Echoes of these sentiments occur in *Dance*, and there is a direct link to Gypsy Jones in what Muggeridge says here about the physical traits of female power maniacs: 'untidy clothes, whispy hair, grubby appearance, slight flush' (20 October 1950). Muggeridge also notes how suitable it is that Sir Stafford Cripps's wife should be the Eno's Fruit Salts heiress, 'because Cripps, like all power-maniacs, is a chronic dyspeptic' (9 February 1948). So of course is Widmerpool, though he puts his faith in pills rather than Eno's.

To say that Muggeridge played Boswell to Powell's Johnson would be to distort their relationship. The fact remains that no other friend of Powell's recorded so much of what he said and did. Here are some examples:

George [Orwell] and Connolly, Tony said, were really like two sides of the same face – one lean and ugly and the other fat and ugly; one phoneyly abstemious and the other phoneyly self-indulgent (23 March 1949).

Tony insisted that marriage was essentially mercenary in concept, and that X's realisation of snobbish and financial aspirations was almost the only element of sanity in his life (8 July 1949).

Tony said that George IV had had the idea of making naval officers wear red waistcoats, but had given it up, remarking: 'Dress them how you will, you can't make them gentlemen' (17 December 1949).

Tony made a very good point that the reason why Churchill's memoirs, like all memoirs of men of action, were so tedious, is that the convention has to be sustained that all the people concerned with him in the war were diligent, conscientious, honest, etc., etc. Writing about writers – e.g. Proust or Stendhal, this is not in the least necessary, so that their lives and adventures are always more interesting (12 February 1949).

Tony told me that fifteen food parcels which the Pakenhams had mysteriously received from America had, in fact, been sent to them by David Astor. As he said, 'It is extraordinary how good the rich are to each other' (2 March 1948).

Tony said he thought Walter Pater would have made a better General than Patton (19 August 1948).

Tony said he regarded the row now going on about 'modern art' as a very good indication of returning to normality (29 April 1949)

Modern art, about which Muggeridge 'knew nothing and cared nothing',[13] was one subject on which he and Powell agreed to disagree. But when he was booked to appear on *The Critics*, a weekly radio programme whose remit included current exhibitions, Muggeridge sought, and received, guidance from Powell, who explained that

[Paul] Nash was really a belated product of French Impressionism, whose development in England had been delayed by that utterly bogus thing, the Pre-Raphaelite Movement. As Tony put it, while English painters were fooling about with the 'Blessed Damozel', French painters were hard at work developing an authentic school of painting.[14]

Soon afterwards they both went to a private view of Powell's old friend, Adrian Daintrey. Muggeridge said he preferred Daintrey's paintings to

Nash's. Powell agreed, 'But said this was rather like saying one preferred Maclaren-Ross's novels to E.M. Forster's.'[15]

Another link between the two of them was Orwell, whom Muggeridge had asked Powell to introduce him to during the war. Muggeridge had naturally been keen to meet another premature anti-Stalinist. Orwell was not so sure. He was aware that in left-wing circles Muggeridge was considered a dangerous reactionary. 'I shall probably sock him,' he told Powell. But the meeting passed off without blows and after the war the three of them began to lunch together once or twice a month in Soho, or at a Spanish restaurant called La Bodega off the Strand. Powell and Muggeridge admired Orwell for the unanswerable case he put against totalitarianism and its intellectual groupies and were later saddened at the lousy hand he was dealt by fate. But as friends of his, and equals, they were not going to defer to him. Powell said more than once that 'one of the basic human rights is to make fun of other people, whoever they are',[16] and there can be no doubt that he and Muggeridge used to wind 'Old George' up from time to time. Julian Symons, who sometimes joined them for lunch, recalled how,

> In a friendly, and even affectionate way, Muggeridge and Powell would often lure Orwell away from sensible empiricism to wild flights of political fancy, like his view that the Labour Government should, in honesty, try to convert the British electorate to the idea that they should accept a lower standard of living in order to get rid of the evils of colonialism. 'Freedom for the Colonies and a Lower Standard of Living for all', that would have been his election rallying cry. It was impossible not to respect the integrity of his ideas and the seriousness with which they were put forward, inevitable that Muggeridge and Powell should see him primarily as an English eccentric with a great fund of out-of-the-way knowledge, and strongly-held opinions about such matters as the proper way of making tea and of cooking steak and kidney pudding.[17]

In 1949 Orwell's health took an irremediable turn for the worse at the very moment when he had everything to live for: fame, fortune and his engagement to a beautiful and intelligent young woman, Sonia Brownell. It must be said that Powell in particular was more intrigued by Orwell's involvement with Sonia Brownell – 'the art tart'[18] – than the impact of *Nineteen Eighty Four*. When Muggeridge told him that according to Fred Warburg, Orwell's publisher, 'a number of booksellers who had read it had been so frightened they had been unable to sleep afterwards ... [he] laughed long. The idea of anything keeping booksellers awake was, to him, irresistibly funny.'[19] They both, however, made the difficult journey to Cranham, the isolated Cotswold sanatorium where Orwell was being treated for TB, walking across country from Stroud station. Muggeridge has recorded that on the way there he and Powell had been laughing over an incident in a novel by Arthur Koestler:

> The hero, in seducing one of the female characters, through being circumcised, reveals that he is a Jew. Orwell was not as amused as we were. Of course it's not true, he said, that in this country only Jews are circumcised; but it is true that, generally speaking, the upper classes are and the lower classes aren't. He cited his own case at Eton, where in the changing-rooms he was very ashamed at being uncircumcised, and kept himself covered.[20]

Muggeridge describes this as 'a vintage Orwell point'. But it seems to have given Powell food for thought. Forty years later he admits in his Journals that at last he has managed to establish when circumcision became fashionable among the upper classes.[21] It was not until the 1890s, lending weight to an American writer's remark that the hero of *Daniel Deronda*, born years before this, would only have had to look to realise that he was Jewish. Powell then implies that unlike Orwell, he was not in the habit of comparing his private parts with other boys'. This may simply have been because, unlike Orwell, he had been circumcised and was therefore à la mode. But it may also reflect his lack of sexual interest in other boys.

When, in September 1949, Orwell's condition deteriorated and he was transferred to University College Hospital in Bloomsbury, Powell and Muggeridge were regular visitors to his bedside. Unwilling to be married in a dressing gown he asked them to get him a smoking jacket, which Powell did, though there is some dispute as to whether it was crimson corduroy, as Powell recalled, or mauve velvet, in Muggeridge's account. Either way it pleased Orwell so much that he wore it right up until his death, which occurred on 21 January 1950.

True to his quirky conservative temperament Orwell wanted a Church of England funeral and burial, the arrangement of which Powell and Muggeridge undertook. Powell chose the hymns, among them 'Guide me, O thou great Redeemer' which would be sung, in its original version,* at his own memorial service, and persuaded his local vicar, whom Violet knew, to take the service. This went off well despite the presence of several mourners who Violet thought were 'obviously distrustful of organised religion'[22] (like those who attend Erridge's funeral). But Powell, who read the lesson from the last chapter of Ecclesiastes (to whom Orwell had once compared Muggeridge), thought it among 'the most harrowing' he had ever attended. The burial took place later, in a graveyard near David Astor's estate in

---

* 'Guide me, O thou great Jehovah'.

Berkshire. Muggeridge produced this pithy epitaph: 'George died on Lenin's birthday, and is being buried by the Astors, which seems to me to carry the full range of his life.'[23]

How much of Orwell did Powell appropriate for Erridge? 'Tramping' for one thing, 'Spain' for another; also shabby clothes, ascetic tastes and a weakness for vintage juvenile reading matter (Orwell loved early issues of the *Girl's Own Paper*). But Erridge is a doctrinaire lefty who would probably have disapproved of *Homage to Catalonia*, particularly if Gypsy Jones, with whom he may briefly have been involved, had any say in the matter. Nor did Orwell share the pacifism that Erridge later espouses; he was a patriot who wanted to take an active part in the war and was bitterly disappointed that his health confined him to the Home Guard. Above all, as we have heard, Orwell inspired affection; Erridge does not. Therein lies the difference.

*

In May 1948 there appeared in the *TLS* a review of Harold Acton's *Memoirs of an Aesthete* which contained the following caution:

> Then comes Eton, and here the book falls off somewhat. Because he cannot remain on the same terms with all his readers, Eton is an extraordinarily difficult subject for a writer. While many of them will be Etonians, to whom the whole picture is familiar, the majority, the non-Etonians, cannot help wasting much reading energy in adapting themselves to Eton's odd vocabulary, and following those customs which are so different from those of other schools. There seems no way out of this quandary.[24]

Powell, who had recently gone on the *TLS* payroll, cannot have failed to see this notice, which must have been written at about the time he was beginning *A Question of Upbringing*. We may never know whether it influenced him, but he found a way out of the quandary, conveying the essence of Eton without overwhelming his readers with jargon or esoteric detail. However a ruminative passage like this, on only the second page, must have surprised those who remembered the direct manner of his early novels:

> As winter advanced in that river valley, mist used to rise in late afternoon and spread over the flooded grass; until the house and all the outskirts of the town were enveloped in opaque, chilly vapour, tinted like cigar-smoke. The house looked on to other tenement-like structures, experiments in architectural insignificance, that intruded upon a central concentration of buildings, commanding and antiquated, laid out in a quadrilateral, though irregular,

style. Silted-up residues of the years smouldered uninterruptedly – and not without melancholy – in the maroon brickwork of these medieval closes: beyond the cobbles and archways of which (in a more northerly direction) memory also brooded, no less enigmatic and inconsolable, among water-meadows and avenues of trees: the sombre demands of the past becoming at times almost suffocating in their insistence.

In the Thirties Cyril Connolly had commended Powell as an exponent of the tough new Vernacular style that was, he said, putting their more precious rivals, the new Mandarins, out of business. But talking out of the side of your mouth is not necessarily the best way to tell a long story. And there was another factor too. In a letter to Evelyn Waugh Powell admitted that his spelling, 'never very sound', was 'now completely ruined by years of 17th century research'.[25] I think it is reasonable to assume that immersion in the seventeenth century may also have made him a more elaborate writer, though it's equally possible that, like Waugh himself when he came to write *Brideshead Revisited*, he was reacting against a surfeit of 'Basic English' during the war. Whatever the explanation, Powell's post-war prose aroused a good deal of comment. Alan Pryce-Jones, writing as 'George Cloyne', thought it had something in common with Widmerpool's overcoat, which 'was only remarkable in itself for the comment it aroused'. His own take on it deserves to be recorded: 'It is as if Gibbon were drafting the text of a valentine, or Sir Thomas Browne writing advertising copy for gin.'[26]

Powell himself wouldn't comment. 'I think the less writers examine themselves in that sort of way, the better. You just want to try and write as well as you can. It's above all a question of *instinct*.'[27] But he admitted that the longer he spent on a novel, the more difficult it was to maintain a sense of proportion about it. This was where Muggeridge came in. Powell tried out the novel on him as he went along. 'Tony read more of his novel to me. Quite excellent, humorous, characteristic' is a typical diary entry for 1948.[28] The following year, when the novel was finished, Powell was faced with the problem of finding a publisher now that he had severed his links with Eyre and Spottiswoode. At Muggeridge's suggestion he submitted the novel to David Higham, who was Muggeridge's agent. Higham, who admired Powell's pre-war novels, particularly *Waring*, was very enthusiastic, but felt he had to have a second opinion. The reader he chose could be savage, but this did not deter good publishers from using her, which is why Higham used her as well. 'It never occurred to me,' he later wrote, 'that she wouldn't know of [Powell] at all, let alone appreciate, at least, what he was up to in this book. But she didn't. She treated it as a first novel, duly tore it to pieces and advised against our offering it.'[29]

Higham claimed in his autobiography that he never used this reader again. But neither does he mention either Powell or *Dance* again, which given that he became Powell's agent is odd. Perhaps he preferred not to acknowledge that it was no thanks to him that Powell found a publisher. The credit for this goes to Muggeridge, in his capacity as literary advisor to Heinemann, then one of Britain's biggest publishers. In *Faces* Powell says that Muggeridge 'persuaded' him to go to Heinemann, the implication being that he had had other offers. If so, no one has admitted it. On 9 December 1949 Muggeridge handed over *A Question of Upbringing* to Heinemann's chairman, A.S. Frere, 'with a very strong recommendation'. Three months later, on 28 February 1950, a contract was signed.*

Powell was fond of the phrase 'Time's revenge', as in 'it is Time's revenge that nowadays [1954] Van Gogh's *Sunflowers* is almost a *sine qua non* of any schoolroom'.[30] His signing for Heinemann could also be seen as an example of this, since as a young man three of the authors he was most hostile to – Galsworthy, Maugham and Priestley – were Heinemann bestsellers. Galsworthy, to borrow another of Powell's expressions, had been 'gathered in', but Priestley and Maugham were still going strong; indeed Powell had made partial amends to the latter by proposing in the *TLS* that 'highbrows who can see no good in him are on the whole those not ranking foremost in their own hierarchy'.[31] Other Heinemann mainstays were Enid Bagnold, Neville Shute and Georgette Heyer, while there was also Graham Greene, who after years in the red, had just begun to show a profit.

As an artist Powell was the equal of any writer on Heinemann's list. But as a commercial property he was undoubtedly a risk, for the reasons advanced here by Alan Ross:

> Just over a decade separates Mr Anthony Powell's new novel from *What's Become of Waring*, the last of the quintet produced in the Thirties. These novels, considering their distinction, their comparative omission in contemporary criticism as well as the extreme difficulty of obtaining them, must be the most neglected of the period. *From a View to a Death*, certainly, was reprinted a year or two ago ...but what of [the others]? They seem to be as extinct, though less deservedly, as the dodo.[32]

The size of Powell's advance is indicative of Heinemann's modest expectations. Although I do not know the exact figure I doubt if it was more than £150, say £3000 in today's money, since five years later his advance for *The*

* The contract was for two novels, a pattern that would be repeated.

Acceptance World was only £300. Nor, to judge from the trade press, was there much in the way of advance publicity, though this may be explained by the effort Heinemann were putting into promoting Boswell's *London Journal*, arguably the main event of the 1950/51 publishing season. Oddest of all is the absence of any fanfare in support of *The Music of Time* (its original title) as a sequence. It's as if Powell and his publisher were too busy holding their breaths to see how the novel itself did to concentrate on the big picture. This probably explains why, when *A Question of Upbringing* was going to press, 'some over-enthusiastic supervisor' at Heinemann's removed *The Music of Time* from the page preceding the opening of the narrative: he hadn't been told about either the sequence or its title.

The jacket copy deserves a mention at this point. It begins by reminding readers that in one of Powell's few autobiographical writings, his essay in *The Old School*, he confessed that he liked looking out of the window in the hope of seeing something of interest. 'His object [in] *A Question of Upbringing*, and subsequent volumes, is to convey what he has seen though the window during the course of these last three strange decades.' Since the novel opens in 1921 this would seem to indicate that Powell had always planned to cover the war, thus gratifying the reader's curiosity about, e.g., Sunny Farebrother, who passes out of Jenkins's life 'for some twenty years'. But it's by no means clear that this was the case. For instance in a letter to Alan Pryce-Jones, dated 12 January 1961, Powell said that he had always intended the sequence to 'continue *until* the war' (my italics), adding that he would agree that 'the planning is otherwise quite unsystematic'.[33] John Russell records him as saying, at about the same time, 'I wonder if I dare tackle the army.'[34]

Powell's reluctance to draw up a blueprint accorded with his belief, expressed in a letter to Jocelyn Brooke a few months earlier, that 'the more one writes, the more one feels that the material largely controls itself'.[35] He did not write for anyone in particular except himself, but had he done so I imagine it would have been the sort of reader for whom the journey was more important than the arrival. He was particularly taken by the metaphor used by Evelyn Waugh, who said he felt 'each volume of this series is like a great sustaining slice of Melton pie. I can go on eating it with the recurrent seasons until I drop.'[36]

A Question of Upbringing was published on 22 January 1951, almost twenty years on from *Afternoon Men*. Within two days 1700 copies had been sold. By 4 March the first edition of 5000 copies had gone and a further 2000 copies were on order. Powell was back in business, a theme plugged by reviewers, many of whom began by reminding their readers that before the war he had been in the frame with Evelyn Waugh and Christopher Isherwood. Old friends like Peter Quennell (*Daily Mail*) and John Betjeman (*Daily Telegraph*) could be relied upon to give him a good chitty. But what must have been particularly encouraging was the welcome he received from younger men like Alan Ross, Francis Wyndham and John Raymond, who said in the *New Statesman* that 'without prejudice to whatever masterpieces may make their appearance later in the year, I have a feeling that *A Question of Upbringing* is the novel I shall have enjoyed reading most in 1951'.[37]

It was, however, in the *TLS* (where else?) that Powell received his longest and most discerning review, from the egregious Maclaren-Ross. With more than 2000 words at his disposal, Maclaren-Ross could afford a lengthy resumé of Powell's work to date, beginning with how, as a young man, he had broken free of the autobiographical stranglehold imposed on his coevals by *Sinister Street*.[38] He notes the absence of sentimentality and self-pity in his early novels and applauds 'his easy mastery of dialogue used as a means of expressing personality as well as a means of communication'. He also instances Zouch as proof of Powell's 'latent preoccupation with the will to power and its visible incarnations'. Some of his comments on *A Question of Upbringing* are so shrewd that one suspects him of 'insider' reviewing. For instance he spots that Stringham, despite his advantages, is riding for a fall, and that Sunny Farebrother's 'air of shabby resignation' conceals a power-complex as formidable as Widmerpool's. He also suggests that Blore-Smith, in *Agents and Patients*, may have served 'as a preliminary sketch' for Widmerpool: 'Blore-Smith, in a dim, groping way, was not devoid of a lust for power, though he lacked the sharp drive of ambition present in Widmerpool; and in the last analysis only his thick-lensed spectacles and slight impediment of speech would appear to have been bequeathed to his successor.'

But having implied that we have not heard the last of Powell's protagonists, Maclaren-Ross fails to mention *The Music of Time*. He merely hopes 'that the author will allow us, in the future, further glimpses of his characters' development'; meanwhile, 'the present volume ... cannot fail to be regarded as a triumph in its own right'. Since he must have known that Powell was hard at work on volume two, I can only assume that Maclaren-Ross had been asked to adopt this approach.

*

In *Strangers* Powell refers to 'the wastage among friends and acquaintances [that] is one of the liabilities of middle-age'. After the war he had ample opportunity to observe this process at work. Two of its most notable victims were John Heygate and Constant Lambert, both of whom found life insupportable without large quantities of drink. This proved their downfall, sooner in Lambert's case, later in Heygate's.

Despite his veneer of urbanity, Heygate had always had his rackety side. In 1926, after failing to get into the Diplomatic Service, he went on a prolonged bender that resulted in DTs, an episode he described as 'when I was mad'. Drink continued to figure prominently in his life; indeed a mutual delight in pubs and road-houses was one of the reasons he and 'She-Evelyn' hit it off. During the Thirties he had to be dried out more than once, and in an effort to turn over a new leaf signed up with the evangelical Oxford Group, forerunners of Moral Rearmament. Confession was part of their therapy, so Heygate wrote a ten-page letter of contrition to Evelyn Waugh, receiving back a postcard which read: 'OK. E.W.'

In 1935 Heygate's father died, leaving him and his sister a half-share each in his estate. By now his marriage to Evelyn Gardner had effectively ended and he had met Gwyneth Lloyd, a young film actress, who became his second wife. Heygate wooed Gwyneth with the promise of a dream house in the country where he could write and she could raise a family. He found a dilapidated Queen Anne house in the Sussex Weald, complete with pond and oast-house, and set about restoring it, a process described in *A House for Joanna*. When his publisher paid a visit and saw the handsome writing room Heygate had created, with views towards the coast, he was unimpressed. 'You'll soon be back in London, scribbling on a bar counter.'[39] So it proved.

War with Germany did nothing to restore Heygate's equilibrium. Powell implies, though without adducing any hard evidence, that he was a Nazi sympathiser. But in *These Germans*, the combination of memoir and character study he wrote in 1939, Heygate rejects Hitler and all his works. On the other hand he probably didn't relish the idea of killing Germans and at the earliest opportunity volunteered to serve in the Far East. Destined for Singapore, his troopship was diverted to Colombo when news reached the convoy that the base had fallen. Heygate spent the rest of the war in India, as a bombardier in an anti-aircraft regiment. There cannot have been many baronets in the ranks, but Harold Acton's anecdote, quoted earlier, indicates a wider off-duty horizon for him than the NAAFI. By the time he was demobbed he was in poor shape, having celebrated winning the war 'unrestrainedly' on the voyage home. With his second marriage on the rocks he blagged his way into UNRAA (the United Nations Relief and Rehabilitation Administration), only to be sent home almost immediately from occupied Germany after a forty-eight-hour binge.

Heygate eventually decamped to Ulster, having inherited, with his title, an estate near Londonderry called Bellarina, from which he eked out a living for the rest of his life. In 1951 he married a widow with five daughters, but not before showing a brief glimpse of his old form. In London to announce the banns (or some such formality), he got drunk in a night-club and proposed to a hostess, which gallantry was duly reported in the press. This was his last hurrah. He dug himself in at Bellarina where Powell, unlike other old friends of his, could not be induced to visit him. They did, however, exchange letters and postcards, in one of which Powell wrote, 'I've killed you off. Sorry about that.' To whom was he referring? Heygate's son Richard is convinced that the answer is Stringham, adducing Powell's obituary of his father in *The Times*: 'Powell used exactly the same words he'd used for Stringham. A lot of people came up to me afterwards and said, "I never knew your father was Stringham", but of course he was.' Well, I have checked that notice against *Dance* and can find no resemblance to it there. But this is not to deny that Stringham may owe as much to Heygate as to Hubert Duggan: drink, melancholia (he eventually shot himself), service in the ranks, even Singapore – Heygate's original destination in 1941 – these tie in. More importantly there is what Powell calls Heygate's brand of wit, e.g. his complaint that 'stupid people thought him intelligent [while] intelligent people found him stupid'.[40] This bears the same hallmark as Stringham's aside that before he joined the army, 'I thought all you had to do when you fired a rifle was to get your eye and the sights and the target all in one line and then blaze away. The army has produced a whole book about it.' Powell concluded Heygate's obituary with the thought that he was someone 'who never quite found himself'.[41] He said something similar about Hubert Duggan: '[At Eton he] seems to have "realised" himself in a way he never quite managed again.'[42] Either could apply to Stringham as well.

Constant Lambert's last decade could not have got off to a more dramatic start. On the morning of 10 May 1940 he and Margot Fonteyn were in bed together in The Hague when German paratroopers began dropping on the city, a *coup de théâtre* that terminated the Sadler's Wells ballet company's Dutch excursion. Somehow they all got home safely and settled down to a punishing round of provincial tours in which Lambert, as Andrew Motion puts it, sustained a 'multiplicity of roles – jester, arranger, player, conductor, director'.[43] Unencumbered by emotional or domestic ties – Flo had moved on and his mother looked after Kit – Lambert played as hard as he worked. He had other lovers besides Fonteyn, but it was drink rather than sex that kept him going while the company was on the road.

Powell used to complain that drink was very hard to come by during the war, and what there was of it was pretty horrible: watery beer, Algerian plonk, Empire port and so on. But those like Lambert for whom it has become a necessity can usually sniff it out, which is what he did. The result was there for all to see. In the Thirties he had become corpulent, but there were still traces of what Margot Fonteyn called his 'seraphic face'.[44] By the time he was forty, at the end of the war, he was gross. Yet according to Michael Ayrton, probably his closest friend at this time, he retained his charisma: 'To be with him raised the pitch of life.'[45] Ayrton later wrote a memoir of Lambert that he included in a book of essays reviewed by Powell. While conceding that Ayrton's reminiscence was 'entertaining, genuine and first-hand', Powell said it emphasised a side of Lambert 'that most certainly existed but [which was] not at the same time by any means the whole story'.[46] I think Powell must have felt that Ayrton, who was only nineteen when introduced to Lambert in 1940, had depicted his old friend as a sacred monster with subversive tendencies rather than the matchless confidant, companion and wit he remembered. There is an anecdote about Lambert and Ayrton covering the whole of a railway carriage, including the ceiling, with drawings of cats and fishes that must have made him squirm.[47]

In October 1947, to the surprise of many including Margot Fonteyn, Lambert married Isabel Delmer, a tall, glamorous and hard-drinking painter and former model who had previously been married to the foreign correspondent and wartime black propagandist, Sefton Delmer. They went to live at Albany Street, not far from the Powells, in a large flat that soon became, in Isabel's words, 'an absolute shambles'. To begin with Lambert cut back on his drinking, probably because, for the first time, it had begun to affect his conducting; but when, in July 1948, he met Powell and Muggeridge for a drink, the latter wrote in his diary: 'great deterioration, nerves etc'[48] after Lambert's name. In 1992, when Isabel died, Powell concluded that 'she was some sort of an answer for Constant Lambert at the close of his life, tho' one was never sure she did not add even worse habits to his heavy drinking, which gave him the horrors at the very end'.[49] As usual, Powell didn't speculate on the nature of those habits, though we can exclude incest and folk-dancing because he says elsewhere that Lambert, like Tallulah Bankhead, would try anything once bar these. In any case Isabel can't be held responsible for her husband's death, which occurred on 21 August 1951, about six weeks after the première of his ballet, *Tiresias*.

Lambert had high hopes for *Tiresias*, his most ambitious work since the ballet version of *Rio Grande*, but it disappointed the critics, two of whom were particularly scathing. To console himself he hit the bottle in a big way, alarming even those who were used to his binges. They would have been more alarmed still had they known that for years he had had diabetes, which due to negligence on the part of his doctor went undiagnosed, though the symptoms must have been apparent. When he failed to join Isabel for lunch with some friends she returned home to find him in the throes of DTs, a direct consequence of his diabetes. He lapsed into a coma and died the next day.*

In his memoir of Lambert Michael Ayrton recalled how fond he was of chewing over 'some exact turn of phrase from among the more improbable paragraphs unearthed from the morning paper'. In the months before he died Lambert had taken to doing this on the phone to Powell, late at night, two or three times a week, usually beginning with a quote from the idiosyncratic column his old friend Sacheverell Sitwell was writing for one of the Sunday papers. Powell writes about this as if it were perfectly natural behaviour on the part of an old friend, though many of us, I imagine, would find it intolerable after a while, however entertaining the caller. In the first week of August the Powells went on holiday for a fortnight, returning home the day Lambert died. Powell takes up the story:

> The following day two friends dined at our house. I mention them merely as witnesses. At a quarter to twelve the telephone bell rang.
> 'It's Constant,' said my wife. I went downstairs and picked up the receiver.
> 'Hello?'
> There was a click. Then the dialling tone.

This was not the only curious incident attendant on Lambert's death. As noted above, Cyril Connolly and Lambert were enemies. On learning that he had died, Connolly 'made some uncharitable comment', and was promptly stung on the big toe by a wasp.[50] Lambert, like God, was not mocked.

*

Maud Powell had two sisters, Cicely and Violet. Cicely died in childbirth, while Violet had what Powell calls an 'adventurous' life before dying at the beginning of the Second World War. She gave a life interest in her estate to Major Henry Inglis, her estranged husband, who like Jenkins's Uncle Giles lived in a private hotel to the west of Queensway. In June 1950 Major Inglis, whom Powell says he 'barely knew', died, and the estate 'such as it was' passed to his nephew by marriage. In fact Powell inherited a tidy little sum

---

* Lambert used to say that he had written an essay which he hoped would be published after his death entitled 'Sir William Walton OM' by Constant Lambert DT.

– £17,000, which even after estate duty amounted to over £300,000 in today's money. This made possible the move to Somerset in 1952.

Before the war Powell would never have dreamt of living anywhere but London. Metropolitan by nature, he would compare himself to Wyndham Lewis's character Tarr, for whom 'the Spring was nameless'. But ten years of war and neglect had left their mark on the capital and its infrastructure, greatly diminishing its charm. 'Everything was shabby,' he recalled, 'in need of a lick of paint, or at the very least a clean. When something went wrong there was no one to fix it. There were bomb sites everywhere, full of rubbish. The parks and squares had lost their railings. And in the winter you got these horrible smogs that made everyone ill.'[51] Nor was Chester Gate the ideal base for a working writer with a young family. Its seven rooms were spread over four storeys, so that people were for ever clattering up and down. Powell worked in the dining room, 'at the mercy,' so Violet wrote, 'of the telephone or any caller'.[52]

Powell had a love-hate relationship with the phone. Once on, he found it difficult to get off, even if, as so often happened, he was in the middle of writing something.* 'In London the phone rang all the time, especially in the mornings when I was trying to work. I do know people with strong enough nerves to take the receiver off or just let it ring, but my nerves have never been up to that. And what used to happen in practice was the telephone went and you answered it and it was a friend and before you knew what the whole bloody morning was gone.'[53]

Wherever they went Powell would still have to spend a day or two a week in London, calling in at the *TLS*, going to a party if one were on offer, seeing old friends, keeping abreast of the gossip. This meant moving not much further than a hundred miles from London, preferably within reach of a main-line station. Because of its Aubrey associations Powell fancied Wiltshire, particularly the south-east near Salisbury, where he had lived in his teens; but prices there were too high, so they looked further north and west, towards the border with Gloucestershire and Somerset. They visited one house simply on the strength of its name – Under-the-Hill House at Wootton-under-Edge, once owned by More Adey, editor of the *Burlington Magazine* and boyfriend of Christopher Millard's benefactor, Robert Ross. Powell wondered whether Adey had named the house after Beardsley's erotic novel, or vice-versa. Evelyn Waugh, who lived nearby, facetiously suggested that Powell ought to buy the place because it was not far from the factory of Messrs Tubbs, famous for their trusses.

---

* In his *Journals* Powell refers to the 'marathon' conversations he had on the phone with Muggeridge.

Powell's reply was worthy of Widmerpool: 'I don't think at my age I shall derive any great convenience from the proximity of Tubbs's factory.'[54]

Eventually, after traipsing up hill and down dale (they didn't own a car), they settled on a grey limestone Regency house called The Chantry, in a village called Chantry not far from Frome in north Somerset. Their first offer was rejected, and thinking that was that they resumed their search. Then the owner, an RAF officer for whom the property was an encumbrance, invited them to make a second, slightly higher bid, which he promptly accepted. Powell had completed his double: a wife with a title and a house with a drive.

Not that the drive was very apparent in 1951. Like the rest of the grounds it was submerged beneath a jungle of vegetation, so thick in parts that from certain angles the house was scarcely visible. Conditions within may be imagined from the uses to which The Chantry had been put since 1940: variously a refuge for bombed-out families, a chocolate factory, and a school that failed to attract a single pupil. Oddly enough the Victorian novelist Helen Mathers depicted it as a girls' school called Charteris in her bestseller *Comin' Thro' the Rye*, though the detail she gives is so scanty that you could be forgiven for missing this. She also describes how the girls donned bloomers to play cricket in the field behind the house, a sight that might have quickened the pulse of Sir Magnus Donners.

Though much too small to be classed as a stately home (an unsympathetic interviewer said it looked as if it had been designed as one, and then shrunk), The Chantry was what another writer called 'pending manorial', in that it had an 'all-important lodge',[55] to say nothing of stables, a lake and two grottoes. Completed just before the Gothic Revival began in earnest, it was built to a design that echoed the Italianate villas of Bath, sixteen miles to the north. In time the Powells would add many neo-classical embellishments of their own, such as busts and urns and pillars; but in the early Fifties their priority was making the place habitable. Fortunately their furniture, mostly Empire or Victorian and bought for a song in the Thirties, would look as well at The Chantry as at Chester Gate, both houses dating from the same epoch. 'Tony has undergone only two conversions,' Violet used to say. 'One was early on in our marriage when he stopped liking modern tubular furniture. The second, when we came here, was to wallpaper.'

12

Bouverie Street

'Life ... holds no more wretched occupation than trying to make the English laugh.'

Malcolm Muggeridge

The Great Upheaval, as Violet called the move to Chantry, took place in July 1952, shortly after the publication of *A Buyer's Market*, the second volume of *Dance*. Set in 1928, it describes how Jenkins, a year or so later than Powell, discovers that there is more to life than deb dances. At Mrs Andriadis's party he gets a glimpse of the Art-Smart world, the ramifications of which are not to be had from *Burke* or *Debrett*. At Stourwater, Sir Magnus Donners's castle *ornée*, he is once again excited by the proximity of Jean Templer, now married to her brother's truculent friend, Bob Duport. And in the back of Mr Deacon's shop he is seduced by the recalcitrant left-wing nymph Gypsy Jones, an experience as dissatisfying in its way as Powell's initiation in Paris, if equally necessary. But although we are made aware of Jenkins's hopes and fears, there are also hints that we shall learn less about the narrator than the circles he inhabits. These circles overlap, so that men of action, socialites and artistic types are thrown together, the usual catalysts being their wives, mistresses or lovers. Observing the way these contradictory social groupings intertwine, and the bizarre human gyrations that result, Jenkins discerns a pattern dictated by the rhythm of life – hence Powell's theme, which is that his characters, like the four figures in Poussin's painting, are all engaged in a ritual dance to the music of time.

A problem Powell faced was how to introduce as many characters as possible in a realistic way. This explains why most of the book consists of four social events: the Huntercombes' dance and the dinner that precedes it, Mrs Andriadis's party, lunch at Stourwater and Mr Deacon's birthday party. In addition to those already mentioned we meet the Walpole-Wilsons, Barbara Goring, Rosie Manasch, Prince Theodoric, Baby Wentworth and Max Pilgrim. Barnby also appears, the first unconventional person his own age with whom Jenkins establishes a rapport. Uncle Giles comes and goes all too briefly, while Stringham, after his fling with Mrs Andriadis, is set to marry a grandee's daughter. However, it is Widmerpool, described in the blurb as 'forlorn', who makes most of the running. Three times he is unseated, three times he remounts, so that even the ranks of Tuscany – well, Jenkins at any rate – can scarce forbear to cheer.

Powell later complained about the obtuseness of reviewers who in the early stages were rather unwilling to grasp that he simply could not explain right away how everybody fitted in. Once again I think that he and/or his publishers must share some of the blame for this because of their reluctance to come clean about his intentions. Most reviewers were aware that *A Buyer's Market* was a sequel to *A Question of Upbringing*, but only Julian Symons, who must have been in the know, was prepared to state that several more volumes were in the pipeline. Writing in the *TLS*, Symons declared Powell's theme to be 'the slow disintegration of an upper middle class', adding that such a theme 'permits many variations ... upon the corrosive vulgarities of commerce and the bewildering intricacies of love'.[1] In the *New Statesman*, V.S. Pritchett elaborated on Symons's remarks about the theme: 'in the background the upper classes start on that peculiar course of chasing after artists, drifting into Bohemia, the demi-monde and the business rackets, which has been typical of our age.' Pritchett concluded that 'The Jazz Age, that high-fed, prosperous, hard-faced period of our recent past, has found what it needed so badly – a straight-faced, muscular historian who works the last drop of irony and alarm out of his documents like some relentless taskmaster, and who will yet remember each separate delicious finger of the loving girl he danced with or the smell of bath salts on old men.'[2] It was left to Philip Toynbee in *The Observer* to sound a cautionary note about style. Powell's 'immense circumlocutory facetiousness' could get out of hand, so that instead of using a 'simple and familiar expression in common use',[3] he came up with this:

> [Barnby stated] in the most formidable terms at hand ... his own ineradicable unwillingness, for that matter suspected actual physical incapacity in face of financial indemnities of the most extravagant order, to be inveigled into any situation that might even threaten approach to intimacy with her.

Powell's usual retort to this sort of criticism was that with any writer, however great, there was a good deal you just had to put up with. Nevertheless, in later editions he did prune this passage considerably. Earlier I suggested that immersion in Aubrey and his contemporaries might explain his more elaborate style. It now occurs to me that his years at the War Office could be equally responsible, the tortuous jargon of minutes and papers hard to shake off, also, perhaps, the habit of enclosing within inverted commas any word or expression not in the Whitehall style book.

*

A few months after *A Buyer's Market* was published the Home Service did a series on 'The Seven Deadly Sins and the Contemporary World'. For a fee of twenty guineas plus expenses Powell was commissioned to give a talk about Lust, presumably on the strength of the tapestry that intrigues Jenkins at Stourwater rather than because he was considered an expert on the subject. His Notebook does, however, contain this wonderful simile: 'Lust gives that grim pounding feeling, like heavy guns in the distance.'[4]

Although not a radio virgin – he had done a month on *The Critics* the year before – Powell was not very comfortable in front of a microphone and only accepted if it was understood that his was 'essentially a subjective view, not that of a spokesman for a system'.[5] He began by explaining about the tapestry he had envisaged and the research necessary to get the detail right, including a visit to the Warburg Institute. There he discovered that although the Seven Deadly Sins were an essentially medieval concept, a tapestry depicting them could 'just' have been fabricated at the period he had imagined them, though by then they were usually represented as being 'interesting and impressive' (as at Stourwater) rather than 'grotesque and repulsive'.[6] Turning to Lust itself he pointed out that although 'it was the first of the Seven to spring to most people's minds' when the Deadly Sins were mentioned, it was, together with Pride, 'one of the least objectionable for the individual, at least outwardly, to admit to possessing. Avarice and Gluttony immediately suggest unattractive social habits, but Lust does not necessarily imply a disagreeable outward appearance. Perhaps, indeed, quite the reverse. Sloth and Anger cannot be concealed, but Lust can get to work secretly, remaining hidden for years, for a lifetime, even,' only being revealed after death by a biographer or hitherto unpublished diaries (probably he had Boswell in mind).

Powell then reminded listeners of the debt owed to Lust by literature: 'It is the Sin beyond all others that has commanded attention ... Remove Lust from literature and a vast gap would be left.' In countless poems and novels it took a leading role, while its dire consequences were a recurrent theme in Shakespeare. By contrast D.H. Lawrence saw it not as a Sin, but a Virtue, commending those who were 'deeply committed to [it]' at the expense of others whose behaviour was 'more circumspect'.

Powell thought there was a curious contradiction in the modern attitude to Lust. On the one hand it was no longer regarded as a moral failing, but as a disease which was probably attributable to 'heredity or environment'. On the other, the 'fear and horror' it inspired 'at certain levels of life' seemed greater than ever before. For instance no public man now could afford to gain a reputation for Lust, though he could indulge in any of the other sins with impunity. He recalled how when Hitler came to power it was said in his favour that he seemed 'almost entirely free from Lust'. His own feeling was that Hitler 'would not have been so great a nuisance to the world if he *had* been less of a stranger to Lust'. He thought we were in far greater danger today 'from the ascetic, quasi-scientific, self-righteous, power-worshipping megalomaniac than from the old-fashioned, easy-going, self-indulgent tyrant who sought power merely to gratify the flesh'.

Powell emphasised that Lust was not simply the preserve of those who were in a position to gratify it, like Jezebel and Casanova: 'it can be indulged in just as much, perhaps even more, by those with no outlet for its satisfaction … There is no knowing what may not be going on in the heart of the mildest of our acquaintances, or people of the most conventional appearance in the street.' But a problem arose when self-control, which everyone ought to be capable of, imposed too severe a restraint so that Lust 'boiled over' and became one of the other Sins – probably Pride or Envy – 'in a particularly virulent form'. He thought those most at risk from this were people 'whose concentration on themselves makes them feel cut off from others'.

Powell concluded with the thought that if you wanted to understand these 'inner forces', you would do better to read poetry than analytical prose. To illustrate this he chose two examples, beginning with the whole of John Betjeman's poem 'Senex', about an old man tormented by his desire for nubile young women: 'Oh would I could subdue the flesh/Which sadly troubles me.' He then quoted 'The Frailty' by Abraham Cowley, the metaphysical poet invoked by Jenkins during the Victory service at St Paul's. Powell admired Cowley who ought, he considered, to be better known than he was, so I shall reproduce the lines he chose in full:

> I know 'tis sordid, and 'tis low;
> (All this as well as you I know)
> Which I so hotly now pursue;
> (I know all this as well as you)
> But while this cursed flesh I bear,
> And all the weakness, and the baseness there,
> Alas, alas, it will be always so.
>
> In vain, exceedingly in vain
> I rage sometimes and break my chain;

For to what purpose do I bite
With teeth which ne'er will break it quite?

Powell said he found this piece 'extremely difficult' to write. I think its chief interest lies in the relationship, as he sees it, between Lust and Power, from which certain conclusions can be drawn in respect of *Dance*. Thus although you might not want your daughter to be mixed up with Sir Magnus Donners, you would probably find him a better boss than Widmerpool because he has come to terms with his desires, something that Widmerpool never really does (except perhaps at the end of his life), hence his determination to take it out on others. Again, there is obviously something rather fishy about Sunny Farebrother's self-righteous scheming, the inference being that his machinations bring him the release that most men get from a good fuck. But Powell does not go all the way with D.H. Lawrence, as is evident from the fate of Peter Templer, who comes to grief because he lets Lust get the better of him.

If Lust ever got the better of Powell himself he was not going to say how, when or with whom. The most he would admit was that 'All sex life sooner or later lands you in what, for want of a better word, I would call trouble.'[7] When Lynn Barber asked him what he *meant* by that, he waffled: 'Well, I honestly think it does, don't you? I don't say utterly *frightful* trouble, but you can't get away with things, you have to pay for it one way or another. But the whole thing is really very difficult, I mean how people ought to behave. I mean one doesn't want to be *queer*, one wants to sort of tick over in the normal way.'[8]

In the same piece Ms Barber said that 'unlike most writers' Powell had avoided the hazard of drunkenness because drink didn't agree with him. At the age of 86, when the interview was done, this was probably the case. But for most of his adult life wine, in particular, agreed with him very well. Had that not been the case he would hardly have chosen a daily bottle of 'ordinary rough' red wine as his luxury item on *Desert Island Discs*. But I think there is a parallel between his attitude to sex and his attitude to drink. To invoke a fan of Powell's, the writer Simon Barnes: 'Drink [in *Dance*] is a very good thing, and then again, a very bad thing.'[9] It is a very good thing for those who can handle it and a very bad thing for those who can't. But those who can't handle it are a danger to themselves, not to other people. It's non-drinking control freaks like Sillery, Widmerpool and Scorpio Murtlock you'd better beware of.

*

199

Malcolm Muggeridge was rarely happy doing the same job for more than a few years and having been at the *Telegraph*, in one capacity or another, since 1946, he was by 1952 beginning to get itchy feet. That autumn he was approached by Messrs Bradbury & Agnew, the proprietors of *Punch*, and offered the Editorship. Once he had got over his surprise he drove a hard bargain: an annual salary of £5000 plus £1000 expenses. He also insisted on a completely free hand, having ascertained that as the first outsider in the magazine's history to become editor, he could expect hostility from the staff, who were, to put it mildly, set in their ways. One of the first things he did was to lure Powell away from the *TLS*.

Powell probably felt the need for a change as well. With *Dance* under way his appetite for new fiction had waned and he must have welcomed the opportunity to broaden his critical horizons, particularly since he had begun to think of publishing a collection of his literary journalism. *Punch* would take up more of his time, requiring him to be in London from Monday afternoon until Wednesday afternoon. But there were fringe benefits: a desk of his own and the use of a secretary, spare theatre and film tickets, the weekly *Punch* lunch ('ample to eat and drink'), and more varied gossip. Furthermore it was perhaps 'appropriate' that he should join the staff of a magazine whose bound volumes he – and so many of his contemporaries – had pored over as a child. A formal offer was made in January 1953. Two months later he became Literary Editor of *Punch* at a salary of £1500 a year. Here is how he struck R.G.G. Price, a regular contributor who was at work on a history of the magazine:

> It is difficult to think of any new man, at least since Phil May, who has arrived with so considerable an outside reputation ... Like the Editor, he enjoys the comedy of the fight for power and the humour of personal idiosyncrasy. He shares his Toryism, though he is less interested in day-to-day politics. His distaste for the old philistinism of *Punch* and his interest in the Arts indicate, together with the caste of mind revealed in his novels, what he probably brings to the making of *Punch* policy in editorial discussions.[10]

Powell's first task was to rid the magazine of 'ungifted' reviewers and assemble a team he could rely on. Some, like R.G.G. Price, were already in place; others, like Maclaren-Ross, were recruited from outside. He next established the principle that while books were to be treated seriously, rather than in a somewhat cursory manner as before, this still allowed the reviewer to make a joke, something he encouraged. He also managed to obtain enough space for one full-page review each week. Price takes up the story again:

[Powell] did most of the long articles ... and with gentle persistence accustomed readers to the scholarly discussion of books that could support scholarship. It was the first time that *Punch* readers had been addressed in that tone. His writing is much quieter than the rest of the paper and until one is used to it, the jokes, often complex, may be invisible. His articles in other parts of the paper are private, amused and sometimes, like his *Steerforth on Copperfield*, brilliant. Where he shows his quality is on the borderland of literary and social observation, as in the article he wrote about the gainful occupation of writers.[11]

'Steerforth on Copperfield' was a parody. This form had undergone a revival since the war and Powell was a dab hand at it, his other targets including Chesterfield, Lear, Kipling, Melville, Connolly (twice) and Greene. The second piece referred to by Price was 'Profession or Occupation?',[12] in which Powell examined the extraneous employment of artists and writers, a topic dear to his heart. He was amused to think of Chateaubriand, Verlaine and Van Gogh teaching English schoolboys, at pains to point out that 'douanier' Rousseau was not a customs officer but a 'municipal rate-collector', and intrigued at the idea of Stendhal issuing passports. In general he thought it was important for writers to keep the literary world at a distance for as long as possible, 'otherwise you become assimilated and end up writing about it, which you don't want to do'. Ideally you needed a territory you could make your own, like 'lower-middle-class Dublin' in the case of Joyce. But of course once you'd written a novel or two, particularly if they were noticed, it was very difficult not to be drawn into the literary world. This was why it was important for writers to get their significant experiences over early in life.

Muggeridge later wrote that the funniest documents which came his way as editor of *Punch* were 'communications from irate readers'.[13] He always intended that the magazine should be subversive, and so, by the deferential standards of the time, it undoubtedly was. Although at one with Muggeridge in believing that the magazine had to be shaken up Powell was more concerned to redefine its saloon-bar attitude towards the arts. He was probably responsible for getting John Betjeman to write about architecture and topography, and for the appointment of Adrian Daintrey as art critic, a lucky break for his old friend whose work was out of favour with galleries and patrons alike. He also advised Muggeridge on the illustrations, encouraging him to make better use of artists 'with more decided personality' like Ronald Searle and André Francois. Mark Boxer, not long out of Cambridge, was another of his finds. Boxer thought Powell 'was responsible for killing the idea that everything in the magazine had to be side-splitting'.[14]

It was one of Powell's maxims that whereas all writing was difficult, at least in a novel you could say something happened and the reader had to believe you, which was not necessarily the case in an autobiography. 'You say, Snooks behaved very badly. But there will always be people who say, "Rubbish. *You* behaved very badly. Snooks behaved perfectly well."'[15] The story of his recruitment of Claud Cockburn to the *Punch* contingent bears this out. A brilliant exponent of agitprop, Cockburn had been 'useful' to the Communist Party, of which he was still a member, for over twenty years. He had coined the phrase 'The Cliveden Set', licked Stalin's boots in the *Daily Worker* and lined up against Muggeridge and Powell in the battle for control of the NUJ chapel. He and Powell did, however, go back a long way – to the Hypocrites Club; and while they were never more than acquaintances, Powell found him 'a pleasant drinking companion'[16] as well as an amusing writer, albeit one who would need to be watched.

Cockburn, living in Ireland by now, knew nothing of the new broom at *Punch*, so that Powell's letter inviting him to become a contributor knocked him sideways:

> What, I had to ask myself, in God's name was he doing in that *galère*? And what, admitting that he personally was aboard that sluggish old hulk, on earth made him suppose that my presence would be welcome. Just making the matter more mysterious was a note in his letter – he was asking for an article about Ireland – saying that he would like the piece to be 'somewhat astringent'. If he were simply trying to do me a good turn by arranging for me to get a small piece of money out of *Punch*, surely, knowing my general line of literary brew would he not instead have put in some cautionary note urging me to draw it mild?[17]

Cockburn claimed that had he known that Muggeridge was in charge he would have thought twice about accepting Powell's offer, however enticing the terms. To someone like himself, CP and proud of it, Muggeridge the apostate was anathema. Apparently – though this is hard to believe – he was still in the dark when at Powell's invitation he called in at Bouverie Street on his next visit to London:

> The *Punch* offices have a peculiarly solid, Edwardian air about them which is agreeable enough to the detached observer, but made me a little nervous. I was a great deal more nervous when Tony, who supposed I knew all about it already, incidentally disclosed that the enterprise was now under the guidance of Malcolm Muggeridge. To my further discomfiture, he made a suggestion that we now walk down the corridor and visit Mr Muggeridge in person. I positively babbled ... 'I have every reason to suppose,' I said, 'that he detests me as deeply as I detest him. Let us keep this whole thing as far as possible in the old boy net – let me deal exclusively with yourself. A meeting with Muggeridge can end only in bitterness and disaster.'

Pooh-pooing and laughing – idiotically I thought – Tony insisted; in fact he actually held me by the arm and steered me down the passage and into the bugbear's den.[18]

Now you would assume from this that Powell was mischief-making, which wasn't his style and might, in any case, have deprived him of Cockburn's services if all hell had broken loose. But far from coming to blows Cockburn and Muggeridge hit it off so well that they became bosom pals (though this didn't stop Muggeridge – 'the biggest garter-snapper in the business' according to Mary MacCarthy – making a heavy pass at Cockburn's wife in the back of a taxi, sustaining a badly bruised finger for his pains). Muggeridge even showed the door to a spook who urged him not to publish material from such a tainted source.

I think Cockburn was almost certainly exaggerating the supposed enmity between him and Muggeridge in order to make a good story. Back in 1948, as he records in his Diary,[19] Muggeridge had opposed the blackballing of Cockburn when he applied to join the Authors' Club. Cockburn might be a Communist, he said, but that was not grounds for excluding him from what was a purely social organisation; indeed he had supported his candidature. Muggeridge would hardly have endorsed Cockburn as a member of his club if he couldn't bear to be in the same room as him. 'I cannot,' he later admitted, 'relate my affections to my principles. A classic case would be Kim Philby ... If I had known what he was doing I would have turned him in. But if I saw him in the street I would say hello and hold nothing against him.'[20]

Powell's take on this incident is curious. In his Journals he admits he made the first approach to Cockburn. He then says that Muggeridge fell for Cockburn, 'seeing much more of him *than formerly*' (my italics), which was regrettable because the latter was a 'thoroughly bad influence', winding Muggeridge up when he needed to be calmed down. Cockburn, he concludes, was out to wreck any institution with which he was associated. But, 'Never apologise. Never explain.' Powell doesn't say why he approached Cockburn in the first place, nor does he blame himself for having taken him to see Muggeridge. It is as if, having lit the blue touch-paper, he won't take the blame for the bang.

Although not sharing either his preoccupation with politics or his growing attachment to television, Powell still found Muggeridge an immensely stimulating friend and colleague. This was very apparent to Peter Dickinson, a young Cambridge graduate who shared an office with Powell. He recalled Violet distinguishing between 'half-hour people' and 'long week-end people'. Muggeridge was definitely a long weekend person:

He was a genuine character. That was really all that mattered to Tony. Of course he was very fond of Malcolm too, but that was beside the point. He was always on the look-out for what was out of the ordinary. I remember him urging me to go and see *Look Back in Anger* and *The Summer of the 17th Doll* when they were on in the West End. You may not like them, he said, but you'll find them of interest. I think that was probably his attitude to something like a really wild party. He wouldn't have given one himself, but he'd have wanted an invitation so as to see what went on.

Dickinson thought Powell was impressed by the liberties Muggeridge took with the language, bending it and shaping it according to his own rules, not those of the grammar book. 'Tony put it down to the fact that Malcolm hadn't done Latin. I remember one day he said to me that he was tired of writing correct English and was going to loosen up a bit. He thought grammarians like Fowler had too much say in the way people wrote.'[21]

According to Dickinson Powell rarely said much at editorial meetings and eventually withdrew from them altogether. But on at least one occasion he sided against Muggeridge and was proved right. This was over *The Punch Review*, an intimate revue partly sponsored by the magazine, which included sketches by some of the contributors. Powell said it wouldn't work and it didn't. The notices varied from lukewarm to derisory and within a few weeks it had been taken off.

Despite his scepticism Powell was at the *Review*'s first night, providing Ann Fleming, who was also present, with a chance to be snide at his expense to Evelyn Waugh: 'Your friend Mr Anthony Powell was outraged because a young man in full mess kit sang "Miss Joan Hunter-Dunn" wearing a white tie – apparently "an unspeakable offence" when wearing military fancy dress.'[22] Waugh's reaction to this is not recorded. A year later Ann Fleming had another dig: 'What do people see in Anthony Powell? I find him a hearty [B]limp – or do you like him because his wife is a catholic?'[23] Waugh corrected her. 'Lady Violet Powell is a pillar of the Church of England. Powell I suspect of agnosticism.'[24] Seven years later, reporting a lunch given by her rival hostess Lady Pamela Berry, Mrs Fleming made another, graver howler. Powell, she told Waugh, had complained that all people talked about these days was politics, 'seldom or never the arts'. She then said that he admitted to knowing nothing about music, 'and I would surmise has never glanced at a painting'.[25]

In bygone days this libel would have earned her a sharp rap over the knuckles, but Waugh now thought of himself as 'just a retired school-master'[26] and all he did was patiently put her right:

Tony Powell knows a lot about painting. In youth he drew Lovat-Fraser-like decorations of military subjects. He slept with Nina Hamnett and attended the L.C.C. School of Arts and Crafts in Southampton Row.

I cannot judge his musical tastes. He was a friend of Constant Lambert and the musical conversations in what was it called? 'The Pagoda of the Amber Moon'? No, something like that. *Casanova's Chinese Restaurant* perhaps – anyway those conversations impressed me with his inside knowledge.* I don't think you appreciate Tony as you should. Of course everyone is at his worst at Grubstreet's table.[27]

Powell knew that he was not Ann Fleming's cup of tea. He considered her a spiteful woman who might well have contributed to Waugh's demise by 'kindly' telling him that some people he had stayed with in the West Indies considered him a great bore.[28] Unlike Waugh, he was never part of her circle, the core of which were old *Horizon* hands like Connolly, Quennell and Spender, and thought her markedly inferior as a hostess to Lady Pamela Berry ('Grubstreet'), who would, he told Muggeridge, adorn the memoirs of their contemporaries.

Muggeridge knew all about the 'shrewd and tough' Lady Pamela, having become her lover at the time he took over at *Punch*. Their tempestuous affair lasted for years and was the talk of Fleet Street, not least because she was the wife of Michael Berry, later Lord Hartwell, the editor and co-proprietor of the *Daily Telegraph*. For whatever reason her husband turned a blind eye to Lady Pamela's infidelity, which involved many men besides Muggeridge. Naturally Powell was aware of all this and it is possible that, consciously or unconsciously, he drew on it when writing of the Widmerpools' equally unconventional marriage. That both errant wives should be called Pamela is too much of a coincidence to be overlooked; but as I have already indicated Barbara Skelton is the obvious model for Powell's Pamela. (It must, incidentally, have been at one of Lady Pamela's celebrated Election Night parties that Widmerpool learns he has lost his seat – and serve him right, given that he could not be bothered to attend the count at his constituency.)

*

In June 1952, in a letter to Evelyn Waugh, Nancy Mitford wrote: 'About Tony – I don't think his novels have enough story, in every other way they are perfection.'[29] I think Powell would have accepted this. Indeed he admitted as much to Waugh himself in May 1953 when at work on *The*

* Powell asked Benjamin Britten to check his musical passages.

Acceptance World: 'At the moment I am hopelessly stuck and can think of nothing for anyone to do.'[30] Another problem, as he explained to Kay Dick, was that he had 'used up so much of that particular period in past novels'.[31] Then there was the move to Somerset and his change of job, both of which were distractions; so it was not until May 1955, almost three years after its predecessor, that *The Acceptance World* was published.

The novel opens in Autumn 1931. The Jazz Age is over; the Pink Decade just begun. In time Jenkins will be as hag-ridden as the next man by the shape of things to come. But for the moment it is Love that keeps him awake at night. What began in volume one as an adolescent crush ignites, two books later, into a full-blown affair:

> The exact spot must have been a few hundred yards beyond the point where the electrically illuminated young lady in a bathing dress dives eternally through the petrol-tainted air ... A few seconds after I had seen this bathing belle journeying, as usual, imperturbably through the frozen air, I took Jean in my arms. Her response, so sudden and passionate, seemed surprising only a minute or two later. All at once everything was changed. Her body felt at the same time hard and yielding, giving a kind of glow as if live current issued from it. I used to wonder afterwards whether, in the last resort, of all the time we spent together, however ecstatic, those first moments on the Great West Road were not the best.

Partly because we're told so little about his marriage, but also because, from first to last, she represents 'the real thing', Nick's affair with Jean Templer is central to *Dance*. It is never plain sailing. Although separated from her philandering husband Bob Duport, Jean may decide to return to him, if only for the sake of their daughter. Then there are the 'inward irritations always produced by love: the acutely sensitive nerves of intimacy: the haunting fear that all may not go well'. But here is what makes it all worthwhile: 'There is, after all, no pleasure like that given by a woman who really wants to see you.'

By volume four the affair has ended and by volume five Nick has married Isobel Tolland. But Jean's ghost is never really laid. For although Nick eventually concludes that she was never any better than a *poule de luxe* like Bijou Ardglass – 'It struck me all at once, confronted by this luxuriance, that ... money was after all what Jean really liked' – he can still recall, forty years on, her soft laugh and the invitation that accompanied it: 'It's the bedroom next to yours. Give it half an hour. Don't be too long.'

The difficulty Powell had in resolving Nick's affair with Jean is apparent from a letter he wrote to Jocelyn Brooke, who had agreed to read the manuscript and, if necessary, make suggestions. The book ended rather abruptly, he explained, because he couldn't make up his mind 'whether or not to attempt more of an "anecdotal" ending, e.g. her husband has had a serious accident and she feels she must go back to him. Sometimes I feel I should attempt a "set form" of that kind – at other moments I recoil from it.'[32] Powell also raised this last point with Evelyn Waugh: 'I am always torn between trying to emphasise the plot in order that the design should not seem woolly (and also for commercial reasons) and, on the other hand, trying to avoid too neatly contrived happenings that detract from its naturalism and may spoil the overall picture.'[33]

That an overall picture was beginning to emerge was apparent to reviewers. 'These books will not, it seems, tell any particular story,' wrote Julian Symons in the *TLS*, 'but will offer glimpses of a number of people at various moments in time … Mr Powell's twin purposes are to expose and comment on the condition of society between the wars, and to illuminate also some aspects of the general human condition.' Symons praised Powell's 'infallible sense of social ironies' and his 'sense of place', as evidenced by his skill in capturing the atmosphere of the Ritz; but he did hazard that 'some of the local colour', like Trotskyites and Surrealism, 'belongs to a slightly later date'.[34] James Stern, in *Encounter*, also thought it was 'a trifle premature' of Powell to bring in a Trotskyite refugee like Guggenbuhl when he did. But he agreed with Symons that '[to] [Mr Powell] the story is not the thing: it is the place, the house, the hotel lounge, the prevailing fashion, the people …On the day my nephew asks me to tell him of the England I knew when I was young, I shall bid him read this history – for that is what this admirable novelist is writing.'[35]

In the *New Statesman* Richard Lister took a dim view of Powell's characters and the 'very narrow' segment of society to which they belonged. 'They are a doomed lot wriggling in a closed circle from which they do not even want to get out.' Lister thought Powell evoked his chosen scene 'brilliantly', but doubted whether he was aware 'that the world he describes is as nasty as it is'.[36] Another reviewer took a more lenient view of the 'restricted world' to which Powell's characters belonged:

'[T]he ruling class' sounds a bit snappish, and not much in the way of ruling evidently gets done; while 'society' sounds a bit something else, and 'the rich' may have the effect, to be avoided if possible, of recalling Miss Nancy Mitford or Miss Angela Thirkell. Anyway, it was unerringly pointed out recently that we find nothing of the working classes in *The Music of Time*, and in addition politics are not taken very seriously – this in the 1930s. Mr Powell is not 'committed', in fact – except to an interest in human behaviour and to the duty of irony and scepticism which confronts every chronicler of an exclusive group. A glance at some contemporary talents 'committed' in other directions will not show that Mr Powell has chosen wrongly.

This reviewer concluded his piece with a word of praise to die for: 'I would rather read Mr Powell than any other English novelist now writing.'[37]

Powell's fan was none other than Kingsley Amis, one of the 'sour young people' responsible, so Evelyn Waugh told Nancy Mitford, for the 'new wave of philistinism' that was threatening to engulf every literate person over forty.[38] Time's revenge (to borrow Powell's phrase) would see to it that thirty years later Amis had become almost indistinguishable from Waugh, at least from a distance; but in the Fifties, following the runaway success of his provocative first novel, *Lucky Jim*, he was regarded by many as a beery underbred lout, equally hostile to fine writing* and fine wines.

Powell knew from the beginning that this was nonsense. Shortly before *Lucky Jim* was published he read a review by Amis in the *Spectator* (the first Amis ever wrote), assessing James Thurber and P.G. Wodehouse, which concluded like this:

The old lesson, that it takes a serious writer to be a really funny writer, is rubbed in once more. Over here we have either popular entertainers who when scrutinised cease to entertain, or serious novelists, like Mr Evelyn Waugh and Mr Anthony Powell, who entertain as well. It is with the second, not the first, that Mr Thurber deserves to be compared.[39]

Powell wrote to Amis c/o the *Spectator*, saying he found his style 'very sympathetic' and suggesting he call in at *Punch*. Amis replied that he lived and worked in Swansea, but hoped to be in London before too long. Powell then issued an open invitation to lunch, which did not take place until the following March, by which time his good opinion of Amis had been reinforced by reading *Lucky Jim*: 'Mr Amis,' he wrote, 'is the first promising young novelist who has turned up for a long time.'[40]

Amis later claimed that he had always doubted Powell's original motives for writing to him about his *Spectator* piece. 'I *don't believe* the story about his curiosity,' he told Philip Larkin, 'tagging me as a bright new shag and wanting to see if he was right. I think he thought, "Huh, 48 in December, not getting any younger, ah, here's a new shag who seems to like me, better get his support right away."'[41] However that might be – and it is worth

* 'What can [these sour young people] hope to make of the undertones and innuendoes, the evocative, reminiscent epithets of, say, Tony Powell or Leslie Hartley?' asked Waugh.

recalling here what Peter Dickinson said about how alert Powell was to new developments in the arts – at the time Amis was flattered to be courted by a writer he much admired. In a letter to Larkin describing how he and Hilly, his first wife, went on a post-publication jaunt to Oxford and London, he wrote,

[Anthony Powell] was the nicest man we met ... He expressed admiration for Proust, affection for Grgr (Graham Greene) though dislike of his books, sorrow about Evelyn Waugh, who apparently gets into fights whenever he goes out and only does one draft of his books with an occasional verbal correction, liking for David Cecil, whose fag he was at Eton, but dislike of his books, and not much else that I can remember, except that he thought nasty Burgundy nicer than nasty Bordeaux. He also wore a ridiculous felt hat pulled down to the level of his eyebrows.[42]

Amis was still a card-carrying Party member in those days, something he would certainly have kept under his hat had he worn one. Nevertheless he and Powell had enough in common to strike up a friendship. Both loathed Bloomsbury, both delighted in South Welsh irony and both reserved the right to laugh at people who in their opinion deserved to be laughed at. They did not, however, meet again until 1957, when the Amises spent a weekend at The Chantry. Amis had already speculated on what sort of kit might be required: 'Shall I have to take white tie, black tie? Hunting pink? Guns, dogs?'[43] he asked Philip Larkin. In the event he was relieved to discover that The Chantry was modest in size, with not a butler in sight, and that Violet was 'as unswanky a Lady as could be imagined'.[44] When the Powells visited them in Swansea, which they did more than once, Violet would always leave a ten-shilling note for the bedmaker which Hilly would pocket.

Soon after visiting The Chantry Amis interviewed Powell for the BBC Third Programme, the subject of a revealing anecdote in his *Memoirs* which Powell did not challenge (as he did others), so presumably it is accurate in all but the date, which Amis gives as 1955, not 1957. No sooner had the interview begun when the producer butted in and insisted that they talk about 'The Novel' rather than Powell's novels; at which point Powell simply said that they would do it their way, or not at all. Collapse of producer. What impressed Amis was 'the placid, conversational delivery'[45] of Powell's response, which he attributed to his upbringing. He could never have taken that line himself without losing his temper in the process.

Once established, the friendship between Powell and Amis, though nothing like as intimate as that between Powell and Muggeridge, remained unbroken. It is true that Powell objected to some of what Amis wrote about him in his *Memoirs*; and he would not have appreciated the aspersions Amis cast on him in letters to Philip Larkin (who in *his* letters to Amis dubbed Powell 'the horse-faced dwarf'). But as he himself admitted, what seems like savagery when quoted out of context in the press is usually understood to be satirical when confined to a small circle of friends. I myself can vouch for the fact that when lunching with Amis, which I did three or four times in the Eighties, his relish for *Dance* was very apparent. Uncle Giles, invoked as far back as 1952 in a letter to Larkin, was a particular favourite of his; so too Moreland, who says something here that Amis himself might have written: 'One of the worst things about life is not how nasty the nasty people are. You know that already. It is how nasty the nice people can be.'

A year or so before he contacted Kingsley Amis, Powell had made overtures to another writer who he thought had dealt intelligently with his work. This was Jocelyn Brooke (1908-66), referred to several times already, who had submitted a piece on *Afternoon Men* to *Time and Tide* without, apparently, realising that Heinemann were reissuing it. Powell said he thought Brooke had caught the tone of the novel 'extraordinarily well (as I now see it)', but insisted, as he always did, that it was meant to be 'a quiet little love story with a contemporary background', not 'a slashing satire'. Powell added that his new job at *Punch* was 'not without its funny side in the light, for example, of your article',[46] which I take to be a reference to the 'sense of inward desolation' Brooke detected in his work.

Three years younger than Powell, educated at Bedales and Oxford, Brooke was a genuine oddity who spent twenty years faffing about before suddenly finding the resolve to write full-time. The son and grandson of wine merchants, he was just old enough to be infected by the Twenties virus, and this, added to his being highly strung, made him virtually unemployable during the Thirties, towards the end of which he had a nervous breakdown. Much to his surprise, since he was sure it would be like going back to school, Brooke rather enjoyed the war, finding fulfilment as the proverbial pox-doctor's clerk in an Army VD unit stationed in North Africa and Italy. So enamoured was he of soldiering that within a year or so of being demobbed he re-enlisted. But meanwhile he had had a novel, *The Military Orchid*, accepted for publication. Its success persuaded him that writing was truly his *métier*, and having bought himself out of the army he went to it with a will, publishing fifteen titles between 1948 and 1955 alone.

Powell did not share Brooke's Proustian preoccupation with childhood or his passion for orchids, both very apparent from his novels, but he still thought he was one of the ablest writers to have surfaced since the war. In a letter to Brooke about his novel, *The Dog at Clamberhorn*, he wrote, 'You manage to bring off the feat of "telling the truth about yourself" without egotism or self-pity, and also with a lightness of touch that never becomes artificial and pretends that life is just a jolly good rag.'[47] Powell also admired the 'easy, conversational style' of Brooke's criticism, believing that it often got to the core of a book in a way that more formal articles never managed to attain. He must have enjoyed what Brooke says here, since it bore out his theory that only novelists understood the technical problems involved in writing a novel:

[A]nyone who has ever attempted to write a novel will know the appalling difficulties which can attend the mere removal of two people from one room to another (Virginia Woolf, for one, is on record as having suffered agonies over this particular fictional chore); but with Mr Powell the whole thing is managed with the smooth efficiency of a change of scene in some beautifully produced review.[48]

Powell and Brooke used to lunch together every few months. Brooke always put a fair amount of drink away and if the lunch had been on Powell at the Travellers would say 'Shall we be *beasts*, and go to *my* club now, and have another glass of port.' A year or two after their first meeting Powell invited Brooke down to The Chantry. Brooke accepted but excused himself thereafter, leaving Powell with the impression that he was unwilling 'to cope too often with face-to-face cordialities that might be acceptable in letters'. This is a curious statement given that their letters were largely about literary topics. I think the answer must be that away from his beloved Elham valley in Kent, Brooke, who never married, was happiest on neutral territory like a club.

Brooke was one of the first critics of *Dance* to take issue with the notion that Powell was an English Proust. It was true, he wrote, that Powell was

engaged upon a long continuous novel, whose title admittedly carries a Proustian echo, and which deals, for the most part, with the higher ranks of society; but there the resemblance ends. One might just as profitably compare Proust with Galsworthy. The point need not be laboured, but it is significant that *The Music of Time* begins at Eton, when the narrator and his friends are already adolescent; Mr Powell is not much – if at all – interested in childhood, nor does he respond (or at least his narrator does not) with much enthusiasm to the beauties of nature: one can hardly, for example, imagine the young Nicholas Jenkins standing rapt before the hawthorn hedge at Tansonville.[49]

No indeed. You could also point out, echoing Powell himself when taxed with the comparison, that unlike Proust (and Brooke) he was neither homosexual nor solipsistic. Nevertheless, I think they are more alike than Brooke, at that stage, was prepared to allow (he died before the sequence was completed). For a start, both were obsessed with Time and its consequences for human beings. Again, both wrote largely about what they had either seen, heard or experienced; you could say of Powell what Louis Auchincloss said of Proust, that there would be 'little point ... in writing so many volumes to recapture a purely invented past'.[50] Then there are the uses to which they both put painting, particularly as a device for capturing people and places. Also their shared acknowledgement of how little we know of other human beings, plus the idea that there is always a real and an imaginary person with whom we fall in love. Powell's prose, though never so contorted as Proust's, is sufficiently labyrinthine in places to deserve the adjective 'Proustian'. It is also the case that Powell, like Proust, made endless alterations and could hardly bear to part with his manuscripts, which were equally messy. Finally, can it be just a coincidence that Nick and Jean, like Swann and Odette, should first come to grips when bowling along in a vehicle?

13

A Legacy

'Riches should come as the reward of hard work, preferably one's forebears'.'
Sir Steven Runciman

'In this country it is rare for anyone, let alone a publisher, to take writers seriously.'
Anthony Powell

In the Queen's Birthday Honours for 1956 Powell was made a Commander of the British Empire (CBE) for his services to literature. With impeccable timing his investiture took place in late November, shortly after the Suez crisis had ensured that there would very soon be no empire left to command. But unlike Evelyn Waugh, who considered the CBE 'a degrading decoration', fit only for 'second grade civil servants',[1] he had no qualms about accepting it. 'After all,' he told Maurice Cranston, 'one lives in the world so why not take pleasure in worldly things?'[2] A year or so later he won his first literary prize when At Lady Molly's was awarded the James Tait Black Memorial Prize for the best novel of 1957.

By now it was apparent to reviewers that Powell was engaged on a long haul, probably ten volumes thought Julian Symons in the *Times Literary Supplement*. But, cautioned Symons, this was no latter-day *Forsyte Saga*: 'It is very likely that the series will end without formal tidiness, leaving the principal characters frozen in single, symptomatic attitudes.'[3] The same conclusion had been reached by Anthony Quinton in the *London Magazine*: 'It is all rather like the steady unwinding of a bolt of cloth of superlative texture but no apparent design.'[4] Both Quinton and Symons also considered that Powell's detachment, so necessary to achieve his comic effects, might impose limitations in other directions. Take what Quinton called 'a serious event' like Jenkins's engagement. This, he said, 'is just not discussable in Powell's dialect'. Quinton then spoilt his case by rashly predicting that 'it would be impossible for anyone to commit suicide in a Powell novel'; but what he said about Jenkins's engagement was spot on in respect of an even more 'serious event', Jenkins's marriage. Anyone hoping for more than the barest details of this is in for a disappointment:

To think at all objectively about one's own marriage is impossible, while a balanced view of other people's marriage is almost equally hard to achieve with so much information available, so little to be believed. Objectivity is not, of course, everything in writing; but, even after one has cast objectivity aside, the difficulties of presenting marriage are inordinate. Its forms are at once so varied, yet so constant, providing a kaleidoscope, the colours of which are always changing, always the same. The moods of a love affair, the contradictions of friendship, the jealousy of business partners, the fellow feeling of opposed commanders in total war, these are all in their way to be charted. Marriage, partaking of such – and a thousand more – dual antagonisms and participations, defies definition.

Powell was asked about this by Kingsley Amis in the second of their radio discussions. He said it all depended on whether or not you were dealing with a happy marriage:

If somebody's married life is in a very bad way then like it or not they'll tell you all about it. But if people are rubbing along all right in their marriage they won't discuss it with you. And I think that if my narrator, who is happily married, were to give immense details about what his married life was like, you would immediately feel a sense of unreality about the rest of the book.[5]

When, many years later, Amis dealt with Jenkins's marriage in a long radio talk he gave on *Dance*, he said he thought that

the *real* difficulty facing the *author* wasn't merely to describe a marriage but to describe it on the same scale as all the other events and characters while going on describing them on that scale. Impossible? No, just foolhardily inadvisable without guarantee of a working life extended well into the next century. But he has no way of saying that, and Jenkins can't say it for him ... *That's* the point about first person narration.[6]

But at the time, 1960, Amis thought Powell was copping out, as indeed did Evelyn Waugh. 'Mr Powell,' he grumbled in the *Spectator*, 'owes us something more solid than this evasion of the novelist's duty if he expects us to sympathise with the anxieties of his creations.'[7]

Had Waugh lived to see the completion of the sequence – it was, he said, one of the few reasons he had to desire longevity – he might have amended his complaint. Because if you read carefully enough you can see how and why Nick and Isobel 'suit each other', as Jeavons would say. On the other hand, you need not read a line to appreciate Powell's dilemma. Jenkins, in most people's eyes, is his alter ego. So were he to examine closely Jenkins's marriage, he would automatically invite readers to confuse it with his own.

Which brings me to *my* dilemma. I should like to say more about Powell's marriage, but I can't. What I can do, however, is draw the reader's attention to how he treats aspects of married life in a couple of reviews. Here he quotes, approvingly I think, the analysis of married love given by the French writer, Marcel Jouhandeau:

> When I think of [Elise], I feel that married love has nothing to do with sympathy, with sensuality, with passion, with friendship, or with love. It alone is adequate to itself and cannot be reduced to one or another of those different feelings. It has its own nature, its particular essence, and its unique mode which depends on the couple that it brings together.[8]

In the next passage he quarrels with Somerset Maugham's belief that the prospect of sex, and sex alone, is what makes one person marry another:

> It would not be difficult to find further instances in Mr Maugham's more solid works of this assumption that marriage is entirely a matter of passion, and that passion is almost entirely a matter of good looks: both postulates resting on decidedly questionable premises. The complicated gradations of community of interest and instinctive attraction seem to play an almost negligible part in the lives of his characters, as does desire to have children for its own sake.[9]

In *Faces* Powell declares that becoming a father changed him – but omits to say how. And while on the subject of children I recall that Cathleen Ann Steg, a speaker at the first Anthony Powell Society conference in 2001, was rather shocked by the 'invisibility' of Nick and Isobel's children, in particular Nick's reference, in *Books Do Furnish a Room*, to making arrangements for 'a son' to go to school. 'I have two sons,' she said. 'I don't call them "a son". They have names.' As this incident takes place immediately after the war I think Nick must be arranging a place for his younger son. So here, to redress the balance, is an anecdote of Violet's about their younger son John that speaks for itself. The Powells had been to see a play in Edinburgh with Henry Green and his wife. By the time it was finished Green was desperate for a drink:

> Before I could intervene, Henry said to John, aged twelve, 'Johnny boy, just run down and see if that's the sign of a pub across the road' and John obligingly skipped across what seemed to me to be the main traffic artery between John O'Groats and Land's End. Mercifully, [our] cars drove up just as John had signalled that it was indeed the sign of a pub, so he was recalled. By then, however, my rage had overcome all good manners, and I bawled into the ear of my husband's oldest school friend, 'Henry, if that boy is run over Tony will thrash you within an inch of your life.'[10]

In his letters to George Lyttelton, Powell's friend Rupert Hart-Davis refers to his mistress and colleague Ruth Simon – later his wife – as 'my beloved prop and stay'. This, it seems to me, is a good description of what Violet was to Powell. Quite apart from ensuring that every morning he could 'strap himself into his desk', unburdened by domestic responsibilities, she was also on hand with suggestions or advice, if required. For instance if he wanted to know what a lady would be wearing to go to a party in a museum in, say, 1936, she would have an answer. Or again, to quote Powell himself, 'She's very helpful if I say, "Two people are arriving on a doorstep; I just want a bit of delay. What would they suddenly have begun to talk about?"'

Violet shared Powell's delight in 'looking people up' and she could, if necessary, put them down just as firmly as well. Her disappointingly discreet memoirs, throughout which she refers to Powell as 'Anthony', not Tony, do occasionally hint that there was very little she missed. Thus describing a visit to Evelyn Waugh at Combe Florey she writes: 'Evelyn was toying with a glass of whisky. He felt that this was appropriate for a country squire at 6 p.m. rather than a cup of tea, or the gin and Italian vermouth which he could be found drinking when off his guard.'[11] Simon Raven recalled the manner in which she demolished the character of someone who came up in conversation. 'Chop, chop, chop – until there was nothing left but a bit of gristle.' Raven also recalled that it was from Violet that he learnt one of the more extravagant excuses Cyril Connolly advanced for his literary sterility. 'He told her he couldn't write for a month after he'd come!'[12] Nevertheless it is in Connolly's *Unquiet Grave*, when he dilates on 'the pleasure of the joint understanding of the human comedy', that you will, I think, find the secret of the Powells' successful marriage:

> The greatest charm of marriage, in fact that which renders it irresistible to those who have once tasted it, is the duologue, the permanent conversation between two people which talks over everything and everyone until death breaks the record. It is this which, in the long run, makes a reciprocal equality more intoxicating than any form of servitude or domination.[13]

Admittedly Connolly went on to warn that because '[the artist] must look alone out of the window', the duologue, by depriving him of 'those much rarer moments which are particularly his own', might prove dangerous. But he must have been thinking of himself, not Powell, whose mornings Violet made inviolate.

*

By 1957 relations between Malcolm Muggeridge and his employers at *Punch*, the Agnew family, had become very strained. While the circulation rose, which it did during his first few years in the chair, the Agnews were prepared to overlook the number of important corns he trod on. But once it began to fall they became increasingly agitated by the howls of pain from the Establishment. That summer a row over a mildly subversive poem about Cheam, the prep school for which Prince Charles was destined, led to a parting of the ways. Muggeridge, with a year's salary in his pocket, reverted to being a freelance, leaving Powell to soldier on under the new editor, Bernard Hollowood, formerly the radio and television critic, whose main interest was cricket. Predictably, Powell found Hollowood unsympathetic. More than twenty years later, when Alan Watkins visited The Chantry, he made some reference to Hollowood. 'Well, is he?' said Powell. 'I had hoped he was starving.'[14]

But however irksome he found the new régime, Powell could not afford to resign. He needed that £1500 a year over and above his royalties to pay for two sons at Eton and the upkeep of The Chantry and its grounds. Then, in the autumn of 1958, Hollowood decided that *Punch* could do without a Literary Editor. Powell, who was on six months' notice, received a golden goodbye of £500. It was, he told Jocelyn Brooke, 'really rather a relief [to leave], though a bore to have to reorganise one's affairs. It was also convenient to have a London office. It looks as if I shall divide my time between the *New York Times* and the *Daily Telegraph*, but I am also going as "literary advisor" to Heinemann's.'[15]

The job of writing for the *New York Times* did not materialise, but in January 1959 he began his fortnightly column in the *Telegraph*, reviewing 'anything from a life of Christina Rosetti in the first half of the month to a book about the reorganisation of the Roman Army in the second'.[16] He would occupy this slot for just over thirty years, only relinquishing it following Auberon Waugh's toxic review of *Miscellaneous Verdicts* in the *Sunday Telegraph*. Whatever he was paid in the beginning – and the Berrys, he would later complain, were always a stingy lot – it can't have approached his stipend at *Punch*, particularly when perks such as review copies are taken into account. Peter Dickinson, with whom he remained on good terms, and who claims to be the source for 'sheet lightning hangovers' in *Hearing Secret Harmonies*, thought he had been 'hard hit financially' by his sacking. But almost a year to the day after his exit from *Punch* he had a totally unexpected windfall that would free him from financial worry for the foreseeable future.

The source of this bounty was none other than Philip Powell, who at his death was found to be worth £174,000, the equivalent today of almost £2.5

million. True, there was duty to pay on this of £97,000, but Powell still pocketed about a million, vastly more, I suspect, than he had earned to date from his books. He doesn't mention this in his Memoirs, but there may be an oblique acknowledgement of it in *The Kindly Ones* when Uncle Giles's estate proves 'unexpectedly large' (though not in the same league as Philip's).

So Philip Powell was a dark horse. For years he had pleaded poverty; now he was revealed as a wealthy man. Small wonder that Powell should add 'secretive' to 'proud' and 'anonymous' when describing the sort of people who, like Uncle Giles and his parents, lived in residential hotels. And yet it must have been obvious to Powell that his parents weren't destitute. After all, Philip belonged to four clubs and Maud, his mother, who died in 1954, left £45,000. Some of this must account for Philip's riches. As for the rest, I think we must assume that he was cannier – or luckier – than Uncle Giles at playing the market, this being about the only prudent way then that someone in his position could accumulate wealth.

What did this money buy for Powell? Peace of mind, obviously. He said more than once, when canvassed about bursaries for young writers, that old writers were far more deserving of help, since by then writing was all they could do. He now knew he could afford to devote himself to completing *Dance*, however many years it took. There would be no need, as there might have been, to look for more remunerative bread-and-butter tasks than reviewing – 'that recurrent disease you've got to deal with every fortnight'.[17] His new-found wealth also strengthened his hand with publishers, enabling him to sever ties with Penguin a few years later. No doubt there were other, more material consequences as well. Powell had his suits and shirts made for him, enjoyed decent wine and liked to travel, which he did for two or three weeks every year, in reasonable style. The cost of such indulgences could now be met with a clearer conscience.

Powell had as little interest in business or finance as in politics, but saddled with a character like Widmerpool he could not afford to display his inexperience of such matters. Fortunately he knew someone to whom he could turn for guidance, Sir Henry ('Harry') d'Avigdor-Goldsmid MP, a man of parts who had already distinguished himself in the City and the wartime army before entering Parliament. It was from Sir Harry that Powell learnt about 'the Acceptance World'. And when he was looking for the kind of job that Widmerpool might aspire to in 1936, Sir Harry obligingly recalled that it was round about then that big industrial firms like Donners-Brebner were creating departments to run their pension funds: 'I think Widmerpool would get a great sense of importance busying himself with fluctuations in the trade cycle and poring over multifarious charts that brokers proliferate.'[18]

Powell next quizzed Sir Harry about a job abroad for Bob Duport, perhaps in the metal market, which could be linked with the outbreak of war. His solution was chrome: 'During the war we went to enormous lengths to pre-empt Turkish production of chrome in order to stop the Germans getting it.'[19] It was also to Sir Harry that Powell applied for the subject of a row between a DAAG* at Division and his opposite number at Corps. Two years later he indicated that 'any information about sergeants embezzling mess funds' would always be welcome.

About half-way through their correspondence Powell joked that Sir Harry's contributions to *Dance* had created the basis for an interesting Bacon/Shakespeare controversy in the future. 'Some will say that Sir Harry – being too great a man to put his name to a novel – hired Powell, a journalist known to stop at nothing, as the vehicle for his work. Others will take the view that there was no such person as Sir Harry d'Avigdor-Goldsmid, and this was Powell's pseudonym during his secret City and political life.'[20] In 1968 he said he was 'rather toying with the idea of sending Widmerpool into politics in the Labour interest'. Sir Harry confirmed that Widmerpool's City background would not be an 'insuperable' problem just after the war. Then in 1970 Powell again asked Sir Harry's advice 'on this perennial subject'.

> I see Widmerpool as being created a Life Peer about 1958 ... this being done, as you once suggested, by a Tory government rather than his own party. This means he would have been out of office since 1951. He was (and this is between ourselves) in some way that never became quite clear, involved in the Burgess and Maclean defections, but all was forgiven and forgotten, so nothing definite was ever alleged. Any suggestions as to what he might have been doing out of office during that period? (The book to appear next year touches on his fellow-travelling tendencies, chiefly in connection with visits to Prince Theodoric's now Communist country.)[21]

Sir Harry replied:

> 1958 was the year when Life Peerages came in. He could make use of his pre-war Donners connections to indulge in very profitable East West barter trade which then sprang up ... profits were made by inducing Iron Curtain countries to purchase such materials as potash – they paid a keen price, but what they sold in return could be sold at a large profit. This would conform very well to Widmerpool.[22]

---

* Deputy-Assistant-Adjutant-General, Widmerpool's job when Jenkins becomes his dogsbody.

Sir Harry was by no means the only friend Powell consulted about *Dance*. Needing a plausible peg on which to hang one of Pamela Flitton's wartime misdemeanours, Powell quizzed Alan Ross, who had served in the navy: 'Could a naval lieutenant or sub-lieutenant be dismissed his ship for an indiscretion with a girl, or does that only happen to the officer in command? ... Perhaps he would just be reprimanded. If you happen to have any scabrous anecdotes about ATS or WRENS at your fingertips they would also be acceptable.'[23] What added spice to this enquiry was that Ross had had an affair with Pamela's prototype, Barbara Skelton, some years before.

Powell sought additional advice on military matters from Rupert Hart-Davis, who had been an adjutant in the Guards, Simon Raven and Peter Fleming (though Powell, a 'conventional soldier', was 'a trifle shocked' to discover that while on active service Fleming had not only kept a diary – 'strictly forbidden' – but had it with him when his glider came down behind Japanese lines).[24] Rupert Hart-Davis also read Powell's galleys, as indeed did Handasyde Buchanan, manager of the toffs' bookshop in Curzon Street, Heywood Hill, and a great promoter of *Dance*. It was however to the Norfolk historian and squire of Felbrigg, Wyndham Ketton-Cremer, an old friend from Balliol, that Powell deferred on matters of style.

Powell's editor at Heinemann for most of the years he was writing *Dance* was Roland Gant, a mysterious figure reputed to be the by-blow of a Scottish nobleman, who left instructions (which were not obeyed) that no obituary of him appear. Of medium height, dapper, fluent in French, Gant had knocked about in Paris and New York before the war, been briefly a medical student, and was then recruited by SOE. Captured on a secret mission in France, he was ordered to dig his own grave. One version has it that he challenged the firing squad on the validity of their orders, convincing them that they would be in deep trouble if they went ahead and shot him without the proper paperwork. Another version is that having dug the grave and removed his clothes he began to sneeze uncontrollably, which made his executioner laugh. 'I can't shoot a man while I'm laughing,' said the German.

Gant's assistant at Heinemann was the poet and Latinist, James Michie, who told me that he and Gant used to call each other Chipchase and Maltravers, after the two rogues in *Agents and Patients*. When, in 1957, Gant left Heinemann (returning there in 1965), Michie became Powell's editor, though his responsibilities did not extend beyond deciphering the manuscripts (which Powell himself was not always able to do) and seeing them into print. Michie thought that Powell would have made a wonderful interrogator. 'Like most Etonians he had superb manners, to which was added great charm and an endearing smile. You were so at ease with him that you said much more than you'd intended, particularly about something like sex. At the same time he managed to be very oblique about himself.'[25] Michie also thought that one of the reasons Powell warmed to Gant – and, for that matter, to Kingsley Amis – was that their backgrounds were so different from his.

In John St John's history of Heinemann Powell is quoted as saying, 'A happy country is said to have no history. The same can be said about a happy relationship with one's publisher, as in my case.'[26] Powell had either forgotten, or chosen to conceal, that in the early Sixties he had thought seriously of moving elsewhere. The first shots were exchanged in 1958, over a division of the spoils when Penguin bought the paperback rights to *Dance* and the five pre-war novels. Heinemann wanted the fee split down the middle, whereas Powell's agent, David Higham, thought the author's contribution was greater than the publisher's and suggested 60/40 in Powell's favour. This enraged Heinemann's choleric chairman, A.S. Frere: 'If we admitted that [the author's contribution was greater] then I can only suggest that we had better get out of business and let authors publish and peddle their own books.' To which Powell replied: 'Yes. Go ahead. The delicacy of the refusal's phrasing makes the negotiation quite acceptable.'[27]

Powell's next complaint was about the 'ludicrous' amount of time it took Heinemann to bring his novels out. Surely, he wrote to David Higham, they could do it in less than six months? 'If they can't get a move on ...I don't know what there is to be said for them. Certainly not financial generosity or the beauty of the books that emerge from their press.'[28] Higham replied that 'actually six months is short indeed these days ... nine months is much more normal'. They then clashed twice over royalties. Powell thought he should received the full 15 per cent on reprints and on copies sold to private circulating libraries like Boot's. Heinemann would only pay 12½ per cent and 10 per cent respectively. 'They are the most cheese-paring buggers,'[29] commented Powell. But what came nearest to severing relations was Heinemann's failure to keep all volumes of *Dance* in print.

In August 1961 Powell learnt that the American writer Arthur Mizener, a great fan of *Dance*, had traipsed all over London trying unsuccessfully to find copies of *A Buyer's Market* and *The Acceptance World*. Having just been assured by Heinemann's managing director, Dwye Evans, that all the sequence was in print, Powell went off the deep end. 'The only possible excuse,' he told David Higham, 'is if they are seriously thinking of doing a three-in-one volume. I perfectly realise that I am not an enormous seller, but I *am* a seller, and certainly give Heinemann's increasingly unattractive list some prestige. Above all, I want a publisher who takes an interest in my books and the series.' In his own hand Powell added: 'This is not written in a sudden rage but in sober fury at the confirmation of Heinemann's crassness.'[30]

It then transpired that Dwye Evans had either lied, or was not in touch with his production department. Powell thought the latter more culpable. He put it to Higham that perhaps the time had come 'to ask very seriously whether it would not suit [Heinemann] better to disembarrass themselves of an author in whom they clearly take no interest'.[31] Higham must have read the riot act, because by Christmas 1961 all of *Dance* was back in print. But it was not until the return of Roland Gant to Heinemann in 1965 that Powell's confidence in his publisher was fully restored. Twenty-one years later, shortly after the publication of Powell's last novel, *The Fisher King*, Gant decided to retire, news that Powell received with 'a distinct pang'.* Roland, he said, was 'a publisher in a million'.[32]

*

Some writers like the sound of their own voice. Powell was not one of them. So a little bit of arm-twisting was necessary to get him to cross the pond for the first time since 1937 and be examined about his work by Ivy League students. He went at the behest of John Meek, the then Vice-President of Dartmouth College, New Hampshire, a man who would not take no for an answer. In conjunction with Powell's American publisher, Little, Brown, Meek made the novelist an offer he couldn't refuse: an undemanding itinerary – no formal lectures, just questions and answers – and his every want supplied.

The visit, which took place shortly after the row with Heinemann, could not have come at a better time for promoting *Dance* in America, where despite having had several different publishers Powell was acknowledged to have 'a small but vocal audience'. This would seem a good moment to see how that audience came about.

Before the war Powell was virtually unknown in America, something he attributed to the Depression, which made American publishers wary of all but the most gilt-edged of British authors like Maugham and Wodehouse. *Afternoon Men* did creditably for a first novel by a foreign writer, but not well enough for the publisher to take *Venusberg. From a View to a Death*, retitled

---

* Gant's son, Dr Vanya Gant, told me how proud his father was to have been associated with *Dance* and its author, a man so different from him in every way, yet with whom he forged 'a close and trusting relationship'.

13. A Legacy

Mr Zouch: Superman, sank without a trace; and that was more or less that for almost twenty years. Scribner's bought the rights to the first two volumes of *Dance*, but declined to bid for any more. Meanwhile an Anglophile Manhattan bookseller called Bob Vanderbilt so enjoyed *Venusberg* and *Agents and Patients* that in 1952 he published them in one volume himself, selling more than 3000 copies, a better result than Scribner's achieved with *Dance*.

Farrar, Strauss were Powell's next American publisher, but they were no more successful with *The Acceptance World* than Scribner's had been with its predecessors, one problem being, as Higham pointed out to Powell, that the book didn't really stand on its own. When Farrar, Strauss turned down *At Lady Molly's* Powell commented to Higham: 'I am obviously fated to be published once by every publisher in America.'[33] Luckily, in the Boston firm of Little, Brown he found a publisher who was prepared to go the distance despite 'modest' sales. For instance in 1970, in response to a request by Higham's that Powell's advance be raised from $3000 to $5000, his editor there, Harry Sions, wrote back 'We at Little, Brown are not unduly concerned with the fact that the Powell novels have not yet made a profit. We are looking forward to the day when there will be a breakthrough in this country and we will be delighted to continue publishing Mr Powell until and indeed after this happy event.' Sions added that 'as a gesture of affection to Mr Higham, we will offer an additional advance of $500, making it $3500'.[34]

That same year, in a piece entitled 'The Relevance of Anthony Powell', Sions put his mouth where his money was. The gist of his argument was that if the relevance of a writer was determined by his engagement with the here and now – Vietnam, race riots, Nixon etc – then Powell was indeed irrelevant. But if, on the other hand, the touchstone was how he dealt with something timeless like the human comedy, then he was 'burningly relevant'.

> I know of no writer who is more sensitive to the special worlds in which his characters live, whether it be publishing, the military, politics, sexual fantasy or whatever; but he treats these worlds and their people in his own special way. Anthony Powell, perhaps more than any other writer in the world today, is not influenced by doctrine, by any special political point of view. His people are not conformists: they are individuals, with their special charms and madnesses. They may infuriate or entrance you, but they never bore you.[35]

It took Little, Brown four years to acquire the rights to the first three volumes of *Dance*. Having done so, they published them in a triple-decker. This was in January 1962, and a very shrewd move it proved to be. Not only did it pander to the American taste for club-sandwich-sized fiction, it also

223

gave reviewers a chance to consider the story so far. As Elizabeth Janeway wrote in the *New York Times Book Review*, 'the first three volumes of the five-volume series, when taken quickly between a single pair of covers ...present an even sharper, more profound and more closely knit picture of the world than when read singly.'[36] The same point was made by *Newsweek*: 'As published singly, [the Powell novels] often seemed disjointed, full of capriciously loose ends, mysterious references. But when they are read in series, the subtlest of joinery appears, the loose ends are tied in fascinating knots, the mysteries lead to captivating exposures.'[37]

Newsweek also ran a short interview with Powell in which he denied that *Dance* was intended to be elegiac, a common assumption among American reviewers, one of whom referred to the sequence as a 'gaga saga'. But this was an argument he could never win. Indeed many British reviewers took the same line. On the other hand he was gratified at the interest American reviewers took in Jenkins, however far-fetched their extrapolations (an early *Time* review took Uncle Giles at his word and identified him as 'a descendant of that Captain Jenkins about whose ear a war was fought in the 18th century').[38] I can suggest two explanations for this. First, in Britain Jenkins tends to be seen, understandably enough, as his master's voice: 'a device rather than a character', in Powell's own words. And that voice is – or at any rate was – familiar enough in manner to inspire like or dislike, but not much in the way of analysis. But as Alison Lurie pointed out, first-person heroes like Jenkins – 'trustworthy, intelligent, modest and sane'[39] – were a rarity for American readers in the Fifties and Sixties. No wonder they were curious about him.

Secondly, whereas British reviewers of Powell were almost exclusively male, in America his books were often dealt with by females, among them Elizabeth Janeway, Elizabeth Hardwick, Naomi Bliven, Joan Didion, Pamela Marsh and Dawn Powell, who reckoned that 'Of all the sad young men alone in all the gay places, Nicholas Jenkins must be the saddest.'[40] I can't imagine a man saying that. Again, I don't recall any British reviewer echoing Naomi Bliven's point that once Jenkins marries, his attitude towards relationships changes: before, 'he understood loves more easily than marriages'; after, 'he becomes more interested in relationships within marriage than in relationships, however alluring, outside it'.[41] Jenkins, incidentally, is 'Nicholas' to most of these ladies, not 'Nick', or 'Nick Jenkins' or, commonest of all in Britain, 'Jenkins'.

Powell did, of course, appeal to American men as well as women. One of them, Benjamin DeMott, provides an instructive vignette of the author rebuking some youthful trespassers:

13. A Legacy

The back-yard acres of The Chantry, near Frome, Anthony Powell's Somerset house, are a splendid tramping ground – wetland, stream, bullrushes, overgrown paths. One midsummer noon while I was visiting, the owner, clad in boots and walking stick and light mac, leading a band of improbables including a former Red Army officer named Tibor [Szamuely] as well as myself, fetched up on trespassers – four or five bejeaned figures in their twenties, lads and lasses picnic-bent, crashing through the bush, shouting Shit. The owner's position was quickly conveyed in a tone severe yet not castigatory, bespeaking awareness that asking permission had gone out, that hanging a man for breaking a branch had no merit, that it was a healthy thing for neighbourhood youngsters to be aware of charming local picnic sites and to use them ... Nevertheless, the trespassers must understand that in future they would have to ask permission at the house, was that understood? And if it were inconvenient to have them then, perhaps another time. Nevertheless – the message underlined – nevertheless, you will need always to *ask at the house*: this is understood? The picnickers, impressed (I thought) by someone standing up for their rights without shrillness, embarrassment, or threat, hauled ass, and a minute later, parting a hedgerow with his stick, our host brought us out onto the lawn.[42]

Powell's academic fans included Arthur Mizener, William Pritchard, Frederick Karl, Samuel Hynes and Arthur Schlesinger Jr, who described him as a 'prosopographer', an eighteenth-century term meaning someone who investigates 'the common background characteristics of a group of actors in history by means of a collective study of their lives'. Powell took this quasi-sociological interpretation in good part, while insisting once more that all he was trying to do was show how people behaved. By and large he was pleased with his reception in America, his only real cause for complaint being 'English reviewers writing for American papers who said how difficult it was for outsiders to understand what I was getting at. That happened a lot in the early days and used to send me absolutely up the wall.'[43]

To whom was Powell referring? Certainly not Elizabeth Bowen or Alan Pryce-Jones ('George Cloyne'), both of whom gave him an enthusiastic write-up in the old *New York Herald Tribune*. Perhaps the culprit is Roger Pippett, identified as 'a former British book critic'. Pippett reviewed *A Question of Upbringing* for the *New York Times Book Review*, describing it as 'completely English – and upper-class English at that'.[44] Some readers, I suppose, might have been put off by that, but it seems a perfectly valid caution to me; after all Henry Swados, in the *New Republic*, thought it would 'not be easy for Americans to grasp the apparent coolness of the relationships between boys of a certain class, or their casual attachment to their families'.[45] Powell used to quote approvingly Conrad's dictum about reviews: 'Measure them. Don't read them.' Could this be what happened here?

One distinguished American critic who thought Powell overrated was Edmund Wilson. In an interview conducted in London but published in the *New Yorker* Wilson was asked about Powell. He said he couldn't see why people made such a fuss about him. 'He's just entertaining enough to read in bed late at night in summer, when his books usually reach me ... It's a pity he ever dipped into Proust.'[46] Powell's immediate reaction to this was recorded in an interview he gave shortly afterwards. 'Some people,' he said, 'simply won't like my books because they don't like my personality.'

> People often put their preferences in literature down to a number of things that don't count, when it's all based on personal preference. Edmund Wilson ... indicated that he had read my books and enjoyed them, but simply didn't understand what all the fuss was about. Somehow one doesn't mind that kind of criticism; it came from a man who had given thought and care to the matter, a man who loves books, and you don't mind that as you mind a good deal of less thoughtful or competent criticism.[47]

Some years later, in a letter to John Monagan, Powell revealed that not long after the *New Yorker* piece appeared he met Wilson at Cyril Connolly's sixtieth birthday party in London. He took the bull by the horns and said he quite understood why Wilson found his books unsympathetic. 'He seemed rather embarrassed, but we got on quite well in the few minutes we talked ... if you start off with the determination that it is imitation Proust, the objection is very understandable.' It reminded him, said Powell, of the arbitrary manner in which an American publishing lady, now deceased, had turned down *From a View to a Death*. In a letter to another lady publisher, also deceased, she wrote: '"He is a homo, I suspect: all these clever kids are, it seems to me and I think it is a pity." It seems to me that Wilson in rather the same way has settled one's status in his own mind before he opens the book.'[48]

Inevitably, Wilson's version of this, their only meeting, is somewhat different:

> Powell, whom I had imagined tall and languid, is a lively intent little Welshman, who began by letting me know that he had seen what I had written about him and hastened to add that people in America could sometimes see things more clearly than people over here where they were all so much closer to it; and he went on to talk eagerly about the sales of his books in America. I asked whether Widmerpool's financial disquisitions were authentic or double talk, and he assured me that they were perfectly accurate – he had got up the bank rate and all the rest.[49]

Powell had his final dig at Wilson in 1993, when contacted by Wilson's biographer, Jeffrey Meyers. After repeating what he had said to Monagan he added: 'He was an odd fish who never had the slightest idea what the British, or life in the UK was like, but was, I think, intelligent in his way.'[50] But although, as so often, Powell had the last word, honours were probably about even, because by being so condescending about 'America's best mind' – Gore Vidal's estimate – he bore out Wilson's criticism of the supercilious English literary elite in *Europe Without Baedecker*.

Other things being equal Powell would probably have found Wilson too earnest for his taste. In a review he called him 'the least frivolous man imaginable'.[51] But had they managed to sink their differences they would have found much to discuss, including Scott Fitzgerald, with whom Wilson overlapped at Princeton; George Orwell, the one English writer of his time for whom Wilson had unqualified admiration; and the American Civil War, the subject of Wilson's *Patriotic Gore*, with which Powell had been fascinated since childhood. I also feel sure that wearing his Aubrey hat Powell would have wished to verify the legend that even as an old man Wilson would line up six martinis and drink them one after the other without losing the thread of his conversation.

14

The Play's the Thing

'Dramatise! Dramatise!'

Henry James

Now that both his parents were 'off the scene', as he put it, Powell could find a place for them in *Dance*. They appear, as Captain and Mrs Jenkins, in the first part of *The Kindly Ones*, the theme of which is, to adapt a line of Valery's quoted by Moreland, *la guerre, la guerre, toujours recommencée.*

Captain Jenkins – his rank, unlike that of his brother Giles, is not in dispute – comes across as a neurotic martinet for whom 'all tragedies were major tragedies', a spot of blood on his riding britches ranking as high as the onset of Armageddon. Keen on power, 'though never in a position to wield it on a notable scale', he has his share of the power-seeker's concomitants, e.g. dyspepsia and 'a hatred of constituted authority'. But like Cyril Connolly, who hated colonels, but also hated those who made fun of them, he cannot bear to hear constituted authority questioned by anyone but himself. Hence his chronic irritation with Uncle Giles, the self-proclaimed radical; and hence, too, the mixed feelings with which he views a visit by his wife's distant relation, General Conyers, with his disdain for 'the powers that be'.

Although described as painfully shy with all but her family and a few close friends, Mrs Jenkins is obviously better able to 'cope' than her husband, and it is clear that he is the cross she has chosen to bear, just as Philip Powell was Maud's. She utters the most portentous line in the book, perhaps in the whole sequence: 'I thought it was the end of the world.' She is referring to the sight of Billson, the maid, standing stark naked on the threshold of the drawing-room at Stonehurst. But the date, Sunday 28 June 1914, tells a different story. The proud tower is about to crumble, the Four Horsemen are at the gate, summoned by what Uncle Giles calls 'a nasty affair' involving 'some royalty in a motor-car'.

Just over twenty-five years later Uncle Giles himself is gathered in while staying at the Bellevue, a mildewed seaside hotel managed by Albert, formerly the Jenkinses' cook. 'Awkward to the end', in the words of his younger brother, he has chosen the worst possible moment to involve his family, for the last time, in his affairs. Jenkins draws the short straw, travelling down to the south coast to attend the cremation, a trip that will also see most of his cherished memories of Jean go up in smoke. This particular pyre is lit by her ex-husband, Bob Duport, a coarse-grained character with a savage turn of phrase who is later revealed to be less of a philistine than Jenkins had supposed.

Besides Albert and Uncle Giles there is, at the Bellevue, another link with that fateful summer Sunday in the shape of Dr Trelawney, the magician and cult-leader. A palsied figure now, hard-up, asthmatic and addicted to heroin, Trelawney is reported by Albert to be trapped in the bathroom, unable to unlock the door. Luckily Jenkins gives the correct response – 'the Vision of Visions heals the Blindness of Sight' – to his habitual salutation – 'the Essence of the All is the Godhead of the True', whereupon Trelawney pulls himself together enough to turn the key in the lock. Once installed in his bedroom the Doctor goes into mystic mode, which results in a comic double-act involving him and Duport, the latter delivering a series of earthy rejoinders to Trelawney's florid transcendental posturings. Then Mrs Erdleigh arrives with the Doctor's fix, but not before he has predicted that 'the sword of Mithras ... will ere long now flash from its scabbard'. Next morning, right on cue, the Nazi-Soviet pact is announced.

Jenkins tars Trelawney with the same brush as Widmerpool: he is sinister and absurd, ludicrous and alarming – precisely the epithets Powell applied to Aleister Crowley (1875-1947), alias the Beast 666, when writing about him. Crowley, the model for Oliver Haddo in Maugham's early novel *The Magician*, a reissue of which Powell reviewed for *Punch*, was part mountebank, part monster. Cyril Connolly thought he 'bridged the gap between Wilde and Hitler'; while his biographer John Symonds, in what Powell calls 'a magnificent piece of understatement', concluded that 'he was not, in the narrow, Victorian sense of the word, "a gentleman"'.[1] Whether Crowley was a genuine mage, or whether magic was just a convenient means to an end for him, is not for me to say. But just as Dr Trelawney has an influence out of all proportion to the time he is on-stage in *Dance*, so Crowley – 'the wickedest man in the world' – aroused the interest of all sorts of people who did not necessarily share his taste for diabolism. Powell would certainly have got some useful background on him from Nina Hamnett, who knew him in her Paris days and was once overheard to warn someone: 'You be very careful if you have anything to do with AC, my dear. He once made fire come out of my studio floor, my dear.'[2] Crowley subsequently sued Nina for libel, a case he lost. It was later rumoured that her gory death was the result of a curse he put on her.

Crowley owed his baleful reputation to the three years he spent at a farmhouse near Cefalu, in Sicily, where he presided over a congregation dedicated to sex, drugs and black magic (not necessarily in that order). Eventually, as Norman Douglas told Nancy Cunard, he was too much even for the Italians, and they kicked him out — but not before he had been accused by the British press of culpability in the mysterious death of one of his followers, an Oxford undergraduate only a year or two older than Powell (Trelawney too was vilified in the press when one of his acolytes, a promising pianist, threw herself over a cliff). A few years later an account of life at Cefalu, by the unfortunate undergraduate's widow, Betty May, was published by Duckworth, as a consequence of which Powell was invited to lunch at Simpson's-in-the-Strand by Crowley himself. Crowley complained bitterly about Betty May's book but never threatened to sue, so that Powell concluded that he may just have wanted an audience. He compared his manner to that of 'a general who had been removed from his command for dropping shells on his own trenches'.[3] One curious detail, anticipating Powell's lunch with Scott Fitzgerald, is that Crowley drank milk. He must have been very off-colour, because this was a man who began the day with a half-pint of ether, drank triple absinthes as an aperitif and usually put away two or three bottles of wine with a meal before hitting the brandy. He was also, right up until his death, a very heavy heroin user.

Crowley died at a comfortable residential hotel just outside Hastings, where he was often visited by John Symonds, whose biography of him Powell reviewed in 1951. This book, which describes how dependent Crowley had become on heroin to alleviate his boredom and self-pity, is the obvious source for Powell's account of Dr Trelawney in old age. It contains a photograph of Crowley, taken about a year before he died, in which he sports a straggly goatee beard like Trelawney's. Another visitor Crowley had at this time was James Laver, who recorded how, after a shot of heroin, Crowley perked up to such an extent that the 'hypnotic fascination he must once have possessed' became very apparent. Perhaps Powell read this as well, because Jenkins says he is soon conscious of Trelawney's 'quasi-hypnotic powers', and although confident he can resist them, is on his guard. Thirty years or more later he is again on his guard when in the presence of Scorpio Murtlock, the spooky young hippie who claims to be a reincarnation of Trelawney.

By no means all Powell's admirers thought the occult scenes in *Dance* worked. Kingsley Amis, for instance, said they were like 'a burst paper bag',[4]

231

while Malcolm Muggeridge described Powell's apparent endorsement of characters like Mrs Erdleigh and Murtlock as 'the only chink in [his] otherwise implacably terrestrial outlook'.[5] Powell did not deny an interest in the occult. He once joked that like Max Beerbohm's character, Enoch Soames, his diabolism might be his most healthy side. And I think that Henchman, in his last novel *The Fisher King*, is speaking for the author when he observes: 'I am superstitious in the sense that I believe the curious synchronisms and juxta-positions, physical and moral, in which we all from time to time find ourselves involved, have meaning.' Powell was also prepared to speculate on what Edwardians called 'The Beyond'. When Duncan Fallowell asked whether he believed in life after death, he replied, 'Generally speaking, not. But I s'pose it is not absolutely inconceivable that maybe sort of quite *odd* things might happen ... later.'[6] But the reason he usually gave for including the occult element was that it had been part of his life from the very beginning:

> Remember we lived in a haunted house. That's the only explanation for some of the decidedly *peculiar* things that went on at Stonedene. And I had various rela-tions who were very keen on that sort of thing and actually told people's fortunes, like my mother's sister Violet and my grandmother on my father's side. My mother also used to talk about it a lot and would visit fortune-tellers, as everyone did in Edwardian times. Osbert Sitwell tells a story in his memoirs about a fash-ionable fortune-teller just before the first war who was in despair because she drew a blank with so many of the young men who consulted her. And then of course after that war you had this tremendous interest in Spiritualism and seances because people wanted to try and get in touch with relations of theirs who had been killed. But really the point of it coming in at what is chronologically the beginning of the book and then coming in again at the end is the fact that nothing ever changes. What is now dished up in a supposedly different form is really exactly the same as the thing one was familiar with as a child.[7]

Trelawney's impact on *Dance* was examined by Timothy d'Arch Smith in what Powell thought was an 'amusing' piece for the *London Magazine*.[8] D'Arch Smith also had an intriguing theory about the antecedents of Canon Paul Fenneau, the equivocal priest who dabbles in alchemy and is an authority on Scorpio Murtlock. He suggested that Fenneau was derived, at one remove, from the Reverend Montague Summers, an equally dubious churchman who was one of the demonologists Dennis Wheatley consulted when he embarked on the occult thrillers for which he is still best remembered.* D'Arch Smith

---

* Wheatley always insisted that his interest in Black Magic was purely academic. Of Crowley, whom he also consulted, he wrote that 'intellectually he is quite wonderful, but I don't believe he could harm a rabbit'.

cited as evidence Wheatley's novel *To the Devil a Daughter*, in which there is a character called Canon Copely-Syle, whose description matches that of Fenneau, and whom Wheatley based upon Summers. Powell, he thought, might have 'dipped into' Wheatley's book for its Satanic detail and come away with a character as well.

In his follow-up letter to d'Arch Smith, Powell said he hadn't read *To the Devil a Daughter* and did not draw on Montague Summers, whom he had never met, for Canon Fenneau. He did, however, admit to being a 'fan' of Wheatley, which may surprise those readers who recall that in his Journals he bracketed Wheatley with Hugh Walpole and the fictional Valentine Beals in *The Fisher King*, all 'relatively intelligent men who write more or less conscious drivel'. They may be even more surprised to learn that in 1972 he applied to Wheatley for help over *Dance*. Widmerpool (he explained) had been implicated in a spy ring. Could Wheatley suggest a plausible device for getting him off the hook? This was the sort of thing Wheatley excelled at and he evidently made several suggestions that Powell said 'clarified' matters with regard to the plot.

When Wheatley died his huge library was found to contain several signed first editions of Powell's novels, including *Afternoon Men* and *A Question of Upbringing*, both collectors' items even then. Appropriately – that word again – their friendship was forged over meals at one of Wheatley's many clubs, the St James's, to which Capel-Dunn – and Widmerpool – had also belonged. No doubt they drank to the post-war spirit, which Wheatley, as a Mayfair wine merchant in the Twenties, had done much to promote. And lest anyone wonder what common ground existed between two such different types of novelist, it is worth recalling one of Powell's dicta. Novelists, he would say, 'are much more like each other than they're like people who don't write novels'. So he had more in common with Wheatley than either of them had with, say, F.R. Leavis or Frank Kermode.

*

In July 1961 *Twentieth Century* magazine ran a substantial interview with Powell by W.J. Weatherby, the first piece of its kind to be published. Over the next thirty years a succession of interviewers, myself included, made their way down to The Chantry, usually arriving after lunch and departing after tea. On arrival one would be ushered into the high-ceilinged library-cum-drawing room with its stripey wallpaper and gallery of ancestral portraits that struck a French journalist as 'awkward and sepulchral'. Powell would measure his length on a large Victorian sofa, where he would often be joined by one of his cats, and the interviewer, perched on the edge of a deep armchair, would begin to poke around. I use that term because Powell gave the impression that submitting to questions about his work from a journalist was like undergoing an intimate medical examination at the hands of someone who was not qualified to perform it. You had to be a novelist yourself to undertake such a delicate task.

Powell did not put it quite like that in his Memoirs. He chose a military parallel instead. 'In the army it is not uncommon for a soldier to keep certain items of kit purely for the eye of the inspecting officer. Small odds and ends that are a trouble to clean or to assemble are stowed away for daily use, an unsullied example presented. That is rather like what writers usually hand out at interviews.' It helped, of course, that the same questions were asked again and again: Why did you decide to write a long novel? How far ahead do you plan? Were you influenced by Proust? Are you Nick Jenkins? Who is Widmerpool? ... etc, etc. Recognising that an indirect approach might yield better results a man from the *Times* recalled Dr Johnson: 'Questioning is not a form of conversation for gentlemen.'[9] This came back to haunt me when I was trying to agree a final draft of the interview I did with Powell for the *Paris Review*'s 'Writers at Work' series.

I had approached Powell after interviewing Kingsley Amis for the same series. George Plimpton (1927-2003), the magazine's founder and editor, was keen, but omitted to tell me that, as Powell put it, 'four (if not five) persons have interviewed me over the years for the *Paris Review*, and nothing has ever appeared'. He instructed me to tell Plimpton, 'in the plainest possible terms', that unless he could guarantee 'in writing' that my interview with him would appear, he would not be prepared to see me.[10] That was in June 1975. Two months later, on the day that *Hearing Secret Harmonies* was published, I interviewed Powell at Heinemann for the BBC World Service. It must have been then, I think, that I produced Plimpton's written guarantee of publication, following which Powell agreed to see me later in the year. He added, however, that while he was quite happy to discuss his writing, he would not talk in great detail about himself 'as I need any material of that sort for the Memoirs I am writing'.[11]

I eventually saw Powell shortly before Christmas, having sent him a rough list of questions in advance. We must have talked for a good two hours before Lady Violet arrived with the tea, over which there was plenty of gossip, particularly about Cyril Connolly, who had died the year before. I thought it had gone pretty well, but was conscious, when I read the fair copy, that it was no more 'an in-depth interview' than had been Julian Jebb's with Evelyn Waugh twenty years before. Never mind, I thought, George will understand.

The son of a diplomat and a graduate of King's College, Cambridge, he would appreciate that a degree of reticence was to be expected from Englishmen of Powell's age and class.

I was wrong. George felt that Powell was not playing the game. He asked me to submit no less than thirteen additional questions, all arising out of Powell's 'inadequate' replies. Some I thought were justified, as when George wanted Powell to give an example of someone whose wit was hard to get across on paper (I suggested Maurice Bowra); or when he asked what Powell meant when he said he had met people in the war 'who carved out careers by just absolutely imposing their will, with nothing else behind it'. But others would, I knew, risk a seizure. For instance talking about Hemingway's influence in the Twenties, Powell said there 'certainly was a feeling that writing had got to change, and I was quite interested in that'. Why? asked Plimpton. Who said so? Who were some of the experimenters? Was it a topic of conversation – 'We must change'? Again, when Powell said that writing, for him, was 'above all a question of *instinct*', Plimpton wondered what he meant. Are writers born? he asked. And what was the link between 'discipline', referred to earlier, and instinct?

As I had feared, the additional questions were not well received. Powell scribbled a few amendments on the typescript I sent him and made his feelings known in a letter:

15 July 1976

Dear Mr Barber,
    Here are some expansions of the answers. Plimpton's questions suggest that he is a man of almost incredible stupidity. I really can't supply a whole history of the Modern Movement, or write a treatise on 'instinct' for him.[12]

I forwarded Powell's 'expansions', but not his letter, to George, who wrote back to say that he was

puzzled, frankly, by Powell's reluctance to embellish or improve his interview. He acts as if the questions were galling, or rude ... which was hardly my intent. The interviews are not 'conversations' (which he seems to think) but in every case are attempts to get as much said as possible about an author's craft. What good is an interview which raises questions which are not pursued and answered. That he refused to answer even *one* query raises the possibility that he may have been confused by what we hoped of him. He sounds out of sorts, to put it mildly ... which made us wonder about the circumstances of your questioning him. Perhaps you reached him during dinner. *Coitus interruptus*? Was there a full moon?[13]

I explained to George that his questions were not put over the phone but typed up and sent in context. I then said I would speak to Powell's editor, Roland Gant, in the hope that he could bring Powell round.

Roland Gant advised against any further approaches to Powell, who was, he said, hard at work on his Memoirs. He said that while he sympathised with Plimpton's intention 'to get as much said as possible about an author's craft', he doubted whether Powell was capable of giving the sort of answers expected of him. 'He says somewhere that he's "a great non-definition man". So when he says that writing is only any good "if the art is there", don't expect him to explain what he means by "art". He thinks writing is a mysterious process which the author himself doesn't really understand.' – A bit like alchemy? – 'Yes, but there's no magic formula, just bloody hard work. You do it over and over again until you're satisfied.'

I passed on Roland Gant's comments to George, together with some amendments of my own. Although still not satisfied George kept his word and the interview was published in the Spring-Summer issue of 1978; but unlike most interviews in the series it has never been republished in one of the collected volumes. On receiving his copy Powell thanked me on a post-card, adding: 'You have brought off a project embarked on well over twenty years ago. Goes all right, I think, don't you?'

At the time I agreed with him. Now I tend to side with George, while doubting whether I could have extracted much else of value. Powell was very difficult to pin down, something even old friends of his had to accept. Here, for instance, James Lees-Milne writes of lunching with the Powells in December 1975:

> I understand how young Hugh Massingberd felt. He longed to talk to Tony about his novels, which he admires intensely, and Tony would only discuss genealogy. He is hipped on the subject, and his shelves are filled with every sort of reference book, *The Complete Peerage* among them ... Some people find him sinister. He is not in the least so; but he is inscrutable behind his very affable manner. It is his form of defence.[14]

I interviewed Powell again in 1983, when his novella, *O, How the Wheel Becomes It*, was published. Rather to my surprise I was invited to lunch – best end of neck, apple pie and cream, plenty to drink. Such occasions are bound to be slightly artificial and I was conscious of the need to keep my end up while avoiding any topic that 'might unknowingly cause offence',[15] the social hazard identified by Alan Watkins in his portrait of Powell that had appeared the year before. Perhaps I was too circumspect, because this is how Powell wrote my visit up in his Journals:

Michael Barber (whose sole distinction that his interview for *Paris Review* was put in, after four or five journalists before him had interviewed me for that periodical, then not published) came from *Books and Bookmen*. An uninspiring figure, to say the least.[16]

That a visit to The Chantry could be intimidating, even for people whom Powell would have hesitated to call uninspiring, was confirmed by the critic John Bayley, who described staying there as 'a bit like a permanent *viva*. You felt you had to have amusing, intelligent or original things to say.' When he and Iris Murdoch were invited down, 'Tony got what he could out of her, which wasn't much, and then rather lost interest.'[17] In fairness it should be said that to those on his wavelength Powell was reckoned the best of company: amusing, generous, loyal, and as eager to hear a good story as to tell one, at which he excelled. The Canadian diplomat, Charles Ritchie, meeting him for the first time in 1971, found him 'unalarming to an almost alarming degree, young in manner, extremely nice, natural and charming'.[18] The novelist Jilly Cooper had equally fond memories of their first meeting: 'We giggled and giggled.' Tony, she said, was 'terribly nice to waiters'.[19]

*

A question Powell was often asked was whether or not he needed a card index to keep track of the literally hundreds of characters he had created. The answer was that in the beginning he had made one but it was 'such hard work' that he concluded, about half-way through the second volume, that if he had the energy to write a card index, 'I really had the energy to write the book. So that was that.'[20] He did, however, concede that it was 'tortuously boring' having to reread the whole thing each time he started work on a new volume.

What was 'tortuously boring' for Powell was a welcome task for many of his readers. Even so, as early as 1957 David Higham unsuccessfully floated the idea of a 'dramatis personae' or index. Three years later, to mark the publication of *Casanova's Chinese Restaurant*, *Time and Tide* published a two-part 'Who's Who of *The Music of Time*', for the benefit of those who simply couldn't keep track. Higham thought this had worked very well and urged Powell to consider including it with *The Kindly Ones*. Once again Powell turned him down, because

I always feel very put off when explanations of that sort appear in a book. It immediately suggests a lowish level of writing. I see that Evelyn Waugh has a resumé of the previous plot in his new one [*Unconditional Surrender*], and I think it starts one off very much on the wrong foot. The point is that mine is the kind of book where the reader is *meant* to make an effort. It is not just to read on the train.[21]

Or, as Edmund Wilson thought, in bed. But I wonder how Powell would have reacted had Higham reminded him of what he wrote, a few years before, in praise of the Pleiade edition of *A la recherche du temps perdu*: '[It] takes up only three volumes, and contains an index of all the characters – an inestimable advantage.'[22] When, in 1977, Hilary Spurling produced her comprehensive 'Handbook' to *Dance*, it was Proust's translator and publishers she set out to emulate.

*

In the summer of 1963 Powell had a new and intoxicating experience: he sat in on the rehearsals of a play based upon his first novel, *Afternoon Men*. By nature resolutely *'un*-stage-struck', he later admitted that he had been 'corrupted' by the production, getting a particular kick out of the 'physical effervescence' it generated. And complementing the drama on-stage was what went on in the wings, 'the complicated human relationships' that were part and parcel of theatrical life.

Two assimilated foreigners were chiefly responsible for the staging of *Afternoon Men*. The adaptation was by Ricardo Aragno, an urbane Italian who after many years as London correspondent of *La Stampa* had successfully branched out into stage and screenwriting. The director was a twenty-seven-year-old American, Roger Graef, now a distinguished documentary filmmaker, but in those days committed to drama. Graef was a young man in a hurry. He had arrived in London in 1961, hoping to repeat here the success he had enjoyed in New York, where he had directed twenty-eight plays and operas in six years. An Anglophile, addicted to the novels of Powell and Waugh, Graef met Aragno soon after his arrival and was so excited by his treatment of *Afternoon Men* that he set his heart on directing it in the West End. He envisaged a cast that included Robert Stephens, Mary Peach and Virginia Maskell, with sets designed by Sean Kenny. But it was not to be. By the time a contract to produce the play had been signed people like Stephens and Kenny were otherwise engaged. And instead of a fully-fledged West End production, Graef had to settle for a cut-price job at the Arts Theatre Club.

Forty years later Graef was still at a loss to know why, when there were better offers on the table, his agent had involved him with David Pelham, an impresario derisively known as 'the King of the Flops'.

He was very *louche*. It was in his flat that Mandy Rice-Davies used to screw VIPs like Douglas Fairbanks. Not that that mattered. But he was also a crook. We had this gentleman's agreement about the money and he reneged. There was never enough. So we couldn't afford a proper set designer and the cast had to wear their own clothes and so on. I should have walked away but I believed in myself. Big mistake. It was a disaster waiting to happen.[23]

Determined to press on regardless, Graef managed to assemble a promising cast, two of whom, Imogen Hassall (Harriet Twining) and Pauline Boty (Lola), died tragically young. James Fox, in his first stage role, played the anti-hero, Atwater, while Georgina Ward was the beautiful, unattainable Susan Nunnery. Graef had wanted Willie Rushton for Fotheringham, the philosophising drunk, but he was not available, so Alan Howard, whom Powell thought excellent, got the part instead. Pringle was played by Peter Bowles, Barlow by Jeremy Kemp.

Graef had been associated with the New York Actor's Studio, where the 'Method' school of acting was taught. This encouraged improvisation on the part of performers, particularly in the beginning, with minimal guidance from the director. Graef's cast were not happy with this. They expected the director to direct. The matter was never really resolved, to the detriment of the production. Graef also gave the play a contemporary setting and socially upgraded the girls from artists' models and adventuresses to debs. The objections to this were put by the novelist and dramatist, John Bowen:

Listening to Mr Powell's dialogue against a background of the 'Twist', one realises that the attempt was bound to fail. Soho drinking clubs are now frequented more by bookies and ad-men than by upper-class drifters dabbling in the arts – and Augustus John is no longer to be seen at the Café Royal.[24]

Powell shared some of Bowen's reservations. But knowing nothing of the stage and being, moreover, immensely grateful to Graef for all he had done, he was in no mood to interfere. Not only was he seduced by the sound of his own lines, he was also reliving his past. There, on the stage, were two attractive young people re-enacting the unhappy love affair that had led to *Afternoon Men*. No wonder he identified with James Fox. No wonder, either, that he fell more than a little in love with Georgina Ward, who was bright as well as beautiful and well-born too. In saying this I am giving away no secrets. Powell's infatuation with the Honourable Miss Georgina Ward, to style her correctly, was apparent to all. It was also perceived to be chaste, like the *amitié amoureuse* between Gibson Delavacquerie and Fiona Cutts. Had this not been the case there would certainly have been comment, since the whole country was in one of its periodic fits of morality over the Profumo affair, which had come to the boil a few weeks before.

It is a measure of how haphazard the whole enterprise was that Powell missed the opening night because, contrary to expectations, this took place on the very day he and Violet flew to Venice for a Mediterranean cruise. Roger Graef expected the worst – 'Theatre is like a soufflé: you know when it's gone wrong' – so he thought there must be some mistake when the first review he read, in the *Telegraph*, was a rave. 'Then I remembered that Tony was the Literary Editor!' In the *Daily Mail* Bernard Levin, not known for his charity, praised the play itself, saying it was 'like [Iris Murdoch's] *A Severed Head*, but without the twaddle, a subtle and oblique study in casual relationships carefully observed and obliquely charted'. The cast, said Levin, was 'full of pretty girls most of whom can't act'. As for Graef, 'his direction is a repertory of every elementary error it is possible to make on the stage, and a good few it is not.' By contrast, *The Guardian*'s Christopher Driver thought the play didn't work, describing it as an 'un-drama'. He was sorry for the cast: 'None try harder than Georgina Ward. Unfortunately she is the girl who goes to America at the end of the second act and her elegant, distrait intensity, though inexplicable, is sadly missed ... The trouble is Mr Powell's dialogue, which is pleasurably dry on the pages of a book, but positively dehydrated in Ricardo Aragno's stage version.'

In addition to lukewarm reviews, *Afternoon Men* laboured under two major handicaps. It opened in August, the least auspicious month in the West End calendar; and it was not a show the public could buy a ticket to see: you had to join the Arts Theatre Club first, a process that took twenty-four hours to arrange. Consequently houses were, in Powell's words, 'thin, not to say gaunt'. On his return from holiday he looked in as often as he could, and came to admire the dedication of the cast who soldiered on as if people were standing in the aisles. When, after a few weeks, the curtain came down for good, he suffered such severe withdrawal symptoms that there was nothing for it but to set aside *Dance* and write a play, a resolution encouraged by Georgina Ward, who wanted a good part for herself.

In the event Powell wrote two plays, without hindrance to the machinery for *Dance*, which proceeded on schedule. Both examine sexual tensions, in particular the arguments for and against continence. In the first play, *The Garden God*, set on a small island in the Aegean, the excavation of a site dedicated to Priapus disturbs the god himself, with traumatic consequences for those in the vicinity. The second play, *The Rest I'll Whistle*, is like a profane variation on de Montherlant's *The Master of Santiago*, with incestuous attraction rather than faith as the determinant. Set in a small and remote National

14. The Play's the Thing

Trust property it explores the relationship between the curator, a misanthropic scholar, and his pretty daughter, a free spirit whom he is determined not to surrender to a wealthy suitor.

Powell showed *The Garden God* to Richard Schulman, manager of the Arts, who passed it on to his friend, Willie Donaldson, producer of *Beyond the Fringe* and a fan of Powell's novels. Donaldson, who later wrote *The Henry Root Letters*, liked what he saw and agreed to become involved. But having gone bankrupt a year or two before he was not in the best position to broker a deal. 'I'm surprised his agent didn't warn him about me. Perhaps he did and Powell ignored him. I dare say he thought that if the worst came to the worst I might say something he could use in a novel.'[25]

In *Strangers* Powell says that throughout the first half of 1966 he and Donaldson and Schulman would lunch together once a week, taking it in turns to choose the restaurant and pay the bill. He enjoyed these outings, at which all sorts of ideas about the play were ventilated. Donaldson, though he 'worshipped' Powell, found him heavy going:

> Doesn't Confucius describe the gentleman as 'courteous, but not pliable'? That was how I remember him. He had exquisite manners, but was absolutely unbending. A bit like royalty. I certainly don't recall him laughing much, though it was clear from the way he talked about Georgina Ward that he had a crush on her. I think I suggested quite early on that nice as it was to meet at places like L'Ecu and The Ivy – we did ourselves proud – we weren't really getting anywhere and ought to call it a day. But Tony – I think we were using christian names by then – insisted we carry on. I remember on one occasion he brought Osbert Lancaster along. It was at the Post Office Tower, which hadn't been open long. And Lancaster didn't say a word. He just stared out of the window.

Eventually another crisis in Donaldson's affairs obliged him to run for cover, and with him went any real hopes Powell may have had of staging *The Garden God*. Nor were the omens propitious for *The Rest I'll Whistle*. The lady at Higham's who dealt with plays pronounced it 'unpleasant' and, what was worse, 'unsaleable'. A more optimistic assessment was, however, given by a colleague of hers who said he would like to knock on a few doors. That autumn the Powells visited India, and it was while staying in Bangalore that Powell received a cable from Highams saying that H.M. Tennent had taken an option on the play. He was elated. 'Binkie' Beaumont, the boss of Tennent's, was the nearest thing to a West End Godfather; if anyone could put your name up in lights, he could. On his return Powell, accompanied by his agent, went to see Mr Beaumont, who behaved as if receiving the Bard

241

himself. No expense, he promised, would be spared in bringing such a masterpiece before the public. Only the very best cast, in the hands of an equally superlative director, would do. Unable to believe his luck, Powell went on his way rejoicing. Weeks passed and there was no word from Binkie, who was always too busy to come to the phone. Nor did he answer letters. Eventually it dawned on Powell that for whatever reason, the West End Godfather had had second thoughts, which it would have been beneath his dignity to acknowledge.

Powell's two plays were published together in hardback in 1971, an event that passed unnoticed except in the *Telegraph*, where the drama critic John Barber praised the ingenuity with which Powell had involved 'so many stunted lives in crises beyond their control'. Unusually, there was no dedication, which given that the plays had been written with Georgina Ward in mind might seem an oversight. But three years before, by which time it was obvious that neither play would be staged, Powell had dedicated *The Military Philosophers* to her. She is the only female to whom he dedicated a volume of *Dance*.

Afternoon Men was the last play Roger Graef directed. Soon afterwards he was invited to make a film about the effects of Thalidomide, an undertaking that convinced him that he had found his *métier*:

> So I suppose you could say that that terrible production changed my life. If it had been a success and had a West End run I might have stayed in the theatre. Or made feature films instead of documentaries. I always thought *Agents and Patients* would have made a good film. It had an existential quality about it that was fashionable then. Who knows?

*

In 1957, reviewing a book of portraits from the National Portrait Gallery, Powell described the Gallery as 'architecturally speaking ... one of the most depressing buildings in London – perhaps in Europe – and its interior is designed with almost uncanny skill to be unsuitable for the display of pictures'. However, he added, 'in the face of insuperable difficulties, the Director, Staff and Trustees put up an heroic effort, and the result is a collection of pictures unlike anything else in the world'.[26] In 1962 Powell himself began to grapple with these difficulties, being appointed to the Board of Trustees under the chairmanship of Maynard Keynes's younger brother, Sir Geoffrey Keynes.

Powell served for fourteen years, his resignation coinciding with an exhibition called 'British Writers of the Thirties', a subject that can't have held much appeal for him since it was largely devoted to the Auden Group. Still, it is a measure of how much more enterprising the National Portrait Gallery had become in that time that such an exhibition could be mounted. When Powell became a Trustee it was more like a mausoleum than a public gallery. No living persons were represented on its walls: candidates must have been dead for ten years before the Trustees could consider them. As for the paintings themselves, they bore out Kenneth Clark's belief that while the English 'are not very fond of art, they are very fond of pedigrees'.[27] It was the status of the sitter, not of the artist, that mattered, resulting in some truly hideous pictures that ought, like the portrait of Dorian Gray, to have been hidden in an attic. This convention gave the Treasury a perfect excuse for keeping the Gallery short of funds; in 1962 the purchase grant was a miserly £4000. It also explains why few of the Trustees laid any claims to connoisseurship; Powell's colleagues included landowners, politicians, several historians and Field-Marshal Sir Gerald Templer, who in 1967 told the newly-appointed Director, Roy Strong, to get a haircut!

Sir Roy Strong, as he later became, is generally given the credit for rejuvenating the National Portrait Gallery. But in Powell's opinion the process really began under Strong's unobtrusive predecessor, David Piper, who as a young man had fought against the Japanese in Malaya, the subject of his autobiographical war novel, *Trial by Battle*. Powell liked Piper, a tall and languid figure whose experiences as a prisoner of the Japanese probably accounted, he thought, for the impression he gave of being somewhat withdrawn. Piper subsequently became Director of the Ashmolean, final resting place of the ceramics collection assembled by Powell's old friend, Gerald Reitlinger.

Powell says nothing about the National Portrait Gallery in his Memoirs, a surprising omission, you might think, in the light of his love of painting. But according to his fellow Trustee, the historian Sir John Plumb, 'Powell was very much sub fusc at [our] meetings. He usually voted with the Duke of Grafton or, at least, that was my impression.'[28] The minutes I have seen support what Sir John says. The only time Powell seems to have held the floor was over the question of photographs versus paintings. He said that in about 1914, 'art' portraiture ceased largely to be a social habit and photographs became the norm. So there was a case to be made for only acquiring a twentieth-century painting of someone if it conveyed a quality of the sitter that a photograph was unable to capture.

When in London Powell would try and attend the 'fascist' lunches that took place every fortnight (later every month) at Bertorelli's Restaurant in Charlotte Street. He went to these at the invitation of Kingsley Amis, who by the mid-Sixties was moving as far to the Right as he had been to the Left. Other regulars included Amis's friend, Robert Conquest, author of *The Great Terror*, the novelist John Braine, the political journalist Anthony Hartley and the Hungarian émigré writer, Tibor Szamuely, who surprised Amis by his familiarity with *Dance*. Anthony Burgess also came for a while, but fell out with Amis and Conquest over Modernism, which they – wrongly in his opinion – associated with political progressivism.

In his *Memoirs* Amis insisted that, despite rumours to the contrary, there was nothing conspiratorial about these lunches, which sometimes went on until 5.30. He claimed to have learnt 'quite a lot of history and politics ... before the rounds of grappa started'.[29] Another fairly regular attender, the historian Donald Cameron Watt, said it was always very competitive, with Amis, closely followed by Conquest, setting the pace. 'Amis would defer to others – once. But he and Bob [Conquest] regarded themselves as top dogs.' He thought that this was the real reason Burgess stopped coming: 'He wasn't prepared to let Bob and Kingsley lay down the law, whereas Tony Powell didn't mind at all.' What struck Professor Watt about Powell was, first, his 'easy manners' and, second, his 'Englishness'.

> He stood out as a product of the pre-war era. He hadn't been coarsened by military service and you couldn't imagine him using the sort of language the others often used, particularly as the afternoon wore on.

Watt thought Powell was as English in his way as the Mosleyite novelist, Henry Williamson – 'though he was definitely not a Fascist'.[30]

15

Mugged

Friendship, like love, carries the seeds of disillusion in it.'
                                                Anthony Powell

Towards the end of Powell's Notebook this melancholy reflection occurs:
'One of the things one did not expect when younger was that friends quite
simply dislike one being even relatively successful.'[1] In the absence of a date
it would be difficult to prove that Powell had Malcolm Muggeridge in mind
when he wrote this. But in 1990, trying to account for the swingeing review
Muggeridge gave *The Valley of Bones* in the *Evening Standard*, he concluded
that 'unbridled envy' was the most likely explanation, probably brought
about by reading the 'laudatory' notices on the jacket:

> I am always unwilling to attribute malice to straight jealousy, especially in
> someone of whom I was as fond as Malcolm, but I'm now pretty sure that was
> the cause: a sudden burst of hysterical rage, induced by envy, which some-
> times used to assail him.[2]

Muggeridge's envy, if that is what it was, has to be seen in context. By
1964, when the review appeared, he could justifiably claim to be one of the
most successful communicators of his time, as at home with the masses as
the chattering classes thanks to his mastery of television. But for someone
who set such great store by the Imagination (as opposed to the Will), it must
have been galling to realise that his own was not up to the challenge of
writing novels; he lacked what Powell called 'creative fantasy', that essential
quality without which even the most intelligent people could not get the job
done. Evelyn Waugh, who had praised his non-fiction, put his finger on it
when reviewing his fourth, and last, novel, *Affairs of the Heart*: 'despite the
high gifts of wit, humour and observation, he cannot tell a story.'[3]

Oddly enough it was Waugh whom Muggeridge invoked when delivering the first of his lashes. Having explained that the novel dealt with a
middle-aged man-at-arms he said a comparison with Waugh's *Sword of
Honour* was inescapable. 'The difference lies in the nature of the narrator.'

245

Waugh's is more involved, in the sense that he actually believes for a while that the war is about something: his snobbishness is more dynamic, even crazy.

Powell's narrator just takes the war for granted, as he does existing social arrangements; his snobbishness has no revivalist or mystical edge to it, but is quiet, steadfast, as it were Anglican in its flexibility and tenacity. It is Snobbishness Ancient and Modern as compared with a Gregorian chant; the Thirty-Nine Articles of Snobbishness rather than an illuminated missal.

There is even, at the beginning of *The Valley of Bones*, an echo of another Waugh book, *Brideshead Revisited*. Jenkins reports for duty in a place where his ancestors have lived and thriven, going back, it seems, to legendary kings. The Jenkins have thus a more ancient, if less definitive, lineage than Lord Sebastian Flyte. With them it is a case of *Stonehenge Revisited*.

After briefly acknowledging Powell's 'unique talent' for comedy Muggeridge took his second swipe:

Stendhal, one of Mr Powell's major admirations, prophesied that posterity would enjoy and appreciate his work, neglected by his contemporaries. The prophecy has been abundantly fulfilled.

We, Mr Powell's contemporaries, have proved less recalcitrant and done him proud. Will posterity be correspondingly less amenable? See in his meticulous reconstruction of his life and times a heap of dust? Despite a strong personal partiality, honesty compels me to admit it might.[4]

This was a surprise attack. To the best of Powell's knowledge he and Muggeridge were still close friends. Indeed, Muggeridge had just invited himself down for the following weekend, a visit cancelled immediately. Powell was deeply hurt and his wounds continued to smart long after he and Muggeridge were reconciled – or at any rate corresponding again. 'I could just about stomach the fact that a close friend of mine had given me a bad review,' he told me in 1982. 'That's something you must learn to put up with in the literary world. But what did annoy me greatly was his assertion that *Dance* belonged "on the ashheap of history". That's a Marxist cliché and it absolutely infuriated me.'

At that time I hadn't seen Muggeridge's review, but even if I had I might have thought twice before trying to correct him. 'Marxist cliché' or no, the message was clear: Powell was wasting his time – and this from the man who had recommended *Dance* to Heinemann. Perhaps Muggeridge realised he had gone too far; at any rate he omitted any reference to 'posterity' from his review of the American edition for *Esquire*. He did, however, repeat the charge of snobbishness, 'the basic English mania',[5] which seems perverse given that most of the book deals sympathetically with a very unsnobbish unit of Welsh miners officered by bank clerks. (Taxed about his love of looking people up in *Burke's Peerage*, Powell used to insist that if there were a *Burke's Bank Clerks* he would look people up in that.)

Today, a review like this would be widely publicised and both parties encouraged to come out fighting. But in 1964 it appears to have gone unnoticed except by Powell and his friends. This must explain why an old Fleet Street hand like Alan Watkins knew nothing about it until he went to see Powell himself. Watkins, who was gathering material for his *Brief Lives*, had been fobbed off by Muggeridge like this: 'I asked him about his quarrel with Powell and he said I'd been misinformed. "My dear boy, as you grow older you will discover that there is no such thing as friends for life. At a certain stage you move on and leave them behind. This was what happened with Tony." He didn't mention the review at all.' Suspecting that Muggeridge was being evasive Watkins contacted Powell, who confirmed that there had been a quarrel. 'He said that if I cared to "come and propose myself" at The Chantry he would show me the review, but would not discuss Malcolm – he called him that – because he would be dealing with him in his memoirs. So I went and proposed myself and he showed me the review and we had a very interesting chat about everything under the sun except Muggeridge.'[6]

Some people, Watkins among them, thought that Powell got his own back on Muggeridge with 'Books-do-furnish-a-room' Bagshaw in *Dance*, the seedy, much-married, all-purpose hack, steeped in left-wing lore, who morphs into 'Lindsay Bagshaw', an early example of the television personality. Powell denied this, but he would have been hard-pressed to deny any connection between Muggeridge and Prosper Bland, a character in his play *The Garden God*. Unlike Bagshaw, Bland is a household name, an 'infinitely famous' talking head who 'enchants millions by his dry wit'. Undeniably plausible, particularly when chatting-up women, he is also a flatulent old humbug who pretends that fame is a bore and that there is nothing he would like more than to escape the demands of the flesh. Stranded on a Greek island while on an assignment, he falls in with some archaeologists, one of whom he seduces, only to be kicked out of her bed for failing to come up to scratch. Public humiliation follows and he is last seen looking for a donkey to take him back to the meretricious world he had earlier disparaged.

Powell did in fact deal brilliantly with Muggeridge in his Memoirs, but without referring to their quarrel. Meanwhile his old friend had made handsome amends in the *New Statesman*, declaring that *Dance* was a 'great work' and that the portrait it gave of the contemporary scene would 'prove to be of lasting interest and an authentic contribution to literature'.[7] A few years later, when selections from Muggeridge's Diaries were published, Powell reviewed them with appreciation in the *Telegraph*. By then they had been in touch again for several years, Muggeridge having written to Powell following Cyril Connolly's death in November 1974. Nevertheless, it is clear from Powell's first two volumes of Journals that the review still rankled and that he took an increasingly jaundiced view of Muggeridge's saintly asceticism. Then in 1990 Muggeridge died, whereupon Bernard Levin wrote a singularly ill-informed piece about their quarrel in the *Times*. Without quoting from the review or giving any dates he said how childish it was that they had not spoken for seventeen years. Salt was rubbed in the wound when the *Times* refused to print Powell's letter of refutation; he had, they said, 'hit below the belt' by telling Levin that he was still young enough to learn that you should not believe all you read in the papers.

Muggeridge did not keep a diary for 1964, and if he confided in anyone at the time there is no record of it; consequently his motives for the attack will probably remain a mystery. He pleaded amnesia to his official biographer, Richard Ingrams; while Ian Hunter's life of him, published in 1980, says nothing about his quarrel with Powell at all. Alan Watkins thought it was not malice, but expediency, that explained what he wrote. 'It's the age-old reviewer's dilemma: "Copy due tomorrow. What line do I take? Ah yes, snobbery. Bring in Waugh as well by way of comparison." And the problem is solved.'[8] But to the end of his days Powell maintained that by attacking him so blatantly – he could easily have made his point more subtly – Muggeridge was serving notice on their friendship.

One other mystery remains. In December 1965, at a time when they were supposed to be estranged, Powell recorded a half-hour conversation with Muggeridge in the latter's BBC TV series, *Intimations*. Alas, no record of this programme survives in the BBC archives, but according to Lady Violet it was 'well-conducted'.[9] Strange to relate, Powell does not mention this tête-à-tête. Readers will draw their own conclusions. I couldn't possibly comment.

*

With *The Valley of Bones* Powell and his publishers finally put their cards on the table. 'It begins,' said the blurb, 'the six volume sequence planned as the second half of [*The Music of Time*] and is itself the first instalment of a trilogy dealing with the Second World War.' Although Jenkins's past is ever before us, so that the war volumes do not stand on their own, I think they are best dealt with collectively.

Jenkins's war, as I have said, is similar in most respects to his creator's. Commissioned by the Grace of God and his Certificate A at the end of 1939, he is soon shipped off to Ulster with his battalion and spends the phoney war trying to justify his arbitrary status as a leader of men. By the time the Germans have reached the Channel ports it is clear that he is not cut out for heroics, except perhaps of the last-ditch variety, a verdict he accepts resignedly. Then Widmerpool, a Major at Divisional HQ, bags him for staff duties – in effect selects him as his fag. The novel ends with the news that Paris is about to fall.

Three new characters catch the eye. One is Jenkins's self-important company commander, Captain Roland Gwatkin, in civvy street a bank clerk, whose aspirations belong to another age:

> I suspected Gwatkin saw himself in much the same terms as those heroes of Stendhal – an aspiring, restless spirit, who, released at last by war from the cramping bonds of life in a provincial town, was about to cut a dashing military figure against a backcloth of Meissonier-like imagery of plume and breast-plate: dragoons walking their horses through the wheat, grenadiers at ease in a tavern with girls bearing flagons of wine.

If keenness were the only criterion Gwatkin would make a good officer. But he can't delegate and is too easily discouraged by rebukes from his superiors. He is also a romantic, a fatal handicap in wartime as Jenkins comes to realise. Eventually he loses his grip altogether and is relieved of his company, his final humiliation being to discover the local barmaid he's in love with smooching with one of his men. Invalided out soon afterwards, he ends his days as a pillar of the local British Legion.

The second newcomer is Lieutenant Bithel ('Bith'), a boozy and shambolic queer, formerly in the Territorials, who is given the benefit of the doubt because his brother, so it's said, won the Victoria Cross and he himself was capped at rugger for Wales. All a dreadful misunderstanding, of course, as he tells Jenkins, but a fellow can't help it if people get the wrong end of the stick. Full of respect for 'varsity men' and frank about his inability to stick at a job – 'Can't bear being tied down'– there is a touch of Captain Grimes about Bithel, who admits to having been a Scoutmaster. When Widmerpool gets him booted out in the next book the assumption is that he will sink without a trace. But thirty years later he reappears as the elderly mascot of Scorpio Murtlock's band and the witness to Widmerpool's death.

The third newcomer, Odo Stevens, is made of infinitely sturdier stuff. He is not just a new face, but a new type. This is immediately apparent from his behaviour on a night exercise he and Jenkins undertake while attending a course at Aldershot. One of their colleagues, a 'muscular neurotic', begins to shower them with gravel. Instead of yelling at him to pack it in Stevens sneaks up on him and belts him in the ribs with his rifle butt. Impossible to imagine any of Jenkins's other associates acting with such brutal decision. The next we hear of him he's in the Commandos and has won the Military Cross.

With a name like Odo, Stevens sounds like one of Evelyn Waugh's gentleman toughs. In fact he was christened Herbert and is from Birmingham, where he was apprenticed to a firm that made artificial jewellery. Aged about twenty, he's cocky, resourceful, attractive to women and decidedly undeferential. Isobel comes to loathe him, holding him responsible for the death of her younger sister Priscilla, whom he detaches from Chips Lovell, another of those seismic shifts in the social strata that occur throughout *Dance*. Jenkins has misgivings too, but his curiosity, as always, gets the better of him, especially when Stevens reveals that he writes poetry and is a fan of Max Pilgrim, the equivocal entertainer. It also helps that he's brave, a quality Jenkins not only respects but would dearly like the chance to exhibit himself. There is a hint of envy in his voice when, in *The Soldier's Art*, he asks Stevens how much hand-to-hand fighting he has done. Years later, when Pamela Flitton calls Stevens, by now married to Rosie Manasch, 'that little ponce', he says at once, 'You must admit his war record was good.'

The Valley of Bones is the most self-contained volume of *Dance*. Like Waugh's *Men at Arms*, it is largely devoted to regimental soldiering. But whereas Waugh confined himself to 'Officers Only', Powell achieves some of his best effects with the troops:

'She was a big woman that gave us that jug of tea, she was,' said Corporal Gwylt.

He addressed Williams, W.H.

'Ah, she was,' agreed Williams, W.H.

He looked thoughtful. Good at running and singing, he was otherwise not greatly gifted.

'She made me afraid, she did,' said Corporal Gwylt. 'I would have been afraid of that big woman in a little bed.'

'Indeed, I would too that,' said Williams, W.H., looking as if he were sincere in the opinion.

'Would you not have been afraid of her, Sergeant Pendry, a great big woman twice your size?'

'Shut your mouth,' said Sergeant Pendry, with unexpected force. 'Must you ever be talking of women?'

Corporal Gwylt was not at all put out.

'I would be even more afeared of her in a *big* bed,' he said reflectively.

Some reviewers thought Powell's Welsh-English dialogue was suspect. One of them, Roy Thomas, said it was a pity Powell didn't have a tape-recorder with him when he served with The Welch. Powell's initial response to this may be inferred from Trapnell's theories about art, quoted above. In *Faces* Powell revealed that at some stage he asked the Liverpudlian Welsh actor and dramatist, Alun Owen, whether he thought the soldiers' dialogue needed revising. Owen replied that while a tape-recording of Welsh soldiers talking might differ from what he had written, that was not the point. The dialogue represented faithfully 'what the narrator heard'. Not being Welsh I cannot comment on the authenticity of the soldier's speech; but I do think there are times when Powell's ear betrays him. For instance when Odo Stevens sees a fellow Commando at the Café Royal and offers him a drink, his chum declines: 'Not going to risk being cashiered for WOASAWL.' Stevens immediately translates the acronym. But surely the other chap would simply have said 'for being absent without leave'? Again, when Widmerpool is trying to put the drunken Stringham to bed after the Old Boys' dinner, the latter, having insisted that getting in and out of your own bed is a fundamental human right, then repeats himself like this: '[I]ngress and egress of one's own bed is unassailable.' I don't see anyone saying this when sober, let alone in Stringham's state.

To the astonishment of Jenkins Stringham turns up as a mess waiter at Divisional HQ. Although cured of drink, he has become 'awfully odd'. Jenkins wants to help him but Stringham insists he's happy where he is, in a job that allows him to examine himself. 'I've come to the conclusion that I'm narcissistic,' he says. Jenkins does not demur; he can barely get a word in edgeways, so determined is Stringham to prove his point. In the process he utters the last of the throwaway lines at which he excels: 'Awfully chic to be killed.' And while there appears to be no danger of that at present, Fate, in the shape of Widmerpool, shortens the odds. He shunts Stringham off to the Mobile Laundry Unit who are, he correctly suspects, bound for Singapore. At that moment – June 1941 – no one knew that within eight months Singapore would be in Japanese hands, but this is a typical instance of Widmerpool's resourceful nastiness paying an unexpected dividend. 'That boy will be the death of me,' says Stringham at school. So it proves. (Melancholy thought: when in 1921 Crown Prince Hirohito, the future Emperor of Japan, visited Eton, he was accorded a salute of *banzai* by the whole school – among them 'Stringham'.)

Other notable casualties include Barnby, a camouflage officer in the RAF, shot down on a reconnaissance flight, and Chips and Priscilla Lovell, both killed during the same air-raid but at different locations. Powell said this really happened. 'I could tell you the names of the people,' he told an interviewer in 1985:

He was out with a girl, taking her somewhere, some roadhouse out of London, and a bomb was dropped. She [the man's wife] was killed the same night in a blitz on London. Unless I knew as an absolute fact that that had taken place, I would have hesitated. I couldn't swear that the real people in the story were each having an affair, but a husband and wife were each out with another person of the opposite sex.[10]

In another interview Powell gave a different version of this incident. 'The husband was out with a girl at the Café de Paris, the wife was out with another chap at the Ace of Spades. A bomb was dropped on both, miles away from each other, at the same time.'[11] That the Café de Paris should have copped it on the same night as the Ace of Spades, a celebrated road-house on the Great West Road where Peter Templer once had a row, is a remarkable coincidence in itself. So it is odd that there is no mention of this in standard histories of the Blitz.

The death of Barnby (exactly like that of Eric Ravilious, a very promising painter whom Powell admired) comes as a shock. Almost his last words to Jenkins are about a wonderful new girl of his 'with one extraordinary trait' it would amuse Jenkins to hear about. It would doubtless amuse us too, but Jenkins can't dine with him that evening and the chance is lost for ever. In his radio talk, Kingsley Amis had a technical point to make about Barnby's sudden exit:

In ordinary novels the rule is that any major-minor character, anyone who does much more than mow the lawn in the next-door garden or say 'Your taxi's here' has got to do or say something of general importance sooner or later, the degree of that importance depending roughly on how much he's done and said that isn't important. And now here's Barnby come and gone without his scene, without any sort of big moment.

It was when he registered this that Amis concluded 'that anybody who might still retain the smallest expectation that *The Music of Time* was going to turn out to be an ordinary novel after all was going to have to lose it'.[12]

*

At the end of *The Soldier's Art* both Jenkins and Widmerpool are Whitehall-bound, Jenkins to liaison duties with the Poles, Widmerpool to the Cabinet Offices, a rich reward for his machinations and proof that you don't neces-sarily have to look the part to get on. In his ill-fitting utility uniform he reminds Jenkins of 'a railway official, perhaps of some obscure country', but there's no denying that the Army suits him. His disobliging manner, far from being a handicap, is actually of more service than his enormous capacity for hard work. And as a veteran hatchet man in civvy street he quickly takes to the backstabbing and intrigue that are part and parcel of advancement on the Staff. 'War,' he tells Jenkins, 'is a great opportunity for everyone to find his own level.' It's also a great opportunity for him to pay off old scores. Templer, as well as Stringham, is undone by him, a reminder that you make enemies for life at school, as well as friends.

Confronted by all this evidence Jenkins at last gets the message about Widmerpool: he's a monster, devoid of feelings for anyone but himself. Useless therefore to expect him to show any mercy towards a pathetic misfit like Bithel, let alone express more than cursory regret over the 15,000 Polish officers murdered by the Russians at Katyn and so inconveniently exhumed by the Germans. But Jenkins is also well aware that Widmerpool's value to the Army is far greater than his. And, although this is implicit rather than explicit, Jenkins the connoisseur of human oddness is obviously as fascinated by Widmerpool as he is repelled by him. What will he do next? Marry Stringham's niece, Pamela Flitton, is the answer.

Widmerpool and Pamela deserve each other. If Widmerpool commands Powell's awkward squad, a body that includes such incorrigibles as Uncle Giles, Gypsy Jones, 'Books-do-furnish-a-room' Bagshaw, Mrs Maclintick, Duport, Quiggin and Baby Wentworth (believed never to speak another civil word to a man after taking him as her lover), then Pamela is his right-marker. A beautiful and insatiable witch, with black hair and a dead white complexion, she is the incarnation of Swinburne's Dolores, 'Daughter of Death and Priapus'. Trapnel says that in bed she goes 'rigid as a corpse', a portentous simile. Another of her lovers croaks in the saddle. It's a lucky man – or woman – who can walk away from her unscathed, as does Duport: 'I only stuffed her once … but even then I could see she might drive you round the bend, if she really decided to.' Most are scarred for life – literally in some cases. She socks Odo Stevens on the jaw and would, you feel, unhesitatingly shoot someone if it came to it. Jenkins thinks she is vicious in the way that a horse is vicious; he gives her a wide berth. Widmerpool tries to exercise his rights, fails dismally, and then settles for a seat in the grandstand.

That Widmerpool is a voyeur seems incontestable. Pamela says he is and she should know. But we're also told that he goes in for whores, and even orgies. So how does this square with his failure to satisfy either Pamela or his first fiancée, Mildred Haycock? Could his fearsome lady mother be the problem? General Conyers hints at this. In his opinion Widmerpool suffers from 'exaggerated narcissism'; but what does this mean in practice? Is he impotent, or merely inept? Perhaps it all hinges on the 'slavish' look he wore when Budd, the captain of cricket at school, hit him full in the face with a ripe banana and which he wore again when Barbara Goring tipped a castor of sugar over him. Masochism would explain why he willingly suffers so much at Pamela's hands; also his compliance with Scorpio Murtlock's unspeakable penances. I'm reminded of the 'man in the mask', that mysterious symbol of upper-class depravity who was often invoked at the time of the Profumo crisis. Rumoured to be a Cabinet Minister, he would wait at table clad in nothing but a frilly apron and a mask. Round his neck hung a card saying, 'Whip me if I am clumsy'. I can see Widmerpool doing something similar, but I think humiliation rather than pain was what he craved.

In Whitehall, while Widmerpool marches on, Jenkins marks time. Although both are engaged in a paper war, the bumf that crosses Jenkins's desk is mostly routine stuff, not the highly sensitive material that Widmerpool traffics in. He tries to console himself with the thought that his Section's focus, while narrower, is easier to monitor and therefore just as satisfying. Nevertheless, while Widmerpool is busy redrawing the map of post-war Europe – how apt that he should describe his promotion to Colonel as 'going red' – Jenkins wrestles with the likes of Mr Blackhead, the embodiment of bureaucratic intransigence, over straw for stuffing hospital palliases in Scotland and screwdrivers for Polish civilians 'temporarily employed at military technical establishments'. Somebody has to do this of course, and there are worse billets than the War Office; but as the tide begins to turn, Jenkins, you feel, would give anything to be swept along with it.

Odo Stevens, with a bar to his MC, reappears as a protégé of Sunny Farebrother, whose rivalry with Widmerpool, dating back to their City days, has intensified to the point where they seem to hate each other more than the Germans. Now at SOE, Farebrother overplays his hand when he and Stevens engage in the 'military bohemianism' described above, using forged documents to remove a Polish hardcase called Szymanski from military prison. In the ensuing stink Widmerpool sees to it that Farebrother loses his job. But within a year the 'downy old bird' is back on his perch. Ten or more years older then his rival, he is every bit as ambitious and every bit as ruthless. If he doesn't seem as nasty it's because he positively oozes charm, a commodity Widmerpool despises. Widmerpool is in your face; Farebrother is up your arse. He's a creep, and a sanctimonious creep at that. But, lest we forget, he did win a 'good' DSO in the last show. It's this, I think, that redeems him in Jenkins's eyes, and also, by definition, in Powell's.

The end of the war finds Jenkins at Olympia where, as a boy, he had watched the Royal Tournament, with its stirring reconstructions of battles long ago. Now it is full of dowdy demob outfits, appropriate clobber for the drab years ahead. Among those come to claim their bounty is a legendary figure from Jenkins's youth, Archie Gilbert, so much a fixture of deb dances in the Twenties, averaging two or three a night, that it was impossible to imagine him wearing anything but a white tie. They exchange notes and Jenkins learns that Gilbert, a Captain in the Gunners, has served with an anti-aircraft battery in north London:

> One pictured a lot of hard, rather dreary work, sometimes fairly dangerous, sometimes demanding endurance in unexciting circumstances. Perhaps experience in the London ballrooms had stood him in good stead in the latter respect.

Jenkins supposes that if Gilbert has a wife, she will be one of the girls he used to dance with in their salad days. Far from it, says Gilbert. Her family lived just across the road from the battery, which is how they met. Whether intended or not, the marriage of a stuffed shirt like Gilbert to a girl from the suburbs seems symbolic, another example of how the social foundations are crumbling. In just the same way it is appropriate that apart from Widmerpool, the character to have done best out of the war is Odo Stevens, who may not necessarily have been braver than 'gentle obsolescent heroes' like Stringham and Robert and George Tolland, but almost certainly got his retaliation in first, which is what was needed against an enemy like the Nazis.

Powell's war trilogy appeared during the Sixties, not the most receptive epoch for war novels, particularly when written from an upper-class perspective. But reviewers were quick to record one vital difference between Powell's protagonist and Waugh's: their attitude to Hitler's invasion of Russia. As Laurence Kitchin explained in *The Listener*: 'When Anthony Powell's narrator ... greets the news of Russia's entry into the war as a blessed relief, he lets us know we're in the presence of a writer in focus on the central issue, however closely he concentrates on the fortunes of an upper-class group. To [Waugh's hero] Crouchback, on the contrary, the news is a disaster.'[13] Roy Fuller thought that where Powell differed from Waugh was that his end was achieved by 'secular and sensible means ... The morality of *The Music of Time* could be extracted (it might in essence be said to be the disastrous effects of human will) but it is very far indeed from that of the Catholic or the gentleman.'[14]

In a letter to Waugh, Powell spoke of the 'agony' of writing about army life and said he now realised 'the awful technical problems you yourself had to cope with'.[15] Reviewers, particularly those who had served in the forces, thought he had managed very well, showing how the military machine worked at various levels, but in a way that would be intelligible to civilians. Kingsley Amis was not alone in singling out for applause the episode in the barn when General Liddament, complete with stick like 'a verger's wand', cross-examines Jenkins and his platoon about what they had for breakfast: '[T]here is nothing of fantasy there,' said Amis, 'in fact it approaches more the grimmest academic literalism.'[16] Simon Raven, another old soldier, described the Liaison Officers' outing to Belgium and France as 'a combination of poetry, reflection, satire and farce which no other living writer could have conceived or carried through'.[17]

The appearance of Pamela Flitton, as lethal a weapon as any bomb, reminded Francis Hope how 'extraordinarily well' Powell wrote about sex, 'by a process of indirection. He emphasises its power by dwelling on its social consequences: people not only go to bed, but forgo money, abandon careers and leave homes in order to do so.'[18] John Braine also admired the Powell approach to sex, quoting the passage in which Jenkins tries to reconcile the chic signora he meets outside St Paul's with the wanton bedmate he had once been mad about. 'How utterly tasteless, how absurdly contrived, this makes other novelists' treatment of sex appear. There is no physical detail ... And yet all the lunatic abandonment, the obsessive hunger of mutual infatuation, are exactly delineated.'[19]

As you would expect, some American reviewers could not resist comparing Powell's understated depiction of war with that of Norman Mailer or James Jones. 'Can one dream of an American war novel without a single battle scene or – even worse – without a single bedroom scene?' asked Melvin Maddocks. But Powell was not a sissy. 'Far from being "soft", he is ambitious for a realism that goes beyond the visceral.'[20] Another American reviewer, Paul Zimmerman, thought Powell's 'beautifully woven prose, its spots of colour perfectly placed as in some semantic English tweed, makes the whole war seem like a monstrous breach of manners, disturbing the routine of those decent people who constitute civilisation'.[21] The anonymous reviewer in *Time* (which with *Newsweek* had covered *Dance* from the beginning) wondered why Powell's 'splendid fictional achievement' was not more popular in the US. Was it because, as some British critics thought, it was too upper-class? And what about the suggestion that in order to get Powell's measure, you needed 'some acquaintance with the flesh-and-blood originals of his fictional characters'? Nonsense, said *Time*, on both counts. You might just as well say that in order to enjoy Proust, 'one needs to be a French homosexual with aristocratic friends'. However, 'Like the peculiar British fondness for cold toast ... a taste for Powell's prose is best acquired through prolonged exposure.'[22]

16

Wits' End

'One felt as if one's Commanding Officer were dead.'

Graham Greene on the death of Evelyn Waugh

'I do not recommend dying.'

Cyril Connolly to Stephen Spender

In April 1966, while Powell was writing *The Soldier's Art*, Evelyn Waugh died. Powell was shocked, but not surprised. The previous November, at a country wedding, he had noticed how feeble his old friend had become, requiring the assistance of his wife and daughter to ascend the modest ramp that led to a marquee. Waugh was only sixty-two, yet he moved like a geriatric. It was Powell's impression that he had lost the will to live. Later that year Powell contributed a brief memoir of Waugh to *Adam*, the first of several such pieces he would write over the next thirty years. He called Waugh 'the most naturally gifted writer of his generation' and said that although they had not met much in later years, 'his going means that a chunk of my own life has gone too'.[1]

Waugh was the first of the Oxford Wits to die of natural causes and it is understandable that his death should have diminished all those, including Powell, who remained. But in Powell's case a distinction must be made between his high opinion of Waugh the writer and his many reservations about Waugh the man. As he once said to Waugh's biographer, Christopher Sykes, 'It is quite impossible to be objective about Evelyn.'[2] Not that Powell had any scars to display. Waugh never turned on him as he did on so many of his friends. Even in the years when they were estranged following his divorce Waugh made a point of praising *From a View to a Death*, and his admiration for *Dance*, though not unbounded, was sincere. Two of his comments deserve to be repeated here. Reviewing *Casanova's Chinese Restaurant* he wrote:

> I do not think these characters exist fully 'in the round'. They can be observed from one position only. We cannot walk round them as statues. They present, rather, a continuous frieze in high relief, deep cut and detailed.[3]

Two years later, reviewing *The Kindly Ones*, he chose a different analogy:

> [W]e watch [the characters] through the glass of a tank; one after another various specimens swim towards us; we see them clearly, then with a barely perceptible flick of a fin or a tail they are off into the murk. That is how our encounters occur in life. Friends or acquaintances approach or recede year by year.[4]

Having known Waugh in his unregenerate 'knockabout' period at Oxford and immediately after, Powell was bound to take his aristocratic pretensions with a pinch of salt. He was quick to point out that Waugh did not like politics or racing, nor did he shoot. He might also have added that Waugh did not share his own familiarity with 'the stud book', *Burke's Peerage*. And yet just as Jenkins is compelled to give Widmerpool his due, so Powell had to give Waugh full marks for effort. In a wartime letter to Malcolm Muggeridge he reports that 'Evelyn Waugh has exchanged from the Marines – and what regiment has he gone into? No one I have yet asked has had the temerity to guess the truth – the answer is, however, the Blues … One cannot but admire such pertinacity of purpose.'[5]

Powell was incapable of acting like that. He didn't have the nerve, or, to be fair, the inclination. His concept of duty did not comprehend the blatant string-pulling that Waugh engaged in. Not that it did Waugh much good in the long run. A natural anarchist in everything but religion, he was neither a leader of men nor a reliable subordinate. He was once rebuked by a general for drinking too much in the Mess before dinner. 'You can't expect me to change the habits of a lifetime for a whim of yours,' retorted Waugh. The notion that you saluted the uniform, not the man, was beyond him and was one of the reasons why his Army career was marked by disillusionment and rancour. I think it is instructive that in his review of Waugh's novel *Officers and Gentlemen* Powell should have quoted this passage: 'In all his military service Guy never ceased to marvel at the effortless transitions of intercourse between equality and superiority.'[6]

Powell was also one of the first to question, albeit very obliquely, Waugh's conduct during the evacuation from Crete, a fictionalised version of which provides the climax to *Officers and Gentlemen*. Like Waugh himself, his protagonist, Guy Crouchback, escapes from Crete after witnessing shameful scenes, notably the desertion of his men by Ivor Claire, 'the fine flower of them all', and the crack-up under fire of his punctilious Brigade Major, 'Fido' Hound. Powell's response to this in his review was mischievous: 'I most enjoyed Major Hound's personal withdrawal from combat, but thought it perhaps a pity that these happenings could not instead have befallen Crouchback himself.'[7] He explained why in a letter to Waugh:

> [Major Hound's withdrawal] is so vivid – and indeed poetic – that one's sympathies – in the wider sense – immediately become engaged with Hound. I see that this would probably have been impossible for a number of reasons, but do rather regret that Crouchback did not have a temporary lapse on this occasion.

Powell added, for good measure, that he didn't like Crouchback's saintly father, 'and was sorry he was not turned out of his room'.[8]

Waugh did not rise to the bait. '"Crouchback" (junior: not so his admirable father) is a prig,' he informed Powell. 'But he is a virtuous, brave prig. If he had funked, the defection of "Ivor Claire" could not have had the necessary impact on him.'[9]

Later Powell took the matter up with Christopher Sykes, who in his biography blandly ignored Waugh's adventures in Crete because 'he told the whole grisly story himself' in *Officers and Gentlemen*. Surely Crouchback, like Claire, was guilty of having deserted his men and disobeying the order to surrender? Sykes replied that whereas Claire commanded a troop, Crouchback had only a small section under him. 'Claire deceived the destroyer captain and left his men. Crouchback gave his men the option.' Powell replied that 'Evelyn created something of a stumbling block in giving Crouchback men, in the light of having had none himself in Crete,* and it did occur to me that there was intended to be a moral dilemma.'[10] He then turned from fiction to fact, and questioned the authority of the senior officer who countermanded the order to surrender in respect of Waugh and his commanding officer, Colonel Robert Laycock, thus allowing them to escape. It now seems probable that he was on to something here. Two historians, Anthony Beevor[11] and Angus Calder,[12] have suggested that Laycock, like Ivor Claire, had no intention of being captured, whatever overtook his men. He persuaded the officer in command of the evacuation that he and his headquarters, including Waugh, should be allowed to leave. Waugh connived at this and felt guilty ever after.

Powell regretted that he never saw action and I am sure that he was jealous of Waugh, whose courage under fire all are agreed upon. But I don't think jealousy accounts for his hostile insinuations. It was something Waugh himself said to him shortly after his return from Crete. Speaking of his experiences there, Waugh said: 'I saw some of your regiment marching

---

* Waugh was his unit's Intelligence officer.

in good order with their equipment.' Powell took this to be a slur on The Welch, who he knew had suffered very heavy casualties, losing the best part of a battalion.

> It does not seem to have occurred to Waugh ... that, had no troops been holding the German line back, it would have been where he was: nor that he himself, a staff-officer personally attached to [Colonel] Laycock, was, without troops under his command to worry about – in a privileged position.[13]

If Powell understood Waugh correctly then it is natural that he should wish to mount a counter-attack. But to me, Waugh's remark sounds like a compliment. It is on a par with what he was to write about Crouchback's old unit, the Halberdiers, who execute a withdrawal in which 'everything was done correctly'. (Incidentally, it is a pity that during the dispersal of Waugh's literary remains an unpublished piece of his called 'Writers at War' should have gone missing. His thoughts on the subject would have been well worth knowing.)

Powell had ample opportunity to re-examine his old friend thanks to the 'Great Waugh Boom', which began with the posthumous publication of his *Diaries* and *Letters*. A fan of the *Diaries*, he thought Waugh was at his 'most gifted' when writing autobiographically, rating *The Ordeal of Gilbert Pinfold* above his other novels. His nastiness (and that of his son, Auberon) he ascribed to heredity, adducing the callous behaviour of his Waugh grandfather, who crushed a wasp on his wife's forehead with the knob of his stick. As an agnostic, Powell probably felt unqualified to comment on Waugh's assertion that without his faith he would have been even nastier. But given his own aesthetic beginnings I am surprised he ignored the significance of Waugh's early excursions into illustration and carpentry. 'These are craftsmen's hands,' Waugh was heard to say. And when asked why he wrote, he replied, 'To make pleasant objects.' Though he did not, like Waugh, use a pen, Powell also saw himself as a craftsman. Writing a novel on the typewriter was, he said, 'like a sculpture coming up in front of one'.[14]

*

Not long after Waugh died Powell was involved in an acrimonious dispute with Penguin Books over their shabby treatment, as he saw it, of Osbert Lancaster, who had designed the covers of the first six volumes of *Dance* to appear in paperback. Without wishing to detract from the portfolio of caricatures subsequently done by Mark Boxer for Fontana, Lancaster's drawings strike me as exemplary. Indeed Boxer himself said this of Lancaster's cover for *At Lady Molly's*: 'As a framed time capsule it evoked the Thirties as brilliantly as a Bill Brandt photograph.'[15]

The trouble was that by the mid-Sixties imagery of the sort that Lancaster excelled at was considered outdated. Paperbacks needed to be as eye-catching as record sleeves, and the simplest way of ensuring this was to give them suggestive covers. Penguin had been slow to cotton on to this, with the result that their primacy had been eroded by less inhibited rivals like Pan, Corgi and Panther, all of whom were prepared to use 'bosoms and bottoms' (Allen Lane's phrase) to sell books. Lane, Penguin's founder, was no prude: in 1960 he had published the unexpurgated *Lady Chatterley's Lover*, the first successful challenge to the Obscene Publications Act. But having been born in 1902 he was understandably out of touch with anyone under thirty.

To try and tap this new market Lane hired a couple of Young Turks. Tony Godwin, the new fiction editor, had made his name as the founder of 'Better Books', an avant-garde bookshop in Charing Cross Road whose basement was one of the early outposts of the counter-culture. Both he and Penguin's new art director Alan Aldridge, soon famous for his collaboration with the Beatles, would try anything, including putting bare breasts on the cover, in order to sell books. 'Covers with naked tits sent the sales up but upset the authors,'[16] recalled Aldridge. Godwin later quarrelled with Lane and was sacked, but by then Powell was resolved to go elsewhere.

Powell's version of what happened is that in the summer of 1966 Osbert Lancaster asked him when a cover would be needed for *The Valley of Bones*, the customary two years between hardback and paperback having almost elapsed. He was going abroad soon and wanted to clear his desk. Powell wrote to Penguin and received no reply. When he wrote again he got a letter back from a secretary saying that someone else would be doing the cover. This 'casualness' infuriated Powell, who felt that to jettison Lancaster without informing either of them first was an appalling breach of good manners. He made his views known in a third letter.

By now news of the row had reached the press. Godwin was quoted as saying that the decision to change the covers had been made because sales of the sequence had been 'so disappointing'. He described Powell's attitude as 'condescending' and said his letters were 'most unpleasant'.[17] Powell agreed that he was 'out of sorts' with Penguin, not least because they had leaked the matter to the press. He insisted that the covers themselves were not an issue: design and production were a matter for the publisher, not the author. What incensed him was that Penguin seemed incapable of grasping that they had behaved 'loutishly' towards a distinguished artist.

In *Strangers* Powell says that having fallen out with his paperback publisher (he names neither Penguin nor Godwin), he went elsewhere; but it took a while to disengage himself. Godwin left Penguin in 1967. In 1968, two years later than planned, Penguin published *The Valley of Bones*, complete with cover by Lancaster. Shortly afterwards Fontana, Powell's new paperback publisher, did *The Soldier's Art* in a completely different format. This must have affected the momentum of the sequence, even if its impact on sales can never be determined. It was Powell's good fortune that when a uniform edition of *Dance* in paperback was published in 1977, he and his publishers could call upon Mark Boxer, who described it as 'probably the sweetest commission'[18] he would ever get.

As it happens Powell had been one of the many distinguished writers who, if called, would have been a witness for the Defence in the Chatterley Trial. Though he didn't think much of the book itself – he thought a novel based on the married life of Mellors and Lady C had much more potential – he was strongly opposed to censorship. Had the censorship laws not been relaxed some of what Pamela Flitton, in particular, says and does could not have been spelt out. Powell admitted this. He also admitted to a taste for Erotica, but drew the line at 'hard porn'. On holiday in Sweden, while walking down a rather smart street, he'd suddenly been confronted by a large picture of a woman's private parts: 'I don't think anyone wants it any more than one wants to leave the door open on a mortuary.'[19] But if that was the price you had to pay for reading *Ulysses*, so be it. 'Art is the true adjudicator, in its complicated relationship with taste.'

*

Powell always insisted that however contrived some of the entanglements he depicted in *Dance* might seem, they did not begin to match the symmetry of those that occurred in real life. The extraordinary love life of Barbara Skelton – 'Skelters' – supports this. 'Do you know her – probably slept with her? Most of one's friends have,' says Chips Lovell of the beautiful Bijou Ardglass. But he might just as well have been speaking of Skelters, who, like Bijou, was briefly a mannequin. However, by 1971, when *Books Do Furnish a Room* came out, it was clear to many people, including the lady herself, that if Skelters had a fictional counterpart it was not Bijou but Pamela Flitton (as I shall continue to call her despite her marriage to Widmerpool).

Skelters was by now back to being Miss Skelton, having changed her name three times in the previous twenty years. We left her in the midst of the Greek Civil War, employed as a cipherine at the British Embassy in Athens. Six years and innumerable lovers later she married Cyril Connolly, who had just tried to use her as bait to get an interview in Biarritz with her old lover, King Farouk, conduct Powell thought 'put [Connolly] within hail of the ponce area'.[20]

It was never going to be an orthodox marriage, any more than the Widmerpools'. Connolly was still half in love with his de facto wife, Lys Lubbock, and pursuing at least one other woman as well. For her part Skelters was being kept by John Sutro, a wealthy Oxford contemporary of Connolly and Powell who had the added advantage, in Skelters's eyes, of being fat and ugly. 'I never really appreciated conventional good looks,' she confessed. 'Erich von Stroheim was my ideal.' Unable to afford a London address the newlyweds retreated to Oak Cottage (nicknamed 'Oak Coffin' by Connolly), Skelters's tiny, primitive bolt-hole near Elmstead in Kent which she had bought for £400 before the war. There, to Connolly's chagrin, Skelters kept a diary, the basis for her memoir *Tears Before Bedtime*. Reviewing this, Powell issued the following warning: 'Anybody contemplating a plunge into bohemian intellectual life should study these pages before making an irrevocable decision.'[21] Here is a typical entry:

This morning I woke to be told, 'Why don't you drop down dead? That's all I wish, that you'd drop down dead.' He was lying half naked on the bed. 'Is there anything that you want?' 'That you will drop down dead.' Writs arrive by almost every post. Cyril remains in his bed, sucking the sheet. The Waugh article has been abandoned. The Third Programme has made suggestions. C just potters about the house in carpet slippers dusting his first editions and cluttering up the tables with cracked Sèvres and chipped faience.[22]

Physically, Skelters did not in the least resemble Pamela. With her green eyes, olive skin, tawny mane and sinuous body she reminded men of a feral cat, rubbing against your leg one minute, lashing out the next. But she and Pamela were certainly sisters under the skin, as witness this testimony by Edmund Wilson, who met her in the Fifties: '[W]hen you talk to her, there is no response in her face, a simple narcissistic mask, petrified by a fundamental sullenness.'[23] Wilson had just read Skelters' novel, *A Young Girl's Touch*, whose beautiful and ruthless heroine, Melinda Paleface, he saw as a self-portrait:

People come to grief on her account but she does not really care. She is sulky and selfish, never seems to have any real fun, is not interested in what she sees … The only thing she has to depend on is the power over men of her prettiness. When she has made proof of this, she repulses them.[24]

Powell applauded *A Young Girl's Touch*: 'Miss Skelton writes like the crack of a whip.' But he added that it 'was not for the easily shocked'.[25] It seems reasonable to suppose that he might have got the idea for Pamela's 'dead-white complexion' from the surname of Skelters's heroine.

In 1955 or thereabouts Skelters fell in love with another fat man, George Weidenfeld, who happened to be Connolly's publisher as well as her own. After a dramatic tug-of-love lasting several months Connolly agreed to a divorce, but by then Skelters had decided that she and Weidenfeld were incompatible out of bed. They married, but lived together for a mere six months. When Weidenfeld later sued for divorce, Connolly was cited as the co-respondent, though by then he had his eye on Deirdre Craven, who became his third wife.

Skelters was over forty by now, rather old to be a penniless *femme fatale*. Her predicament was underlined when Andy Warhol offered her the part of a nude grandmother in one of his early porn epics. It must have been a relief when the millionaire physicist, Derek Jackson, installed her at the Paris Ritz as his fifth wife. Briefly though this liaison lasted, it proved a nice little earner. She emerged with a pension for her mother and a Provençal farmhouse which she shared with cats, coatis and an incorrigible French writer called Bernard Frank, several years her junior, who was also carrying on with Françoise Sagan. Connolly, however, retained the key to her heart. On one of the last occasions they met before his health failed he paid her this unambiguous compliment: 'You certainly were a sexpot in your day.'[26]

Given her indiscriminate taste in lovers it is not inconceivable that Skelters could have had a fling with Julian Maclaren-Ross, particularly in the days before she took a fancy to fat men. But there is no evidence that they even met. On the other hand Maclaren-Ross did have an unrequited passion for Sonia Brownell, which Powell certainly knew about since he's supposed to have said that they 'were made for each other'.[27] This may have been in the back of his mind when he had X. Trapnel fall for Pamela, a cause that seems equally hopeless in the beginning. But in a twist worthy of grand opera Pamela walks out on Widmerpool and moves in with Trapnel, whose sordid digs in Maida Vale provide the backdrop to the electrifying moment when Widmerpool tracks them down and Trapnel rises from his sickbed, unsheaths his sword-stick, and expels him (in an opera he would run him through). This is followed by an even more sensational denouement, Trapnel's discovery that the manuscript in the nearby canal is his masterpiece, *Profiles in String*, deposited there by Pamela who has left him. Cue the final aria, following which Trapnel throws not only his sword-stick (as in the novel) but himself as well into the canal, thus bringing down the curtain on a suitably melodramatic note.

The fate of *Profiles in String* is in stark contrast to that of *Sad Majors*, Odo Stevens's war memoir, which Gypsy Jones tries to 'liquidate' on account of its unflattering view of 'the Comrades'. Gypsy, by now married to Stevens's publisher, Howard Craggs, destroys the typescript and its duplicate. But Stevens outwits her by making two duplicates, the second of which he is able to place with a different publisher. The example of *Animal Farm*, though not identical, is relevant. Soviet sympathisers in publishing and the Ministry of Information did their damnedest to suppress it. Who can doubt that given the chance to strangle the story at birth, one of these stooges would have obliged? On a lighter note, it is amusing to learn from Paul Willetts's biography that Maclaren-Ross once fobbed off a publisher to whom he owed a book by claiming that it was at the bottom of the Regent's Canal, thrown there by his current girlfriend after a row.[28]

Up until now we have had to take Jenkins's writing largely on trust. But in *Books Do Furnish a Room* we see him at work on *Borage and Hellebore*, his study of the seventeenth-century scholar Robert Burton. Burton stands for Aubrey, whom Powell was writing about at that moment, notwithstanding the objection made by 'a very *serious* American scholar' that Burton was an unsuitable choice because he was a man of Death, whereas Aubrey was a man of Life.[29] Powell's interest in Burton dated back to his early days at Duckworth, where he found an edition of *The Anatomy of Melancholy* on the office shelves. In idle moments he would read a few pages, the best method, he thought, of tackling an author whom some found heavy going. This paid off in a curious way. Not only did he light upon the title for his first novel, he also noted down for future reference one of Burton's 'torrential' passages. It would be almost fifty years before he could find a use for it.

When he is not writing about Burton, Jenkins is editing the book pages of *Fission*, a new monthly magazine 'for the Atomic Age'. Enlisted under *Fission*'s banner are Quiggin, in his new role as a publisher, Widmerpool, who is on the board, Trapnel, a regular contributor, and the editor, 'Books-do-furnish-a-room' Bagshaw, a self-styled professional rebel mentioned earlier in connection with Malcolm Muggeridge. At *Fission*'s threadbare launch party there is one notable absentee, Isobel's eldest brother Erridge, who was to have backed the magazine. Believed by his family to be a hypochondriac, Erridge confounds them by dropping dead shortly after his younger brother George has succumbed to wounds sustained three years before in North Africa.

Powell rarely allows Jenkins to express explicit moral judgements, but he makes an exception in the case of Erridge and George Tolland. The latter dies, as he lived, unobtrusively, whereas Erridge receives 'some little notice' by way of obituaries, which disseminate the fantasy that he 'fought' in Spain. This valedictory imbalance strikes Jenkins as unjust:

> Musing on the brothers, it looked a bit as if, in an oblique manner, Erridge, at least by implication, had been given the credit for paying the debt that had in fact been irrefutably settled by George. The same was true, if it came to that, of Stringham, Templer, Barnby – to name a few casualties known personally to one – all equally indifferent to putting right the world.

Another reference to the audit of war occurs at the end of the book when Jenkins returns to his old school to register his younger son there. He meets Le Bas, his former housemaster, now temporarily employed as the school Librarian. At first Le Bas can't place him, but once Jenkins mentions Templer and Stringham, the old man has him in his sights. 'Sad about those fellows who were killed,' he says. 'I sometimes think of the number of pupils of mine who lost their lives. Two wars. It adds up.'

What doesn't add up – on the available evidence – is how Jenkins makes ends meet. Apart from the job at *Fission*, which only lasts about eighteen months, he has no visible means of support after leaving the Army; yet his sons are down for Eton and there is nothing to suggest that he is worse off than anyone else. 'I wonder sometimes,' wrote Philip Larkin, 'how much money he has, and where it comes from.'[30] So do I. By revealing so little about his narrator's professional and domestic life Powell invited these questions, which he never, as far as I know, answered properly.* Jenkins, he would say, 'is somebody like me'. End of story. We must assume, therefore, that in addition to his professional earnings – from novels and reviews – Jenkins has sufficient private means to educate his sons and keep his wife in a style that befits her rank.

While on the subject of Jenkins I think we can learn something from the way people address him, particularly in the early books, before the universal adoption of Christian names, something Powell deplored. His intimates call him Nick, as do most women; to everyone else he is either Jenkins, Mr Jenkins or, chilliest of all, Nicholas. Eventually just about everyone, including Widmerpool, calls him Nick, further evidence, if you like, of the crumbling of social foundations. Powell himself was always Tony to his friends, never Anthony, which was why I drew attention to the fact that Violet calls him Anthony in her autobiography, *The Departure Platform*.

---

* V.S. Pritchett had 'the irritating impression that Jenkins ... has no other profession but to run about collecting the news.'

*

Two months before the publication of *Books Do Furnish a Room*, Powell celebrated his sixty-fifth birthday, entitling him to a State pension. He would continue to collect it for the next thirty years, comfortably outliving all his contemporaries, some of whom had already shot their bolt. At the head of the field was Powell's oldest friend, Henry Green, whose last novel had appeared in 1952. Green had never had to live by his pen alone, being gainfully employed since Oxford in his family's engineering business, Pontifex. He had also remained married to Dig, despite having had a succession of affairs. After the war, in which he served as a London fireman, he took to drink in a big way, beginning with a gin and tonic at ten in the morning. One reason for this was resentment of his elderly father, who still regarded himself as head of the firm; another was his failure to complete a novel based on his experiences in the Blitz. In 1958 his brother discovered that the tumbler Green was drinking from at a board meeting contained neat gin. He was quietly pensioned off. That same year Powell met him for the last time at a party given by the American Institute. Green said he wasn't well, but insisted drink was not to blame. 'I think I'm going to die,' he told Powell, which was premature because he hung on for another fifteen years, until December 1973.

At Green's memorial service a month later Powell met Cyril Connolly and asked, 'Who's next?' With 'elaborate politeness', Connolly replied, '*You* come to mine.'[31] The following December this is exactly what Powell did. Unlike Green, Connolly went downhill very rapidly. He can't have known in January that he had less than a year to live. But that spring, after years of neglect, his body began to seize up and by the autumn he was ready to board the ferry, which docked on 26 November. Powell was not there to wave him off, nor did he rush into print with a tribute, having earmarked Connolly for his Memoirs. He retained a passionate interest in him to the end of his days. Alan Ross recalled that one of the last conversations they had concerned a new Connolly story that was circulating.

Ross, born 1922, probably knew Connolly and Powell as well as any man of his generation. What he says here about Connolly could also apply to Powell: 'As some need a drink to get going, Connolly needed gossip. It brought him up to par, released some essential juices. He could not bear to think of his friends, or enemies, enjoying a world outside his knowledge.'[32] The difference was that Connolly himself generated gossip, whereas Powell didn't. Ross was struck by the fact that so many of Powell's close friends – Adrian Daintrey, John Heygate, Malcolm Muggeridge and Constant

Lambert – were promiscuous. He thought Powell took a vicarious delight in their exploits.

Connolly died at about the time Powell was completing *Dance*. In a valedictory piece written for *Encounter*, Jack Lambert, Connolly's literary editor on the *Sunday Times*, said 'he had been looking forward to writing at some length about the whole twelve volumes'. This might have taxed even Connolly's powers of dissimulation, since according to his widow, Deirdre Levi, he had never managed to finish a single volume, which was why he had dodged reviewing it up until then. 'He would flip through each new instalment as they arrived, so as to get the gist, and liked trying to work out who was really who, but he much preferred Tony's early novels. He thought *The Music of Time* was droning.'[33]

Connolly came up with one of the more bizarre theories about Widmerpool's prototype. He fingered an old enemy of his, Douglas Cooper, the choleric art historian and collector. John Richardson, for many years Cooper's companion, rejected this. 'Douglas could be a shit, but not that sort of shit. He was anything but cold. Perhaps this was one of Cyril's jokes.'[34] In his memoir of life with Cooper, Richardson quotes Connolly as saying 'I could do without all painting,'[35] a statement he insists was not a tease. If so, it suggests another reason why Connolly couldn't get on with *Dance*, so much of which is concerned with painting and its symbolism. It may also explain why, in a long piece about the Wallace Collection, an 'old love' of his, Connolly says practically nothing about the art and ignores Poussin altogether.

It is a measure of the different roads they travelled after Eton and Balliol that Powell and Connolly never wrote for the same publication at the same time. But when their old friend and mentor Maurice Bowra died they both composed tributes that were later included in the *Celebration* edited by Hugh Lloyd-Jones. Powell's piece, one of the longest in the collection, was a mixture of analysis and autobiography that he put straight into *Infants*. Connolly's was more intimate, as befitted someone with whom Bowra had been little short of in love, so Powell thought. On this they were agreed: the unbridgeable chasm that separated those, like Bowra, who had fought in the Great War, from those who hadn't. Powell told how, after he and Bowra had made up, they went on a Mediterranean cruise together that passed within sight of Gallipoli, where a wreath was committed to the waves. This gesture moved Powell considerably, as he later admitted to Bowra. Bowra's response was forthright:

Had to go below. Lie down for *half-an-hour* afterwards in my cabin.

*

At the beginning of *Temporary Kings*, the penultimate volume of *Dance*, we learn that Jenkins is 'in difficulties about a book', which is why he succumbs to Mark Members' blandishments – 'You'll live like a king once you get there' – and signs up for a writers' shindig in Venice, where most of the story takes place. Members is now a professional *conférencier*, an epithet I once heard applied to Stephen Spender, traces of whom are to be found in another delegate, Quentin Shuckerley, formerly a 'committed' poet, now the celebrated author of *Athlete's Footman*, 'the best queer novel since *Sea Urchins*', according to Members. (Powell's titles – books, paintings, even a cocktail: 'Death Comes for the Archbishop' – are as pithy as his throwaway lines.)

Jenkins doesn't seem to have heard of *Athlete's Footman*. His intelligence-gathering system is in disarray. 'You must live absolutely out of the world,' says a younger colleague, the last thing you ever supposed someone would say of him. On practically the last page we learn that he has moved to the country, so the Venetian jaunt is a plausible way of reimmersing him in the social swim. Conveniently, it overlaps with the Biennale and the Film Festival, which explains the presence of Pamela Flitton and her latest beau, Louis Glober, a colourful American film producer who began life as a publisher, in which capacity Jenkins met him thirty years before. Glober, an unreconstructed Jazz Age type, peps up the narrative. He is the first man to get the better of Pamela; also the first to throw a punch at Widmerpool, already on the ropes after the arrest and trial of his Stalinist associates in the Balkans.

In complete contrast to Glober is another American, Russell Gwinnett, as buttoned-up as Glober is expansive. Whereas Glober is a life-force, Gwinnett, a young lecturer, is unnaturally keen on death. He may even, while a student, have had congress with a corpse, though like Widmerpool's involvement in the Burgess and Maclean affair, this was never proved. Gwinnett is writing a book about the now deceased X. Trapnel, in connection with which he meets Pamela, who selects him as the agency of her apotheosis. Quite why she should sacrifice herself in order to satisfy Gwinnett's fetish is one of those mysteries that Powell delights in. Surely she hasn't given all for love – she's not the type. Perhaps she did not intend to take a fatal overdose, merely enough to cause a scandal and embarrass her husband, who may have been under the bed or behind the curtain (something Powell did not 'absolutely rule out'). In a letter to Frederick Bradnum, who did the radio adaptation of *Dance*, Powell said, 'I think one must always allow for *no one* quite knowing what happens on certain occasions, including the participants.'[36]

Equally mysterious – to jump to the final volume – is the manner in which all the dirt, including Widmerpool's spying (if that is what it was), is swept under the carpet without anyone raising more than an eyebrow. People blame the CIA for framing Widmerpool and, conceivably, murdering Pamela, which sounds anachronistic in the late Fifties, when it's all supposed to have happened. Then one remembers that Powell wrote *Temporary Kings* and its successor in the early Seventies, the Watergate era, by which time cover-ups and conspiracy theories were all the rage. It is also the case that in disposing of Pamela, Powell eliminated his most candid witness, the one person who consistently flouts Lady Warminster's rule that 'only the discipline of infinite obliquity made it lawful to examine the seamy side of life'. Did she, as a girl, seduce her Uncle Charles? Was Templer really unable to satisfy her? What did she and Widmerpool talk about when they were alone together? When she dies, so does any chance of our getting an answer to these questions.

I think the file on Pamela's death ought to remain open. The post-mortem would surely have detected the presence of semen in her vagina, even if in those days it couldn't prove whose it was or when it was deposited there. Consequently the inquest would not have been the formality Jenkins says it was. This is not to say that everything ought to be spelt out. What could be more eloquent than the brief exchange, at a military reunion dinner, between Jenkins and Cheesman, the commander of the Mobile Laundry Unit in which Stringham served?

'Surely you fetched up in Singapore?'
Cheesman nodded.
'In fact you were a Jap POW?'
'Yes.'
Cheesman gave the answer perfectly composedly, but for a brief second, something much shorter than that, something scarcely measurable in time, there shot, like forked lightning, across his serious unornamental features that awful look, common to those who speak of that experience.

For his own peace of mind Jenkins does not press Cheesman for details of Stringham's death, but we can be sure that there was nothing remotely 'chic' about it. Again, in the final volume, we don't need a description of the ghastly penances Scorpio Murtlock orders Widmerpool to enact with Bithel; enough has already been said about Murtlock's cult to imagine them. Widmerpool's death is another matter: it is meet and right that we hear all about that, not least because it bears out one of Jenkins' favourite dicta, that in the end 'most things in life – perhaps all things – turn out to be appropriate.'

At the end of *Temporary Kings* Moreland dies. In poor health for years he was never going to make old bones, but you sense that he's been living on borrowed time since 1939, when his wife Matilda left him and the world he cherished vanished for good. 'I've turned my back on contemporary life,' he tells Jenkins just after the war. Increasingly afflicted by nostalgia – 'They say you lose your head for it as you grow older' – he never recovers from the massive draught of it he swallows at Rosie Manasch's charity concert. Jenkins visits him in hospital and in the last few months of his life their old conversational intimacy is briefly restored. Moreland's last recorded words – 'I'll have to think about that song' – always bring a lump to my throat when I read them. He belongs on the same roll of honour as Stringham, Templer and Barnby, all victims of the large, impersonal forces unleashed the day Billson gave notice in her birthday suit.

Weighing in at 280 pages *Temporary Kings* is the thickest volume of *Dance*. It won the 1974 W.H. Smith Prize, worth £1000 to the author, and left readers in suspense about Widmerpool, who assures Jenkins on the last page that he will rise above his misfortunes and continue to 'assail the limitations of contemporary empiricism, and expose the bankruptcy of cold-war propagandists'. No hint here of what is to come. Reviewing the novel in the *TLS* Alan Brownjohn pronounced it 'the saddest in the sequence', adding that the author had 'never combined high comedy and the sense of impending tragedy so capably'. Shortly afterwards Brownjohn wrote a 9000 word article on Powell for *The New Review*, probably the longest piece about him ever published. Although billed as a profile it was more in the nature of a meditation, with very little in the way of direct speech. Powell's Burmese cat, described as 'serene but friendly, faintly inscrutable [and] of daunting pedigree', might almost be taken for the author himself, who responds to straight questions with 'an infectious smile and a steadily matter-of-fact answer'.[37] A better approach, suggests Brownjohn, would be to try and work a flanker on him, though as an old soldier his position is chosen carefully, with a good field of fire all round. Occasionally a frontal assault does pay off. Asked point-blank why he lists no recreations, 'not even a whimsical or unbelievable one', in *Who's Who*, he counters, 'How can you have recreations if your work is reading and writing?' (But what about genealogy?)

A line of attack Brownjohn identifies, but does not seem to have pursued, concerns the code by which Jenkins judges his fellow men. It is, he says, 'that of an upper-class Englishman of open-minded, humanistic leanings, immaculately reticent, not shockable, who feels an inherent security in his status and in the values of art, believing that ambitious striving towards the goals of worldly power and success is ridiculous'. Thus equipped, Jenkins 'is able to observe the contortions of others as the exercise of efforts in which he has little share; little share because most of such efforts must be adjudged vain and comic, forms of behaviour unbecoming in the light of the code'. Vain and comic perhaps; but for most of us, *necessary*, if we are to survive. We come back to Larkin's question about money. Is Jenkins's 'metropolitan detachment' (as a hostile critic described it) a reflection of his bank balance as well as his code?

Powell was aware that his narrator's serenity might irk some readers. In a letter to Kingsley Amis he admitted to 'some uneasiness about Jenkins being relatively too much on top of the world (tho' he does, for instance, speak of his despair at Castlemallock), but the alternative here – and so often – is to write quite a different sort of novel about the hero's sufferings'. The matter had arisen after Amis's long radio talk on *Dance*. A listener had written to Amis about Jenkins, and he had forwarded the letter to Powell. 'I suspect,' concluded Powell, 'that [your listener] is really yearning for the self-pity novel.'[38]

Powell said he never gave much thought to the reader over his shoulder. 'I think that's rather the sort of thing I would prefer *not* to do ... If you possibly can avoid being self-conscious about your writing, I do think it is ever so much better.'[39] But in the speech of thanks he made at the W.H. Smith Prize dinner he decided to have a go at all those people who thought *Dance* was just a *roman à clef*. Unfortunately the weapon he chose was irony, which as any experienced public speaker could have told him is double-edged. 'It is very generally known,' said Powell,

> that of all creatures in the community, novelists have the least imagination. All they do is to write down things that have happened to themselves, linking these things with their own friends and acquaintances, whose names they slightly alter. It is easy to know that, because even people who've never read a given novel – perhaps never read books at all – will always be able to tell you who all the characters in a contemporary novel are 'meant to be'.[40]

What of course happened was that this passage was quoted out of context and had exactly the opposite effect he intended.

Although less of an issue than who was really who, the obscurity of Nick Jenkins exercised many of Powell's fans. Would he eventually colour him in? The answer was no. Keen on having his own portrait painted, Powell vetoed any likeness of Jenkins. Had he not been such a visual writer this might have passed unnoticed; but given the care with which he delineates the other leading characters it draws the eye like an empty space on a gallery wall. Consequently Powell had only himself to blame if people assumed Jenkins was his doppelgänger. Malcolm Muggeridge, who was in a better position than most to separate fact from fiction in *Dance*, quoted X. Trapnel's theory that writers disclose more about themselves in fiction than in autobiographies:

> People think because a novel's invented, it isn't true. Exactly the reverse is the case. Because a novel's invented, it is true. Biography and memoirs can never be wholly true, since they can't include every conceivable circumstance of what happened. The novel can do that. The novelist himself lays it down ... In a sense you know more about Balzac and Dickens from their novels, than Rousseau and Casanova from their Confessions.

'Certainly,' pursued Muggeridge, 'for those that have eyes to see, the life story and character of Powell is unfolded with extraordinary clarity and vividness in Nicholas's narration.'[41]

17

The Music Dies

'I have never believed that characters in fiction vanish after the last page is turned.'

Paul Theroux: *The Consul's File*

In 1957 Julian Symons, with uncanny foresight, had predicted that *Dance* would end 'without formal tidiness, leaving the principal characters frozen in single, symptomatic attitudes'. Turn to the last sentence of *Dance* and what do you find? 'Even the formal measure of the Seasons seemed suspended in the wintry silence.' Powell subsequently endorsed the wider implications of Symons's prediction in an interview with his sister-in-law, Elizabeth Longford, who recalled his telling her 'some time ago' how hard it would be to tie up all the loose ends. He said he'd since decided that he 'didn't want an "end" of that sort ... It was very important that the reader should *not* feel there was not a single other word to be said.' This was why it fell to the drunken Bithel to describe Widmerpool's death – 'like light refracted through water'.[1]

But, however opposed to 'slickness', Powell could not round off the sequence without tying some knots. Just as he relished seeing 'the end of a few stories', so his readers had the same expectations. They would feel cheated if a character they liked disappeared without trace or was left dangling, like one of the author's participles. Although the days are long gone when not a social item escaped Jenkins's notice he still manages to file a final report on old favourites like Dicky Umfraville, Bob Duport, Sunny Farebrother and Members and Quiggin, 'nowadays disputing with each other only who had enjoyed the more modest home'. Gypsy Jones is dead, and Jean might as well be, so glacial is she towards her old lover when they meet for the last time. There is also an interesting newcomer, Gibson Delavacquerie, a poet and PR man of Creole descent who might, you feel, have filled the void left by Moreland were he and Jenkins closer in age.

Another problem was that *Dance* had at last caught up with contemporary life, some aspects of which Powell, after more than twenty years in the boondocks, was understandably remote from. Galsworthy had found himself in the same boat and, in Powell's opinion, was shipwrecked as a consequence: 'In the end, when he begins to bring in the younger generation, it's ludicrous beyond words what he writes down.'[2] If Powell was determined to bring everything up to date, he would need to steer very carefully, since there was all the Sixties to be negotiated.

Novelists, like generals, need luck. When Powell christened Widmerpool 'Kenneth', he could not have foreseen how redolent of trendy classlessness 'Ken' would sound in the Seventies. Nor can he have divined that in the late Sixties a new generation of 'crackpot' visionaries would arise, no less dedicated to building 'a New Heaven and a New Earth' than their Edwardian predecessors, and no less 'sinister or comic' according to your tastes. As Jenkins says somewhere, 'Everything alters, yet does remain the same.' Here was the justification, if it were needed, for characters like Dr Trelawney and Mrs Erdleigh. And here too was a serendipitous solution to the problem of Widmerpool, who returns from California convinced that the future lies with young drop-outs, hence his involvement with Scorpio Murtlock, whom he thinks, mistakenly, he can control. (To me, Widmerpool's high standing in the counter-culture is no more credible than his pre-war association with the Prince of Wales, but as Trapnel might say, the author's decision is final.)

It was not, however, luck, but good management that explained Canon Fenneau, last encountered almost fifty years before as 'Paul', a speechless young pupil of Sillery's. In volume one Powell deliberately introduced more characters than he needed because a few of them, he felt sure, might come in useful later on (he called them 'cards of re-entry'). Possibly he also had hopes for Honthorst, a rich American Rhodes scholar, and Vaalkiipaa, an earnest Finn. But it was Paul who got the nod. On the other hand, there were certain things he couldn't plan for. *Hearing Secret Harmonies* contains a description of a literary prize-giving, the Magnus Donners Memorial award, at which Widmerpool launches a vitriolic attack on 'the great industrialist' and all he stood for. This owed something to the notorious Booker Prize dinner of 1972, at which Powell was present, when the winner, John Berger, said that because Booker Brothers' wealth was derived from slavery, he would give half his winnings to the Black Panthers. Then Powell was awarded the W.H. Smith Prize, by which time he had written about the Donners award. To an uninformed witness it would look, he told his agent, as if he had acted 'in very bad taste'.[3]

The Donners award dinner is one of three set pieces in *Hearing Secret Harmonies*, the other two being a Royal Academy banquet and a smartish wedding at Stourwater, now a fashionable girls' school. Each marks a stage in the rapid deterioration of Widmerpool, from seditious Chancellor of a new university, where he keeps open house for student radicals, to deranged and decrepit votary of Harmony, Holy Grail of the cult led by his nemesis, Scorpio Murtlock, Dr Trelawney's self-styled heir. Murtlock, in my opinion, doesn't come off. Unlike Powell's other bogeymen, he is creepy but not in the least grotesque, which goes against the grain. Jenkins may be wary of him, but I'm not. The hold he has over people as different as Jimmy Stripling and Isobel's wayward niece, Fiona Cutts, has to be taken on trust.

Fiona escapes Murtlock's clutches by marrying Russell Gwinnett, which bothered Kingsley Amis. In his radio talk on *Dance*, broadcast in 1979, he said Jenkins ought to have warned Fiona's mother that she was getting a necrophile for a son-in-law. Powell's response to this was that while he understood Amis's concern,

> I don't think in practice one would interfere about a niece's wedding, if she had rather a background of hippy life. It so happens that most of our innumerable nephews and nieces have not gone that way, but we have quite a collection of friends who could produce parallel cases, and I think one would very much think twice before sticking one's nose in – just in case something worse then happened. But I agree it is anybody's guess.[4]

A previous criticism Amis had made was not so well received by Powell. At the lunch Heinemann gave to mark the completion of *Dance* he gave Amis a 'ballocking' for citing Fowler in support of his objection to this sentence: 'If Murtlock liked sex at all, he preferred his own.' As Amis recalled, 'Tony and I were among the first to arrive. His opening words to me were, "Hallo Kingsley, and I think you should realise that Fowler has no authority at all and was merely expressing his personal preferences."' Amis thought this illustrated a 'faintly comic and egotistical' side of his character that was 'rarely in evidence'.[5] But it surfaced again during the lunch itself. Jilly Cooper, who was sitting next to Powell, said he complained bitterly that Amis thought the sex in his books was 'rather pedestrian'.[6] If Amis did think this, he omitted it from the *Observer* review to which Powell took exception.

In fact, as Amis pointed out in his *Memoirs*, he gave *Hearing Secret Harmonies* a very good write-up, comparing the feeling he had when he laid the book down to 'the sadness that descends when the last chord of a great symphony fades into silence'.[7] Paul Scott, in *Country Life*, also regretted that the performance had come to an end. But 'the compensation will be felt later when I have got used to the idea that the music has not stopped, because it can always be replayed.'[8] The addictive quality of the sequence was emphasised by John Bayley in the *TLS*, who said that there were not many stories 'which when finished one immediately wishes to begin again'. He attributed this to the curiosity aroused by the cast: 'They are always the same and yet we always want to meet them.' But only on the page. 'We should run a mile from a real Alfred Tolland, Bob Duport, or Mrs Maclintick.'[9] Michael Frayn, in a celebratory essay, compared his discovery of *Dance* in the Sixties to the discovery of 'a complete civilisation – and not in some remote valley of the Andes or the Himalayas, but in the midst of London, in the midst of my own life. It altered my perception of the world ... I began to see in my own life the kind of patterns which were emerging in Jenkins's life.'[10] Most surprising of all was this puff from the *Guardian*'s dour literary editor, W.L. Webb, whose superlatives were usually reserved for East European fiction: 'Achieved is the glorious work. Buy it now; we won't be able to afford this kind of writing again.'

There was, however, one loud dissenting voice. It belonged to Evelyn Waugh's son, Auberon, who had this to say about Nick Jenkins: 'I see him as an odious poseur, a ponderous and conceited public-school show-off whose ludicrous one man act can appeal only to the socially and intellectually insecure.' Then, echoing what Powell himself had said in respect of Evelyn Waugh's Guy Crouchback and Major Hound, he said he wished 'that what happened to poor Widmerpool might have happened to Jenkins'.[11] This was not the first time that Bron, as I shall call him, had attacked *Dance* (he admired Powell's pre-war novels). In his review of *Books do Furnish a Room* he urged him to give up the sequence while there was still time for him to attempt something else. It would not, he maliciously surmised, ruin his chances of a CH, since the 'philistine hacks' in Government who awarded such honours had already pencilled him in.[12]

Bron and Powell went back a long way. They first met in October 1952, during Bron's first half-term at Downside, just down the road from Chantry. Evelyn Waugh, who had not seen the Powells' new abode, asked if he could call in with his 'well-conducted son'. For the next fifteen years Bron was *persona grata* with the Powells. He and Tristram overlapped at Oxford and had many friends in common; Bron attended parties at The Chantry. Then Evelyn Waugh died and shortly afterwards Bron, in his own words, set about 'cultivating the vituperative arts'.[13] Powell thought it was a case of 'post hoc, propter hoc'. In a letter of commiseration to Christopher Sykes, who had been roughly handled by Bron over his biography of Evelyn, he said,

[Bron], I think, really loathed his father, but it does not suit him to say so for professional reasons, and I think any of Evelyn's friends are therefore Bron's most hated people, because, if of that generation, they are identified as father figures, particularly yourself as being a close friend, and I read the [*Books and Bookmen*] review with fascinated horror at how right my theory seemed to be, after you had gone out of your way to be agreeable about Bron yourself. Bron is also, in my view, very *stupid* – as may be seen when he wants to praise something – tho' I must admit that he has an extraordinary capacity for pouring out journalism, indifferent as it may be ... Incidentally, isn't it rather odd to describe yourself in books of reference (*Modern Novelists*, St James Press) as 'wounded' when I always understood he shook the gun, and it went off into himself. His feelings, perhaps.[14]

There, for the moment, matters rested. Bron continued to snipe away at Powell in publications like *Private Eye*. Powell, for his part, could console himself with the thought that, as Kingsley Amis later reminded him, 'You've gone on writing novels and he hasn't.'[15] It probably did not escape his notice that the year Bron launched his first salvo was also the year he gave up novel-writing.

*

Powell knew that the completion of *Dance* would create a vacuum. He proposed to fill it by writing his Memoirs, *To Keep the Ball Rolling*, four volumes of which were published between 1976 and 1982. An appetiser had already appeared in October 1974, when the *Times* published his contribution to Hugh Lloyd-Jones's *Maurice Bowra*. But included in this vivid eulogy was the following admission: 'One learns in due course ... that, more often than not, it is better to keep deeply felt views about oneself to oneself.' Those hoping that 'Mr Powell-Jenkins' would bare his soul were doomed to disappointment. 'It is not Jenkins's creator we meet,' said James Delany in the *London Review of Books*, 'but Jenkins's ghost.'[16]

A substantial ghost, nevertheless (to borrow a title of Violet's). You cannot write four volumes of memoirs without describing your life in some detail, and this Powell does. But just as Jenkins, in 'telling the story over the dinner table', is allowed the occasional lapse in memory, so Powell nods from time to time as well. For instance in *Messengers of Day* he mentions a boozy friend of his called Desmond Ryan, 'later to give a party greatly to influence my own life; but that was some years on, and subject for a subsequent volume of these Memoirs'. The reader will search in vain for any further reference to either the party or Desmond Ryan. Again, as noted earlier, he says that becoming a father 'had a profound effect upon the manner in which one looked at the world' – and leaves it at that. I suppose you could make an educated guess as to what he means (bearing in mind that this happened in April 1940), but a clue would have been helpful.

Luckily, Powell's reticence about himself was more than matched by his willingness to discuss his contemporaries, distinguished and otherwise, particularly those in thrall to a 'personal myth', like Connolly, Orwell and Waugh. It helped, of course, that so many of them were safely dead. 'I don't think I could have written about John [Heygate] like that if he was still alive,' he told a mutual friend. I am reminded of Ashenden's comment, in *Cakes and Ale*, that it is very hard to be a gentleman and a writer (Heygate would have agreed). For much of his life Powell, it seems to me, struggled to come to terms with this dichotomy. Writing of Conrad, whose idealistic parents died when he was a boy and who was brought up by a hard-headed uncle, he said he 'could be seen in the characteristic situation of the novelist, pulled in two contrary directions by temperament and upbringing'. Born an artist, Powell was brought up to be a gentleman. Hugh Massingberd has a revealing anecdote about his fear of stepping out of line. He and Powell were discussing Waugh's *Diaries*, extracts from which were being serialised in the *Observer*:

> 'I don't care in the slightest what Evelyn may or may not have jotted down in a drunken moment about me,' said Tony. 'I can take it. But what one really dreads is being quoted by him making some disobliging remark about a third party who might be very much still with us.'[17]

An 'infinitely remote' kinsman of Powell's on the Dymoke side and a keen genealogist himself, Hugh Massingberd was one of the select few who, as Powell himself put it, could 'stomach' the forty pages of raw genealogical material at the beginning of *Infants*. Addressing the Anthony Powell Society (whose first president he became), Massingberd insisted that genealogy was 'absolutely fundamental to understanding Powell's life and work'.[18] As may be apparent by now I do not go all the way with this. While accepting that his interest in genealogy accounts for the authenticity of his characters' names, I am sure that Powell's interest in other people and their funny ways was there from the beginning, though it may have been stimulated by some of the stuff he unearthed in his researches. Nor do I think that *Dance* demonstrates what Powell considered to be the chief lesson of genealogy: 'how extraordinarily close the classes are – and have always been – together.' True, Barbara Goring's granddaughter marries a pop-star. But what about the Cutts-Akworth wedding near the end of the book at which all the rather well-bred guests seem to be related to each other? Not much evidence of social mobility there. One can't help feeling that when the fruit of that particular union marry in their turn they will choose people of the same background.

Perhaps now is the time to consider whether, as many have alleged, Powell was a snob – and if so, what sort of snob? The case for the prosecution is strong. Not only did he write about the upper classes, he shared their preoccupation with kinship. It was because they were so 'interested in each other',[19] he said in his Notebook, that he identified with them. It is also the case that as a young man he belonged to a set for whom social climbing was virtually a condition of entry. '[W]e were greatly impressed, in a Ninetyish way, by money and titles and the necessity of coming into closer contact with them,'[20] recalled Cyril Connolly. Though not so determined as most of his fellows Powell rose nevertheless. And having risen, he was not slow to chastise other writers, e.g. Balzac, Dickens and Maugham, whose depiction of the upper classes he found wanting.

So Powell had a case to answer. But I think the plea he enters in *Messengers* on behalf of Rosa Lewis could also be used in his own defence:

> It has been asserted that Rosa Lewis was a great snob. The indictment is unde-niable if the word – one of many meanings – is used merely in the sense of being interested in the ramifications of aristocratic life: who engaged to whom; who running away with someone else; who blessed with grandchildren; who resigning from the Brigade of Guards after matrimonial disaster.
>
> On the other hand, Rosa Lewis could not have been less of a snob in the sense that she liked only the grand or successful; nor would she have hesitated for a moment to order from her hotel anyone of whatever rank or station, if bored or displeased by them. When she found people amusing, or they other-wise took her fancy, neither class, race, colour nor tongue, would create a barrier. She liked the feeling of belonging to a huge family, the sort of gossip too subtle to reach the ears of a professional gossip-writer.

Powell was undoubtedly an intellectual snob, which may be another reason why, as a young man, he did not climb so high as some of his contem-poraries. Though he did, by his own admission, try and 'ingratiate' himself with grandees, he preferred High Bohemia to High Society, his turf being the neutral territory where they met. There is a revealing entry right at the end of his Journals when he reports the death of his Somerset friend and neigh-bour, Lees Mayall, formerly Head of Protocol at the Foreign Office and Ambassador to Venezuela. 'Sympathetic as one found Lees, occasionally one came up against a difference from what, for want of a better term, I call "bohemian" friends, though some of these could not, in a way, be less "bohemian".'[21] I take this to mean that at bottom, Powell preferred the company of those who were somewhat raffish to those Lady Molly Jeavons would have called 'correct'.

When Powell died the issue of his snobbery was once again debated, prompting a robust defence of his uncle by Ferdinand Mount, who pointed out that much of *Dance* is concerned with 'people and places' that are 'shabby or past their best (if they had one)'.[22] This in turn was answered by Paul Johnson, who commended Mount's loyalty, but thought it unnecessary. A degree of snobbery, he argued, 'in one or other of its many manifestations, is essential to novel-writing. All great novelists are, and must be, snobs.'[23] A few years earlier the novelist John Lanchester anticipated both Mount and Johnson when reviewing the final volume of Powell's Journals. Having quoted the entry for Albert, the Stonehurst cook, in Hilary Spurling's *Handbook*, he declared that 'no snob, in the conventional sense of the word, could have written that character'. But, Lanchester went on,

> Perhaps there is a kind of snobbery in Powell's work, but it is a kind shared by many writers (and perhaps by all good ones). This is the snobbery of finding some things more worthy of attention than other things, and of choosing to find a character's quirks interesting in and for themselves. Snobs are like novelists, and vice versa, in the way they choose to invest certain people, and certain worlds, with interest. In other words, all exclusive attention (and all attention in fiction is necessarily exclusive) is structurally similar to snobbery, whether being lavished on a whisky priest, Mrs Dalloway or the Duke of Buccleuch. To put it another way, for a novelist, qua novelist, snobbery is not necessarily the sin of sins.[24]

I am sure Powell would have agreed with Lanchester. Commenting on a collective memoir called *Evelyn Waugh and His World*, he wrote: 'I suppose it is hopeless to expect people to be interested in how good a writer he was, rather than whether or not he was a snob.'[25]

*

In his Diaries Malcolm Muggeridge describes how he once made the mistake of allowing over the threshold a complete stranger who had written a letter to him and who took ages to dislodge. When he told Powell about this, 'Tony said it all went to show the importance of maintaining the sanctity of the home.'[26] Powell applies this principle to his Memoirs, which are as devoid of domestic detail as *Dance*. All we learn of his two sons is that Tristram, the elder, produces arts programmes for the BBC and is married to the granddaughter of 'the last officer in the British army to obtain a captaincy "by purchase"', while John, six years younger, is destined for Cornell University in America. (Why Cornell? Powell, whose idea this apparently was, doesn't say.) Scattered throughout the text are occasional references to books by Violet, but no indication as to when she began to write or what difference, if any, this made to Powell.

Ink ran in Violet's veins. Through her mother she was not only related to Jane Austen, but also, much further back, to Dryden's 'Zimri', George Villiers, the Second Duke of Buckingham, a dissolute cavalier and author of at least one successful play, whose *Commonplace Book* is full of worldly jottings like this: 'Wenches are like fruit, only dear at their first coming in. Their price falls apace afterwards.' Her father, she used to say, 'shared blood' with the novelist Maria Edgeworth and her nephew, Thomas Lovell Beddoes, who wrote the poem that begins, 'If there were dreams to sell/What would you buy?' In her twenties Violet progressed from writing occasional pieces about riding to doing the 'Mary Grant' shopping column in the *Evening Standard*, a by-line inherited from her elder sister Mary, who wrote novels under the pseudonym of Hans Duffy. After the war she reviewed and sometimes wrote articles for *Punch*. Then, in about 1958, she began to write her first volume of autobiography, *Five Out of Six*, a light-hearted account of her privileged but dysfunctional childhood. Although he said it was 'lamentably lacking in sex, scandal or bad taste', Frere, Heinemann's chairman, accepted *Five Out of Six*, which was published in 1960. Violet's new career, intimated some years before by a palmist, was launched.

Over the next twenty-five years she wrote two further volumes of autobiography; a life of her grandmother, Lady Jersey, the only grown-up she was close to as a child; and studies of among others Jane Austen, Somerville and Ross, E.M. Delafield and Ivy Compton-Burnett. Nobody undertakes such work for fun, yet it would appear that professionally, she was content to remain in her husband's shadow: 'I have never felt the need to be someone in my own right,'[27] she told a journalist in 1998. It also emerged from this interview that although, like Powell, she preferred to use a typewriter, she wrote her books in longhand because the noise of her typing irritated him.

Violet emerges from the shadows in Powell's Journals, begun when he was seventy-six. So do other members of his family, notably John, his unmarried younger son, who is often to be found at The Stables, The Chantry's converted stable block which he and Tristram owned jointly. Tristram's teenage children, Georgia and Archie – 'great charm, nice manners, general air of being bright' – also make increasingly frequent appearances as the years unfold. They have their lives before them, unlike the steady stream of those characterised by the suffix 'obit'. Long before his own death Powell would write in despair to John Monagan that 'the trouble is almost everyone I know is *dead*'.[28]

*

Astonishing as it must seem to devotees of *Dance* the sequence has never had a big following, even among supposedly literate people. For example when, in 1975, Frederick Bradnum put forward the idea of adapting the sequence for radio, he discovered that with one exception, none of the management of BBC Radio Drama had read a word of it. The exception said he had read all the books but the last, and thoroughly disliked them, 'a feat of reader's masochism', said Bradnum, 'that would take some beating (no pun intended)'.[29] Nor did Bradnum fare any better with the producers he canvassed; only one, Graham Gauld, expressed any interest. Bradnum, a busy man, dropped the idea and got on with other things. About eighteen months later he received a call from the editor of BBC Radio 4's Classic Serial, 'a communist with Albanian connections'. This character said there was now some interest in serialising *Dance*, so would Bradnum take it on? He added that 'they' wanted volume two done first, 'and if it worked, return to volume one'. Bradnum failed to discover the reasoning behind this 'bizarre decision', putting it down to 'editorial imperiousness or the like'.

A few months later Bradnum bumped into the then boss of BBC Radio, Aubrey Singer, who asked how he was getting on. When he learnt that Bradnum had been told to start with volume two, Singer, who had been responsible for the renewal of interest in *Dance*, smelt a rat. He thought it was an attempt to stall the whole process and said he would take appropriate action. Bradnum was commissioned to dramatise the whole sequence, but not at one fell swoop. The idea was to break it up into four trilogies, going out at yearly intervals, with two one-hour episodes to each volume. Bradnum did however manage to obtain an extra episode each for *Temporary Kings* and *Hearing Secret Harmonies*, making twenty-six hours of broadcasting in all.

Powell had naturally consented to the project but was not involved with either the production or the script. However in June 1981, half-way through the production, he and Bradnum began to correspond. Powell was delighted with Bradnum's adaptation but less happy about some of the cast. For instance he thought it a pity that Gareth Johnson, who played Jenkins as a young man, hadn't 'a glimmering of the throwaway line' and sounded 'resentful in exactly the way Jenkins ought *not* to sound'.[30] Even worse was the actress who played Pamela – 'she merely sounded like a bad-tempered chorus girl, not a cold and cosmically fed-up enchantress.'[31] Gwinnett was 'not sinister enough (tho' otherwise good)'[32] and Mrs Erdleigh too 'matter of fact': she ought to sound 'dreamy',[33] like all fortune-tellers. He thought the actor who played Colonel Flores 'didn't manage to make him sound attractive enough, or anyway dominating enough', adding that he didn't think 'Flores gave a damn about Jean's past'.[34] Bradnum subsequently set the TV quiz show 'Mastermind' questions on *Dance* – rightly so, according to Powell, who admitted that he could remember 'little or nothing about the detail, which adds to the enjoyment of the radio version'.[35]

Powell reported to Bradnum that he had heard, via a friend, that a bookseller had mentioned a distinct movement in sales resulting from the broadcasts. But he knew that if *Dance* were ever to become a bestseller, it would need to be seen on television. 'It does make this *colossal* difference in sales,' he told an interviewer. 'Really absolutely colossal. For a respectable writer to sell well you've almost got to be on television.'[36] Aware that an adaptor would face special problems with *Dance*, not least in respect of the 'invisible' Nick Jenkins, he was prepared, in principle, to give them a free hand. 'I don't much care what approach the adaptor takes to the book,' he told me in 1983. 'In fact I think the more independent a line the better. But what I am clear about is that there's enough *stuff* there to require more than eight ninety-minute episodes, which is all the BBC say they can afford at the present time. I think it might be presented in a hundred different ways, but what I don't think is that you can boil the thing down. Freddy Bradnum absolutely went down on his knees to get a bit more time for the radio version. And all the additional stuff he did – naturally one's prejudiced – did seem to improve the thing.'

One of the first to show an interest in adapting *Dance* for television was Dennis Potter, then on a roll following the success of *Pennies from Heaven*. Potter, who as a young man hoped to lead the Labour Party, might seem an odd enthusiast of *Dance*; but according to his friend and collaborator, the producer Ken Trodd, he saw it as 'a window on a class that ought to be flung open for all to see. It was a challenge, like going to Oxford as a working-class student and making people take notice of you. I remember he said to me once that of course Oxford was really just a façade – anybody who'd been there knew that – but it was worth conquering all the same. So you spoke at the Union and wrote for *Isis* and so on. And I think he saw the *Music of Time* in those terms too. He wanted to prove that someone like him could make it intelligible to people who wouldn't dream of reading it.'[37]

Potter, said Trodd, was 'all attitude', and it may be that this was a little too apparent when they went to lunch at The Chantry. Hard though Violet tried to put them at their ease it was 'all a bit of a strain – like evacuees having tea at the manor instead of the gardener's cottage'. At one point Powell said he would expect to be consulted. 'About what in particular?'

asked Trodd. 'Unfamiliar things', said Powell, meaning the upper classes. 'He obviously thought,' said Trodd, 'that we couldn't be trusted to get them right.'

Years later Powell described Potter as 'a very tricky customer', who made him feel that novelists as a class were not up to much.[38] But at the time, 1978, he was prepared to give Potter and Trodd the benefit of the doubt, not least because they said they intended to devote two hours to each volume, enough to satisfy his requirements with regard to length. Then the BBC tried to make Potter and Trodd sign exclusive contracts, which they were not prepared to do, whereupon plans to televise *Dance* were put on indefinite hold. But according to Trodd, he and Potter had already had second thoughts. 'The BBC was serialising something by Arnold Bennett – *Clayhanger*, possibly – anyway it was clear after only a few episodes that nobody was watching. And we both felt that might happen with the *Music of Time*. It didn't have the sort of universal appeal that would guarantee a decent audience.'

Sadly for Powell, who hoped that the televising of *Dance* would provide an ongoing interest for his declining years, such disappointments became the order of the day. Over the next decade a succession of producers and directors made their way to The Chantry, options were taken up, treatments approved, contracts signed, scripts written – all to no avail. It was not until 1996 that Channel 4 began to shoot Hugh Whitemore's script, by which time Powell, confined to a wheelchair, was in no position to 'keep an eye' on it, as he had once hoped to do.

*

Powell used to say that while writing was never easy, the alternative, not writing, was far, far worse. So having finished his Memoirs, he took serious thought as to what he might attempt next. His preference was for fiction. But the story would need to be written from the point of view of someone his age – 'otherwise you sound absurd' – and this did not allow much room for manoeuvre, since at seventy-six you were no longer cut out for action of the sort that gave point to novels. His solution was to offer a different perspective on the world he depicted in *Afternoon Men*, taking as his theme an (unattributed) maxim of La Rochefoucauld's invoked by Jenkins in *Dance*: 'Though love may die, vanity lives on timelessly.' This is certainly true of Shadbold, the ageing protagonist of *O, How The Wheel Becomes It*, at 143 pages comfortably Powell's shortest work of fiction.

A sort of all-purpose bookman, Shad (as he's universally known) had knocked about in his hot youth with Winterwade, a reluctant stockbroker with Bohemian connections and the author of an obscure social-realist novel, *The Welsons of Omdurman Terrace*. So dated in approach was Winterwade's novel that Shad, an ardent Modernist, decided he would have to drop his old friend or risk the derision of his professional associates. The war separated them for good: Shad dodged the column, while Winterwade died on active service. Decades later Shad is commissioned to read and report on the coded diary which, unknown to him, Winterwade had kept until his death. Once he has broken the code Shad has to concede that whatever his shortcomings as a novelist, Winterwade had real talent as a diarist. This is bad news for someone as envious as he, but much worse is to come. Winterwade reveals that he spent a dirty weekend in Paris with Isolde Upjohn, the ravishing model-cum-illustrator whom Shad himself had long lusted after in vain. No matter that she was 'contumaciously frigid and uncooperative'; Winterwade still had her 'three or four times'. This knowledge so unhinges Shad that notwithstanding the carrot dangled before him of editing what could become a minor classic, he rubbishes the manuscript in his reader's report, thereby ensuring that it will be returned to sender, unpublished.

Shad is well paid out for his spite. First, an old enemy of his, an academic with Structuralist leanings, says he's so impressed by the 'unexpected culture-codes and utterance types' to be found in Winterwade's novel that he intends to use it as a set book. Then Isolde Upjohn herself, whom Shad imagined long dead, barges in on him shortly before the arrival of a television crew to record what he hopes will be a flattering interview. She wants Shad to write an introduction to her memoirs, in which Winterwade has a place of honour. Sensing Shad's discomfiture, the interviewer eggs her on. Shad is well and truly stitched up, goes into a decline and dies not long afterwards.

Although a bagatelle, *Wheel* is sly, witty and comic. Shad may be a toad, but like Quiggin, whom he somewhat resembles, he is very entertaining in a ghastly sort of way:

> By now, broadly speaking, Shadbold's attitude to the war was that even if it had unquestionably taken place (which he never went so far as to deny) the whole episode had been grossly exaggerated by those with a vested interest in making capital out of wartime experiences.

As for Isolde Upjohn – 'some people thought I was a beauty a thousand years ago' – she is in a line that stretches back to Susan Nunnery, taking in Mona Templer and Roberta Payne on the way. Whatever torments Powell suffered at the hands of their prototypes, he evened the score in his novels, recording for posterity their empty narcissistic chatter. Unfortunately, as more than one reviewer complained, he seemed suddenly to lose interest in Shad and his problems, 'remaindering' him in a couple of pages. I for one would have liked more of Rod Cubbage, the ghastly interviewer, and 'Major' Jock Crowter, the bogus landlord of Shad's local, both of whom had obviously escaped from a Kingsley Amis novel and were none the worse for that.

In a letter to his agent Powell said he was 'amused' by the 'extraordinary pile of sour reviews' of *Wheel* that he had received. He thought 'an awful lot of critics must regard themselves as present or future Shadbolds'.[39] My impression is that considering its length *Wheel* did remarkably well in terms of coverage, even if the notices themselves were not all he could have wished for. One of the most judicious was by J.K.L. Walker in the *TLS*, who wrote: 'It may be as readers we should cease secretly to sigh for the great harmonies and praise Mr Powell in his seventy-eighth year for attempting a new genre: his Late Quartets, perhaps?'[40] What no one could have foreseen was that Powell still had plenty of shots in his locker. His eighth decade would prove to be one of the most productive – and provocative – of his career.

Last Words

'The thing that counts in writing is staying power. It's that, more than anything, that gives you a reputation.'

Anthony Powell

Cyril Connolly thought that provided a promising young writer did not burn himself out before he was forty, then given a tolerably fair wind he 'becomes a master in his prime, one who can pass into old age as a sage, a prophet or a venerated, carefree and disreputable figure'. Powell was not carefree or disreputable, nor did he see himself as a prophet. But *Dance* was recognised as the work of a master, who in old age received many tangible reminders of the esteem in which he was held, both at home and abroad. For instance in 1984, at the age of seventy-eight, he brought off a remarkable left and right, potting two prestigious American literary awards, the *Hudson Review* Bennett Award and the Ingersoll Foundation T.S. Eliot Award for Creative Writing, each worth $15,000. Here was acknowledgement of the fact that his profile in the States deserved to be higher, since both prizes were in the gift of panels whose remit was to reward writers who had not received the recognition there that they merited.

Unable to face the journey to Chicago, where the Ingersoll Foundation conferred their award, Powell arranged for Robert Conquest, who lived in America, to accept on his behalf. This passed off without incident, unlike the Bennett Award lunch, which was held at the American Embassy in Grosvenor Square. This was hosted by Raymond Seitz, the newly-arrived Deputy Chief of Mission, who opened the proceedings with 'a lighthearted remark that turned out to be made of lead'. Mr Powell, he said, might be better known in America if he didn't insist on people calling him 'Pole'. He then went on to praise *Dance*, which he had recently read, but the damage had been done. Luckily Powell had a standard retort to Seitz's quip, with which he prefaced his acceptance speech. He would, he said, cease to insist on people rhyming Powell with 'Pole' when the 'Lowells of Massachusetts' – which he pronounced to rhyme with 'bowels' – 'did the same'. Seitz, who was US Ambassador here from 1991 to 1994, later described this as 'perhaps the greatest *faux pas*' he committed in Britain, 'which given my many other *faux pas*, is a considerable distinction'.[1]

Powell did not lack for honours at home. Several universities, including Oxford, awarded him an Honorary D.Litt., and in 1974 he became an Honorary Fellow of Balliol. He was also offered a knighthood, which he turned down. At first sight Powell's decision seems strange, since not long after receiving the CBE he quoted with approval Stendhal's belief that the more a man has the gifts of a great artist, the more he should aspire to titles and decorations as a protective rampart against the world.[2] But he was by no means the first author to decline a knighthood. Kipling refused one, as did Galsworthy; Maugham may also have done so, though this is disputed. There was a feeling, which Powell shared, that it was inappropriate for a writer to be knighted for services to literature alone. And in any case, he had been brought up, he said, to regard knights (even more so their ladies) as really rather 'awful'. A knighthood would also make it doubly difficult to explain to 'unsophisticated people' why Violet was 'Lady Violet Powell', not Lady Powell. The latter was the correct form of address for the wife of a knight or baronet, but Violet, as the daughter of an Earl, would always be 'Lady Violet'.[3]

Having rejected a knighthood Powell assumed that he was out of the running for anything else of that sort. But in November 1987 he received a letter from the Prime Minister, Margaret Thatcher, asking if he would consent to being made a Companion of Honour. Willingly, replied Powell. He knew that this 'quiet medal', though unrecognised by the man in the street, ranked well above a knighthood. He would be one of only sixty-five recipients, all of whom enjoyed national renown in their chosen fields. (In 2002 Powell's nephew by marriage, Harold Pinter, was also made a CH after turning down a 'squalid'[4] knighthood. The mischievous thought occurs that being married, like Powell, to the daughter of an Earl, he too had envisaged problems with 'unsophisticated people'.)

Powell had met Mrs Thatcher on several occasions, once sitting at her right hand when dining at 10 Downing Street. As a High (and Dry) Tory he approved of her policies. As a connoisseur of style he admired her attack. And as a heterosexual male he found her 'very attractive', though without saying exactly what it was about her that caught his fancy. He admitted, however, that she was 'not at all easy', reminding him of occasions when, as a youth, he had sat next to a beautiful girl and could think of nothing to say.[5] One feels that in Cabinet she must have been a little like Dame Emily Brightman presiding over the Donners Prize committee, though as a physical presence probably owing more to Mrs Widmerpool.

*

In July 1985, a few months before his eightieth birthday, Powell finished *The Fisher King*, his final novel. The title refers to a dim Arthurian legend of great interest to Powell but not, I suspect, to most of his readers. Fortunately it is possible to enjoy the novel without paying much attention to the symbolism which is, in any case, often rather far-fetched. The setting is the good ship *Alecto*, bound for Orkney on a Swan-Hellenic-type cruise that takes in sites like Hadrian's Wall. Among the passengers are Saul Henchman, the notoriously rebarbitive crippled photographer, and his beautiful companion, Barberina Rookwood, who some years before gave up the chance of a dazzling career in ballet to become Henchman's handmaiden – literally so: the German shell that crippled Henchman also unmanned him, so Barberina, seventeen when she quit dancing, remains *intacta*. But for how much longer? For the spell that Henchman cast over Barberina has begun to wane, and it looks as if someone aboard the *Alecto* will break it. The question is, who? Most would bet on her old admirer Gary Lamont, the dynamic Fleet Street editor. But as Henchman himself observes – and he should know – 'in love, nothing is impossible'.

True to his belief that a story is better told at one remove, Powell uses Valentine Beals, bestselling author of bodice-rippers like *Mistress to Maximus* and *Lancelot's Love Feast*, in the role of raisonneur. Beals, though shrewd and intelligent, is inclined to let his taste for 'pin-pointing archetypes' run away with him. When this happens he is reined in by his old chum Piers Middlecote, an amazingly erudite adman whose ability to quote ex tempore even Moreland might envy. Both men have excellent foils in their wives, sympathetic women who ensure that this never becomes a smoking-room yarn.

Fittingly, it is Henchman who dominates the proceedings. 'Is he perhaps not a photographer at all, but a magician?' wrote Powell of Cecil Beaton.[6] You could say the same of Henchman, though there is more of Dr Trelawney in him than Beaton. 'We all have our crutches in one form or another,' he says at one point, 'although not everyone needs the kind I use. That sounds rather like the beginning of one of those long sermons I found so wearisome as a boy.' Trelawney says something similar when rescued from the bathroom by Jenkins and Duport: 'I am too weak to walk unaided. That sounds like the beginning of an evangelical hymn.' Another source for Henchman is John Hayward, T.S. Eliot's crippled flatmate, who was of interest to Powell because at parties he was always surrounded by pretty women, his 'somewhat terrifying manner and appearance' notwithstanding.[7]

Surprisingly, given his contempt for most of humanity, Henchman befriends Mr Jack, a seedy old soak whose life has been one long dirty story which he delights in retelling. 'You must never leave me,' says Henchman to Mr Jack.

> Become my male Scheherazade, eternally relating a chronicle of aimless amatory encounters, unspeakably wearisome to everyone but yourself, while I photograph, stage by stage, your rapid descent on the escalator of senile degradation. You shall be Falstaff to my Prince Hal.

Mr Jack is one of Powell's best comic turns, though his fellow passengers might not agree. One of the funniest scenes in the book occurs at dinner, when a learned American professor tries to shake off Mr Jack and take part in a more rewarding conversation just along the table. All of us must have endured such moments, when good manners are tested to the limit, but it takes an artist like Powell to make you laugh out loud at the victim's increasingly desperate attempts to grab a lifeline, however precarious.

If Powell had been disappointed by *Wheel*'s reception, he must have been cheered by what reviewers said about *The Fisher King*. John Bayley, Malcolm Bradbury and A.S. Byatt all gave it the thumbs-up, Bayley confessing that he 'could read whatever Powell writes from here to eternity'. One of the most measured responses came from Peter Levi in the *Literary Review*, who admitted that he was 'still unable to make up his mind about [Powell]', having stayed up all night arguing about him with a friend, only to find that next morning they had changed sides: 'There are few novelists who are that interesting and puzzling.' One thing was for sure: 'he is certainly the greatest portraitist of bores ... Their personal prose style is like bad breath, lightly differentiated.' Levi thought *The Fisher King* would make a good film, but said he would 'regret the loss of the only purple patch, which is the last sentence'. Since this rings down the curtain on Powell's fiction I shall do as Levi does and quote it:

> On the other side of the waters, low rounded hills, soft and mysterious, concealed in luminous haze the frontier of Thule: the edge of the known world, man's permitted limits; a green-barriered checkpoint, beyond which the fearful cataract of torrential seas cascaded down into Chaos.

Possibly Powell thought the world was like that, suggested Levi, and 'only the novelist imposes some temporary order'.[8]

*

Powell's Memoirs are notable for their absence of spleen. Reading them, you never feel that the port went round once too often the night before. But near the end of the final volume there is a hint that his serenity cannot be taken for granted. Visiting India, he and Violet pay a call on the Monkey Temple at Benares, so-called because it is overrun with monkeys who mingle with the worshippers and priests. From a vantage point overlooking the interior, Powell spies a monkey apparently reading a tattered sheet of newspaper. Suddenly – 'as if all at once uncontrollably exasperated with the world as it is today' – the monkey casts aside the paper and makes a rapid ascent to a secluded niche on the roof where he can chill out.

> In that parade of utter dissatisfaction with things I became aware of a strong fellow feeling. How often do the papers report some item that seems to demand just such energetic and immediate form of self-release – had one the monkey's agility – as the only practical means of discharging inward discontents, rage, contempt, despair at what one reads in the papers.

I take that to have been written in about 1980, when even many to the left of Powell thought the country had become ungovernable. Though the news, from Powell's point of view, would get better under Mrs Thatcher, he seems to have decided that after seventy years of gentlemanly reticence he had earned the right to let off steam. In future, if someone says something he disagrees with, then regardless of who they are, he will tell them where to get off. So it is that when the Chancellor of Bristol University, Dorothy Hodgkin, the Nobel prize-winning biologist, says she hopes a time will come when the Government spends more on education than armaments, Powell, who has just received an honorary degree from her, tells her she is talking balls. 'I have rarely seen anyone look so surprised.'[9]

We learn this from his Journals, which he began writing in 1982 and which were published in three volumes between 1995 and 1997. To say that they are a caution is to put it mildly. One reviewer, the *Sunday Times*'s John Carey, even suggested that they were an elaborate joke played on the reader: 'If you did not know that they were the work of one of our most respected senior novelists, you might take them for the private cogitations of a blimpish old party with a rather restricted allowance of grey matter.' Powell, he said, had mischievously converted himself into 'a "character", whose opinions and adventures, though passed off as his own, are as funny as anything encountered in his fiction'.[10]

Professor Carey gave some examples of Powell's comic persona in action. His irritation with journalists and the photographers who trailed in their wake. His low opinion of other writers (always excepting Shakespeare). His exhaustive excursions into genealogy and his determination to record every bottle of wine that comes his way. His brusque classifications – 'more or less the usual army wife of the better kind' – and his 'cantankerous insistence' on the difference between, e.g., Lord Snooks and Lord John Snooks. Fortunately, added Carey, Powell's 'uncanny ear for dialogue' was still in evidence: V.S. Naipaul is reported as saying that he is off to Brazil 'to interview a couple of dagos', while Harold Macmillan insists that one would have no difficulty talking to Cicero 'if he came into Pratt's'.

Professor Carey's review is what Powell would have called 'knockabout'. He was, after all, writing for readers many of whom, I imagine, had only the dimmest idea of who Powell was or what he was like. To be told that this was the first time he had been so free with his opinions would probably not have excited their interest. But for someone like James Lees-Milne, who liked Powell but found him 'inscrutable', the Journals were 'out of the ordinary ... very sharp and painful'.

> He does not emerge as sympathetic. There is a hard wooden superiority about him, a censoriousness, and immense snobbishness. Very self-centred, like most literary stars; most of the engagements are for newspapers and television interviews. Curious that he should accuse Diana Mosley of encouraging the press to refer to her as Lady Diana Mosley, when only at Xmas she was complaining to me about this ignorant and prevalent habit. For someone not nobly born, and hailing from a frightfully unimportant family, he is remarkably obsessed with genealogy. Really very boring, and much less funny than Harold Nicolson on the McCrackells of Scottish antiquity. I would never mention my own forbears in such a way.[11]

Reading this one can understand why Powell's nephew, Ferdinand Mount, later admitted that some at least of Powell's family regarded the publication of his Journals with 'consternation'.[12] But first it must be stressed that the snobbish material, if snobbish it is, amounts to only a small proportion of the Journals. Over 700 pages in length, they comprehend gossip, commentary, speculation, reminiscence, meditation, anecdote and autobiography. As must already be apparent, my own debt to them is considerable. They provide either a solution, or a substantial clue, to many of the mysteries of Powell's life, e.g. the girl who inspired *Afternoon Men*. They also show what might be called his human face, as in this entry about the death of his beloved Cornish Rex, Trelawney:

> V[iolet] and John [Powell] took him in today to the vet to make an end of things. I felt ashamed that this unpleasant job fell on them. Dreadfully distressing. The

most intelligent cat I have ever known, in some ways the most affectionate, jumping on one's back, nuzzling under one's chin in the evening after his supper. He hated the smallest alteration to his routine, such as not being picked up in the morning, said 'Good Morning' to. A very, very sad day.[13]

Written in an increasingly staccato style that recalls Uncle Giles and Dan Tokenhouse at their most laconic, Powell's Journals are as addictive in their way as *Dance*; so it is interesting to note that he did not regard himself as a natural journal-keeper. In an interview he gave in 1970 he described it as a gift that he was 'entirely without'.[14] Clearly he was mistaken. You would never say of him, as he said of Siegfried Sassoon, that his weakness as a diarist lay in 'not being able to convey in a couple of words individual character'.[15] But I am not convinced by Violet's explanation, in her introduction to volume one, that the Journals were a temporary expedient that became a habit. I think that once he had convinced himself that he did have the knack Powell set out to emulate the success of Evelyn Waugh's *Diaries*, which triggered the Great Waugh Boom that continues to this day. Despite protestations to the contrary he was, where writing was concerned, very competitive. He may also have relished the prospect of rubbing people up the wrong way. Near the end of volume three he quotes approvingly a remark made to him by Edith Sitwell: 'It's wonderful being able to make people so angry when one is so old.'[16]

Unblinkingly judgmental about the living, Powell was also quite prepared to speak ill of the dead. In a canting age this is refreshing, but it does leave you with the initial impression that he knew more than his fair share of shits. It even occurred to me that a slight adjustment to the title of volume three of his Memoirs could provide a collective title for the Journals: *Faeces in My Time*. Rereading them I realised that this was unfair. But first impressions, as Powell admitted, are important. For years he had either pulled his punches or delivered them so unobtrusively that his opponent was on the canvas before you were aware that he'd been hit. Now he was in there slugging like a streetfighter – which will serve to introduce what might be termed his final round with Bron Waugh.

It is a mistake to suppose that writers crave only good notices from reviewers. A certain amount of abuse, even the occasional ripe tomato, can be equally good for business because of the interest it arouses. But when in 1990 Bron reviewed *Miscellaneous Verdicts*, Powell's first volume of collected journalism, he attacked not only the book but the author, denigrating his achievements and mocking his 'socially and intellectually insecure' fans.[17] Although uncalled-for, this was predictable. What came as a horrible surprise was that Bron's piece should appear in the *Sunday Telegraph*, which had just run a laudatory interview with Powell by Hugh Massingberd. As Bron's review had been commissioned by Nicholas Shakespeare, who was also the literary editor of the *Daily Telegraph*, Powell, for thirty years the *Telegraph*'s chief reviewer, resigned on the spot. He could not, he told the *Telegraph*'s editor, Max Hastings, deal in future with a literary editor who did this kind of thing.

In his memoir, *Editor*, Hastings describes what Shakespeare did as 'a moment of madness'.[18] But he didn't sack him, which suggests that he thought there was method in his madness. Since becoming editor he had been trying to attract younger readers; the loss of Powell, now in his eighty-fifth year, was unlikely to impede this process. Amends were made a year or so later when, at Hastings's urging, the *Telegraph* forked out £5000 for a large bust of Powell by the sculptor, Bill Pye. Powell thanked Hastings for this, but soon afterwards was quoted as saying that he thought the paper had 'gorn a bit downmarket lately'.[19] He repeated this in his Journals, to the annoyance of Hastings who refers to it acidly in *Editor*.

Powell's opinion of Bron was literally unprintable: Bron is in the index of *Journals 1990-1992*, but absent from the text. Not much imagination is required to remedy this deficiency. The question is, why did Bron have it in for Powell? As well ask what song the sirens sang. Nobody who knew him that I have talked to can convincingly account for his animus, though Bron's friend Susan Crosland thought he dropped a hint in his autobiography, *Will This Do?* Writing about his father's old friends he divides them into those, like Graham Greene, John Betjeman and Harold Acton, who were prepared 'to take a friendly interest in him', and those, including Powell and Cyril Connolly (another victim) who 'conspicuously weren't'.[20] Another friend of Bron's, Alan Watkins, writes that Bron thought Powell grossly overrated as a novelist and snobbish to boot[21] (which coming from Bron was a bit rich). Possibly the fact that Powell's fans included Clive James, also on Bron's blacklist, should be taken into account.

Powell later claimed that it came as a relief 'not to have to read some frightfully boring book every fortnight'.[22] Yet only a few years before he had admitted that although poorly paid, it was agreeable work, 'without which I should go bankrupt buying books, or mad from having nothing to read'.[23] No doubt he had begun to flag by the time Bron shafted him; but I think that at the very least you could say of him, as he said of Cyril Connolly, that it is rare to read a review of his and find nothing of interest. He also, like Connolly, put a lot of himself into his reviews: you recognise his voice immediately. But he never hectors, being more interested in conveying what other people say and think than shouting them down. The result, as John Bayley said, 'is that his extraordinary richness of fact and detail' is far more rewarding to read than 'the theoretical pronouncements of modern academic criticism'.[24]

Bayley also pointed out that Powell was at his most fascinating when discussing authors and their personal 'myths'. But what, one wonders, was his? How about 'The Man Without Characteristics' or even 'The Invisible Man' (as Nick Jenkins has been called), both of which would accord with his assertion that he had no picture of himself at all? His Journals suggest an alternative: 'The Poor Boy Made Good'. Powell says he was 'pleased' by this estimation, which occurs in the introduction to Professor Robert L. Selig's study, *Time and Anthony Powell*.[25] Some may wonder if this is not another of those jokes referred to by John Carey, but Powell did think of himself as poor by comparison with most of the people he knew at Eton and Oxford. In one of the last interviews he gave he explained to Lynn Barber that the reason why he, alone of his peers, had not lost his virginity at Chabanais, the famous Parisian brothel, was because he felt he 'wasn't rich enough, really'.[26]

*

'Growing old,' says Dicky Umfraville, 'feels like being increasingly penalised for a crime you haven't committed.' These words, written when he was still spry enough to contemplate old age with equanimity, must have haunted Powell as his clock, like the century's, ran down. His Journals end with this sombre acknowledgement: 'I realise more than ever how much I depend on V, and on the rest of my immediate family.' In particular, it should be emphasised, his younger son John, who had long since given up his job as a financial journalist in order to help manage the house and its ninety acres of grounds. Quiet and unobtrusive, but extremely capable, he selflessly shared, with Violet, the role of carer during his father's declining years. These dated from a fall in early 1993, following which he wrote to John Monagan, 'Do persuade anyone you can *not* to come and see me.'[27]

The news was not all bad. Between 1990, when *Miscellaneous Verdicts* was published, and 1997, when the final volume of the Journals appeared, Powell had five books out, which must be a record for someone of his age. Also in 1997, after twenty years of disappointments, *Dance* finally reached the screen, fulfilling Powell's prophecy to Frederick Bradnum that it would be 'just in time for our great-grandchildren'. Unfortunately production costs had risen at the rate of house prices; so instead of twelve two-hour episodes, as Powell had originally hoped, Channel Four could only afford four, which left the adaptor, Hugh Whitemore, no room for manoeuvre. Despite the best efforts of a distinguished cast, which included John Gielgud (St John Clarke), Alan Bennett (Sillery), Miranda Richardson (Pamela) and Simon Russell Beale (Widmerpool), it failed to hold its audience and was not even repeated. Powell, however, declared himself satisfied. 'It's really not too bad, is it?' he said to Hugh Massingberd. And he delighted Hugh Whitemore by asking, 'Did you write that joke, or was it one of mine?'[28]

Powell outlasted the century, dying in the early hours of 28 March 2000, aged ninety-four. His friend, the bibliophile Anthony Hobson, described his funeral in a note to Stuart Preston.

5.4.2000

I went yesterday to Tony's funeral service at Holy Trinity, Chantry. There were sprinklings of snow on the hills outside Warminster and by the time I reached The Chantry the earth was covered with a thick white cloak of mourning. It has all gone today. *Julius Caesar* came to mind: 'When beggars die there are no comets seen/The heavens themselves blaze forth the death of princes.' Or signal in other ways the death of writers.

The church was full, but not packed. No address. A short reading from the *Dance* by Tony's granddaughter. Otherwise a traditional, understated, service, very much in his style. Baked meats in the house afterwards.

According to his wishes Powell's ashes were scattered on The Chantry's lake, where they were joined in January 2002 by those of Violet. His estate was valued at £1,603,403 net. The 'poor boy' had indeed made good.

Endnotes

Author's note: Endnotes are a necessary evil in a book like this. To prevent them from getting out of hand I have not identified the many quotations from Powell's novels and memoirs, most of which are already flagged in the text.

1. In the Beginning

The primary source for Chapters 1-3 is *Infants of the Spring* (*Infants*).

1. Anthony Powell (A.P.) to Waugh 6 September 1964, British Library (BL). Copyright 2004, Estate of Violet Powell.
2. *Melton Mowbray Mercury* (4 July 1912).
3. John Baynes, *Morale* (Cassell, 1967), pp. 210-11. This book provides an invaluable guide to the code of an Edwardian subaltern.
4. *New Yorker* (3 July 1965), p. 18.
5. A.P., *Under Review: Further Writings on Writers* (Heinemann, 1990), p. 304.
6. *New Yorker* (3 July 1965), p. 18.
7. A.P., *Under Review*, p. 52.
8. A.P., *Journals 1987-89* (Heinemann, 1996), p. 207.
9. Jocelyn Brooke, 'From Wauchop to Widmerpool', *London Magazine* (September 1960).
10. Christopher Isherwood, *Kathleen and Frank* (Methuen, 1971), p. 241.
11. Tony Gould, 'Master of the Dance', *New Society* (13 December 1985), p. 468.
12. Interview with Paul Fussell for 'A Question of Class', August 1986.
13. Major-General Sir Thomas Marden, *The Welch Regiment 1914-1918* (Western Mail, 1932), pp. 312-27.
14. Henry Green's account of Mr Norman and his school are in his *Pack My Bag* (Oxford Paperbacks, 1984), pp. 16-48.

2. The Best of Schools

1. Richard Ollard, *An English Education* (Collins, 1982), p. 103. Ollard's book was of great help in writing this chapter.
2. A.P., interview with Paul Fussell for 'A Question of Class', August 1986.
3. Cyril Connolly, *Enemies of Promise* (Penguin Modern Classics, 1979), p. 266.
4. Interview with the author, 12 December 1975.
5. Connolly, *Enemies of Promise*, p. 189.
6. Graham Greene (ed), *The Old School* (Oxford Paperbacks, 1984), pp. 127-8.
7. Charles Castle, *Oliver Messel* (Thames & Hudson 1986), pp. 31-2.
8. Peter Lawrence to the author. Lawrence is described in Powell's *Journals 1982-86* (Heinemann, 1995) as 'a fairly typical example of Eton beakdom'.

9. See Hugh Cecil, 'My Father at Eton', in Hannah Cranborne (ed), *David Cecil: A Portrait* (Dovecote Press, 1990), p. 20.

10. Malcolm Muggeridge, *Diaries*, 24 March 1950.

11. Cecil, 'My Father at Eton', in Cranborne (ed), *David Cecil*, p. 20.

12. John Bayley, interview with the author, 2 November 2000.

13. Simon Raven, 'On the Margin', *Spectator* (3 October 1976).

14. Muggeridge, *Like It Was* (Collins, 1981), p. 288.

15. Harold Acton, *Memoirs of an Aesthete* (Hamish Hamilton, 1984), p. 70.

16. John Heygate, *Decent Fellows* (Gollancz, 1930), p. 166.

17. Clive James, 'They Like It Here', *New Review* 3 (1976).

18. A.P., *Journals 1982-86*, p. 121.

19. Greene (ed), *The Old School*, p. 132.

20. D. Thorpe, *Alec Douglas-Home* (Sinclair-Stevenson, 1996), p. 20.

21. Muggeridge, *Diaries*, 16 June 1948.

22. Acton, *Memoirs of an Aesthete*, p. 91.

23. Jeremy Treglown, *Romancing: The Life and Work of Henry Green* (Faber, 2000), p. 78.

24. Green, *Pack My Bag*, pp. 163-72.

25. Ibid, p. 107.

26. Acton, *Memoirs of an Aesthete*, p. 92.

27. A.P., *Journals 1990-92* (Heinemann, 1997), p. 7.

28. Greene (ed), *The Old School*, pp. 141-2.

29. A.P., *Journals 1982-86*, p. 101.

30. Greene (ed), *The Old School*, p. 128.

31. H. Howarth, 'Discords in the Music of Time', *Commentary* (January 1972).

32. *New Review* 2 (September 1975).

33. Lucy Butler (ed), *Robert Byron: Letters Home* (John Murray, 1991), p. 3.

34. Edward Whitley, *The Graduates* (Hamish Hamilton, 1986), p. 44.

35. Paul Fussell, *Abroad* (Oxford University Press, 1980), p. 13.

36. Millard's appearance and way of life are described in Michael Davidson's *The World, The Flesh and Myself* (Ernest Barker, 1962), pp. 133-40.

37. A.P., *Journals 1990-92*, p. 140.

38. Davidson, *The World, The Flesh and Myself*, pp. 146-7.

3. Oxford Blues

1. A.P. to Waugh, 6 September 1964, BL. Copyright 2004, Estate of Violet Powell.

2. A.P., 'Pessimists v Dandies', *Daily Telegraph* 9 June 1977.

3. *Oxford* (1967), pp. 61-6.

4. Interview with the author, 21 April 1983.

5. *Isis*, 15 June 1973.

6. Interview with the author, 1983.

7. Alan Pryce-Jones, *The Bonus of Laughter* (Hamish Hamilton, 1988), p. 221.

8. Norman Sherry, *The Life of Graham Greene*, Vol 1 (Penguin, 1990), p. 120.

9. 'The Jowler', *Punch*, 30 October 1957.

10. Jeremy Lewis, *Cyril Connolly A Life* (Jonathan Cape, 1997), p. 100.

11. Philip Mason, *A Shaft of Sunlight* (Deutsch, 1978), Ch 4 'Bliss Was It …', *passim*.

12. Kenneth Clark, *Another Part of the Wood* (John Murray, 1974), pp. 95-6.

13. Dominick Harrod, 'Illusion and Reality', in George Lilley and Keith Marshall (eds), *Proceedings of the Anthony Powell Conference 2001* (The Anthony Powell Society, 2001), pp. 78-9.

14. *Balliol Record* (1952), p. 28.

15. Brian Harrison, *History of Oxford University*, Vol 8 (Clarendon Press, 1994), p. 83.
16. Sherry, *Life of Graham Greene*, Vol 1, p. 129.
17. A.P., *Miscellaneous Verdicts: Writings on Writers 1946-1989* (Heinemann, 1990), p. 443.
18. Marie-Jacqueline Lancaster (ed), *Brian Howard: Portrait of a Failure* (Blond, 1968), p. 203.
19. Whitley, *The Graduates*, p. 37.
20. Green, *Pack My Bag*, p. 206
21. Evelyn Waugh, *A Little Learning* (Chapman and Hall, 1964), p. 169.
22. Duggan to Waugh, 30 June 1963, BL.
23. Charles Ritchie, *An Appetite for Life* (Macmillan Canada, 1977), p. 118.
24. *Isis* (14 February 1924), p. 4.
25. Sir Kingsley Amis to the author.
26. 'C.M.B.', *Times Literary Supplement* (23 June 1972).
27. Osbert Lancaster, *With an Eye to the Future* (John Murray, 1967), p. 71.
28. Hugh Lloyd-Jones (ed), *Maurice Bowra: A Celebration* (Duckworth, 1974), p. 44.
29. Clark, *Another Part of the Wood*, pp. 100-1.
30. Maurice Bowra, *Memories, 1898-1939* (Weidenfeld & Nicolson, 1966), p. 161.
31. 'Stuff of the Twenties', *Balliol Record* (1976), p 30.
32. Alan Watkins, *Brief Lives* (Hamish Hamilton, 1982), p. 143.
33. Peter Lewis: 'The Dance Goes On Forever', *You* magazine (13 September 1987).
34. A.P., *Journals 1987-89*, p. 163.
35. Acton, *Memoirs of an Aesthete*, p. 132.
36. Muggeridge, *Diaries*, 20 December 1948.
37. John Monagan, 'A Visit with Anthony Powell', *American Scholar* (Autumn 1996).
38. Noel Blakiston (ed), *A Romantic Friendship: The Letters of Cyril Connolly to Noel Blakiston* (Constable 1975), p. 75.
39. 'Autumn or Fall?' *Punch* (27 May 1953).
40. *Cherwell* (14 June 1924).
41. Cyril Connolly, *The Evening Colonnade* (David Bruce & Watson, 1973), p. 24.
42. Peter Quennell, *The Marble Foot* (Collins, 1976), p. 137.
43. 'Stuff of the Twenties', *Balliol Record* (1976), p 30.
44. Mason, *A Shaft of Sunlight*, p. 51
45. Muggeridge, *Diaries*, 12 September 1948.
46. *Balliol Record* (1952) op. cit.
47. Cyril Connolly, *The Condemned Playground* (Hogarth Press, 1985), p. 218.
48. Ibid.
49. John Betjeman, *Summoned By Bells* (John Murray, 1960), p. 93
50. A.P., *Miscellaneous Verdicts*, p. 9.
51. Interview with Paul Fussell for 'A Question of Class', August 1986.
52. A.P., 'Youth in the Twenties', *Times Literary Supplement* (9 November 1951).

4. A Good Time Everywhere

The primary source for Chapters 4 and 5 is *Messengers of Day* (*Messengers*).

1. A.P., *Under Review*, p. 284
2. A.P., 'Poetry and Action', *Times Literary Supplement* (21 December 1951).
3. Noel Annan, 'The Mood of the Twenties', *Listener* (8 February 1951).
4. Interview with the author, 1975.
5. Lynn Barber, 'Voyeur at the Ball' *Independent on Sunday* (8 March 1992).

6. Mary Pakenham, *Brought Up and Brought Out* (Cobden Sanderson, 1938), p. 199.

7. Antony Knebworth in a letter to his mother, quoted by his father Lord Lytton in *Antony* (Peter Davies, 1935), p. 205.

8. Daphne Fielding, *Mercury Presides* (Eyre & Spottiswoode, 1954), p. 102.

9. Lynn Barber, 'Voyeur at the Ball', *Independent on Sunday* (8 March 1992).

10. Cyril Connolly, 'Going Down Well', *Harpers & Queen* (June 1973).

11. A.P. interviewed by Treglown, 23 November 1992.

12. A.P., *Journals 1990-92*, p. 95.

13. Treglown, *Romancing*, p. 76.

14. Christopher Matthew, 'At Home with Anthony Powell', *Observer Magazine* (17 December 1972).

15. Patrick Balfour, *Society Racket* (John Long, 1932), p. 277.

16. *Night and Day* (8 July 1937).

17. A.P. to Muggeridge, 1 August 1942, Buswell Memorial Library, Wheaton College, Illinois (Wheaton). Copyright 2004, Estate of Violet Powell.

18. Interview with the author, 1975.

19. A.P. to David Higham, 11 June 1970, Harry Ransom HumanitiesResearch Centre, The University of Texas at Austin (Austin). Copyright 2004, Estate of Violet Powell.

20. Information from Richard Ingrams.

21. Andrew Motion, *The Lamberts* (Hogarth Press, 1987), p. 131.

22. Humphrey Searle, MS memoir of Lambert, BL.

23. Michael Ayrton, *Golden Sections* (Methuen, 1957) p. 123.

24. Ibid.

25. Motion, *The Lamberts*, pp. 178-9.

26. Humphrey Searle: MS memoir of Lambert, BL.

27. Motion, *The Lamberts*, p. 211.

28. Denise Hooker, *Nina Hamnett* (Constable, 1986), p. 187.

29. Ibid.

30. Maurice Richardson, 'Sculptress in Wax', *Books and Bookmen* (November 1978).

31. A.P. to Monagan, 6 February 1979, Georgetown University Library, Washington D.C. (Georgetown). Copyright 2004, Estate of Violet Powell.

32. Hooker, *Nina Hamnett*, p. 112

33. Recalled by Alan Ross.

34. A.P., Review of *Is She a Lady, Punch* (16 November 1955).

35. Hooker, *Nina Hamnett*, p. 158.

36. A.P., *Under Review*, p. 194.

37. Adrian Daintrey, *I Must Say* (Chatto & Windus, 1963), p. 95.

38. A.P., 'The great Bohemian', *Time and Tide* (9 November 1961).

39. Adrian Daintrey, 'Augustus and Viva', *London Magazine* (August/September 1976).

40. Michael Luke to the author.

41. Daintrey, *I Must Say*, p. 212.

42. Alan Ross to the author.

43. A.P., *Journals 1982-86*, p. 207.

44. Ibid.

45. Robert Cecil, *A Divided Life* (Bodley Head, 1988), p. 51.

5. The Party's Over

1. A.P., *Under Review*, p. 104

2. *Writers at Work*, Third Series (Viking, 1967), p. 264.

3. A.P., *Miscellaneous Verdicts*, p. 225.
4. Interview with the author, 1975.
5. A.P., *Miscellaneous Verdicts*, p. 227.
6. Cyril Connolly, *The Unquiet Grave* (Hamish Hamilton, 1945), p. 64.
7. *Writers at Work*, Third Series (Viking, 1967), p. 111.
8. *Cherwell* (6 June 1931).
9. R.S. Foreman, 'First Novels', *The Bookman* (July 1931).
10. Harold Nicolson, *Evening Standard* (30 May 1931).
11. L.P. Hartley, 'Novels', *Week End Review* (4 July 1931)
12. A.P., *Journals 1987-89*, p. 154.
13. Interview with the author, 1975.
14. Jocelyn Brooke, 'Wauchop Agonistes', *Time and Tide* (1 September 1953).
15. Alec Waugh, *1931: A Year to Remember* (W.H. Allen, 1975), p. 152.
16. Ibid, p. 177.
17. 'Cocktail Fiction', *New York Times Book Review* (14 February 1932).
18. Interview with the author, 1975.
19. A.P., *Journals 1987-89*, p. 28.
20. A.P., Review of *Harbottle* by John Hargrave, *Cherwell* (31 May 1924).
21. A.P. to Waugh, 28 May 1962 BL. Copyright 2004, Estate of Violet Powell.
22. Harold Acton, *More Memoirs of an Aesthete* (Hamish Hamilton, 1986), p. 124.
23. John Heygate, 'The Creation of a Class', *Horizon* (September 1941).
24. Mark Amory (ed), *The Letters of Evelyn Waugh* (Weidenfeld & Nicolson), p. 38.
25. John Heygate, *These Germans* (Hutchinson, 1940), pp. 70-81.
26. John Heygate, *Talking Picture* (Cape, 1934), p. 9.
27. Ibid, p. 219-20.
28. A.P., *Now and Then* (Summer 1934), p. 14.
29. A.P., *Journals 1982-86*, p. 197.
30. A.P., *Under Review*, p. 104.
31. Ibid, p. 173.
32. A.P., 'Thus Spake Nietzsche', *Punch* (5 June 1957).
33. A.P., *A Writer's Notebook* (Heinemann, 2000), p. 79.
34. Interview with Douglas Davis, *College English* (June 1962), pp. 533-6.
35. Interview with the author, 1975.
36. Waugh, *Harper's Bazaar* (December 1933), p. 71.
37. Stephen Spender, 'Politics and Literature in 1933', *The Bookman* (December 1933).
38. A.P., *Miscellaneous Verdicts*, pp. 332-3.
39. Roy Fuller, 'Comedy, Realism and Poetry in The Music of Time', *Summary* (Autumn 1970).
40. Interview with Douglas Davis, *College English* (June 1962), pp. 533-6.
41. Lewis, *Cyril Connolly: A Life*, p. 289.

6. The Coming Struggle For Power

The primary sources for Chapters 6-11 are *Faces in My Time* (*Faces*) and the military volumes of *Dance*.

1. 'George Cloyne' (Alan Pryce-Jones), 'Three-fifths of a set of five', *New York Herald Tribune* (11 February 1962).
2. Amory (ed), *The Letters of Evelyn Waugh*, p. 34.

3. A.P., 'Exiles', *Spectator* (31 March 1939).
4. Connolly, *The Condemned Playground*, p. 116.
5. Jocelyn Brooke, 'Wauchop Agonistes', *Time and Tide* (1 September 1953).
6. V.S. Pritchett, 'Books in General', *New Statesman* (28 June 1962).
7. A.P., *A Writer's Notebook*, p. 62.
8. Ibid, pp. 17, 18, 25, 50.
9. A.P., *Under Review*, p. 420.
10. A.P., *Journals 1990-92*, p. 50.
11. James Lees-Milne, *Through Wood and Dale* (John Murray, 1998), p. 22.
12. Mark Boxer, 'Anthony Powell at Eighty', *Spectator* (21 December 1985).
13. A.P. to Frederick Bradnum, 1 November 1982. Copyright 2004, Estate of Violet Powell.
14. Interview with the author, 1975.
15. A.P., *A Writer's Notebook*, p. 51.
16. A.P., *Journals 1982-86*, p. 278.
17. William Chappell (ed), *Well, dearie! The Letters of Edward Burra* (Gordon Fraser, 1985), p. 45.
18. Ibid, p. 44.
19. Artists' Lives, National Life Story Collection BL.
20. Sherry, *The Life of Graham Greene*, Vol 1, p. 492.
21. Ibid, p. 450.
22. Greene (ed), *The Old School*, pp. vii, viii.
23. Ibid, p. 137.
24. Ibid, p. 65.
25. Ibid, p. 135.
26. Edward Garnett, 'Books of the Day', *New Statesman* (25 August 1934).
27. A.P., *Under Review*, p. 296.
28. Greene (ed), *The Old School*, pp. 229-30.
29. Violet Powell, *Within the Family Circle* (Heinemann, 1976), p. 223.
30. AP to John Monagan, 26 June 1984. Copyright 2004, Estate of Violet Powell.
31. *Bystander* (4 December 1934).
32. Lady Violet Powell to John Monagan, 9 July 1990. Copyright 2004, Estate of Violet Powell.
33. Violet Powell, *Within the Family Circle*, pp. 163-4.
34. Ibid, p. 5.
35. Fussell, *Abroad*, p. 78.
36. Selina Hastings, *Nancy Mitford* (Papermac, 1986), p. 90.
37. Clive James, 'They Like It Here', *New Review* 3 (1976).
38. *Daily Telegraph* (10 January 1936).
39. A.P., *Journals 1987-89*, p.121.
40. Walter Allen, *As I Walked Down New Grub Street* (Heinemann, 1981), p. 68.
41. James Lees-Milne, *Harold Nicolson*, Vol 2 (Chatto & Windus, 1981), p. 276.
42. Ibid.
43. A.P., *Under Review*, p. 149.
44. James Lees-Milne, *Deep Romantic Chasm* (John Murray, 2000), p. 48.
45. David Pryce-Jones (ed), *Cyril Connolly, Journal and Memoir* (Collins, 1983), p. 271.
46. Peter Quennell, 'Books in General', *New Statesman* (11 January 1936).
47. A.P., 'Romantic Realism', *Punch* (18 June 1968).
48. A.P., 'Dostoevsky en Touriste', *Punch* (11 May 1955).
49. A.P., *Messengers of Day* (Heinemann, 1975), p. 117. See also A.P., *Under Review*, pp. 400-12.
50. A.P., 'Russian Despot', *Punch* (1 December 1954).

51. Interview with the author, 1975.

52. A.P., 'A Reporter in Los Angeles – 2', *Night and Day* (19 August 1937).

53. A.P., 'A Reporter in Los Angeles – 1', *Night and Day* (12 August 1937).

54. Matthew Bruccoli, *Some Sort of Epic Grandeur* (Cardinal 1991), pp. 507-9.

55. Quoted by Neal Gabler in *An Empire of Their Own* (W.H. Allen, 1989), p. 326.

56. A.P., 'Educating Aldous', *Punch* (17 February 1954).

57. 'Desert Island Discs', BBC Radio 4, 18 October 1976.

58. Kingsley Amis, 'Writing for a TV Series', *Listener* (19 December 1974).

7. Later Than We Thought

1. Bevis Hillier, *John Betjeman: New Fame: New Love* (John Murray, 2002), pp. 77-9.

2. A.P., *Journals 1987-89*, p. 147.

3. A.P., 'Marginal Comment', *Spectator* (21 December 1937).

4. A.P. to John Monagan 24 April 1992, Georgetown. Copyright 2004, Estate of Violet Powell.

5. Quoted in Martin Stannard, *Evelyn Waugh: The Early Years* (Paladin, 1988), p. 452.

6. Christopher Hitchens, 'Powell's Way', *New York Review of Books* (28 May 1998).

7. Harold Nicolson, *Diaries and Letters 1930-39* (Nigel Nicolson ed.) (Collins, 1966), p. 396.

8. 'Pooter', *The Times* (21 March 1970).

9. Lady Violet Powell to the author, 30 September 2001.

10. A.P. to Pryce-Jones, 5 May 1954, Bienecke Library, Yale University. Copyright 2004, Estate of Violet Powell.

11. Interview with the author, 1975.

12. A.P., 'Inez Holden: A Memoir', *London Magazine* (October/November 1974).

13. C. Goodman, 'Inez Holden: A Memoir', *London Magazine* (December/January 1994).

14. 'Novels in Sequence', BBC Third Programme, 28 August 1960.

15. Motion, *The Lamberts*, p. 177.

16. *Times Literary Supplement* (28 January 1939).

17. Fussell, *Abroad*, p. 217.

18. G.U. Ellis, *Twilight on Parnassus* (Michael Joseph, 1939), p. 182.

19. Ibid, p. 377.

20. A.P., *John Aubrey and His Friends* (Eyre and Spottiswoode, 1948), p. 13.

21. Ibid, p. 10.

22. John Aubrey, *Brief Lives* (Folio Society, 1976), p. 18.

23. Ibid, p. 11.

24. A.P., *Spectator* (13 October 1939).

25. Motion, *The Lamberts*, p. 208.

26. A.P., *Journals 1990-92*, p. 95.

27. Malcolm Muggeridge, 'Valley of Lost Things', *New Statesman* (12 September 1975).

28. Malcolm Muggeridge, *The Green Stick* (Collins, 1972), p. 203.

29. Muggeridge, *Like It Was*, p. 197.

30. Muggeridge, *The Green Stick*, p. 268.

31. Muggeridge, *Diaries*, 9 February 1950.

32. George Orwell, *Collected Essays, Journalism and Letters*, Vol 1 (Penguin, 1970), p. 589.

33. Geoffrey Household, *Against the Wind* (Michael Joseph, 1958), p. 99.

34. Christopher Isherwood, *Lions and Shadows* (Hogarth Press, 1938), p. 75.

35. Michael Davie (ed), *The Diaries of Evelyn Waugh* (Weidenfeld & Nicolson, 1976), p. 548.

36. Frederick Stopp, *Evelyn Waugh* (Chapman and Hall, 1958), p. 39.

37. Evelyn Waugh, *Men at Arms* (Penguin, 1964), p. 26.

38. 'Lost Leaders or Strayed Revellers', *New Statesman* (17 February 1940).

39. A.P., *Journals 1990-92*, p. 115.

40. Charles Trueheart, 'The Gentleman Author', *Washington Post* (21 January 1990).

8. The Natural Profession

1. Interview with Paul Fussell for 'A Question of Class', August 1986.

2. Tony Gould, 'Master of the Dance', *New Society* (13 December 1985), p. 468.

3. A.P., *Journals 1987-89*, pp. 79-80.

4. A.P., *A Writer's Notebook*, p. 89.

5. A.P. to Monagan, 24 April 1992, Georgetown. Copyright 2004, Estate of Violet Powell.

6. A.P. to Sykes, 19 November 1963, Georgetown. Copyright 2004, Estate of Violet Powell.

7. A.P. to Monagan, 22 February 1990, Georgetown. Copyright 2004, Estate of Violet Powell.

8. He later moved to Sloane Mansions.

9. A.P., *Infants of the Spring* (Heinemann, 1976), p. 131 *passim*.

10. A.P. to Orwell, 18 May 1936, UCL Orwell collection. Copyright 2004, Estate of Violet Powell.

11. Orwell, *Collected Essays, Journalism and Letters*, Vol 1, pp. 252-3.

12. George Orwell, *Homage to Catalonia* (Secker & Warburg, 1986), p. 188.

13. Inez Holden, *Diaries*, 11 September 1941.

14. A.P., 'Orwell', *Punch* (15 July 1953).

15. Julian Symons, 'Orwell, a Reminiscence', *London Magazine* (September 1963), p. 41.

16. Unpublished MS, Wheaton.

17. Bernard Crick, *George Orwell: A Life* (Secker & Warburg, 1980), p. 47.

18. A.P., 'The Lot Fell Upon Jonah', *Punch* (22 January 1958).

19. Unpublished MS, Wheaton.

20. Interview with the author, 1975.

9. Gall and Wormwood

1. Noel Annan, *Changing Enemies* (HarperCollins, 1995), p. 17.

2. AP to Muggeridge, 1 August 1942, Wheaton. Copyright 2004, Estate of Violet Powell.

3. 'Dennis Wheatley at 80': Interview with the author for BBC World Service, 5 January 1977.

4. A.P., *Journals 1982-86*, p. 260.

5. Public Record Office, WO 165/43, *passim*.

6. Paul Kronacker, *Souvenirs de Paix et de Guerre* (Fayard, 1973), p. 75.

7. A.P., *Journals 1982-86*, p. 65.

8. A.P. p/c to Sykes, 4 April 1975, Georgetown. Copyright 2004, Estate of Violet Powell.

9. George Rylands: letter to the author, 27 March 1988.

10. Cyril Connolly, 'The Thistles', p. 116.

11. Quennell was interviewed by the author for 'Connolly's Masterpiece', BBC Radio 4, 24 April 1988, passim.

12. Michael Shelden, *Friends of Promise* (Hamish Hamilton, 1989), p. 30.

13. Hugh Massingberd, *Daydream Believer* (Macmillan, 2001), p. 208.

14. Peter Quennell, *The Wanton Chase* (Collins, 1980), pp. 34-36.

15. Nicolson, *Diaries and Letters*, Vol 2, p. 388.

16. Charles Trueheart, 'The Gentleman Author', *Washington Post* (21 January 1990)

17 Cassandra Jardine, 'In bellowing distance of a genius', *Daily Telegraph* (3 September 1998).

18. A.P., *New English Review* (August 1947), p. 172.

19. Robert Blake, 'Book Review' *Cambridge Review* (30 January 1976).

20. A.P., *Journals 1987-89*, p. 98.

21. Amory (ed), *The Letters of Evelyn Waugh*, p. 206.

22. *Spectator* (29 June 1962).

10. The World Turned Upside Down

1. Tony Gould, 'Master of the Dance', *New Society* (13 December 1985), p. 468.

2. Hugh Hebert, 'A Word in Jenkins's Ear', *Guardian* (15 February 1971).

3. A.P., *A Writer's Notebook*, p. 84.

4. A.P., *Journals 1982-86*, p. 111.

5. A.P., *John Aubrey and His Friends*, p. 13.

6. Muggeridge, *Like It Was*, p. 267.

7. Ibid, p. 274.

8. A.P., *Journals 1990-92*, pp. 105-6.

9. A.P., *Under Review*, p. 144.

10. A.P., *Journals 1982-86*, pp. 225-8.

11. *Spectator* (21 December 1991).

12. Interview with the author, 1975.

13. *New English Review* (May 1946), p. 472.

14. Doris Lessing, *The Four-Gated City* (Knopf, 1969), p. 124.

15. Telephone conversation with the author, 23 May 2001.

16. A.P. to Brooke, 30 July 1962, Austin. Copyright 2004, Estate of Violet Powell.

17. Wilfred De'Ath, 'Episodes in Time', *Illustrated London News* (June 1973).

18. Telephone conversation with the author, 23 May 2001.

19. Ibid.

20. Paul Willetts, *Fear and Loathing in Fitzrovia* (Dewi Lewis, 2003), p. 193.

21. Ibid.

22. Muggeridge, *Diaries*, 1 March 1948.

23. Willetts, *Fear and Loathing in Fitzrovia*, p. 198 *passim*.

24. Maclaren-Ross papers, Austin.

25. A.P., 'Exploration XI', National Sound Archives, British Library.

26. Letter to the author, 30 January 2003.

27. A.N. Wilson, *Daughters of Albion* (Sinclair-Stevenson, 1991), p. 245

28. Paul Gaston, 'This Question of Discipline', *Virginia Quarterly Review* (Autumn 1985).

29. A.P., *A Writer's Notebook*, p. 39 *passim*.

30. Julian Jebb, 'Anthony Powell's dreams', *Listener* (11 September 1975).

31. John Kuehl and Jackson R. Bryer (eds), *Dear Scott: Dear Max* (Cassell, 1973), p. 82.

32. A.P. to Brooke 7 July 1970, Austin. Copyright 2004, Estate of Violet Powell.
33. Interview with the author, 1975.
34. A.P. to Higham 21 November 1961, Austin. Copyright 2004 *Estate of Violet Powell*.
35. Interview with the author.
36. 'Anthony Powell: A Symposium', *Summary* (Autumn 1970), p 131, and elsewhere.
37. 'Mr Douglas Looks Back' *Spectator* 20 December 1946.
38. A.P., *John Aubrey and His Friends*, p. 13.
39. Interview with the author, 1975.
40. A.P. to Waugh 24 October 1957, BL. Copyright 2004, Estate of Violet Powell.
41. Amory (ed), *The Letters of Evelyn Waugh*, p. 538.
42. 'Time's Laughing Stocks', *Times Literary Supplement* (29 June 1962).
43. Letters, *Times Literary Supplement* (20 July 1962).
44. Lucy Hutchinson, *Memoirs of the Life of Colonel Hutchinson* (Bell, 1906), p. 138.
45. A.P., *John Aubrey and His Friends*, p. 290.
46. Ibid.
47. A.P., *New English Review* (June 1946), p. 584.
48. George Orwell, *Collected Essays, Journalism and Letters*, Vol 4 (Penguin, 1971), p. 212.

11. Invitation to the Dance

1. Malcolm Muggeridge, *The Infernal Grove* (Collins, 1973), p. 253.
2. Muggeridge, *Diaries*, 4 April 1948.
3. Muggeridge, *Like It Was*, p. 275.
4. Muggeridge, *Diaries*, 20 May 1948.
5. Ibid, 23 August 1948.
6. Ibid, 29 October 1949.
7. Ian Hunter, *Malcolm Muggeridge A Life* (Hamish Hamilton, 1987), p. 151.
8. Muggeridge, *Like It Was*, p. 356.
9. Muggeridge, *Diaries*, 4 June 1948.
10. Ibid, 5 April 1949.
11. H.D. Ziman, 'The Private and Public Powell', *Summary* (Autumn 1970), p. 118.
12. Richard Ingrams, *God's Apology* (Deutsch, 1977), p. 116.
13. Muggeridge, *Diaries*, 7 May 1949.
14. Ibid, 23 March 1948.
15. Ibid, 1 April 1948.
16. A.P., *A Writer's Notebook*, p 145.
17. Julian Symons, 'Orwell, a Reminiscence', *London Magazine* (September 1963), pp. 41-2.
18. Muggeridge, *Like It Was*, p. 350.
19. Ibid, p. 330.
20. Muriel Gross (ed), *The World of George Orwell* (Weidenfeld & Nicolson, 1971), p. 173.
21. A.P., *Journals 1982-86*, p. 6.
22. Violet Powell, *The Departure Platform* (Heinemann, 1998), p. 6.
23. Muggeridge, *Like It Was*, p. 375.
24. 'A Citizen of the World', *Times Literary Supplement* (8 May 1948).
25. A.P. to Waugh, 14 March 1951, BL. Copyright 2004, Estate of Violet Powell.
26. 'George Cloyne' (Alan Pryce-Jones), 'Three-fifths of a set of five' *New York Herald Tribune* Books (11 February 1962).

27. Interview with the author, 1975.

28. Muggeridge, *Diaries*, 13 March 1948.

29. David Higham, *Literary Gent* (Cape, 1978), p. 141.

30. A.P., 'Change at Rugby', *Punch* (10 November 1954).

31. A.P., 'Stirring the Mixture', *Times Literary Supplement* (21 August 1948).

32. Alan Ross, 'Anthony Powell's Novels', *Time and Tide* (10 February 1951).

33. AP to Pryce-Jones, Bienecke Library, Yale University. Copyright 2004, Estate of Violet Powell.

34. John Russell, *Reading Russell* (Thames and Hudson, 1989), p. 156.

35. AP to Brooke, 7 July 1960, Austin. Copyright 2004, Estate of Violet Powell.

36. Amory (ed), *The Letters of Evelyn Waugh*, p. 440.

37. John Raymond, 'New Novels', *New Statesman* (27 January 1951).

38. Julian Maclaren-Ross, 'From A Chase To A View', *Times Literary Supplement* (16 February 1951), *passim*.

39. Richard Heygate to the author, *passim*.

40. A.P., *Messengers*, pp. 99-100.

41. *The Times* (25 March 1976).

42. A.P., *Infants*, p. 102.

43. Motion, *The Lamberts*, p. 223.

44. 'Remembering Constant Lambert', National Sound Archive, BL.

45. Ibid.

46. A.P., 'Artist at Large', *Punch* (16 October 1957).

47. Ayrton, *Golden Sections*, p. 130.

48. Muggeridge, *Diaries*, 1 July 1948.

49. A.P., *Journals 1990-92*, p. 169.

50. Cyril Connolly, 'March of Time', *Sunday Times* (23 September 1973).

51. Interview with the author, 1975.

52. Violet Powell, *The Departure Platform*, p. 5.

53. Interview with the author, 1975.

54. A.P. to Waugh, 14 March 1951. Copyright 2004, Estate of Violet Powell.

55. Duncan Fallowell, 'Classical with Grottoes', *Vanity Fair* (June 1984).

12. Bouverie Street

The primary source for Chapters 12-16 is *The Strangers All Are Gone* (*Strangers*).

1. Julian Symons, 'Men About Town', *Times Literary Supplement* (27 June 1952).

2. V.S. Pritchett, 'Books in General', *New Statesman* (28 June 1952).

3. Philip Toynbee, 'Comic Intentions', *The Observer* (22 June 1952).

4. A.P., *A Writer's Notebook*, p. 100.

5. A.P. to Talks Department, 15 October 1952, BBC Sound Archives Caversham. Copyright 2004, Estate of Violet Powell.

6. Studio Script, Caversham, *passim*.

7. Lynn Barber, 'Voyeur at the Ball', *Independent on Sunday* (8 March 1992).

8. Ibid.

9. Simon Barnes, 'Anthony Powell and "Drink"', in George Lilley and Keith Marshall (eds), *Proceedings of the Anthony Powell Conference 2001* (The Anthony Powell Society, 2001).

10. R.G.G. Price, *A History of Punch* (Collins, 1957), p. 330.

11. Ibid.

12. *Punch* (27 April 1955).

13. Malcolm Muggeridge, *Tread Softly For You Tread On My Jokes* (Fontana, 1966), p. 14.

14. Mark Boxer, 'Anthony Powell at Eighty', *Spectator* (21 December 1985).

15. *Summary* (Autumn 1970), p. 138

16. A.P., *Journals 1982-86*, pp. 282-3 *passim*.

17. Claud Cockburn, *Cockburn Sums Up* (Quartet, 1981), p. 178

18. Ibid, p. 179.

19. Muggeridge, *Like It Was*, p 262.

20. Nicholas Wapshot, 'A stalls seat at the farce of history', *Times* (2 March 1981).

21. Interview with the author, 15 March 2000.

22. Mark Amory (ed), *The Letters of Ann Fleming* (Harvill Press, 1985), p. 156.

23. Ann Fleming to Waugh, 20 October 1956, BL.

24. Amory (ed), *The Letters of Evelyn Waugh*, p. 477.

25. Amory (ed), *The Letters of Ann Fleming*, p. 324.

26. Amory (ed), *The Letters of Evelyn Waugh*, p. 591.

27. Ibid, p. 606.

28. A.P., *Journals 1982-86*, p. 202.

29. Charlotte Mosley (ed), *The Letters of Nancy Mitford* (Hodder, 1993), p. 298.

30. A.P. to Waugh, 23 May 1953, BL. Copyright 2004, Estate of Violet Powell.

31. A.P. to Kay Dick, 23 June 1953, Austin. Copyright 2004, Estate of Violet Powell.

32. A.P. to Brooke, 17 March 1953, Austin. Copyright 2004, Estate of Violet Powell.

33. A.P. to Waugh, 28 April 1955, BL. Copyright 2004, Estate of Violet Powell.

34. Julian Symons, 'Society Ritual', *Times Literary Supplement* (13 May 1955).

35. James Stern, 'A Variety of Satire', *Encounter* (July 1955).

36. Richard Lister, 'The Strange Case of Mr Powell', *New Statesman* (28 May 1955).

37. 'Afternoon World', *Spectator* (13 May 1955).

38. Evelyn Waugh, 'An Open Letter to the Hon. Mrs Peter Rodd', *Encounter* (December 1953).

39. Kingsley Amis, 'Talk About Laugh', *Spectator* (20 November 1953).

40. A.P., *Punch* (3 February 1954).

41. Zachary Leader (ed), *The Letters of Kingsley Amis* (HarperCollins, 2000), p. 950.

42. Ibid, p. 337.

43. Ibid, p. 483.

44. Kingsley Amis, *Memoirs* (Hutchinson, 1991), p. 150.

45. Ibid, p. 152.

46. A.P. to Brooke, 23 January 1953, Austin. Copyright 2004, Estate of Violet Powell.

47. A.P. to Brooke, June (?) 1956, Austin. Copyright 2004, Estate of Violet Powell.

48. Jocelyn Brooke, 'From Wauchop to Widmerpool', *London Magazine* (September 1960).

49. Ibid.

50. Louis Auchincloss, 'Proust's Picture of Society', *Partisan Review* (August 1960).

13. A Legacy

1. Amory (ed), *The Letters of Evelyn Waugh*, p 473.

2. A.P. to Maurice Cranston, 1 June 1956, Austin. Copyright 2004, Estate of Violet Powell.

3. Julian Symons, 'Time Marches On', *Times Literary Supplement* (1 November 1957).

Endnotes

4. Anthony Quinton, Untitled review, *London Magazine* (February 1958), *passim*.

5. 'Novels in Sequence', BBC Third Programme, 28 August 1960.

6. Kingsley Amis, 'The Music of Time', BBC Radio 3, 29 August 1979, Huntington Library, San Marino, California (Huntington).

7. Evelyn Waugh, 'Marriage à la Mode – 1936', *Spectator* (24 June 1960).

8. A.P., 'Man and Wife', *Punch* (12 October 1955).

9. A.P., 'Stirring the Mixture', *Times Literary Supplement* (21 August 1945).

10. Violet Powell, *The Departure Platform*, p. 140.

11. Ibid, p. 121.

12. Simon Raven to the author.

13. Connolly, *The Unquiet Grave*, p. 39.

14. Alan Watkins to the author, 15 May 2000.

15. A.P. to Brooke, 12 December 1958, Austin. Copyright 2004, Estate of Violet Powell.

16. Interview with the author, 1975.

17. Richard Boston, 'A Talk With Anthony Powell', *New York Times Book Review* (9 March 1969).

18. Sir Harry to A.P., 17 May 1958, courtesy of Mrs Chloe Teacher.

19. Ibid, 18 March 1961.

20. A.P. to Sir Harry, 1 April 1961. Copyright 2004, Estate of Violet Powell.

21. Ibid, 14 November 1970.

22. Sir Harry to A.P., 19 November 1970, courtesy of Mrs Cloe Teacher.

23. A.P. to Alan Ross, 29 September 1967, Austin. Copyright 2004, Estate of Violet Powell.

24. A.P., *Miscellaneous Verdicts*, p. 359.

25. Michie to the author, 26 April 2001.

26. John St John, *William Heinemann – A Century of Publishing* (Heinemann, 1990), pp. 340-1.

27. A.P. to Higham, ? October 1958, Austin. Copyright 2004, Estate of Violet Powell.

28. A.P. to Higham, 21 April 1960, Austin. Copyright 2004, Estate of Violet Powell.

29. A.P. to Higham, 22 February 1961, Austin. Copyright 2004, Estate of Violet Powell.

30. A.P. to Higham, 4 September 1961, Austin. Copyright 2004, Estate of Violet Powell.

31. A.P. to Higham, 18 September 1961, Austin. Copyright 2004, Estate of Violet Powell.

32. A.P., *Journals 1982-86*, p. 251.

33. A.P. to Higham, 28 August 1957, Austin. Copyright 2004, Estate of Violet Powell.

34. Sions to Higham, 21 July 1970, Austin.

35. Harry Sions, 'The Relevance of Anthony Powell', *Summary* (Autumn 1970).

36. Elizabeth Janeway, 'A World That Is Almost Our Own', *New York Times Book Review* (21 January 1962).

37. 'Work in Progress', *Newsweek* (22 January 1962).

38. 'Corpse in the Garden', *Time* (20 February 1956).

39. 'Up Jenkins', *Summary* (Autum 1970).

40. Dawn Powell, 'Somebody Else's Crowd', *The Nation* (25 October 1958).

41. Naomi Bliven, 'The Marriage State', *New Yorker* (31 December 1960).

42. Benjamin DeMott, 'Ask at the house', *Atlantic Monthly* (April 1976).

43. A.P. to the author, 1975.

44. Roger Pippet, 'Four Schoolboys', *New York Times Book Review* (8 July 1951).

45. Henry Swados, *New Republic* (20 August 1951).

46. 'An Interview with Edmund Wilson', *New Yorker* (2 June 1962).

47. Douglas Davis, 'An Interview with Anthony Powell', *College English* (June 1962).
48. A.P. to Monagan, 28 June 1971. Copyright 2004, Estate of Violet Powell.
49. Edmund Wilson, *The Sixties* (Farrar, Strauss & Giroux, 1993), p. 259.
50. Jeffrey Meyers, *Edmund Wilson* (Houghton Mifflin, 1995), p. 425.
51. A.P., *Miscellaneous Verdicts*, p 205.

14. The Play's the Thing

1. A.P., 'Life With Crowley', *Times Literary Supplement* (14 December 1951).
2. Maurice Richardson, *Fits and Starts* (Michael Joseph, 1979), p. 117 *passim*.
3. A.P., '666', *Punch* (19 September 1956).
4. 'Anthony Powell: his dance, his music, his times', BBC Radio 3, 14 December 1985.
5. Malcolm Muggeridge, 'Valley of Lost Things', *New Statesman* (12 September 1975).
6. Duncan Fallowell, 'Classical with Grottoes', *Vanity Fair* (June 1984).
7. Interview with the author, 1975.
8. T. d'Arch Smith, '"Dr Trelawney" and Aleister Crowley', *London Magazine* (March 1988).
9. 'Pooter', *The Times* (21 March 1970).
10. A.P. to the author, 30 June 1975. Copyright 2004, Estate of Violet Powell.
11. A.P. to the author, 8 December 1975. Copyright 2004, Estate of Violet Powell.
12. A.P. to the author, 15 July 1976. Copyright 2004, Estate of Violet Powell.
13. Plimpton to the author, 7 September 1976.
14. Lees-Milne, *Through Wood and Dale*, p. 66.
15. Watkins, *Brief Lives*, p. 143.
16. A.P., *Journals 1982-86*, p. 61.
17. John Bayley, interview with the author, 2 November 2000.
18. Charles Ritchie, *Storm Signals* (Macmillan, Canada 1983), entry for 12 July 1971.
19. Jilly Cooper, interview with the author, 6 May 2000.
20. Interview with the author, 1975.
21. A.P. to Higham, 27 November 1961, Austin. Copyright 2004, Estate of Violet Powell.
22. A.P., 'Kind Hearts Less Than Coronets', *Punch* (15 February 1956).
23. Roger Graef, interview with the author, *passim*, 22 May 2003.
24. John Bowen, 'Everybody's Drifting', *New York Times Book Review* (20 October 1963).
25. Roger Graef, interview with the author, *passim*, 22 May 2003.
26. A.P., 'National Faces', *Punch* (1 May 1957).
27. Clark, *Another Part of the Wood*, p. 237.
28. Sir John Plumb to the author, 13 September 2000.
29. Amis, *Memoirs*, p. 147.
30. Interview with the author, 15 June 2000.

15. Mugged

1. A.P., *A Writer's Notebook*, p. 127.
2. A.P., *Journals 1990-92*, p. 82.
3. Evelyn Waugh, *The Tablet*, 5 February 1949.
4. Malcolm Muggeridge, 'Snobs and Comic Heroes in the Thick of the Phoney War', *Evening Standard* (3 March 1964).
5. Malcolm Muggeridge in *Esquire* (June 1965).

6. Alan Watkins, interview with the author, 15 May 2000.

7. Malcolm Muggeridge, 'Valley of Lost Things', *New Statesman* (12 September 1975).

8. Alan Watkins, interview with the author.

9. Lady Violet Powell to the author, 30 September 2001.

10. Paul Gaston, 'This Question of Discipline', *Virginia Quarterly Review* (Autumn 1985).

11. Octavio Roca, 'Dancing to the music of time', *Washington Times* (16 April 1990).

12. Kingsley Amis, 'The Music of Time', BBC Radio 3, 29 August 1979, Huntington Library.

13. Laurence Kitchen, 'Snobs' Wars', *The Listener* (21 November 1968).

14. Roy Fuller, 'Selected Books', *London Magazine* (May 1964).

15. A.P. to Waugh, 28 May 1962, BL. Copyright 2004 *Estate of Violet Powell*.

16. Kingsley Amis, 'The Music of Time', BBC Radio 3, 29 August 1979, Huntington Library.

17. Simon Raven, 'Around the battlements', *The Observer* (19 October 1968).

18. Francis Hope, 'Marching Orders', *New Statesman* (18 October 1968).

19. John Braine, 'The River Flows', *National Review* (6 May 1969).

20. Melvin Maddocks, 'A Different Drummer', *Atlantic Magazine* (March 1969).

21. Paul Zimmerman, 'Bottom Brass', *Newsweek* (13 March 1967).

22. 'Powell's Piano Concertos', *Time* (28 March 1969).

16. Wits' End

1. A.P., 'A Memoir', *Adam*, no 301-3 (1966).

2. A.P. to Sykes, 22 December 1975, Georgetown. Copyright 2004, Estate of Violet Powell.

3. Evelyn Waugh, 'Marriage à la Mode – 1936', *Spectator* (24 June 1960).

4. Evelyn Waugh, 'Bioscope', *Spectator*, 29 June 1962.

5. A.P. to Muggeridge, 1 August 1942, Wheaton. Copyright 2004, Estate of Violet Powell.

6. A.P., *Punch* (13 July 1955).

7. Ibid.

8. A.P. to Waugh, 1 July 1955. Copyright 2004, Estate of Violet Powell.

9. Amory (ed), *The Letters of Evelyn Waugh*, p 443.

10. A.P. to Sykes, 12 September 1979, Georgetown. Copyright 2004, Estate of Violet Powell.

11. Anthony Beevor, *Crete: The Battle and the Resistance* (John Murray, 1991), pp. 218-23.

12. Angus Calder, 'Mr Wu and the Colonials', *A Time to Kill* (Pimlico 1997) pp 129-46.

13. A.P., 'Evelyn's Diary', *London Magazine* (August/September 1973).

14. A.P., 'Exploration XI', National Sound Archives, British Library.

15. Mark Boxer, 'Anthony Powell at Eighty', *Spectator* (21 December 1985).

16. Tom Dyckhof, 'They've Got It Covered', *Guardian Weekend* (15 September 2001).

17. 'Penguins and Powell – a rupture', 'Londoner's Diary', *Evening Standard* (8 September 1966).

18. Mark Boxer, 'Anthony Powell at Eighty', *Spectator* (21 December 1985).

19. Whiteley, *The Graduates*, p. 41.

20. A.P., *Journals 1987-89*, p. 44.

21. A.P., *Miscellaneous Verdicts*, p. 309.

22. Barbara Skelton, *Tears Before Bedtime* (Hamish Hamilton, 1987), pp. 115-6.
23. Edmund Wilson, *The Fifties* (Farrar, Strauss and Giroux, 1986), p. 374.
24. Ibid.
25. A.P., *Punch* (11 July 1956).
26. Barbara Skelton, *Weep No More* (Hamish Hamilton, 1989), p. 146.
27. Willetts, *Fear and Loathing in Fitzrovia*, p. 281.
28. Ibid, p. 310.
29. Interview with the author, 1975.
30. Philip Larkin, 'Mr Powell's Mural', *New Statesman* (19 February 1971).
31. A.P. to Muggeridge, 16 December 1974, Wheaton. Copyright 2004, Estate of Violet Powell.
32. Alan Ross, 'Before the Women', *London Magazine* (December 1975/January 1976).
33. Deirdre Levi to the author, 20 December 2001.
34. John Richardson to the author, 15 June 2001.
35. John Richardson, *The Sorcerer's Apprentice* (Cape, 1999), p. 150.
36. A.P. to Frederick Bradnum, 5 December 1981. Copyright 2004, Estate of Violet Powell.
37. Alan Brownjohn, 'Profile 6', *New Review* (1 September 1974), *passim*.
38. A.P. to Amis, 20 September 1979, Huntington Library. Copyright 2004, Estate of Violet Powell.
39. A.P., interview with the author, 1975.
40. Quoted by Antony Lejeune: 'An Acquired Taste', *National Review* (11 June 1976).
41. Malcolm Muggeridge, 'Valley of Lost Things', *New Statesman* (12 September 1975).

17. The Music Dies

The primary source for Chapters 17-18 is Powell's three volumes of Journals.

1. Elizabeth Longford, 'A Talk with Anthony Powell', *New York Times Book Review* (11 April 1976).
2. Julian Jebb, 'Anthony Powell's dreams', *Listener* (11 September 1975).
3. A.P. to David Higham, 1 March 1974. Copyright 2004, Estate of Violet Powell.
4. A.P. to Amis, 30 January 1980, Huntington Library. Copyright 2004 *Estate of Violet Powell*.
5. Amis, *Memoirs*, p. 154.
6. Jilly Cooper to the author, 6 May 2000.
7. Kingsley Amis, 'The final cadence', *Observer* (7 September 1975).
8. Paul Scott, 'Turning the Full Circle', *Country Life* (11 September 1975).
9. John Bayley, 'A family and its fictions', *Times Literary Supplement* (12 September 1975).
10. Michael Frayn, 'The End of the Dance', *Observer* (7 September 1975).
11. Auberon Waugh, *Evening Standard* (9 September 1975).
12. Auberon Waugh, 'Auberon Waugh and the Music of Time', *Spectator* (20 February 1971).
13. Auberon Waugh, *Will This Do?* (Century, 1991), p. 222.
14. A.P. to Sykes, 22 December 1975, Georgetown. Copyright 2004, Estate of Violet Powell.
15. Amis to Powell, 3 June 1990, Huntington Library.
16. James Delany, 'Voyeur', *London Review of Books* (5 May 1983).

17. Massingberd, *Daydream Believer*, p. 198.

18. Hugh Massingberd, 'A.D. Powell's "pleasure in genealogical investiga-tion"', in Lillley and Marshall (eds), *Proceedings of the Anthony Powell Conference 2001*, pp. 107-18.

19. A.P., *A Writer's Notebook*, p. 86.

20. Cyril Connolly, 'London Diary', *New Statesman* (16 January 1937).

21. A.P., *Journals 1990-92*, p. 226.

22. Ferdinand Mount, 'The Passing of Powell', *Prospect* (May 2000).

23. Paul Johnson, 'And Another Thing', *Spectator* (27 May 2000).

24. John Lanchester, 'D&O', *London Review of Books* (5 June 1997).

25. A.P. to Monagan, 2 April 1974, Georgetown. Copyright 2004, Estate of Violet Powell.

26. Muggeridge, *Diaries*, 1 September 1948.

27. Cassandra Jardine, 'In bellowing distance of a genius', *Daily Telegraph* (3 September 1998).

28. A.P. to Monagan, (?) June 1993, Georgetown. Copyright 2004, Estate of Violet Powell.

29. Frederick Bradnum to the author, *passim*, May 2001.

30. A.P. to Bradnum, 5 December 1981. Copyright 2004, Estate of Violet Powell.

31. A.P. to Bradnum, 6 September 1982. Copyright 2004, Estate of Violet Powell.

32. Ibid.

33. A.P. to Bradnum, 'St David's Day' 1982. Copyright 2004, Estate of Violet Powell.

34. A.P. to Bradnum, 18 August 1981. Copyright 2004, Estate of Violet Powell.

35. A.P. to Bradnum, 6 September 1982. Copyright 2004, Estate of Violet Powell.

36. Charles Trueheart, 'The Gentleman Author', *Washington Post* (21 January 1990).

37. Kenneth Trodd to the author, *passim*, 29 August 2003.

38. Jeremy Treglown, 'Class Act', *New Yorker* (18 December 1995).

39. A.P. to Bruce Hunter, (?) June 1983. Copyright 2004, Estate of Violet Powell.

40. J.K.L. Walker, 'Chamber Music', *Times Literary Supplement* (24 June 1983).

18. Last Words

1. Raymond Seitz to the author, 21 October 2003.

2. A.P., *Under Review*, p. 368.

3. A.P., *Journals 1987-89*, p. 54.

4. Pinter's views on Honours were given in an interview in 'G2', *The Guardian* (28 August 2002).

5. A.P., *Journals 1982-86*, pp. 140-1.

6. A.P., Review of *The Best of Beaton*, *Apollo* (December 1968).

7. A.P., *Journals 1982-86*, p. 80.

8. Peter Levi, 'Bores Well-Described', *Literary Review* (April 1986).

9. A.P., *Journals 1982-86*, p. 28.

10. John Carey, 'Character Forming', *Sunday Times* (5 February 1995), *passim*.

11. James Lees-Milne, unpublished diary, 29 January 1995.

12. Ferdinand Mount, 'The Passing of Powell', *Prospect* (May 2000).

13. A.P., *Journals 1987-89*, p. 103.

14. *Summary* (Autumn 1970), p. 138

15. A.P., *Under Review*, p. 171.

16. A.P., *Journals 1990-92*, p. 42.

17. Auberon Waugh, 'Judgement on a Major man of letters', *Sunday Telegraph* (27 May 1990).

18. Max Hastings, *Editor* (Pan, 2003), p. 252, *passim*.
19. Lynn Barber, 'Voyeur at the Ball', *Independent on Sunday* (8 March 1992).
20. Auberon Waugh, *Will This Do?*, pp. 222-3.
21. Alan Watkins, *A Short Walk Down Fleet Street* (Duckbacks, 2001), p. 95.
22. Lynn Barber, 'Voyeur at the Ball', *Independent on Sunday* (8 March 1992).
23. A.P., *Journals 1982-86*, p. 244.
24. John Bayley, 'Books and Bookmen', *Sunday Times* (1 March 1992).
25. A.P., *Journals 1990-92*, p. 92.
26. Lynn Barber, 'Voyeur at the Ball', *Independent on Sunday* (8 March 1992).
27. A.P. to Monagan, 20 March 1993, Georgetown. Copyright 2004, Estate of Violet Powell.
28. Massingberd, *Daydream Believer*, pp. 208-9.

If you enjoyed this book, the Anthony Powell Society can be contacted at
76 Ennismore Avenue, Greenford, Middlesex, UB6 0JW, UK
Email: secretary@anthonypowell.org.uk
Website: www.anthonypowell.org.uk

The Society is a charitable literary society devoted to the life and
works of Anthony Powell, 1905-2000.

Works by Anthony Powell

A Dance to the Music of Time

A Question of Upbringing (London: Heinemann, 1951; New York: Scribner's, 1952).
A Buyer's Market (London: Heinemann, 1952; New York: Scribner's, 1953).
The Acceptance World (London: Heinemann, 1955; New York: Farrar, Strauss and Cudahy, 1956).
At Lady Molly's (London: Heinemann, 1957; Boston: Little, Brown, 1958).
Casanova's Chinese Restaurant (London: Heinemann, 1960; Boston: Little, Brown, 1960).
The Kindly Ones (London: Heinemann, 1962; Boston: Little, Brown, 1962).
The Valley of Bones (London: Heinemann, 1964; Boston: Little, Brown, 1964).
The Soldier's Art (London: Heinemann, 1966; Boston: Little, Brown, 1967).
The Military Philosophers (London: Heinemann, 1968; Boston: Little, Brown, 1969).
Books Do Furnish a Room (London: Heinemann, 1971; Boston: Little, Brown, 1971).
Temporary Kings (London: Heinemann, 1973; Boston: Little, Brown, 1973).
Hearing Secret Harmonies (London: Heinemann, 1975; Boston: Little, Brown, 1976).

Other Fiction

Afternoon Men (London: Duckworth, 1931; New York: Henry Holt and Company, 1932).
Venusberg (London: Duckworth, 1932; Boston: Little, Brown, 1965).
From a View to a Death (London: Duckworth, 1933; New York: published as *Mr Zouch, Superman: From a View to a Death*, Vanguard, 1934).
Agents and Patients (London: Duckworth, 1936; New York: Popular Library, 1978).
What's Become of Waring (London: Cassell, 1939; Boston: Little, Brown, 1963).
Two Plays: The Garden God, The Rest I'll Whistle (London: Heinemann, 1971; Boston: Little, Brown, 1972).
O, How the Wheel Becomes It! (London: Heinemann, 1983; New York: Holt, Rinehart and Winston, 1983).
The Fisher King (London: Heinemann, 1986. New York: Norton, 1986).

Biography

John Aubrey and His Friends (London: Eyre and Spottiswoode, 1948; new and revised edition: Hogarth Press, 1988. New York: Scribner's, 1948; new and revised edition: Barnes and Noble, 1963).

Memoirs

To Keep the Ball Rolling: The Memoirs of Anthony Powell
Volume 1: *Infants of the Spring* (London: Heinemann, 1976; New York: Holt, Rinehart and Winston, 1977).

Volume 2: *Messengers of Day* (London: Heinemann, 1978; New York: Holt, Rinehart and Winston, 1978).
Volume 3: *Faces in My Time* (London: Heinemann, 1980; New York: Holt, Rinehart and Winston, 1981).
Volume 4: *The Strangers All Are Gone* (London: Heinemann, 1982; New York: Holt, Rinehart and Winston, 1983).

Diaries

Journals 1982-1986 (London: Heinemann, 1995).
Journals 1987-1989 (London: Heinemann, 1996).
Journals 1990-1992 (London: Heinemann, 1997).

Criticism

Miscellaneous Verdicts: Writings on Writers 1946-1989 (London: Heinemann, 1990; Chicago: University of Chicago Press, 1992).
Under Review: Further Writings on Writers 1946-1989 (London: Heinemann, 1991; Chicago: University of Chicago Press, 1993).

Other Non-Fiction

'The Watr'y Glade'. Contribution to Graham Greene (ed), *The Old School: Essays by Divers Hands* (London: Jonathan Cape, 1934).
A Writer's Notebook (London: Heinemann, 2000).

Poetry

Caledonia, A Fragment. (Privately printed, 1934. Reprinted in Kingsley Amis (ed), *The New Oxford Book of Light Verse* (London: OUP, 1978)).

Bibliography

Absent from this list are any academic studies of Powell, which I purposely avoided. But my task would have been made immeasurably more difficult without Hilary Spurling's *Handbook to Anthony Powell's Music of Time* (Heinemann, 1977) and George Lilley's *Anthony Powell: A Bibliography* (St Paul's Bibliographies, 1993). Also very helpful was 'Anthony Powell: A Symposium' in the Autumn 1970 edition of *Summary*.

Editions referred to here are those I have consulted.

Acton, Harold, *Memoirs of an Aesthete* (Hamish Hamilton, 1984).
———, *More Memoirs of an Aesthete* (Hamish Hamilton, 1986).
Allen, Walter, *As I Walked Down New Grub Street* (Heinemann, 1981).
Amis, Kingsley, *The Letters of Kingsley Amis* (ed. Zachary Leader) (HarperCollins, 2000).
———, *Memoirs* (Hutchinson, 1991).
Annan, Noel, *Our Age* (Fontana, 1991).
———, *Changing Enemies* (HarperCollins, 1995).
Ayrton, Michael, *Golden Sections* (Methuen, 1957).
Balfour, Patrick, *Society Racket* (John Long, 1932).
Baynes, John, *Morale* (Cassell, 1967).
Beevor, Anthony, *Crete – The Battle and the Resistance* (John Murray, 1991).
Betjeman, John, *Summoned by Bells* (John Murray, 1960).
Bowra, Maurice, *Memories, 1898-1939* (Weidenfeld & Nicolson, 1966).
Burra, Edward, *Well, dearie! The Letters of Edward Burra* (ed. William Chappell) (Gordon Fraser, 1985).
Carpenter, Humphrey, *The Brideshead Generation* (Weidenfeld & Nicolson, 1989).
Clark, Kenneth, *Another Part of the Wood* (John Murray, 1974).
Clayton, Anthony, *Forearmed: The History of the Intelligence Corps* (Brassey, 1993).
Cockburn, Claud, *Cockburn Sums Up* (Quartet, 1981).
Connolly, Cyril, *The Unquiet Grave* (Hamish Hamilton, 1945).
———, *Previous Convictions* (Hamish Hamilton, 1963).
———, *The Evening Colonnade* (David Bruce & Watson, 1973)
———, *Enemies of Promise* (Penguin Modern Classics, 1979).
———, *The Condemned Playground* (Hogarth Press, 1985).
Cranborne, Hannah (ed), *David Cecil: A Portrait* (Dovecote Press, Wimborne 1990).
Crick, Bernard, *George Orwell: A Life* (Secker & Warburg, 1980).
Daintrey, Adrian, *I Must Say* (Chatto & Windus, 1963).
Davidson, Michael, *The World, The Flesh and Myself* (Ernest Barker, 1962).
Ellis, G.U., *Twilight on Parnassus* (Michael Joseph, 1939).
Fleming, Ann, *The Letters of Ann Fleming* (ed. Mark Amory) (Harvill Press, 1985).
Fussell, Paul, *Abroad* (Oxford University Press, 1980).

Gallagher, Donat, *The Essays, Articles and Reviews of Evelyn Waugh* (Methuen, 1983).

Green, Henry, *Pack My Bag* (Oxford Paperbacks, 1989).

Green, Martin, *Children of the Sun* (Constable, 1977).

Greene, Graham (ed), *The Old School* (Oxford Paperbacks, 1984).

Hamnett, Nina, *Laughing Torso* (Constable, 1932).

————, *Is She A Lady* (Allen Wingate, 1955).

Hart-Davis, Rupert, *The Lyttelton – Hart-Davis Letters*, Vols 1-6 (John Murray 1978-1984).

Hawtree, Christopher (ed), *Night and Day* (Chatto & Windus, 1985).

Heygate, John, *Decent Fellows* (Gollancz, 1930).

————, *Talking Picture* (Cape, 1934).

————, *These Germans* (Hutchinson, 1940).

Hillier, Bevis, *John Betjeman New Fame: New Love* (John Murray, 2002).

Hooker, Denise, *Nina Hamnett* (Constable, 1986).

Hyde, Montgomery, *Christopher Millard* (New York: Global Academic Publishers,1990).

Hynes, Samuel, *The Auden Generation* (Bodley Head, 1976).

Ingrams, Richard, *God's Apology* (Deutsch, 1977).

————, *Malcolm Muggeridge* (Collins, 1995).

Knox, James, *Robert Byron* (John Murray, 2003).

Lambert, Constant, *Music Ho!* (Hogarth Press, 1985).

Lancaster, Marie-Jacqueline (ed), *Brian Howard: Portrait of a Failure* (Blond, 1968).

Lancaster, Osbert, *All Done From Memory* (John Murray, 1963).

————, *With an Eye to the Future* (John Murray, 1967).

Lees-Milne, James, *Deep Romantic Chasm* (John Murray, 2000).

————, *Harold Nicolson, A Biography*: Vol. 2 (Chatto & Windus, 1981).

————, *Through Wood and Dale* (John Murray, 1998).

Lewis, Jeremy, *Cyril Connolly: A Life* (Jonathan Cape, 1997).

Lilley, George, and Keith Marshall (eds), *Proceedings of the Anthony Powell Conference 2001* (The Anthony Powell Society, 2001).

Lloyd-Jones, Hugh (ed), *Maurice Bowra: A Celebration* (Duckworth, 1974).

Maclaren-Ross, Julian, *Memoirs of the Forties* (Alan Ross, 1965).

Mason, Philip, *A Shaft of Sunlight* (Deutsch, 1978).

Massingberd, Hugh, *Daydream Believer* (Macmillan, 2001).

May, Derwent, *Critical Times: A History of the TLS* (Collins, 2001).

Motion, Andrew, *The Lamberts* (Hogarth Press, 1987).

Muggeridge, Malcolm, *Tread Softly for You Tread on My Jokes* (Fontana, 1968).

————, *The Green Stick* (Collins, 1972).

————, *The Infernal Grove* (Collins, 1973).

————, *Like It Was* (Collins, 1981).

————, *The Thirties* (Weidenfeld & Nicolson, 1989).

Ollard, Richard, *An English Education* (Collins, 1982).

Orwell, George, *Collected Essays, Journalism and Letters*, Vols 1 & 4 (Penguin, 1970).

Powell, Violet (ed), *The Album of Anthony Powell's* Dance to the Music of Time (Thames and Hudson, 1987)

Powell, Violet, *The Departure Platform* (Heinemann, 1998).

————, *Five Out of Six* (Heinemann, 1960).

————, *Within the Family Circle* (Heinemann, 1976).

Price, R.G.G., *A History of Punch* (Collins, 1957).

Pryce-Jones, Alan, *The Bonus of Laughter* (Hamish Hamilton, 1988).

Pryce-Jones, David (ed), *Cyril Connolly, Journal and Memoir* (Collins, 1983).

Quennell, Peter, *The Marble Foot* (Collins, 1976).

————, *The Wanton Chase* (Collins, 1980).

Ritchie, Charles, *An Appetite for Life* (Macmillan Canada, 1977).

Shead, Richard, *Constant Lambert* (Simon Publications, 1973).

Sherry, Norman, *The Life of Graham Greene*, Vol. 1 (Penguin, 1990).

Skelton, Barbara, *Tears Before Bedtime* (Hamish Hamilton, 1987).

————, *Weep No More* (Hamish Hamilton, 1989).

Stannard, Martin, *Evelyn Waugh: The Early Years* (Paladin, 1988).

————, *Evelyn Waugh: No Abiding City* (Dent, 1992).

Sykes, Christopher, *Evelyn Waugh* (Collins, 1975).

Symonds, John, *The Great Beast* (Rider, 1951).

Treglown, Jeremy, *Romancing: The Life and Work of Henry Green* (Faber, 2000).

Watkins, Alan, *Brief Lives* (Hamish Hamilton, 1982).

————, *A Short Walk Down Fleet Street* (Duckbacks, 2001).

Waugh, Alec, *A Year to Remember* (W.H. Allen, 1975).

Waugh, Auberon, *Will This Do?* (Century, 1991).

Waugh, Evelyn, *Brideshead Revisited* (Penguin, 1962).

————, *The Diaries of Evelyn Waugh* (ed. Michael Davie) (Weidenfeld & Nicolson, 1976).

————, *The Letters of Evelyn Waugh* (ed. Mark Amory) (Weidenfeld & Nicolson, 1980).

————, *Men at Arms* (Penguin, 1964).

————, *Officers and Gentlemen* (Penguin, 1964).

————, *A Little Learning* (Chapman and Hall, 1964).

Whitley, Edward, *The Graduates* (Hamish Hamilton, 1986).

Willetts, Paul, *Fear and Loathing in Fitzrovia* (Dewi Lewis, 2003).

Wilson, Edmund, *The Fifties* (Farrar, Strauss, Giroux, 1986).

————, *The Sixties* (Farrar, Strauss, Giroux, 1993).

Permissions

This is an unauthorised biography so I am particularly grateful to David Higham Associates, Random House and the Estate of Anthony Powell for permission to quote from the author's novels, essays, memoirs, journals and reviews, and to reproduce his drawing, *The Four Seasons*. I am also grateful for permission to quote from Powell's unpublished letters © 2004 Estate of Violet Powell, and for permission to reproduce eleven photographs from his memoirs, courtesy of Tristram and John Powell.

I should like to thank the editors and publishers of the *Times Literary Supplement* and the *Spectator* for permission to quote from their publications. My thanks also to the following authors and/or their estates for kind permission to quote from the works cited: Sir Kingsley Amis (Jonathan Clowes Ltd, Huntington Library, California) – *The Music of Time*, *The Amis Collection*, *Memoirs* © Kingsley Amis 1979, 1990 and 1991 and *The Letters of Kingsley Amis* © the Estate of Kingsley Amis 2000; Sir John Betjeman (John Murray Publishers) – *Summoned by Bells*, *Senex*; Cyril Connolly (Rogers, Coleridge and White Ltd) – *Enemies of Promise*, *The Unquiet Grave*, *The Condemned Playground*, *The Evening Colonnade*, *Journal and Memoir* © Estate of Cyril Connolly; Ann Fleming (Mark Amory) – three letters to Evelyn Waugh; James Lees-Milne (Michael Bloch) – *Through Wood and Dale*, *Deep Romantic Chasm*, unpublished Diary entry; Doris Lessing (Jonathan Clowes Ltd) – *The Four Gated City* © 1969 Doris Lessing; Malcolm Muggeridge (Leonard Muggeridge) – unpublished Diaries and Memoir; Evelyn Waugh (Peters, Fraser and Dunlop Ltd) – *A Little Learning* © 1964 Evelyn Waugh, *Diaries* © The Estate of Evelyn Waugh 1976, *Letters* © the Estate of Laura Waugh 1980, *Essays, Articles and Reviews* © 1983 The Estate of Laura Waugh; A.N. Wilson – *Daughters of Albion*; Edmund Wilson (Farrar, Straus & Giroux LLC) – *The Fifties* © 1986 Edmund Wilson, *The Sixties* © 1993 Helen Miranda Wilson.

Ronald Searle very kindly gave me permission to reproduce, gratis, the drawing of Anthony Powell which forms the frontispiece. I must also thank Lady Lancaster and John Murray Publishers for permission to reproduce two drawings by Sir Osbert Lancaster, and Ms Anna Ford and Mark Amory for permission to reproduce two of Mark Boxer's cover designs for the Fontana edition of *Dance*.

Index of Characters

Author's Note: In *A Dance to the Music of Time* Anthony Powell created several hundred characters, many of whom I refer to in my text. To avoid confusion, I have given them a separate index which begins below. (The 'see also' references below refer to the main index.)

General Index